PERSPECTIVES
IN PSYCHOLOGY

Edward Joseph Shoben, Jr.
Teachers College, Columbia University

Floyd L. Ruch
University of Southern California

Scott, Foresman and Company
Chicago   Atlanta   Dallas   Palo Alto   Fair Lawn, N. J.

CONTENTS

L. C. #63-20553
Copyright © 1963 by Scott, Foresman and Company
Printed in the United States of America

INTRODUCTION

Psychological science and human understanding

Man is a puzzling animal. Neither the strongest, the swiftest, nor the most self-sufficient of the beasts that populate the globe, he has nevertheless come to dominate the earth. He has changed the courses of great rivers to irrigate his fields; where once impregnable forests stood, he has built his cities; and, like the Prometheus of legend, he has plundered the dormant sources of energy in his universe — coal and oil, the power of steam and electricity, and the potent forces of the atom and of the sun's rays — to drive his cars and planes, light his towns, operate his enormous factories, and let him communicate almost instantaneously by radio and satellite-relayed television across thousands of miles. At the same time, he has shown himself to be the only organism preoccupied with both the creation and the appreciation of art. Wherever one finds people, one finds a concern for adornment and decoration, a notion of beauty or elegance to set beside a concept of utility or efficiency. The human conquest of the planet has often involved an ideal of loveliness as well as a yearning both to wrest secrets from nature and to make the land, sea, and air yield a less toilsome or dangerous way of life.

Parallel to these bright achievements, there runs a darker thread. In his distinctive use of tools, man has been fascinated since his beginnings with weapons, instruments of destruction that he has consistently turned on his own kind as well as on the game animals on which he has fed. Unlike any other living thing, he has institutionalized self-protection and aggression into organized warfare, and this capacity for militarized quarrelsomeness has now reached a point where it is a commonplace to say that men are presently in imminent danger of making themselves extinct in a cobalt doomsday. Similarly, in the uniquely human development of language, men have not only been able to transcend time through recording the past and envisioning the future, thus making possible a sense of history and the imaginative enterprise called science; they have also been able to deceive each other and themselves. Lying and cheating, made possible by linguistic inventiveness, are also attributes of man; and in complex ways, they have troubled him throughout his existence.

Indeed, the recognition of such perversions of his gifts and powers is one of the sources of the social rules under which man has always agreed, more or less reluctantly, to live. As James Madison put it, perceiving the age-old rift between the triumphant potentialities of human beings and their persistent tendencies toward deception and destruction, ". . . what is government itself but the greatest of all reflections on human nature? If men were angels, no government would be necessary." Restlessly (and by no means unsuccessfully) seeking to control the world in which they live, men have yet to find a fully effective way of controlling themselves.

On the one hand, then, we have a species blessed with a brain that makes possible language and therefore thought of a precise and far-ranging kind. It has a hand so structured as to permit the use of tools of striking delicacy or enormous power. It is responsive to esthetic values; and its capacity for foresight — the ability to imagine situations and circumstances that have never occurred in actuality — embraces ideals, concepts of a better life and a better world than any yet enjoyed in reality. On the other hand, we have a species marked by destructive tendencies unmatched elsewhere in the animal kingdom and by a propensity for deceit that is as distinctive as its symbolic capability. If men possess ideals universally, they just as universally (and almost by definition) fail to live up to them, and they suffer anxiety and guilt in ways and to an extent unduplicated in lower organisms.

To this brief and sketchy characterization of our kind, we must add one further item — human self-consciousness. Men think about themselves and their fellows, observe and judge each other, and reflect on the possible consequences of what they could have done in the past or what they can do in the future. Their attention is commanded not only by the environment of things and natural events, but also by other people and those private occurrences that seem to take place within one's own skin — the experience of pain, an emotion like fear or joy, or the train of associations touched off by an idea.

Here, of course, is the source of our puzzle. As men, we not only embody unresolved conflicts and contradictory traits and tendencies; we *know* we do. Such self-knowledge arouses our curiosity and, because we must somehow live in reasonable comfort with ourselves and our fellows, defines a region of very practical concern for us. On both counts — our curiosity and our anxiety to conduct our affairs more contentedly and happily — we are motivated to enlarge our *understanding* of ourselves in the hope of exercising greater *control* over our lives and over human events in general. If we are to enjoy greater control, however, we must have some notion of the different consequences of the alternatives available to us. In short, we must have some power to *predict* what different people will do, given some set of conditions acting on them as a result of either their personal histories or their circumstances at a particular time.

Fairly simple questions (which require, however, quite complex answers) illustrate these two broad classes of predictive problems. Interested in the effects of personal history on subsequent career, we can ask what kinds of family life and child-rearing practices are most likely to produce children who grow up to be successful scientists. Or, to exemplify the impact of momentary circumstances on behavior, we can pose this query: Which type of television advertising induces the larger number of people to buy more of a particular toothpaste — the sort that threatens painful decay of one's teeth if the dentifrice is not used, or the sort that promises dental health and a winningly bright smile if it is? In each of our two problems, any increase in our ability to predict the outcome is likely to rest on an enlargement of our understanding and is apt to provide a basis for greater control.

The main point is that the pattern of understanding, prediction, and control is the central pattern of science generally. When applied to human behavior, it defines the discipline of psychology, which may be characterized as man's effort, through the medium of science, to solve the puzzle of himself. As such, psychology represents a more or less systematic means for satisfying the curiosity and allaying some of the anxiety evoked by our awareness of our own conflicts and contradictions. Two broad observations must be made on this score.

First, there are ways other than that of scientific psychology by which the human puzzle can be attacked. For example, there is the way of poetic insight. To develop some sense of how difficult it is for a man to know himself thoroughly under emotionally distressing conditions, it is hard to find a more instructive text than Shakespeare's *Hamlet,* and jealousy has rarely been so profoundly examined as in his *Othello.* But one need not turn only to the verse drama. In nine short lines, Robert Frost says a great deal about the nature of human passion:

Some say the world will end in fire,
Some say in ice.
From what I've tasted of desire
I hold with those who favor fire.
But if it had to perish twice,
I think I know enough of hate
To say that for destruction ice
Is also great
And would suffice.

Anyone who reads English is likely to gain from this compact statement, for all its lack of "science," a deeper comprehension of hatred and the various lusts — for sex, for money, for power, for knowledge — that men are typically heir to.

Similarly, there is the way of philosophy, which proceeds essentially by two routes. One is through the analysis of language in an effort to clarify meanings. When we assert, for instance, that democracy is better than communism or that premarital sex relations make for mental health, what kinds of statements are we really making? With language such a central aspect of human behavior, the light that such philosophers as Stevenson (1945) and Pepper (1960) have shed on the surprisingly complex issues bound up in propositions of this sort is extremely helpful. To solve the human puzzle, we must become better acquainted with the tricks our language can play on us, and much of the aid we need here comes from the so-called analytic philosophers. But there is another philosophical approach which attempts to order human experience by systematizing it under general principles. A relatively simple illustration is the golden rule of Christianity, which specifies the conditions under which social life would presumably be most comfortable and productive and the personal experience of guilt and shame would presumably be least. Such readings of man's circumstances can give important direction to our lives, sharpen our appreciation of the alternatives confronting us, and permit our formulating in clearer terms the character of the human puzzle. After all, what we recognize as wisdom, the primary concern of philosophy, existed long before psychology was explicitly conceived and remains the ultimate goal of the psychological route to coping with the puzzle of ourselves.

In a sense, the way of religion is akin to the way of philosophy in that both seek wisdom through reflection on human experience and the attempt to identify those behavioral principles which, if followed, would lead to a life that is somehow better than the one we now know. The religious approach is distinctive, however, in at least two major respects. First, it is founded on a belief in a divinity which is outside ourselves and, indeed, outside all nature, and which is a source of both knowledge and power. Through the disciplines of prayer or mystical devotions and through the sincerity of our worship, we may gain both knowledge and strength. For example, faced with a decision we feel unable to make because we simply do not understand its potential consequences, we can pray for guidance and acquire from the Godhead either the knowledge we need to decide wisely or the fortitude to endure uncomplainingly the results of our action, whatever it may be. Second, most religions teach that our understanding of the human puzzle is greatest when we have achieved the highest degree of identification with divinity itself. In some religious systems, this state of ultimate comprehension is reserved to heaven, where we may live unshackled by our bodies and other trappings of mortality; but even during our earthly existence we may always increase our understanding through "the practice of the presence of God." By careful study of sacred documents, by prayerful efforts to discover the will of the divine being, and by keeping always before us the behavioral ideals of divinity, we may approximate (although we can never in human form actually attain) the kind of understanding that God Himself possesses and conduct ourselves more completely according to His rules and wishes. Around the globe and for long ages, in spite of many instances of corruption and barbarism, the way of religion has produced men of wisdom, kindness, and great personal influence tempered by an intense feeling of responsibility to their communities. Whatever the difficulties that may beset many of us in the twentieth century with respect to the basic beliefs of some of the great religions, the fact remains that, for many people, this route to a functional understanding of the human puzzle has been a personally enriching and socially useful one.

Finally, there is the way of history. In a famous aphorism, George Santayana once remarked that those who remain ignorant of history are condemned to repeat it. While it is noteworthy that he did *not* say that a knowledge of past mistakes is a sufficient guarantee against their recurrence, Santayana was nevertheless underscoring two important facts about human beings. One is that we can and do profit immensely from vicarious as well as direct experience. We need not learn anew in every generation how to use cold temperatures for the preservation of food or that tobacco is a crop which wears out soil. Even when the issues are more complicated and less clear than these, we can save ourselves trouble and hedge against error by examining what our forebears did (and with what consequences) in confronting similar problems. The success of the American Constitution, for example, derives in no small part from the way in which its drafters levied on previous governmental experience, sifting it thoroughly for the promising and workable as opposed to the dubious and dangerous.

The other implication of Santayana's comment is that our perspective on events is often as important as the nature of the events themselves for our comprehension of them and our ability to cope with them fruitfully. Knowing that the difficulties we face, personally or socially, have been faced before often reduces the emotional intensity they arouse, enabling us to confront them somewhat more calmly and ably. General George Marshall, during the war in Korea in 1951, put it this way: "I doubt seriously whether a man can think with full wisdom and deep convictions regarding certain of the basic international issues today who has not at least reviewed in his mind the period of the Peloponnesian Wars and the fall of Athens." General Marshall was not, of course, arguing that history literally repeats itself. Rather, he was saying that history is a mine of relevant case histories which can help one develop a broader point of view, more suggestive of new solutions and less likely to encourage old failures than is the angle of regard that ignores the record of the past. History does not in itself resolve the human puzzle, but it facilitates our taking a firmer stance toward it and our construing it with a more wisely informed eye.

Poetry, philosophy, and history all contribute, then, to our richer comprehension of ourselves. Each has its own validity, and each generates its own brand of insight to be checked against the kind produced by the others and by psychology. Distinctively, psychology represents the attempt to bring the methods of science, of such clearly demonstrable power in other spheres, to bear on human affairs, and this

reminder of psychology's status as a science brings us to our second broad observation.

As a science, although it adheres tightly to the processes of understanding, prediction, and control, psychology faces special problems. Some are obvious. The human ethical sense forbids certain kinds of experimentation that could lead to more exact knowledge. Psychologists may not, for example, take newborn infants from their parents and raise them under rigidly controlled conditions in order to study the effects of different patterns of child care on the development of intellectual skills or personality. Our society, to its credit, even insists that certain humane rules be followed in the experimental treatment of lower animals. Beyond these restrictions, there is the great complexity of organismic behavior itself. Anybody who has kept a pet joins with accomplished animal trainers in testifying to the fact that cats and dogs and monkeys are enormously variable in their activity, always capable of unpredicted surprises and unforeseen departures from their accustomed ways of responding. At the human level, this obdurate unpredictability of behavior is still further heightened. The range of possible reactions is so great among people that it may be impossible to achieve the same precision in understanding and controlling human behavior that physicists have been able to win in relation to the behavior of gas molecules or atomic particles.

But it is not ethical restrictions and the factor of behavioral complexity alone that make difficult the scientific job of psychology. There is a more fundamental problem. When a chemist or a biologist studies the properties of heavy water or the genetics of orchids, the natural world is unaltered by his observations and interpretations. The discovery of the processes of nature does not change their character however much it may provide men with greater leverage in the manipulation of them. In psychology (and the other behavioral sciences), however, the case is somewhat different. One way to put it is that the student and the object of study are the same things. Both are behaving human beings, and whatever generalizations may be formulated from investigation should apply equally to the investigator and his subjects. Even when lower animals are used for experimental purposes, there is a strong tendency to regard the principles adduced from their behavior as applicable to men. In this context, "men" applies as much to psychologists and those familiar with the reports of their work as it does to "other people," the unnamed masses whom we tend to think of at times as analogous to the impersonal nature from which physics and biology extract more profound understanding without changing its basic processes.

The point, of course, is that what men know — or believe they know — is an important determinant of their conduct. In the words of W. I. Thomas (Volkart, 1951), "If men define situations as real, they are real in their consequences." All of us are familiar with this widely pertinent observation. The bright student, for example, who becomes convinced, for a variety of reasons, that he is likely to fail an examination spends more time worrying than studying; consequently, he performs poorly. In more socially important terms, if a dominant ethnic group, like the British in parts of once-colonial Africa or American whites in our own country, develop the idea that Negroes are intellectually inept, then the dominant group provides little for the Negro in the way of schools or opportunities for intellectual growth; as a consequence, Negroes do show, *on the average,* less intellectual cultivation than Caucasions in the same nations. The knowledge, whether true or false according to some criterion, that men have about themselves and each other has the character of a self-fulfilling prophecy (Merton, 1957), affecting in some significant degree the very processes of behavior to which the knowledge applies.

Psychology, of course, is in the business of producing knowledge about behavior; and, to the extent that its propositions partake of the self-fulfilling prophecy, it shares an important characteristic with poetry, philosophy, religion, and history, the other disciplines through which we may gain some enlightenment about ourselves and our institutions. What concerns us here is that psychology *as a science* differs in this regard from the enterprises of physics and biology. The latter have no effect on the processes studied; the former certainly may.

The ideas of Freud, holding that the basic motives of men are universally sexual and aggressive, repressed and sublimated through the demands of social necessity, have had profound effects on our mores and our laws, on our ways of thinking about ourselves as expressed in our arts, and on the way in which we define personal relationships as "real." It is hard to find a reasonably educated person nowadays who is not influenced seriously by the Freudian conception of man as a tangle of repressed psychic energies, struggling to find some behavioral outlet through the "mental mechanisms" that Freud first systematically described. Similarly, one can say much the same thing about the ideas of behaviorism as formulated originally by John B. Watson and more recently by B. F. Skinner. According to this psychological tradition, human conduct is the result of complex conditioning, the product of the way patterns of response are "shaped" by controlling stimuli in the environment. Thus, the actions of men can be "engineered" by the planned application of designated stimulus conditions.

In his Utopia, *Walden Two* (1948), and in his *Science and Human Behavior* (1953), Skinner outlines at length the way in which not only individual behavior but an entire culture can be designed and realized without reference to any self-determining, self-directing elements in the human organism. Man is thus conceived as essentially a reactive machine whose behavioral output can be governed by the types of stimuli which are fed into it. Obviously, the implications of this view are in sharp conflict with the Christian image of man as an imperfect but authentic embodiment of divine spirit, the humanist image of man as a responsible person enjoying a degree of free choice, and the democratic image of man as a participant in the determination of his own social destiny. How one resolves such conflicts makes a difference in the way he lives his own life and in the utility he finds in psychology as a contributor to his understanding. However much they may entail other issues, the older, "natural" sciences do not pose problems of this kind for their students.

We have, then, a kind of dilemma. Science is supposed to produce durable knowledge and reliable laws which throw light on natural processes and increase man's power to control them. Yet psychology, deeply committed to the methods of science, is likely to affect the very thing it studies in such a way as to make its resulting knowledge and ideas neither more or less applicable than its original investigations would suggest. The implicit images of man in any significant psychological idea are things to which we are likely to react, sometimes strongly and on valid grounds, thus altering the utility of the concept. In light of this state of affairs, how can we best approach whatever psychology has to tell us about the human condition?

There are several approaches, of course, three of which seem to be most important. The first is through a straightforward faith in the power of science. For those who elect this course, there is no need for defense or apology. Faith in science has been handsomely vindicated throughout the history of the modern world. Little more than forty years ago, so distinguished a chemist as E. E. Slosson (1919), in discussing the power of atomic energy, could write categorically, "The atom is as much beyond our reach as the moon. We cannot rob its vault of its treasure." In no more than twenty-five years after these words were printed, the vault of the atom, through the efforts of those whose faith in science exceeded Slosson's own, was richly plundered; and the moon is no longer a symbol of the inaccessible. It is quite possible that the techniques of science will become still more applicable to the behavioral domain and that the problem of psychological investigation's changing the processes it investigates will be solved. Such a possibility, at any rate, constitutes a reasonable article of faith, not without warrant in experience. It remains, however, an article of faith, not a demonstrably sure development in the foreseeable future.

The second approach, chosen by a considerable number of psychologists themselves, is not only to invest one's faith in science generally, but to become a partisan of a particular scientific position. This choice, of course, flies in the face of the ideals of open-mindedness and "objectivity" that are supposed to characterize the practitioners of science. The fact remains, however, that many of the greatest achievements in both the physical and the behavioral sciences have resulted from the stubborn persistence of one man and his followers in a single point of view which they straightforwardly attempted with great vigor and ingenuity to demonstrate as true rather than merely to "test." Freud, for example, was not unusual in his refusal to brook criticism of his psychoanalytic theory or in his unremitting efforts to prove its universality. Nevertheless, it must be remembered that when such a doctrinaire stance has been productive, it has been taken by a man of genius, whole-heartedly dedicating his brilliance to a carefully formulated set of ideas. For most of us more ordinary mortals, this kind of allegiance to a particular point of view among the many available in psychology is likely to lead to mere dogmatism, more provocative of empty debate than rich innovation. Generally, it is wise to wait before committing oneself to the special brands of psychoanalysis, behaviorism, or phenomenology that occupy posts along the psychological frontiers.

Finally, there is a third approach, not very fashionable as yet and only hazily formulated. This course involves regarding psychological science less as cut from the same cloth as physics and more as the first of the humanistic studies to learn how to use systematic observation in considering the human condition. It asks not so much for definitive answers as for significant questions and for techniques by which they can be thought about more fruitfully, especially in the light of observations of how organisms, especially human beings, actually do behave. Those who approach psychology in this spirit are not likely to forget or to deprecate the values of poetry, philosophy, or history as routes to enlarged understanding of themselves and others, but they are interested in subjecting these insights to the discipline of direct and systematic evidence and eager to work back and forth in their own thought between the general wisdom that can be derived from other sources and the more precise (if often more limited) propositions of psychological science. For those who travel this avenue, psychology will hardly *furnish* an image of man, but it will *contribute* to one's own evolving conception of an answer to the ancient question of what, then, is man; it will not solve the human puzzle, but it will help present it in more manageable terms.

Whatever approach one takes to it, scientific psychology makes two requirements of those who would use it as a tool for increasing their own understanding. One has to do with its procedures; the other is concerned with its major categories.

On the procedural side, psychology must, in order to follow the methods of science, translate some of the great human questions with which it is concerned into "operations" over which it can exercise more precise controls. Without this reduction of its subject matter to situations that can be either manipulated or measured, psychology can achieve nothing of that special clarity which is the hallmark of science. For example, if we are interested in what makes men ambitious, we can study the biographies of ambitious men, attempting to extract from their histories what generalizations we can from their common experiences or from the circumstances that impress us as somehow most important in their personal development. Such an attack is likely to have a liveliness and a degree of relevance that are compelling, but the evidence it yields is almost sure to be susceptible to divergent readings. Two students, reading the same biographical records, can quite possibly come to very different ideas of how to account for human ambition, and there is no way for them to determine which is the more correct if, indeed, either of them is.

Let us consider another way of focusing on the same problem. We begin by selecting some relatively ambiguous pictures of people in a variety of situations, and we ask college students to make up brief stories to account for what is happening in these scenes, instructing them to tell us what the background is for what is presumably occurring in each picture, what is happening at the moment, and how it is all going to turn out. Once the stories are collected, we subject them to a scoring scheme which permits different scorers to arrive at highly similar evaluations. For instance, our scoring arrangements enable us to count with high accuracy and agreement between judges such things as the proportion of times each student tells a story in which his hero wins out over odds, is driven to do something by a powerful urge to improve himself, or is commended by others for his high aspirations. Assuming that the characteristics the subject imputes to his hero are indicative of his own traits, we now have a score defining each person's degree of

"need-achievement" (McClelland, 1961) or an index of his ambitiousness. Parenthetically, we should note that making this assumption is dangerous; it could be wrong. But the risk is simply part of the adventure of psychological science, and we have ways of checking on ourselves to determine whether we are in serious error.

Equipped with our need-achievement scores, we can now do several things. We can ask, for example, whether the persons telling ambitious stories are themselves regarded as ambitious by their teachers or their peers. In such a case, we can devise a questionnaire or an interview schedule and in standardized and systematic ways sample the opinions and judgments of those who know the subjects well. By statistical procedures, we can then estimate the degree to which our subjects' stories, scored according to our scheme, are related to the estimates of ambition that their actual behavior evokes from other people. Or we can ask whether, in fact, those who tell highly ambitious stories work harder at tasks involving obstacles than do those who tell stories that are not suggestive of strong need-achievement. In this instance, we may devise a problem-solving situation, set our two groups of subjects—one high and the other low on our index of ambition—to working at it, and carefully note such things as how long they persist in their effort to find a solution in the face of failure, how many different ways of attacking the problem they invent, the extent to which they report themselves as troubled or bothered by their inability to do the problem, etc. Or—for a third illustration—we can ask a different kind of question: What kinds of family backgrounds produce people with high need-achievement as opposed to those with low need-achievement? Here we are likely either to go directly to the parents of our subjects or to ask our subjects for biographical data about their early life and their relationships with their mothers and fathers. Again, by using statistical techniques, we can determine the kinds of relationships that may occur between our index of ambition and the kinds of familial experience they have had insofar as we are able to characterize that experience.

Several points are worth thoughtful consideration here. In the first place, our work with need-achievement has none of the high drama of the lives of such great men of ambition as Caesar or Napoleon. Instead, we are concerned with some not very exciting stories told by quite ordinary people, the ways in which they are judged by others who know them reasonably well, their performance in a quite artificial laboratory situation, and the descriptions they or their parents (or both) give of their early lives in, for the most part, very usual families. But if we have been careful in our methods, we have some empirical information, expressed in quantitative terms, about the range of ambition in an important segment of our population, about the impact of need-achievement on people's judgments of each other, about the relationship of the stories told about ambiguous pictures to actual behavior in a problem-solving situation, and about the influence of early family life on our index of ambition. Such knowledge is by no means irrelevant or lacking in provocative power, and it is almost certain to lead, when gathered in the way described, to improved ideas about how still more useful observations can be made of ambition, its antecedents, and its correlates. Further, studies of this sort permit our going back to the biographies of Caesar and Napoleon with a sharper sense of what to look for in order to understand more fully the sources and consequences of ambition in the giants who have marched with telling strides through our history.

In the second place, our little inquiries into the nature of human ambition have demanded some risk and adventuresomeness. Assumptions have been necessary; creative ingenuity has been required in the construction of our questionnaires and interview schedules, the problem-solving task for use in our laboratory, and our scoring scheme for the subjects' stories; and we have constantly been working back and forth between connotatively rich ideas and some relevant operations of measurement and manipulation over which we could keep systematic and standardized control. The practice of science levies heavily on imagination and inventiveness, but it is imagination disciplined by the requirement of controls that will permit scientists to agree on what they observe (not necessarily on how they interpret their observations), including the observation of relationships as well as of discrete events. We

have been interested throughout, for example, in the antecedents or possible causes of ambition in early family life—an interest in a relationship—as well as in the range and variability of our need-achievement scores—a discrete event.

In the third place, we have encountered some important new puzzles. Concerned with the sources of ambition in early family experience, we asked our subjects or their parents for reports of what happened during the childhoods of our students. The procedure is a reasonable one, but it is filled with sources of error. Both our subjects and their fathers and mothers may make mistakes in recalling events that occurred several years ago. They may have forgotten crucial things which, if remembered, would go far toward explaining the growth of ambition. On the other hand, there may be important happenings which are well recalled but, because they evoke embarrassment or are regarded as private, are suppressed. In any case, the remembrance of things past is typically colored by intervening events so that, from a scientist's point of view, memory as a source of data is a less than desirable route to secure knowledge. What, then, are the alternatives? One possibility is to study children over time, making direct observations of parent-child interactions in relation to appropriate indices of the development of ambition. Another is to think of analogues to potentially relevant parental practices and, in the laboratory, subject youngsters to these experiences in controlled ways, taking measures of their need-achievement before and after these experimental manipulations. Both of these modifications would require, of course, that we invent new instruments of observation and that we create some new ideas on which to base the design of our investigations.

We are learning that if we are to solve the larger human puzzle, we must also be able to cope with the smaller puzzles of method and procedure and that to do so taxes our imagination and demands the most creative thought of which we are capable. There are times when we fail, when our operations lack the necessary degree of relevance to the issues which first commanded our interest or when we cannot refine our techniques of observation to a point where they meet the criterion of agreement between observers that science imposes. On such occasions, if we would profit from the contributions of scientific psychology, we must go back to our original ideas and try again to reduce them to properly manageable but still humanly cogent dimensions. In short, like many of the worth-while enterprises of men, the practice of scientific psychology poses its own puzzles *en route* to casting light on the larger one, and they must be dealt with while they are at the same time kept in proper perspective and not allowed to obscure our central and longer-range business of enlarging our human understanding.

This brings us to our second major requirement, having to do with the categories with which psychology is primarily concerned. At this stage of the science's history, it is accurate to say that its primary focus is on *behavior*, but on behavior so construed as to include thinking, feeling, and emotion — those acts which are internal and private, subject to observation by only one person, the actor himself — as well as overt motor reactions or physiological processes that can be observed by means of various kinds of special apparatus. Oddly enough, the terms *behavior* and *response* tend to be a trifle slippery and not entirely clear. If we define a response, for example, as any contraction of a muscle or gland, we are immediately faced with the problem of whether a thought is a response. To say that it is commits us to a theory of thought as implicit speech, entailing minimal contractions of the larynx. Not only is the theory open to some challenge, but such a commitment still leaves us with the issue of sensory images, those "pictures in the head" which all of us experience in varying degree and which, for many of us, constitute at times our primary reaction to certain events in our environment. They involve no contractions of muscles or glands, but they certainly fall under the category of behavior as most of us, including most psychologists, conceive it.

Another way of defining these basic terms is as changes that an organism produces in its relationship to its surroundings. Thus, a rat's pressing a lever in its cage, a college student's telling a story about an ambiguous picture, and a woman's getting angry all qualify without our having to specify what muscles or glands are activated. Even our sensory image seems well taken care of. And yet in what sense does the occurrence of a sensory image change one's relationship to the environment? Driving along a busy street, one suddenly "sees" briefly a "picture" of one's mother's face. Except under the most unusual circumstances, one's relation to the car, the traffic, the signal lights, etc., is not at all altered, and even one's flow of private thoughts is unlikely to be interrupted. The image simply occurs and fades, all very quickly. The changed relationship to the environment would be hard to specify; yet there is no doubt that one has "behaved" in a rather interesting fashion. Many psychologists would find a particular challenge and importance in just such instances of the momentary images of significant people where their occurrence has no discernible bearing on the relationship of the person experiencing the image to the world about him.

The point is that, to profit from the enterprise of scientific psychology, one must tolerate — at present, at any rate — a certain fuzziness in some of its basic categories. They are precise enough to be useful, and the search for increased sharpness of definition is a vigorously ongoing one; but some acceptance of ambiguity is still necessary. In one sense, this state of affairs simply defines the room yet remaining in psychology for a Linnaeus or a Newton to systematize and order its major concepts through the hard work that only a genius can perform; in another sense, it may represent only the elusiveness of human conduct, the tendency of men to escape in some degree the scientific nets of their own weaving.

Whatever else it may suggest, this situation not only entitles but obligates those who come to psychology as consumers, no less than those who are its practitioners, to attend both to the patterns of behavior under consideration in a particular study *and* those neglected by the specific definitions employed by the investigator. To do its job, psychology must analyze, fractionate, and choose observational units on the basis of their specific rather than their general usefulness. In following this necessary procedure, it must exclude other possibilities. Those other possibilities, however, may be fraught with potential new insights, and many experiments and theoretical conceptualizations may be as fruitful by virtue of what they deliberately exclude as by virtue of what they deal with directly. Any sound evaluation of a psychological study or idea entails some attention to the alternatives that were either rejected or not thought of.

The selections in this book are offered for two main purposes. One is to provide some exposure to specific formulations and empirical investigations as a supplement to the synthetic treatment of the field by a standard textbook. Most of the work collected here has involved some controversy; all of it is illustrative of high competence brought to bear on particular problems of real relevance to increasing our fund of human understanding. None of it, however, is definitive. In every case, there are alternatives to be considered, new questions to be raised, and issues to be met in order to fit the ideas and findings reported to other concepts and other observations. For the interested student, each selection is a starting point from which, by tracking down the subsequent literature on the same specific topic, he can develop a reasonably firm comprehension of how psychological science grows, corrects itself, and over time resolves the arguments that occur among its practitioners.

The second purpose is simply to indicate, over a rather narrow spectrum of traditional and fundamental topics, some of the wide range of differences among psychologists as they attack the human puzzle. The authors of the fourteen articles collected in this volume represent all three of the approaches to psychology discussed here, and they vary widely in the breadth and articulateness of their vision and in the degree to which they are directly concerned with the major issues we have tried to clarify in this introduction in the hope of making psychology more useful as a contributor to human understanding. Their work is representative only of diversity, but in that diversity may lie both the challenge to the reader and the impetus for future psychologists to convert psychological science into the groundwork of wisdom, which probably always contains room within itself for diverse ideas about so diverse a creature as man.

part 1

HABIT – THE UNIT OF BEHAVIOR

As human beings, we share with other organisms the tendency to behave in regular, patterned ways. We wake up when an alarm clock goes off; we take our meals, often whether we are hungry or not, according to a time schedule; we dress according to well-established customs. We also show more idiosyncratic regularities in our behavior – holding a cigarette or a coffee cup in a special way, speaking with a distinctive accent or using a certain turn of phrase, checking the doors and windows in a particular sequence before going to bed at night. These consistencies in our conduct, whether widely shared or particular little trademarks of our own, are known, of course, as *habits*. We apply the same term to pathological forms of behavior like drug addiction or the symptoms of a compulsion neurosis. We also use it to designate complex patterns of action which are so highly practiced that we rarely are conscious of performing them; the movements involved in driving a car are illustrative.

Habit, then, pervades our lives. It embraces many of the important behaviors that we engage in as part of a culture; like all Americans, we speak English. It comprises many of our actions as members of a particular group; like most students at a given college, we stay after football games to sing the Alma Mater. It includes the features of our conduct that make us unique as persons; each of us has a distinctive smile, walk, way of expressing anger, etc. At all three levels, it is appropriate to say that we are creatures of habit. Were it otherwise, our behavior would be so chaotic that other people would find it difficult to recognize us, and we would have to spend a great deal of time in thinking about actions that can be carried out through the mechanism of habit while our minds are free to consider other things. Brushing our teeth, filling a pipe, using a knife and fork at the dinner table are commonplace examples.

As a result of this pervasiveness of habit, most of us are prone to use the word as an explanatory concept. "Why do you smoke?" asks a friend. "Just out of habit," we reply. But the matter is not so simple as can be illustrated by revising the question to, "Why do you have the smoking habit?" Exactly the same thing is being asked, but we are now forced to search for a new answer. Far from furnishing an explanation, the concept of habit poses interesting and important problems. How are habits formed, and how do they function in the behavioral economy of an organism? Once formed, how are habits changed? What is the relationship between sets of habits that are very similar, like those involved in playing the piano and those used in typing? Are there behavioral regularities that are *not* habits?

One of the first attempts to deal systematically with such questions appeared in 1890, when William James, later to become one of America's most distinguished philosophers, published his two-volume *Principles of Psychology*. His characterization of habit as "the great flywheel of society" remains memorably relevant, and it placed psychology squarely within the tradition of evolutionary ideas that had been taking form during the latter half of the nineteenth century—since the publication of Darwin's *Origin of Species* in 1859.

Just forty years after James' book appeared, Clark L. Hull attempted to reduce the notion of knowledge and the experience of purpose or intention to the working of habit mechanisms. In doing so, he was working toward a comprehensive theory of behavior that would satisfy all the criteria of scientific thought. His was a highly formalized system, deductive in its structure and moving like Euclidean geometry from a small number of axioms and postulates to a series of theorems which formed the skeleton of the theory. Few psychologists have generated more fundamental research than Hull, and few have enjoyed a greater vision of scientific elegance in their theorizing. Whether the elegance and the investigations have enlarged our understanding to a degree commensurate with the effort expended is a question that is better kept in mind for mature reflection than answered prematurely.

The comparison of Hull's and James' treatments of the topic of habit affords a good opportunity to observe very different styles of psychological thought at work and to study the advantages and disadvantages of each. There is little point in trying to determine which man is "right" in some final and absolute sense. Probably neither is. But some of the problems and the foci of the psychological enterprise will become much clearer if these selections are read in an effort to find what each man was trying to do, how well he accomplished his objective and what he contributes to our improved understanding of habit as a widely adopted unit of behavior.

Habit

WILLIAM JAMES

When we look at living creatures from an outward point of view, one of the first things that strike us is that they are bundles of habits. In wild animals, the usual round of daily behavior seems a necessity implanted at birth; in animals domesticated, and especially in man, it seems, to a great extent, to be the result of education. The habits to which there is an innate tendency are called instincts; some of those due to education would by most persons be called acts of reason. It thus appears that habit covers a very large part of life, and that one engaged in studying the objective manifestations of mind is bound at the very outset to define clearly just what its limits are.

The moment one tries to define what habit is,

one is led to the fundamental properties of matter. The laws of Nature are nothing but the immutable habits which the different elementary sorts of matter follow in their actions and reactions upon each other. In the organic world, however, the habits are more variable than this. Even instincts vary from one individual to another of a kind; and are modified in the same individual, as we shall later see, to suit the exigencies of the case. The habits of an elementary particle of matter cannot change (on the principles of the atomistic philosophy), because the particle is itself an unchangeable thing; but those of a compound mass of matter can change, because they are in the last instance due to the structure of the compound, and either outward forces or inward tensions can, from one hour to another, turn that structure into something different from what it was. That is, they can do so if the body be plastic enough to maintain its integrity, and be not disrupted when its structure yields. The change of structure here spoken of need not involve the outward shape; it may be invisible and molecular, as when a bar of iron becomes magnetic or crystalline through the action of certain outward causes, or India-rubber becomes friable, or plaster 'sets.' All these changes are rather slow; the material in question opposes a certain resistance to the modifying cause, which it takes time to overcome, but the gradual yielding whereof often saves the material from being disintegrated altogether. When the structure has yielded, the same inertia becomes a condition of its comparative permanence in the new form, and of the new habits the body then manifests. *Plasticity,* then, in the wide sense of the word, means the possession of a structure weak enough to yield to an influence, but strong enough not to yield all at once. Each relatively stable phase of equilibrium in such a structure is marked by what we may call a new set of habits. Organic matter, especially nervous tissue, seems endowed with a very extraordinary degree of plasticity of this sort; so that we may without hesitation lay down as our first proposition the following, that *the phenomena of habit in living beings are due to the plasticity*[1] *of the organic materials of which their bodies are composed.* . . .

If habits are due to the plasticity of materials to outward agents, we can immediately see to what outward influences, if to any, the brain-matter is plastic. Not to mechanical pressures, not to thermal changes, not to any of the forces to which all the other organs of our body are exposed; for nature has carefully shut up our brain and spinal cord in bony boxes, where no influences of this sort can get at them. She has floated them in fluid so that only the severest shocks can give them a concussion, and blanketed and wrapped them about in an altogether exceptional way. The only impressions that can be made upon them are through the blood, on the one hand, and through the sensory nerve-roots, on the other; and it is to the infinitely attenuated currents that pour in through these latter channels that the hemispherical cortex shows itself to be so peculiarly susceptible. The currents, once in, must find a way out. In getting out they leave their traces in the paths which they take. The only thing they *can* do, in short, is to deepen old paths or to make new ones; and the whole plasticity of the brain sums itself up in two words when we call it an organ in which currents pouring in from the sense-organs make with extreme facility paths which do not easily disappear. For, of course, a simple habit, like every other nervous event—the habit of snuffling, for example, or of putting one's hands into one's pockets, or of biting one's nails—is, mechanically, nothing but a reflex discharge; and its anatomical substratum must be a path in the system. The most complex habits, as we shall presently see more fully, are, from the same point of view, nothing but *concatenated* discharges in the nerve-centres, due to the presence there of systems of reflex paths, so organized as to wake each other up successively—the impression produced by one muscular contraction serving as a stimulus to provoke the next, until a final impression inhibits the process and closes the chain. The only difficult mechanical problem is to explain the formation *de novo* of a simple reflex or path in a pre-existing nervous system. Here, as in so many other cases, it is only the *premier pas qui coûte.* For the entire nervous system *is* nothing but a system of paths between a sensory *terminus a quo* and a muscular, glandular, or

From *The Principles of Psychology* by William James (New York: Dover Publications, Inc., 1950) pp. 104-127.
1 In the sense above explained, which applies to inner structure as well as to outer form.

other *terminus ad quem.* A path once traversed by a nerve-current might be expected to follow the law of most of the paths we know, and to be scooped out and made more permeable than before;[2] and this ought to be repeated with each new passage of the current. Whatever obstructions may have kept it at first from being a path should then, little by little, and more and more, be swept out of the way, until at last it might become a natural drainage-channel. This is what happens where either solids or liquids pass over a path; there seems no reason why it should not happen where the thing that passes is a mere wave of rearrangement in matter that does not displace itself, but merely changes chemically or turns itself round in place, or vibrates across the line. The most plausible views of the nerve-current make it out to be the passage of some such wave of rearrangement as this. If only a part of the matter of the path were to 'rearrange' itself, the neighboring parts remaining inert, it is easy to see how their inertness might oppose a friction which it would take many waves of re-arrangement to break down and overcome. If we call the path itself the 'organ,' and the wave of rearrangement the 'function,' then it is obviously a case for repeating the celebrated French formula of *'La fonction fait l'organe.'*

So nothing is easier than to imagine how, when a current once has traversed a path, it should traverse it more readily still a second time. But what made it ever traverse it the first time?[3] In answering this question we can only fall back on our general conception of a nervous system as a mass of matter whose parts, constantly kept in states of different tension, are as constantly tending to equalize their states. The equalization between any two points occurs through whatever path may at the moment be most pervious. But, as a given point of the system may belong, actually or potentially, to many different paths, and, as the play of nutrition is subject to accidental changes, *blocks* may from time to time occur, and make currents shoot through unwonted lines. Such an unwonted line would be a new-created path, which if traversed repeatedly, would become the beginning of a new reflex arc. All this is vague to the last degree, and amounts to little more than saying that a new path may be formed by the sort of *chances* that in nervous

material are likely to occur. But, vague as it is, it is really the last word of our wisdom in the matter.[4]

It must be noticed that the growth of structural modification in living matter may be more rapid than in any lifeless mass, because the incessant nutritive renovation of which the living matter is the seat tends often to corroborate and fix the impressed modification, rather than to counteract it by renewing the original constitution of the tissue that has been impressed. Thus, we notice after exercising our muscles or our brain in a new way, that we can do so no longer at that time; but after a day or two of rest, when we resume the discipline, our increase in skill not seldom surprises us. I have often noticed this in learning a tune; and it has led a German author to say that we learn to swim during the winter and to skate during the summer. . . .

Thus Dr. Carpenter's phrase that *our nervous system grows to the modes in which it has been exercised* expresses the philosophy of habit in a nutshell. We may now trace some of the practical applications of the principle to human life.

The first result of it is that *habit simplifies the movements required to achieve a given result, makes them more accurate and diminishes fatigue.*

The beginner at the piano not only moves his finger up and down in order to depress the key, he moves the whole hand, the forearm and even the entire body, especially moving its least rigid part, the head, as if he would press down the key with that organ too. Often

2 Some paths, to be sure, are banked up by bodies moving through them under too great pressure, and made impervious. These special cases we disregard.

3 We cannot say *the will,* for, though many, perhaps most, human habits were once voluntary actions, no action . . . can be *primarily* such. While an habitual action may once have been voluntary, the voluntary action must before that, at least once, have been impulsive or reflex. It is this very first occurrence of all that we consider in the text.

4 Those who desire a more definite formulation may consult J. Fiske's *Cosmic Philosophy,* vol II. pp. 142-146 and Spencer's *Principles of Biology,* sections 302 and 303, and the part entitled "Physical Synthesis" of his *Principles of Psychology.* Mr. Spencer there tries, not only to show how new actions may arise in nervous systems and form new reflex arcs therein, but even how nervous tissue may actually be born by the passage of new waves of isometric transformation through an originally indifferent mass. I cannot help thinking that Mr. Spencer's data, under a great show of precision, conceal vagueness and improbability, and even self-contradiction.

a contraction of the abdominal muscles occurs as well. Principally, however, the impulse is determined to the motion of the hand and of the single finger. This is, in the first place, because the movement of the finger is the movement *thought of,* and, in the second place, because its movement and that of the key are the movements we try to *perceive,* along with the results of the latter on the ear. The more often the process is repeated, the more easily the movement follows, on account of the increase in permeability of the nerves engaged.

But the more easily the movement occurs, the slighter is the stimulus required to set it up; and the slighter the stimulus is, the more its effect is confined to the fingers alone.

Thus, an impulse which originally spread its effects over the whole body, or at least over many of its movable parts, is gradually determined to a single definite organ, in which it effects the contraction of a few limited muscles. In this change the thoughts and perceptions which start the impulse acquire more and more intimate causal relations with a particular group of motor nerves.

To recur to a simile, at least partially apt, imagine the nervous system to represent a drainage-system, inclining, on the whole, toward certain muscles, but with the escape thither somewhat clogged. Then streams of water will, on the whole, tend most to fill the drains that go towards these muscles and to wash out the escape. In case of a sudden 'flushing,' however, the whole system of channels will fill itself, and the water overflow everywhere before it escapes. But a moderate quantity of water invading the system will flow through the proper escape alone.

Just so with the piano-player. As soon as his impulse, which has gradually learned to confine itself to single muscles, grows extreme, it overflows into larger muscular regions. He usually plays with his fingers, his body being at rest. But no sooner does he get excited than his whole body becomes "animated," and he moves his head and trunk, in particular, as if these also were organs with which he meant to belabor the keys.[5]

Man is born with a tendency to do more things than he has ready-made arrangements for in his nerve-centres. Most of the performances of other animals are automatic. But in him the number of them is so enormous, that most of them must be the fruit of painful study. If practice did not make perfect, nor habit economize the expense of nervous and muscular energy, he would therefore be in a sorry plight. As Dr. Maudsley says:[6]

If an act became no easier after being done several times, if the careful direction of consciousness were necessary to its accomplishment on each occasion, it is evident that the whole activity of a lifetime might be confined to one or two deeds—that no progress could take place in development. A man might be occupied all day in dressing and undressing himself; the attitude of his body would absorb all his attention and energy; the washing of his hands or the fastening of a button would be as difficult to him on each occasion as to the child on its first trial; and he would, furthermore, be completely exhausted by his exertions. Think of the pains necessary to teach a child to stand, of the many efforts which it must make, and of the ease with which it at last stands, unconscious of any effort. For while secondarily automatic acts are accomplished with comparatively little weariness—in this regard approaching the organic movements, or the original reflex movements—the conscious effort of the will soon produces exhaustion. A spinal cord without . . . memory would simply be an idiotic spinal cord. . . . It is impossible for an individual to realize how much he owes to its automatic agency until disease has impaired its functions.

The next result is that *habit diminishes the conscious attention with which our acts are performed.*

One may state this abstractly thus: If an act require for its execution a chain, A, B, C, D, E, F, G, etc., of successive nervous events, then in the first performances of the action the conscious will must choose each of these events from a number of wrong alternatives that tend to present themselves: but habit soon brings it about that each event calls up its own appropriate successor without any alternative offering itself, and without any reference to the conscious will, until at last the whole chain, A, B, C, D, E, F, G, rattles itself off as soon as A occurs, just as if A and the rest of the chain were fused into a continuous stream. When we are learning to walk, to ride, to swim, skate, fence, write, play, or sing, we interrupt ourselves at every step by unnecessary movements and false notes. When we are proficients, on the contrary, the results not only follow with the very minimum of muscular action requisite to bring them forth, they also follow from a single instan-

5 G. H. Schneider: *Der menschliche Wille* (1882), pp. 417-419 (freely translated). For the drain-simile, see also Spencer's *Psychology*, part V, chap. VIII.
6 *Physiology of Mind*, p. 155.

taneous 'cue.' The marksman sees the bird, and, before he knows it, he has aimed and shot. A gleam in his adversary's eye, a momentary pressure from his rapier, and the fencer finds that he has instantly made the right parry and return. A glance at the musical hieroglyphics, and the pianist's fingers have rippled through a cataract of notes. And not only is it the right thing at the right time that we thus involuntarily do, but the wrong thing also, if it be an habitual thing. Who is there that has never wound up his watch on taking off his waistcoat in the daytime, or taken his latch-key out on arriving at the door-step of a friend? Very absent-minded persons in going to their bedroom to dress for dinner have been known to take off one garment after another and finally to get into bed, merely because that was the habitual issue of the first few movements when performed at a later hour. The writer well remembers how, on revisiting Paris after ten years' absence, and, finding himself in the street in which for one winter he had attended school, he lost himself in a brown study, from which he was awakened by finding himself upon the stairs which led to the apartment in a house many streets away in which he had lived during that earlier time, and to which his steps from the school had then habitually led. We all of us have a definite routine manner of performing certain daily offices connected with the toilet, with the opening and shutting of familiar cupboards, and the like. Our lower centres know the order of these movements, and show their knowledge by their 'surprise' if the objects are altered so as to oblige the movement to be made in a different way. But our higher thought-centres know hardly anything about the matter. Few men can tell off-hand which sock, shoe, or trousers-leg they put on first. They must first mentally rehearse the act; and even that is often insufficient—the act must be *performed*. So of the questions, Which valve of my double door opens first? Which way does my door swing? etc. I cannot *tell* the answer; yet my *hand* never makes a mistake. No one can *describe* the order in which he brushes his hair or teeth; yet it is likely that the order is a pretty fixed one in all of us.

These results may be expressed as follows:

In action grown habitual, what instigates each new muscular contraction to take place in its appointed order is not a thought or a perception, but the *sensation occasioned by the muscular contraction just finished.* A strictly voluntary act has to be guided by idea, perception, and volition, throughout its whole course. In an habitual action, mere sensation is a sufficient guide, and the upper regions of brain and mind are set comparatively free. A diagram will make the matter clear:

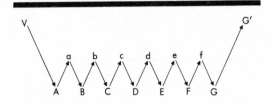

Let *A, B, C, D, E, F, G* represent an habitual chain of muscular contractions, and let *a, b, c, d, e, f* stand for the respective sensations which these contractions excite in us when they are successively performed. Such sensations will usually be of the muscles, skin, or joints of the parts moved, but they may also be effects of the movement upon the eye or the ear. Through them, and through them alone, we are made aware whether the contraction has or has not occurred. When the series, *A, B, C, D, E, F, G,* is being learned, each of these sensations becomes the object of a separate perception by the mind. By it we test each movement, to see if it be right before advancing to the next. We hesitate, compare, choose, revoke, reject, etc., by intellectual means; and the order by which the next movement is discharged is an express order from the ideational centres after this deliberation has been gone through.

In habitual action, on the contrary, the only impulse which the centres of idea or perception need send down is the initial impulse, the command to *start.* This is represented in the diagram by *V*; it may be a thought of the first movement or of the last result, or a mere perception of some of the habitual conditions of the chain, the presence, e.g., of the keyboard near the hand. In the present case, no sooner has the conscious thought or volition instigated movement *A*, than *A*, through the sensation *a* of its own occurrence, awakens *B* reflexly; *B* then excites *C* through *b*, and so on till the chain is ended, when the intellect generally takes cognizance of the final result. The process, in fact, resembles the passage of a wave of 'peristaltic' motion down the bowels. The intellectual perception at the end is indicated in the diagram by the effect of G being represented, at G', in the ideational centres above the merely sensational line. The sensational impressions, a, b, c, d, e, f, are all supposed to have their seat below the ideational lines. That our ideational centres, if involved at all by a, b, c, d, e, f, are involved in a minimal degree, is shown by the fact that the attention may be wholly absorbed elsewhere. We may say our prayers, or repeat the alphabet, with our attention far away.

A musical performer will play a piece which has become familiar by repetition while carrying on an animated conversation, or while continuously engrossed by some train of deeply interesting thought; the accustomed sequence of movements being directly prompted by the *sight* of the notes, or by the remembered succession of the *sounds* (if the piece is played from memory), aided in both cases by the guiding sensations derived from the muscles themselves. But, further, a higher degree of the same 'training' (acting on an organism specially fitted to profit by it) enables an accomplished pianist to play a difficult piece of music at sight; the movements of the hands and fingers following so immediately upon the sight of the notes that it seems impossible to believe that any but the very shortest and most direct track can be the channel of the nervous communication through which they are called forth. The following curious example of the same class of *acquired aptitudes,* which differ from instincts only in being prompted to action by the will, is furnished by Robert Houdin:

"With a view of cultivating the rapidity of visual and tactile perception, and the precision of respondent movements, which are necessary for success in every kind of prestidigitation, Houdin early practised the art of juggling with balls in the air; and having, after a month's practice, become thorough master of the art of keeping up *four* balls at once, he placed a book before him, and, while the balls were in the air, accustomed himself to read without hesitation. 'This,' he says, 'will probably seem to my readers very extraordinary; but I shall surprise them still more when I say that I have just amused myself with repeating this curious experiment. Though thirty years have elapsed since the time I was writing, and though I have scarcely once touched the balls during that period, I can still manage to read with ease while keeping *three* balls up.'" (*Autobiography*, p. 26.)[7]

We have called a, b, c, d, e, f, the antecedents of the successive muscular attractions, by the name of sensations. Some authors seem to deny that they are even this. If not even this, they can only be centripetal nerve-currents, not sufficient to arouse feeling, but sufficient to arouse motor response.[8] It may be at once admitted that they are not distinct *volitions*. The will, if any will be present, limits itself to a *permission* that they exert their motor effects. Dr. Carpenter writes:

There may still be metaphysicians who maintain that actions which were originally prompted by the will with a distinct intention, and which are still entirely under its control, can never cease to be volitional; and that either an infinitesimally small amount of will is required to sustain them when they have been once set going, or that the will is in a sort of pendulum-like oscillation between the two actions — the maintenance of the train of *thought,* and the maintenance of the train of *movement.* But if only an infinitesimally small amount of will is necessary to sustain them, is not this tantamount to saying that they go on by a force of their own? And does not the experience of the *perfect continuity* of our train of thought during the performance of movements that have become habitual, entirely negative the hypothesis of oscillation? Besides, if such an oscillation existed, there must be *intervals* in which each action goes on *of itself*; so that its essentially automatic character is virtually admitted. The physiological explanation, that the mechanism of locomotion, as of other habitual movements, *grows to* the mode in which it is early exercised, and that it then works automatically under the general control and direction of the will, can scarcely be put down by any assumption of an hypothetical necessity, which rests only on the basis of ignorance of one side of our composite nature.[9]

But if not distinct acts of will, these immediate antecedents of each movement of the chain are at any rate accompanied by consciousness of some kind. They are *sensations* to which we are *usually inattentive,* but which immediately call our attention if they go *wrong*. Schneider's account of these sensations deserves to be quoted. In the act of walking, he says, even when our attention is entirely off,

---

7 Carpenter's *Mental Physiology* (1874), pp. 217, 218.
8 Von Hartmann devotes a chapter of his *Philosophy of the Unconscious* (English translation, vol. I, p. 72) to proving that they must be both *ideas* and *unconscious*.
9 *Mental Physiology*, p. 20.

we are continuously aware of certain muscular feelings; and we have, moreover, a feeling of certain impulses to keep our equilibrium and to set down one leg after another. It is doubtful whether we could preserve equilibrium if no sensation of our body's attitude were there, and doubtful whether we should advance our leg if we had no sensation of its movement as executed, and not even a minimal feeling of impulse to set it down. Knitting appears altogether mechanical, and the knitter keeps up her knitting even while she reads or is engaged in lively talk. But if we ask her how this be possible, she will hardly reply that the knitting goes on of itself. She will rather say that she has a feeling of it, that she feels in her hands that she knits and how she must knit, and that therefore the movements of knitting are called forth and regulated by the sensations associated therewithal, even when the attention is called away.

So of every one who practises, apparently automatically, a long-familiar handicraft. The smith turning his tongs as he smites the iron, the carpenter wielding his plane, the lace-maker with her bobbin, the weaver at his loom, all will answer the same question in the same way by saying that they have a feeling of the proper management of the implement in their hands.

In these cases, the feelings which are conditions of the appropriate acts are very faint. But none the less are they necessary. Imagine your hands not feeling; your movements could then only be provoked by ideas, and if your ideas were then diverted away, the movements ought to come to a standstill, which is a consequence that seldom occurs.[10]

Again:

An idea makes you take, for example, a violin into your left hand. But it is not necessary that your idea remain fixed on the contraction of the muscles of the left hand and fingers in order that the violin may continue to be held fast and not let fall. The sensations themselves which the holding of the instrument awakens in the hand, since they are associated with the motor impulse of grasping, are sufficient to cause this impulse, which then lasts as long as the feeling itself lasts, or until the impulse is inhibited by the idea of some antagonistic motion.

And the same may be said of the manner in which the right hand holds the bow:

It sometimes happens, in beginning these simultaneous combinations, that one movement or impulse will cease if the consciousness turn particularly toward another, because at the outset the guiding sensations must *all* be strongly *felt*. The bow will perhaps slip from the fingers, because some of the muscles have relaxed. But the slipping is a cause of new sensations starting up in the hand, so that the attention is in a moment brought back to the grasping of the bow.

The following experiment shows this well: When one begins to play on the violin, to keep him from raising his right elbow in playing a book is placed under his right armpit, which he is ordered to hold fast by keeping the upper arm tight against his body. The muscular feelings, and feelings of contact connected with the book, provoke an impulse to press it tight. But often it happens that the beginner, whose attention gets absorbed in the production of the notes, lets drop the book. Later, however, this never happens; the faintest sensations of contact suffice to awaken the impulse to keep it in its place, and the attention may be wholly absorbed by the notes and the fingering with the left hand. *The simultaneous combination of movements is thus in the first instance conditioned by the facility with which in us, alongside of intellectual processes, processes of inattentive feeling may still go on.*[11]

This brings us by a very natural transition to the *ethical implications of the law of habit*. They are numerous and momentous. Dr. Carpenter, from whose *Mental Physiology* we have quoted, has so prominently enforced the principle that our organs grow to the way in which they have been exercised, and dwelt upon its consequences, that his book almost deserves to be called a work of edification, on this account alone. We need make no apology, then, for tracing a few of these consequences ourselves:

"Habit a second nature! Habit is ten times nature," the Duke of Wellington is said to have exclaimed; and the degree to which this is true no one can probably appreciate as well as one who is a veteran soldier himself. The daily drill and the years of discipline end by fashioning a man completely over again, as to most of the possibilities of his conduct.

There is a story, which is credible enough, though it may not be true, of a practical joker, who, seeing a discharged veteran carrying home his dinner, suddenly called out, 'Attention!' whereupon the man instantly brought his hands down, and lost his mutton and potatoes

---

10 *Der menschliche Wille*, pp. 447, 448.
11 *Der menschliche Wille*, p. 439. The last sentence is rather freely translated — the sense is unaltered.

in the gutter. The drill had been thorough and its effects had become embodied in the man's nervous structure.[12]

Riderless cavalry-horses, at many a battle, have been seen to come together and go through their customary evolutions at the sound of the bugle-call. Most trained domestic animals, dogs and oxen, and omnibus- and car-horses, seem to be machines almost pure and simple, undoubtingly, unhesitatingly doing from minute to minute the duties they have been taught, and giving no sign that the possibility of an alternative ever suggests itself to their mind. Men grown old in prison have asked to be readmitted after being once set free. In a railroad accident to a travelling menagerie in the United States some time in 1884, a tiger, whose cage had broken open, is said to have emerged, but presently crept back again, as if too much bewildered by his new responsibilities, so that he was without difficulty secured.

Habit is thus the enormous fly-wheel of society, its most precious conservative agent. It alone is what keeps us all within the bounds of ordinance, and saves the children of fortune from the envious uprisings of the poor. It alone prevents the hardest and most repulsive walks of life from being deserted by those brought up to tread therein. It keeps the fisherman and the deck-hand at sea through the winter; it holds the miner in his darkness, and nails the countryman to his log-cabin and his lonely farm through all the months of snow; it protects us from invasion by the natives of the desert and the frozen zone. It dooms us all to fight out the battle of life upon the lines of our nurture or our early choice, and to make the best of a pursuit that disagrees, because there is no other for which we are fitted, and it is too late to begin again. It keeps different social strata from mixing. Already at the age of twenty-five you see the professional mannerism settling down on the young commercial traveller, on the young doctor, on the young minister, on the young counsellor-at-law. You see the little lines of cleavage running through the character, the tricks of thought, the prejudices, the ways of the 'shop,' in a word, from which the man can by-and-by no more escape than his coat-sleeve can suddenly fall into a new set of folds. On the whole, it is best he should not escape. It is well for the world that in most of us, by the age of thirty, the character has set like plaster, and will never soften again.

If the period between twenty and thirty is the critical one in the formation of intellectual and professional habits, the period below twenty is more important still for the fixing of *personal* habits, properly so called, such as vocalization and pronunciation, gesture, motion, and address. Hardly ever is a language learned after twenty spoken without a foreign accent; hardly ever can a youth transferred to the society of his betters unlearn the nasality and other vices of speech bred in him by the associations of his growing years. Hardly ever, indeed, no matter how much money there be in his pocket, can he even learn to *dress* like a gentleman-born. The merchants offer their wares as eagerly to him as to the veriest 'swell,' but he simply *cannot* buy the right things. An invisible law, as strong as gravitation, keeps him within his orbit, arrayed this year as he was the last; and how his better-bred acquaintances contrive to get the things they wear will be for him a mystery till his dying day.

The great thing, then, in all education, is to *make our nervous system our ally instead of our enemy*. It is to fund and capitalize our acquisitions, and live at ease upon the interest of the fund. *For this we must make automatic and habitual, as early as possible, as many useful actions as we can,* and guard against the growing into ways that are likely to be disadvantageous to us, as we should guard against the plague. The more of the details of our daily life we can hand over to the effortless custody of automatism, the more our higher powers of mind will be set free for their own proper work. There is no more miserable human being than one in whom nothing is habitual but indecision, and for whom the lighting of every cigar, the drinking of every cup, the time of rising and going to bed every day, and the beginning of every bit of work, are subjects of express volitional deliberation. Full half the time of such a man goes to the deciding, or regretting, of matters which ought to be so ingrained in him as practically not to exist for his consciousness at all. If there be such daily duties not yet ingrained in any one of my readers, let him begin this very hour to set the matter right.

12 Huxley's *Elementary Lessons in Physiology*, lesson XII.

In Professor Bain's chapter on "The Moral Habits" there are some admirable practical remarks laid down. Two great maxims emerge from his treatment. The first is that in the acquisition of a new habit, or the leaving off of an old one, we must take care to *launch ourselves with as strong and decided an initiative as possible.* Accumulate all the possible circumstances which shall re-enforce the right motives; put yourself assiduously in conditions that encourage the new way; make engagements incompatible with the old; take a public pledge, if the case allows; in short, envelop your resolution with every aid you know. This will give your new beginning such a momentum that the temptation to break down will not occur as soon as it otherwise might; and every day during which a breakdown is postponed adds to the chances of its not occurring at all.

The second maxim is: *Never suffer an exception to occur till the new habit is securely rooted in your life.* Each lapse is like the letting fall of a ball of string which one is carefully winding up; a single slip undoes more than a great many turns will wind again. *Continuity* of training is the great means of making the nervous system act infallibly right. As Professor Bain says:

The peculiarity of the moral habits, contradistinguishing them from the intellectual acquisitions, is the presence of two hostile powers, one to be gradually raised into the ascendant over the other. It is necessary, above all things, in such a situation, never to lose a battle. Every gain on the wrong side undoes the effect of many conquests on the right. The essential precaution, therefore, is so to regulate the two opposing powers that the one may have a series of uninterrupted successes, until repetition has fortified it to such a degree as to enable it to cope with the opposition, under any circumstances. This is the theoretically best career of mental progress.

The need of securing success at the *outset* is imperative. Failure at first is apt to dampen the energy of all future attempts, whereas past experience of success nerves one to future vigor. Goethe says to a man who consulted him about an enterprise but mistrusted his own powers: "Ach! you need only blow on your hands!" And the remark illustrates the effect on Goethe's spirits of his own habitually successful career. Prof. Baumann, from whom I borrow the anecdote,[13] says that the collapse of bar-

barian nations when Europeans come among them is due to their despair of ever succeeding as the new-comers do in the larger tasks of life. Old ways are broken and new ones not formed.

The question of 'tapering-off,' in abandoning such habits as drink and opium-indulgence, comes in here, and is a question about which experts differ within certain limits, and in regard to what may be best for an individual case. In the main, however, all expert opinion would agree that abrupt acquisition of the new habit is the best way, *if there be a real possibility of carrying it out.* We must be careful not to give the will so stiff a task as to insure its defeat at the very outset; but, *provided one can stand it,* a sharp period of suffering, and then a free time, is the best thing to aim at, whether in giving up a habit like that of opium, or in simply changing one's hours of rising or of work. It is surprising how soon a desire will die of inanition if it be *never* fed.

One must first learn, unmoved, looking neither to the right nor left, to walk firmly on the straight and narrow path, before one can begin 'to make one's self over again.' He who every day makes a fresh resolve is like one who, arriving at the edge of the ditch he is to leap, forever stops and returns for a fresh run. Without **unbroken** advance there is no such thing **as accumulation** of the ethical forces possible, and to make this possible, and to exercise us and habituate us in it, is the sovereign blessing of regular **work.**[14]

A third maxim may be added to the preceding pair: *Seize the very first possible opportunity to act on every resolution you make, and on every emotional prompting you may experience in the direction of the habits you aspire to gain.* It is not in the moment of their forming, but in the moment of their producing *motor effects,* that resolves and aspirations communicate the new 'set' to the brain. As the author last quoted remarks:

The actual presence of the practical opportunity alone furnishes the fulcrum upon which the lever can rest, by means of which the moral will may multiply its strength,

13 See the admirable passage about success at the outset, in his *Handbuch der Moral* (1878), pp. 38-43.
14 J. Bahnsen: *Beitrage zu Charakterologie* (1867), vol. I. p. 209.

and raise itself aloft. He who has no solid ground to press against will never get beyond the stage of empty gesture-making.

No matter how full a reservoir of *maxims* one may possess, and no matter how good one's *sentiments* may be, if one have not taken advantage of every concrete opportunity to *act,* one's character may remain entirely unaffected for the better. With mere good intentions, hell is proverbially paved. And this is an obvious consequence of the principles we have laid down. A 'character,' as J. S. Mill says, 'is a completely fashioned will'; and a will, in the sense in which he means it, is an aggregate of tendencies to act in a firm and prompt and definite way upon all the principal emergencies of life. A tendency to act only becomes effectively ingrained in us in proportion to the uninterrupted frequency with which the actions actually occur, and the brain "grows" to their use. Every time a resolve or a fine glow of feeling evaporates without bearing practical fruit is worse than a chance lost; it works so as positively to hinder future resolutions and emotions from taking the normal path of discharge. There is no more contemptible type of human character than that of the nerveless sentimentalist and dreamer, who spends his life in a weltering sea of sensibility and emotion, but who never does a manly concrete deed. Rousseau, inflaming all the mothers of France, by his eloquence, to follow Nature and nurse their babies themselves, while he sends his own children to the foundling hospital, is the classical example of what I mean. But every one of us in his measure, whenever, after glowing for an abstractly formulated Good, he practically ignores some actual case, among the squalid 'other particulars' of which that same Good lurks disguised, treads straight on Rousseau's path. All Goods are disguised by the vulgarity of their concomitants, in this work-a-day world; but woe to him who can only recognize them when he thinks them in their pure and abstract form! The habit of excessive novel-reading and theatre-going will produce true monsters in this line. The weeping of a Russian lady over the fictitious personages in the play, while her coachman is freezing to death on his seat outside, is the sort of thing that everywhere happens on a less glaring scale. Even the habit of excessive indulgence in music, for those who are neither performers themselves nor musically gifted enough to take it in a purely intellectual way, has probably a relaxing effect upon the character. One becomes filled with emotions which habitually pass without prompting to any deed, and so the inertly sentimental condition is kept up. The remedy would be, never to suffer one's self to have an emotion at a concert, without expressing it afterward in *some* active way.[15] Let the expression be the least thing in the world—speaking genially to one's aunt, or giving up one's seat in a horsecar, if nothing more heroic offers—but let it not fail to take place.

These latter cases make us aware that it is not simply *particular lines* of discharge, but also *general forms* of discharge, that seem to be grooved out by habit in the brain. Just as, if we let our emotions evaporate, they get into a way of evaporating; so there is reason to suppose that if we often flinch from making an effort, before we know it the effort-making capacity will be gone; and that, if we suffer the wandering of our attention, presently it will wander all the time. Attention and effort are, as we shall see later, but two names for the same psychic fact. To what brain-processes they correspond we do not know. The strongest reason for believing that they do depend on brain-processes at all, and are not pure acts of the spirit, is just this fact, that they seem in some degree subject to the law of habit, which is a material law. As a final practical maxim, relative to these habits of the will, we may, then, offer something like this: *Keep the faculty of effort alive in you by a little gratuitous exercise every day.* That is, be systematically ascetic or heroic in little unnecessary points, do every day or two something for no other reason than that you would rather not do it, so that when the hour of dire need draws nigh, it may find you not unnerved and untrained to stand the test. Asceticism of this sort is like the insurance which a man pays on his house and goods. The tax does him no good at the time, and possibly may never bring him a return. But if the fire *does* come, his having paid it will be his salvation

---

15 See for remarks on this subject a readable article by Miss V. Scudder on "Musical Devotees and Morals," in the *Andover Review* for January 1887.

from ruin. So with the man who has daily inured himself to habits of concentrated attention, energetic volition, and self-denial in unnecessary things. He will stand like a tower when everything rocks around him, and when his softer fellow-mortals are winnowed like chaff in the blast.

The physiological study of mental conditions is thus the most powerful ally of hortatory ethics. The hell to be endured hereafter, of which theology tells, is no worse than the hell we make for ourselves in this world by habitually fashioning our characters in the wrong way. Could the young but realize how soon they will become mere walking bundles of habits, they would give more heed to their conduct while in the plastic state. We are spinning our own fates, good or evil, and never to be undone. Every smallest stroke of virtue or of vice leaves its never so little scar. The drunken Rip Van Winkle, in Jefferson's play, excuses himself for every fresh dereliction by saying, 'I won't count this time!' Well! he may not count it, and a kind Heaven may not count it; but it is being counted none the less. Down among his nerve-cells and fibres the molecules are counting it, registering and storing it up to be used against him when the next temptation comes. Nothing we ever do is, in strict scientific literalness, wiped out. Of course, this has its good side as well as its bad one. As we become permanent drunkards by so many separate drinks, so we become saints in moral, and authorities and experts in the practical and scientific spheres, by so many separate acts and hours of work. Let no youth have any anxiety about the upshot of his education, whatever the line of it may be. If he keep faithfully busy each hour of the working-day, he may safely leave the final result to itself. He can with perfect certainty count on waking up some fine morning, to find himself one of the competent ones of his generation, in whatever pursuit he may have singled out. Silently, between all the details of his business, the *power of judging* in all that class of matter will have built itself up within him as a possession that will never pass away. Young people should know this truth in advance. The ignorance of it has probably engendered more discouragement and faint-heartedness in youths embarking on arduous careers than all other causes put together.

Knowledge and purpose as habit mechanisms

CLARK L. HULL

It is only with the greatest difficulty that scientists are able to maintain a thoroughly naturalistic attitude toward the more complex forms of human behavior. Our intellectual atmosphere is still permeated in a thousand subtle ways with the belief in disembodied behavior functions or spirits. The situation is aggravated by the fact that the details of the more complex action patterns are so concealed as to be almost impossible of observation. Even so, the outlook is hopeful. The work of many ingenious investigators is bringing to light important details of the hidden processes, and enough evidence has already accumulated to enable us in a number of cases to discern with tolerable clearness the broad naturalistic outlines of their operation.

1

One of the oldest problems with which thoughtful persons have occupied themselves concerns the nature and origin of knowledge. How can one physical object become acquainted with the ways of another physical object and of the world in general? In approaching this problem from the point of view of habit, it is important to recognize that knowledge is mediated by several fairly distinct habit mechanisms. In the present study but one of these will be elaborated.

Let us assume a relatively isolated inorganic world sequence taking place as shown in Fig. 1.

From *Psychological Review*, 1950, 37, 511-525.

Fig. 1

THE WORLD: $S_1 \longrightarrow S_2 \longrightarrow S_3 \longrightarrow S_4 \longrightarrow S_5 \longrightarrow \cdots$

Here S_1, S_2, etc., represent typical phases of a sequential flux, the time intervals between successive S's being uniform and no more than a few seconds each. Let us suppose, further, that in the neighborhood of this world sequence is a sensitive redintegrative organism. The latter is provided with distance receptors and is so conditioned at the outset as to respond characteristically to the several phases of the world sequence. Each S accordingly becomes a stimulus complex impinging simultaneously on numerous end organs. As a result, each phase of the world sequence now becomes a cause, not only of the succeeding phase in its own proper series, but also of a functionally parallel event (reaction) within the neighboring organism. The organismic responses of the series thus formed have no direct causal relationship among themselves.[1] R_1 in itself has no power of causing (evoking) R_2. The causal relationship essential in the placing of R_2 after R_1 is that of the physical world obtaining in the S-sequence; R_2 follows R_1 because S_2 follows S_1. The situation is represented diagrammatically in Fig. 2.

Fig. 2

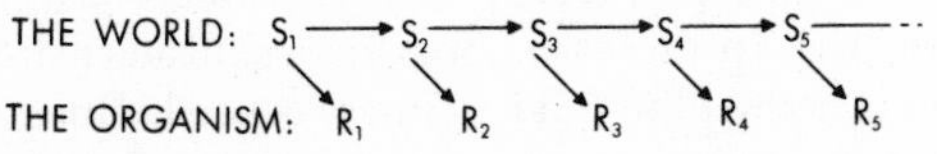

THE WORLD: $S_1 \longrightarrow S_2 \longrightarrow S_3 \longrightarrow S_4 \longrightarrow S_5 \longrightarrow \cdots$

THE ORGANISM: $R_1 \quad R_2 \quad R_3 \quad R_4 \quad R_5$

Now a high-grade organism possesses internal receptors which are stimulated by its own movements. Accordingly each response (R) produces at once a characteristic stimulus complex and stimuli thus originated make up to a large extent the internal component of the organism's stimuli complexes. Let these internal stimulus components be represented by s's. If we assume, in the interest of simplicity of exposition, that the time intervals between the phases of the world flux selected for representation are exactly equal to those consumed by the $S \to R \to s$ sequences, the situation will be as shown in Fig. 3, S_2 coinciding in time with s_1, S_3 with s_2 and so on.

Fig. 3

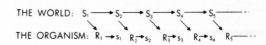

THE WORLD: $S_1 \longrightarrow S_2 \longrightarrow S_3 \longrightarrow S_4 \longrightarrow S_5 \longrightarrow \cdots$

THE ORGANISM: $R_1 \to s_1 \quad R_2 \to s_2 \quad R_3 \to s_3 \quad R_4 \to s_4 \quad R_5 \longrightarrow \cdots$

Now, by the principle of redintegration, all the components of a stimulus complex impinging upon the sensorium at or near the time that a response is evoked, tend themselves independently to acquire the capacity to evoke substantially the same response. We will let a dotted rectangle indicate that what is enclosed within it constitutes a redintegrative stimulus complex; and a dotted arrow, a newly acquired excitatory tendency. After one or more repetitions of the world sequence, the situation will be as shown in Fig. 4.

Fig. 4

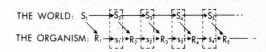

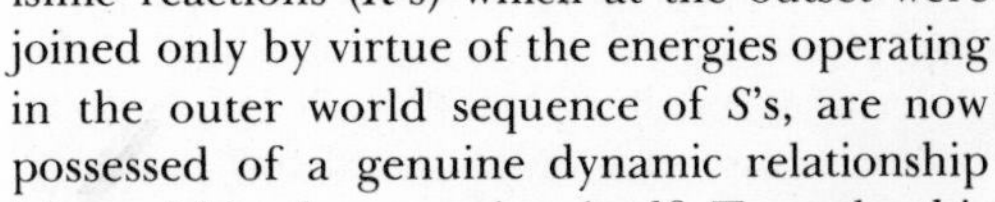

THE WORLD: $S_1 \longrightarrow \overline{S_2} \longrightarrow \overline{S_3} \longrightarrow \overline{S_4} \longrightarrow \overline{S_5} \longrightarrow \cdots$

THE ORGANISM: $R_1 \to s_1 \to R_2 \to s_2 \to R_3 \to s_3 \to R_4 \to s_4 \to R_5 \longrightarrow \cdots$

As a result of the joint operation of the several factors summarized in Fig. 4, the organismic reactions (R's) which at the outset were joined only by virtue of the energies operating in the outer world sequence of S's, are now possessed of a genuine dynamic relationship lying within the organism itself. To make this clear, let it be assumed that the world sequence begins in the presence of the organism, but is at once interrupted. The resulting situation is

1 This neglects the original dynamic influence of the ever-present internal component of the organismic stimulus complex into which each phase of the world sequence enters to evoke the corresponding organismic reaction. The excitatory potency of this internal component is here supposed to be minimal. Its influence is neglected in the interest of simplicity of exposition. Its undeniable presence clearly introduces an element of subjectivity into reactions which appear superficially to be evoked purely by the external world.

shown diagrammatically in Fig. 5. The newly acquired excitatory tendencies, unless interrupted by some more potent influence, should continue the organismic sequence of responses very much as when they were first called forth as the result of the stimulation by the world sequence.

Fig. 5

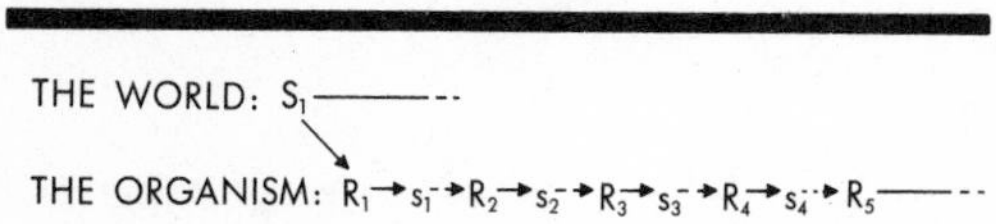

THE WORLD: S_1————--

THE ORGANISM: $R_1 \rightarrow s_1^- \rightarrow R_2 \rightarrow s_2^- \rightarrow R_3 \rightarrow s_3^- \rightarrow R_4 \rightarrow s_4^- \rightarrow R_5$————--

In summary it may be said that through the operation of a variety of principles and circumstances, the world in a very important sense has stamped the pattern of its action upon a physical object. The imprint has been made in such a way that a functional parallel of this action segment of the physical world has become a part of the organism. Henceforth the organism will carry about continuously a kind of replica of this world segment. In this very intimate and biologically significant sense the organism may be said to know the world. No spiritual or supernatural forces need be assumed to understand the acquisition of this knowledge. The process is entirely a naturalistic one throughout.

II

Once the organism has acquired within its body this subjective parallel to the ways of the physical world, certain other activity patterns or habit mechanisms at once become operative. One of the more important of these is the power of foresight or fore-knowledge. A great deal of mystery has surrounded this problem. Foresight may be defined for our present purpose as *the reaction to an event which may be impending, but which has not as yet taken place.* The difficulty seems largely to have been concerned with the problem of how an organism can react to an event not yet in existence. The reasoning runs: An event not yet in existence cannot be a stimulus; and how can an organism react to a stimulus which does not exist? In terms of our diagram, how can R_5, which is a reaction to the stimulating event S_5, take place before S_5 itself has occurred?

An important circumstance connected with foresight is the fact that the tempo of the acquired subjective parallel to the outer world sequence is not limited to that of the latter. Indeed, there is evidence indicating a tendency for a primary conditioned reaction to run off at a higher speed than that of the master world sequence which it parallels.[2] Thus it comes about that, even when both series begin at the same instant, the end-reaction of the subjective series may actually antedate the stimulus in the world sequence which exclusively evoked it previous to the conditioning shown in Fig. 4. It is evident that this possibility of the heightened tempo on the part of the organismic act sequence is intimately connected with the possession by the organism of knowledge of events before they actually take place.

The biological advantage of antecedent knowledge of impending events is great. This is particularly clear in the case of defense reactions. These latter fall into two main types—flight and attack. Let us suppose that in the example elaborated above, S_5 is a seriously nocuous stimulus and R_5 is a successful flight reaction. Foresight will result from the reeling off of the R-series faster than the S-series so that s_4 will evoke R_5 before S_5 has occurred. In this event S_5, when it does occur, will not impinge on the organism for the reason that the latter will have withdrawn from the zone of danger as the result of the act R_5. In case R_5 is an act of attack rather than flight it must, to be successful, bring the organismic series into contact with the world sequence in such a manner as to interrupt the latter before S_5 is reached. In this case also, the organism clearly escapes the injury. Thus the supposed impossibility of an organismic reaction to a situation before it exists as a stimulus is accomplished quite naturally through the medium of an internal substitute stimulus.

---

2 C. L. Hull, A functional interpretation of the conditioned reflex, *Psychol. Rev.*, 1929, **36**, p. 507 ff. A quite distinct mechanism serving much the same function as that here emphasized has its basis in the peculiar advantage afforded by distance receptors. The stimulus of a distant object through a distance receptor is often sufficiently like that when the object is near and nocuous to evoke a successful defense reaction before the source of danger can get near enough to produce injury. This has been discussed in detail by Howard C. Warren, *J. Phil., Psychol. & Scient. Meth.*, 1916, **13**, p. 35 ff.

A reflective consideration of the habit mechanisms involved in anticipatory defense reactions reveals a phenomenon of the greatest significance. This is the existence of acts whose sole function is to serve as stimuli for other acts. We shall accordingly call them *pure stimulus acts*. Under normal conditions practically all acts become stimuli, but ordinarily the stimulus function is an incidental one. The consideration of the approach of an organism to food may clarify the concept. Each step taken in approaching the food serves in part as the stimulus for the next step, but its main function is to bring the body nearer the food. Such acts are, therefore, primarily instrumental. By way of contrast may be considered the anticipatory defense sequence presented above. R_5, the actual defense reaction, obviously has instrumental value in high degree. R_4, on the other hand, has no instrumental value. This does not mean that it has no significance. Without R_4 there would be no s_4, and without s_4, there would be no R_5 *i.e.* no defense. In short, R_4 is a pure stimulus act. In the same way R_3 and R_2 serve no instrumental function but, nevertheless, are indispensible as stimulus acts in bringing about the successful defense response.

A simple experiment which can be performed by anyone in a few moments may still further clarify the concept of the pure stimulus act. Ask almost any psychologically naïve person how he buttons his coat with one hand — which finger, if any, he puts through the buttonhole, what the last act of the sequence is — and so on. The average person can tell little about it at first. If wearing a coat, he will usually perform the act forthwith. If warned against this, the hand may quite generally be observed to steal close to the position at which the buttoning is usually performed and to go through the buttoning behavior sequence *by itself*. After this the nature of the final buttoning act may be stated with some assurance. Clearly, the earlier acts of this pseudo-buttoning sequence are pure stimulus acts since they serve no function whatever, except as stimuli to evoke succeeding movements and ultimately the critical final movement which is sought.

It is evident upon a little reflection that the advent of the pure stimulus act into biological economy marks a great advance. It makes available at once a new and enlarged range of behavior possibilities. The organism is no longer a passive reactor to stimuli from without, but becomes relatively free and dynamic. There is a transcendence of the limitations of habit as ordinarily understood, in that the organism can react to the not-here as well as the not-now. In the terminology of the *Gestalt* psychologists, the appearance of the pure stimulus act among habit phenomena marks a great increase in the organism's 'degrees of freedom.' The pure stimulus act thus emerges as an organic, physiological — strictly internal and individual — symbolism.[3] Quite commonplace instrumental acts, by a natural reduction process, appear transformed into a kind of *thought* — rudimentary it is true, but of the most profound biological significance.

Thus the transformation of mere action into thought, which has seemed to some as conceivable only through a kind of miracle, appears to be a wholly naturalistic process and one of no great subtlety. Indeed, its obviousness is such as to challenge the attempt at synthetic verification from inorganic materials. It is altogether probable that a 'psychic' machine, with ample provision in its design for the evolution of pure stimulus acts, could attain a degree of freedom, spontaneity, and power to dominate its environment, inconceivable alike to individuals unfamiliar with the possibilities of automatic mechanisms and to the professional designers of the ordinary rigid-type machines.

Pure stimulus-act sequences present certain unique opportunities for biological economy not possessed by ordinary instrumental-act sequences. In the first place, there is the ever present need of reducing the energy expenditure to a minimum while accomplishing the ordinary biological functions in a normal

---

3 This peculiarly individual form of symbolism is not to be confused with the purely stimulus acts of social communication. Neither is it to be confused with what appears to be a derivative of the latter by a reduction process, the subvocal speech emphasized by Watson. The special stimulus-response mechanisms by which the evolution of these latter forms of symbolism take place, together with their peculiar potentialities for mediating biological adjustment and survival, are so complex as to preclude consideration here.

manner. It is clear that pure stimulus-act sequences, since they no longer have any instrumental function, may be reduced in magnitude to almost any degree consistent with the delivery of a stimulus adequate to evoke the final instrumental or goal act.[4] Observation seems to indicate that this economy is operative on a very wide scale. It may even be observed in the buttoning experiment previously cited. The hand while going through the buttoning sequence by itself will ordinarily make movements of much smaller amplitude than when performing the instrumental act sequence with a real button.

A significant observation made by Thorndike in the early days of animal experimentation illustrates the same tendency, though in a very different setting. He placed cats in a confining box from which they sought to escape. Some he would release only when they licked themselves, others only when they scratched themselves. After an unusually long training period the cats finally learned to perform the required acts and thus to escape fairly promptly. In this connection, Thorndike remarks:

There is in all these cases a noticeable tendency, of the cause of which I am ignorant, to diminish the act until it becomes a mere vestige of a lick or a scratch. After the cat gets so it performs the act soon after it is put in, it begins to do it less and less vigorously. The licking degenerates into a mere quick turn of the head with one or two motions up and down with tongue extended. Instead of a hearty scratch the cat waves its paw up and down rapidly for an instant.[5]

The ordinary scratch of a cat is an instrumental act. It must have a certain duration and intensity to serve its function. In the present instance the scratch served only as a visual stimulus to Dr. Thorndike. As such, a small movement was presumably quite as effective as a large one.

In the second place there is, particularly in the case of primitive defense acts, the need to economize time so as to increase the promptness of the defense reaction. This desideratum appears to be accomplished by the same means as the first—the reduction in the magnitude of the acts. A movement of small amplitude should be more quickly performed than one of large amplitude.

But the maximum of economy, both as to energy and as to time, demands not only that the units of the stimulus-act sequence shall be small in amplitude, but that they shall also be as *few* as possible. If a single stimulus-act is sufficient to furnish the necessary stimulus for the defense reaction, the existence of all the other stimulus acts in the series is a sheer waste, both of time and energy. This means that biological efficiency demands on two separate counts the dropping out of large sections of purely stimulus-act sequences.

V

The importance of the serial-segment elimination tendency in pure stimulus-act and other complex learning sequences raises very insistently the question as to what stimulus-response mechanisms may bring it about. Observation suggests that one condition favorable for 'short circuiting' is that the process shall be strongly 'purposive.' *In the present study the purpose mechanism shall be understood as a persisting core of sameness in the stimulus complexes throughout the successive phases of the reaction sequence.* We will symbolize this persisting stimulus by S_p. This may be thought of concretely as a continuous strong red light, or a continuous gripping of a dynamometer, or the continuous knitting of the brows, or (more typically) the continuously recurring crampings of the digestive tract as in hunger.

When the principle of the persisting stimulus is joined to the set of principles represented as operating in Fig. 5, a number of novel consequences at once appear. The situation is represented in Fig. 6. An examination of this diagram shows that S_p has a unique advantage over all the other components in the several stimulus complexes. Thus, S_1, S_2, etc. and s_1, s_2, etc. can get conditioned, except for remote

---

4 Movements greatly reduced in magnitude tend to become vestigial. This suggests a possible explanation of the extreme subjectivity of imagery. Just how far the weakening of pure stimulus acts may go and still serve their stimulus function is a question which may yield to experimental approach. That they should diminish to an actual zero, with nothing but a neural vestige remaining to perform the stimulus function, is conceivable though hardly probable. It is believed that the present hypothesis is general enough to fit either alternative.

5 E. L. Thorndike, *Animal intelligence*, Macmillan, 1911, p. 48.

associative tendencies,[6] only to the response in each case which immediately follows, *i.e.* to but a single response each. But S_p, since it is present in all the stimulus complexes of the series, *gets conditioned to all the reactions* taking place in it.

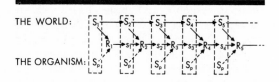

Fig. 6

THE WORLD:

THE ORGANISM:

This multiplicity of excitatory tendencies resulting from the situation shown in Fig. 6, is represented diagrammatically in Fig. 7.

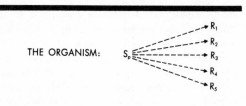

Fig. 7

THE ORGANISM:

VI

It is evident that in a situation such as is presented in Fig. 7, a competition of the several excitatory tendencies will follow. Since this competition must be between the several parts of the series, it will be called *intraserial competition.* We may safely assume that the several excitatory tendencies radiating from S_p will have varying strengths. There also enter into this competition, of course, the stimulus elements which may be present in the stimulus complex from other sources at any particular moment. We will simplify the stimulus situation somewhat by assuming that the world sequence is interrupted at once after its first phase, S_1. What, then, will be the state of this intraserial competition at the second stimulus complex of the diagram?

If we assume that s_1 has an excitatory tendency toward R_2 of 2 units, that S_p also has an excitatory tendency toward R_2 of 2 units, toward R_3 of 3 units, towards R_4 of 4 units and towards R_5 of 5 units, the competition among the several segments of the series will be that shown in Fig. 8. From this diagram it may be

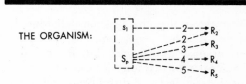

Fig. 8

THE ORGANISM:

seen that the immediately following reaction (R_2) in the original action sequence has the advantage of a double excitatory tendency, whereas the more distant reactions such as R_3, R_4, and R_5, have but a single excitatory tendency each, that arising only from S_p. But if at any time one of the single (S_p) excitatory tendencies should chance to be stronger than the combination of the two tendencies leading to the immediately following act of the original sequence, the elimination of a segment of the pure stimulus-act sequence will take place.

In order to understand how the purposive mechanism, through intraserial competition, may bring about serial segment elimination, let us observe the sequel to the following hypothetical situation. It may very well prove to be the case that S_p gets conditioned more strongly as the final or critical response in a behavior cycle is approached.[7] Accordingly a rough

6 These are here neglected in order to simplify the exposition. Ultimately they must, of course, be taken fully into account.
7 It would not appear to be an over difficult task to test this hypothesis experimentally. If it should prove true it would have extensive theoretical implications and would clear up a number of questions in the theory of learning. However, almost any other hypothesis which provides considerable variation in the strength of the excitatory tendencies radiating from S_p will produce substantially similar results. It may be added that an irregular distribution of intensities of excitatory tendencies from S_p offers special opportunities for backward serial segment elimination as contrasted with the more usual forward variety here emphasized.

approximation to such a system of excitatory tendencies has been assigned to the bonds presented in Fig. 8. We may summarize the several competing excitatory tendencies radiating from the second stimulus complex as follows:

$$R_2 = 4,$$
$$R_3 = 3,$$
$$R_4 = 4,$$
$$R_5 = 5.$$

This shows that the reaction following the second stimulus complex must be, not R_2 as in the original act sequence, but R_5. But if R_5 follows immediately after R_1, the behavior segment shown in Fig. 9 drops completely out of the series. This is inevitable because no stimulus now remains in the series adequate to evoke it.

Fig. 9

THE ORGANISM: $R_2 \longrightarrow s_2 \dashrightarrow R_3 \longrightarrow s_3 \dashrightarrow R_4 \longrightarrow s_4$

One of the most baffling theoretical problems related to experimental psychology has been that of explaining how errors or unnecessary acts in behavior sequences get eliminated. Nevertheless, few psychological phenomena are more common. One is asked the product of 49 × 67. He writes the numbers down on paper, certain multiplication-table and addition-table habits of childhood are evoked in an orderly succession, and at length there is written down by successive stages the number, 3283. If, not too long afterwards, the individual is again asked the product of 49 × 67, he may respond by saying 3283 at once. In thus passing directly from the question to the answer, the behavior sequence of pure stimulus acts which constituted the detailed multiplication of 49 × 67 has completely dropped out of the sequence.

The difficulty of accounting for this phenomenon has been due to a considerable extent to the fact that the serial segment elimination must take place in the face of the so-called law of use or frequency. According to this principle

(alone) practice or repetition might be expected blindly to fix the undesirable behavior segment in its place more firmly than ever. Perhaps such inadequacies as these have contributed much to bringing the simple chain reaction theory into its deserved ill repute as a universal explanatory principle. As a matter of plain fact, the principle of redintegration from which may be derived the simple chaining of reactions, implies with equal cogency the evolution of a stimulus-response mechanism which appears to be capable on occasion of completely transcending the chaining tendency.[8] According to this principle any stimulus such as an organic craving which persists as a relatively constant component throughout the otherwise largely changing stimulus complexes of a behavior sequence, must become conditioned to every act of the series. The implications of this for complex adaptive behavior are far reaching. It is our present concern only to point out that the persisting stimulus, through the sheaf of excitatory tendencies emanating from it to every act of the series, provides a unique dynamic relationship between each part of the series and every other part. This, as we have seen above, gives rise to a significant competition among the several potential action tendencies within the series. While final decision must be reserved until the facts are determined by experiment, the probability seems to be that this intraserial competition may easily become sufficiently potent to over-ride the simple chain-reaction tendency and produce a leap in the behavior sequence from the beginning of a series at once to the final or goal reaction, thus eliminating the intervening unnecessary action segment.

VII

The results of the present inquiry may be briefly summarized.

Sequences in the outer world evoke parallel reaction sequences in sensitive organisms. By the principle of redintegration the organismic sequences acquire a tendency to run off by themselves, independently of the original world sequences. The organism has thus ac-

8 See E. L. Thorndike, *The original nature of man*, New York, 1913, 186-187.

quired an intimate functional copy of the world sequence, which is a kind of knowledge.

In case the two sequences begin at the same time but the organismic or behavior sequence runs off at a faster rate, the knowledge becomes fore-knowledge or foresight. This has great significance in terms of biological survival.

The possibility of more or less extended functional habit sequences being executed by the organism with an instrumental act only at the end, gives rise to the concept of the pure stimulus act. Such behavior sequences have great biological survival significance because they enable the organism to react both to the not-here and the not-now. Incidentally it accounts for a great deal of the spontaneity manifested by organisms.

The concept of the pure stimulus act appears to be the organic basis of symbolism but is believed to be a more fundamental one than that of symbolism as ordinarily conceived.

Pure stimulus-act sequences offer possibilities of biological economy, both of energy and of speed, through the reduction in the amplitude of the acts in the sequence. Further analysis reveals the fact that both energy and time would be economized with no incidental sacrifice if the acts between the beginning of an action cycle and its goal act should drop out of the sequence. Observation seems to show that the dropping out of such intervening pure stimulus acts occurs very extensively.

The problem arises as to how this dropping out of undesirable behavior segments may come about, since it appears to be a violation of the 'law of use.' A plausible explanation is found in the peculiar potentialities of stimuli which persist relatively unchanged throughout a behavior sequence. A persisting stimulus component is regarded as one of the characteristic mechanisms of purposive behavior. We should expect such a stimulus to get conditioned to every act of the sequence, presumably most strongly to the goal act and those acts immediately preceding the goal act. The resulting multiplicity of excitatory tendencies emanating from the persisting stimulus is found to generate an important phenomenon—the competition among the several potential segments of the behavior series. This intraserial competition, if sufficiently strong, could easily over-ride the simple chaining of contiguous acts produced by the 'law of use' and enable the final act of the original series to be evoked at once after the first act of the series, thus producing what is rather inappropriately called 'short-circuiting.' Thus may a persistent problem in the theory of mammalian adaptive behavior be on its way to solution.

The general plausibility of the foregoing theoretical deductions as well as the probable biological significance of several of the deduced mechanisms, suggests strongly the desirability of an intensive program of experimental research designed to test their actuality. In that way the true function of theoretical analysis may be realized.

part 2

ENERGIZING BEHAVIOR – NEEDS AND MOTIVES

If it is fair to say that all of us are creatures of habit, it is also fair to ask how habits are activated. How do behavioral sequences get started in the first place, and once we are started on a habitual process, how are we diverted from it into some other kind of activity? This is the problem of motivation, of how behavior is energized and given direction.

Most textbooks in psychology are rich in information about primary drives and their elaboration into more subtly operating motives. In the present section, our aim is to examine some particular empirical studies and theoretical ideas that illustrate the different ways in which the problem of motivation can be attacked in specific terms. As the selections indicate, the range of differences is large, and it is evident that psychologists can legitimately conceive of motivation in widely divergent ways. Rather than suggesting chaos and ignorance, this state of affairs indicates the breadth and complexity of the field.

Under these circumstances, where motivation is concerned, one test that is always relevant although never ultimately persuasive or definitive is how well a formulation or an interpretation of evidence corresponds with one's own experience. The other side of this coin, of course, is the question of whether one is able to be both honest and discerning in examining one's own experience. To the extent that one can – and the selections offered here may be helpful on this score – it is always possible to consider oneself a test case for a particular formulation; then the question is posed of what changes or modifications must be introduced to improve it, and hard thinking along these lines can be productive of new ideas for empirical investigations and new conceptualizations.

A second test is what behavioral processes other than the specific ones explored in a specific study are more readily understood as a result of the work reported. Does Atkinson's analysis of risk-taking behavior, for example, throw any light on President Kennedy's handling of the Cuban crisis of 1962, the high-tension lives of decision-making business executives, or the fascination of gambling for certain classes of people? Similarly, does White's conception of curiosity and mastery help explain why some people are zestful and widely interested in their jobs, the persons with whom they interact, and world affairs, whereas others seem apathetic or only narrowly interested? Thinking of particular cases of one's own acquaintance often infuses otherwise dispassionate studies with a cogency and relevance that may otherwise be missed.

A third test here is the logical consistency of the ideas that are advanced in the light of the evidence presented to support them. Given Feshbach's findings, what can be said about aggressive fantasy as an expression of hostility as against its serving as a reducer of hostile affects? Are there any necessary contradictions in these two functions of fantasy? Under what conditions is it probable that fantasy can operate both to facilitate and reduce the likelihood of overt aggression or merely to inhibit overt hostility? In Taylor's case, in what sense is manifest anxiety, defined by a score on her Manifest Anxiety Scale, a motive, and in what sense is it a pattern of responses energized by some other drive?

Finally, there is always the dream of some overarching theory that will coordinate and harmonize diverse findings and points of view. Are there any broad conceptual schemes that will order the observations and the ideas presented in these four selections within a unified scheme of thought? Or do the differences reflect real issues that must be resolved before our understanding of the wellsprings of human motivation can be expressed in a single theory?

Motivational determinants of risk-taking behavior

JOHN W. ATKINSON[1]

There are two problems of behavior which any theory of motivation must come to grips with. They may finally reduce to one; but it will simplify the exposition which follows to maintain the distinction in this paper. The first problem is to account for an individual's selection of one path of action among a set of possible alternatives. The second problem is to account for the amplitude or vigor of the action tendency once it is initiated, and for its tendency to persist for a time in a given direction. This paper will deal with these questions in a conceptual framework suggested by research which has used thematic apperception to assess individual differences in strength of achievement motivation (Atkinson, 1954; McClelland, 1955; McClelland, Atkinson, Clark, & Lowell, 1953).

The problem of selection arises in experiments which allow the individual to choose a task among alternatives that differ in difficulty (level of aspiration). The problem of accounting for the vigor of response arises in studies which seek to relate individual differences in strength of motivation to the level of performance when response output at a particular task is the dependent variable. In treating these two problems, the discussion will be constantly focused on the relationship of achievement motivation to risk-taking behavior, an important association uncovered by McClelland (1955) in the investigation of the role of achievement motivation in entrepreneurship and economic development.[2]

Earlier studies have searched for a theoretical

From *Psychological Review*, 1957, **64**, 359-372.

1 I wish to acknowledge the stimulation and criticism of colleagues at the Center for Advanced Study in the Behavioral Sciences (1955-56), and also the current support for this research by a grant from the Ford Foundation.

2 McClelland, D. C. Interest in risky occupations among subjects with high achievement motivation. Unpublished paper, Harvard University, June 1956.

principle which would explain the relationship of strength of motive, as inferred from thematic apperception, to overt goal-directed performance. The effect of situation cues (e.g., of particular instructions) on this relationship was detected quite early (Atkinson, 1954), and subsequent experiments have suggested a theoretical formulation similar to that presented by Tolman (1955) and Rotter (1954). It has been proposed that n Achievement scores obtained from thematic apperception are indices of individual differences in the strength of achievement motive, conceived as a relatively stable disposition to strive for achievement or success. This motive-disposition is presumed to be latent until aroused by situation cues which indicate that some performance will be instrumental to achievement. The strength of *aroused* motivation to achieve as manifested in performance has been viewed as a function of both the strength of motive and the *expectancy* of goal-attainment aroused by situation cues. This conception has provided a fairly adequate explanation of experimental results to date, and several of its implications have been tested (Atkinson, 1954; Atkinson & Reitman, 1956).

The similarity of this conception to the expectancy principle of performance developed by Tolman, which also takes account of the effects of a third variable, *incentive*, suggested the need for experiments to isolate the effects on motivation of variations in strength of expectancy of success and variations in the incentive value of particular accomplishments. The discussion which follows was prompted by the results of several exploratory experiments. It represents an attempt to state explicitly how individual differences in the strength of achievement-related motives influence behavior in competitive achievement situations. A theoretical model will be presented first, then a brief summary of some as yet unpublished experimental evidence will be introduced in order to call the reader's attention to the kinds of research problems it raises and the scope of its implications.

Three variables require definition and, ultimately, independent measurement. The three variables are *motive, expectancy,* and *incentive*. Two of these—expectancy and incentive—are similar to variables presented by Tolman (1955) and Rotter (1954). An expectancy is a cognitive anticipation, usually aroused by cues in a situation, that performance of some act will be followed by a particular consequence. The strength of an expectancy can be represented as the subjective probability of the consequence, given the act.

The incentive variable has been relatively ignored, or at best crudely defined, in most research. It represents the relative attractiveness of a specific goal that is offered in a situation, or the relative unattractiveness of an event that might occur as a consequence of some act. Incentives may be manipulated experimentally as, for example, when amount of food (reward) or amount of shock (punishment) is varied in research with animals.

The third variable in this triumvirate—motive—is here conceived differently than, for example, in the common conception of motivation as nondirective but energizing *drive* (Brown, 1953). A motive is conceived as a disposition to strive for a certain kind of satisfaction, as a capacity for satisfaction in the attainment of a certain class of incentives. The names given motives—such as achievement, affiliation, power—are really names of classes of incentives which produce essentially the same kind of experience of satisfaction: pride in accomplishment, or the sense of belonging and being warmly received by others, or the feeling of being in control and influential. McClelland (1951, pp. 341-352 and 441-458; McClelland et al., 1953) has presented arguments to support the conception of motives as relatively general and stable characteristics of the personality which have their origins in early childhood experience. The idea that a motive may be considered a *capacity for satisfaction* is suggested by Winterbottom's (McClelland et al., 1953; Winterbottom, 1952) finding that children who are strong in achievement motive are rated by teachers as deriving more pleasure from success than children who are weak in achievement motive.

The general aim of one class of motives, usually referred to as appetites or approach tendencies, is to maximize satisfaction of some kind. The achievement motive is considered a disposition to approach success.

The aim of another class of motives is to minimize pain. These have been called aversions, or avoidant tendencies. An avoidance motive represents the individual's capacity to experience pain in connection with certain kinds of negative consequences of acts. The motive to avoid failure is considered a disposition to avoid failure and/or a capacity for experiencing shame and humiliation as a consequence of failure.

The principle of motivation. The strength of motivation to perform some act is assumed to be a multiplicative function of the strength of the motive, the expectancy (subjective probability) that the act will have as a consequence the attainment of an incentive, and the value of the incentive: Motivation = f(Motive × Expectancy × Incentive). This formulation corresponds to Tolman's (1955) analysis of performance except, perhaps, in the conception of a motive as a relatively stable disposition. When both motivation to approach and motivation to avoid are simultaneously aroused, the resultant motivation is the algebraic summation of approach and avoidance. The act which is performed among a set of alternatives is the act for which the resultant motivation is most positive. The magnitude of response and the persistence of behavior are functions of the strength of motivation to perform the act relative to the strength of motivation to perform competing acts.

Recent experiments (Atkinson & Reitman, 1956) have helped to clarify one problem concerning the relationship between measures of the strength of a particular motive (n Achievement) and performance. Performance is positively related to the strength of a particular motive only when an expectancy of satisfying that motive through performance has been aroused, and when expectancies of satisfying other motives through the same action have not been sufficiently aroused to confound the simple relationship. This is to say no more than that, when expectancies of attaining several different kinds of incentives are equally *salient* in a situation, the determination of motivation to perform an act is very complex. Performance is then overdetermined in the sense that its strength is now a function of the several different kinds of motivation which have been aroused. The *ideal situation* for showing the relationship between the strength of a particular motive and behavior is one in which the only

reason for acting is to satisfy that motive.

The theoretical formulation which follows pertains to such an *ideal achievement-related situation*, which is at best only approximated in actual experimentation or in the normal course of everyday life. The discussion will deal only with the effects of the two motives, to achieve and to avoid failure, normally aroused whenever performance is likely to be evaluated against some standard of excellence.

Behavior directed toward achievement and away from failure. The problem of selection is confronted in the level-of-aspiration situation where the individual must choose among tasks which differ in degree of difficulty. The problem of accounting for the vigor of performance arises in the situation which will be referred to as *constrained performance.* Here there is no opportunity for the individual to choose his own task. He is simply given a task to perform. He must, of course, decide to perform the task rather than to leave the situation. There *is* a problem of selection. In referring to this situation as constrained performance, it is the writer's intention to deal only with those instances of behavior in which motivation for the alternative of leaving the situation is less positive or more negative than for performance of the task that is presented. Hence, the individual does perform the task that is given. The level of performance is the question of interest.

Elaboration of the implications of the multiplicative combination of motive, expectancy, and incentive, as proposed to account for strength of motivation, will be instructive if we can find some reasonable basis for assigning numbers to the different variables. The strength of expectancy can be represented as a subjective probability ranging from 0 to 1.00. But the problem of defining the positive incentive value of a particular accomplishment and the negative incentive value of a particular failure is a real stickler.

In past discussions of level of aspiration, Escalona and Festinger (see Lewin, Dembo, Festinger, & Sears, 1944) have assumed that, within limits, the attractiveness of success is a positive function of the difficulty of the task, and that the unattractiveness of failure is a negative function of difficulty, when the type of activity is held constant. The author will go a few steps farther with these ideas, and assume that degree of difficulty can be inferred from the subjective probability of success (P_s). The task an individual finds difficult is one for which his subjective probability of success (P_s) is very low. The task an individual finds easy is one for which his subjective probability of success (P_s) is very high. Now we are in a position to make simple assumptions about the incentive values of success or failure at a particular task. Let us assume that the incentive value of success (I_s) is a positive linear function of difficulty. If so, the value $1 - P_s$ can represent I_s, the incentive value of success. When P_s is high (e.g., .90), an easy task, I_s is low (e.g., .10). When P_s is low (e.g., .10), a difficult task, I_s is high (e.g., .90). The negative incentive value of failure (I_f) can be taken as $- P_s$. When P_s is high (e.g., .90), as in confronting a very easy task, the sense of humiliation accompanying failure is also very great (e.g., $- .90$). However, when P_s is low (e.g., .10), as in confronting a very difficult task, there is little embarrassment in failing (e.g., $- .10$). We assume, in other words, that the (negative) incentive value of failure (I_f) is a negative linear function of difficulty. It is of some importance to recognize the dependence of incentive values intrinsic to achievement and failure upon the subjective probability of success. One cannot anticipate the thrill of a great accomplishment if, as a matter of fact, one faces what seems a very easy task. Nor does an individual experience only a minor sense of pride after some extraordinary feat against what seemed to him overwhelming odds. The implications of the scheme which follows rest heavily upon the assumption of such a dependence.

In Table 1, values of 1 have been arbitrarily assigned to the achievement motive (M_s) and the motive to avoid failure (M_f). Table 1 contains the strength of motivation to approach success ($M_s \times P_s \times I_s$) and motivation to avoid failure ($M_f \times P_f \times I_f$) through performance of nine different tasks labeled A through I. The tasks differ in degree of difficulty as inferred from the subjective probability of success (P_s). The incentive values of success and failure at each of the tasks have been calculated directly from the assumptions that incentive value of success equals $1 - P_s$ and that incentive value

of failure equals $- P_s$; and P_s and P_f are assumed to add to 1.00.

Table 1 may be considered an extension of ideas presented in the *resultant valence* theory of level of aspiration by Escalona and Festinger (Lewin et al., 1944). The present formulation goes beyond their earlier proposals (*a*) in making specific assumptions regarding the incentive values of success and failure, and (*b*) in stating explicitly how individual differences in strength of achievement motive and motive to avoid failure influence motivation.[3] *When the achievement motive is stronger ($M_s > M_f$).* The right-hand column of Table 1 shows the resultant motivation for each of the tasks in this special case where achievement motive and motive to avoid failure are equal in strength. In every case there is an approach-avoidance conflict with resultant motivation equal to 0. This means that if the achievement motive were stronger than the motive to avoid failure — for example, if we assigned M_s a value of 2 — the resultant motivation would become positive for each of the tasks and its magnitude would be the same as in the column labeled *Approach.* Let us therefore consider only the strength of approach motivation for each of the tasks, to see the implications of the model for the person in whom the need for achievement is stronger than his disposition to avoid failure.

One thing is immediately apparent. Motivation to achieve is strongest when uncertainty regarding the outcome is greatest, i.e., when P_s equals .50. If the individual were confronted with all of these tasks and were free to set his own goal, he should choose Task E where P_s is .50, for this is the point of maximum approach motivation. The strength of motivation to approach decreases as P_s increases from .50 to near certainty of success ($P_s = .90$), and it also decreases as P_s decreases from .50 to near certainty of failure ($P_s = .10$).

---

3 In the resultant valence theory of level of aspiration, the resultant force (*f**) for a particular level of difficulty equals probability of success (P_s) times valence of success (Va_s) minus probability of failure (P_f) times valence of failure (Va_f). It is assumed that the valence of a goal [$Va(G)$] depends partly on the properties of the activity and specific goal (G) and partly on the state of need [$t(G)$] of the person, [$Va(G) = F(G,t(G))$] (Lewin, 1951, p. 273). In the present conception, the relative rewarding or punishing properties of specific goals (i.e., incentives) and the more general disposition of the person toward a class of incentives (i.e., his motive) are given independent status.

Table 1 *Aroused motivation to achieve (approach) and to avoid failure (avoidance) as a joint function of motive (M), expectancy (P), and incentive (I), where $I_s = (1 - P_s)$ and $I_f = (-P_s)$*

| | Motivation to achieve | | | | Motivation to avoid failure | | | | Resultant motivation (approach − avoidance) |
	$M_s \times$	$P_s \times$	I_s =	Approach	$M_f \times$	$P_f \times$	I_f =	Avoidance	
Task A	1	.10	.90	.09	1	.90	−.10	−.09	0
Task B	1	.20	.80	.16	1	.80	−.20	−.16	0
Task C	1	.30	.70	.21	1	.70	−.30	−.21	0
Task D	1	.40	.60	.24	1	.60	−.40	−.24	0
Task E	1	.50	.50	.25	1	.50	−.50	−.25	0
Task F	1	.60	.40	.24	1	.40	−.60	−.24	0
Task G	1	.70	.30	.21	1	.30	−.70	−.21	0
Task H	1	.80	.20	.16	1	.20	−.80	−.16	0
Task I	1	.90	.10	.09	1	.10	−.90	−.09	0

If this person were to be confronted with a single task in what is here called the constrained performance situation, we should expect him to manifest strongest motivation in the performance of a task of intermediate difficulty where P_s equals .50. If presented either more difficult tasks or easier tasks, the strength of motivation manifested in performance should be lower. The relationship between strength of motivation as expressed in performance level and expectancy of success at the task, in other words, should be described by a bell-shaped curve.

When the motive to avoid failure is stronger ($M_f > M_s$). Let us now ignore the strength of approach motivation and tentatively assign it a value of 0, in order to examine the implications of the model for any case in which the motive to avoid failure is the stronger motive. The resultant motivation for each task would then correspond to the values listed in the column labeled *Avoidance*.

What should we expect of the person in whom the disposition to avoid failure is stronger than the motive to achieve? It is apparent at once that the resultant motivation for every task would be negative for him. This person should want to avoid all of the tasks. Competitive achievement situations are unattractive to him. If, however, he is constrained (e.g., by social pressures) and asked to set his level of aspiration, he should *avoid* tasks of inter-

mediate difficulty ($P_s = .50$) where the arousal of anxiety about failure is greatest. He should choose either the easiest ($P_s = .90$) or the most difficult task ($P_s = .10$). The strength of avoidant motivation is weakest at these two points.

In summary, the person in whom the achievement motive is stronger should set his level of aspiration in the intermediate zone where there is moderate risk. To the extent that he has any motive to avoid failure, this means that he will voluntarily choose activities that *maximize* his own anxiety about failure! On the other hand, the person in whom the motive to avoid failure is stronger should select either the easiest of the alternatives or should be extremely speculative and set his goal where there is virtually no chance for success. These are activities which *minimize* his anxiety about failure.

How does the more fearful person behave when offered only a specific task to perform? He can either perform the task or leave the field. If he chooses to leave the field, there is no problem. But if he is constrained, as he must be to remain in any competitive achievement situation, he will stay at the task and presumably work at it. But how hard will he work at it? He is motivated to avoid failure, and when constrained, there is only one path open to him to avoid failure—success at the task he is presented. So we expect him to manifest the strength of his motivation to avoid failure in performance of the task. He, too, in other words, should *try hardest*[4] when P_s is .50 and less hard when the chance of winning is either greater or less. The 50-50 alternative is the last he would choose if allowed to set his own goal, but once constrained he must try hard to avoid the failure which threatens him. Not working at all will guarantee failure of the task. Hence, the thought of not working at all should produce even stronger avoidant motivation than that aroused by the task itself.

In other words, irrespective of whether the stronger motive is to achieve or to avoid failure, the strength of motivation to perform a task when no alternatives are offered and when the individual is constrained should be greatest when P_s is .50. This is the condition of greatest uncertainty regarding the outcome. But when there are alternatives which differ in difficulty, the choice of level of aspiration by persons more disposed to avoid failure is diametrically opposite to that of persons more disposed to seek success. The person more motivated to achieve should prefer a moderate risk. His level of aspiration will fall at the point where his positive motivation is strongest, at the point where the odds seem to be 50-50. The fearful person, on the other hand, must select a task even though all the alternatives are threatening to him. He prefers the least threatening of the available alternatives: either the task which is so easy he cannot fail, or the task which is so difficult that failure would be no cause for self-blame and embarrassment.

The tendency for anxious persons to set either extremely high or very low aspirations has been noted over and over again in the literature on level of aspiration (Lewin et al., 1944). Typically, *groups* of persons for whom the inference of greater anxiety about failure seems justified on the basis of some personality assessment show a much greater variance in level of aspiration than persons whose motivation is inferred to be more normal or less anxious. When the details of behavior are examined, it turns out that they are setting their aspiration level either *defensively* high or *defensively* low.

Without further assumptions, the theory of motivation which has been presented when applied to competitive-achievement activity implies that the relationship of constrained performance to expectancy of goal-attainment

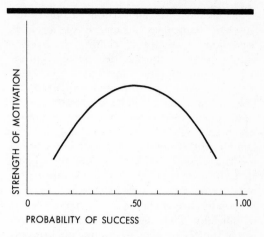

Fig. 1 *Strength of motivation to achieve or to avoid failure as a function of the subjective probability of success, i.e., the difficulty of the task.*

should take the bell-shaped form shown in Fig. 1, whether the predominant motive is to achieve or to avoid failure. Further, the theory leads to the prediction of exactly opposite patterns for setting the level of aspiration when the predominant motivation is approach and when it is avoidant, as shown in Fig. 2.

Both of these hypotheses have been supported in recent experiments. The writer[5] offered female college students a modest monetary prize for good performance at two 20-minute tasks. The probability of success was varied by instructions which informed the subject of the number of persons with whom she was in competition and the number of monetary prizes to be given. The stated probabilities were 1/20, 1/2, 1/2, and 3/4. The level of performance was higher at the intermediate probabilities than at the extremes for subjects having high thematic apperceptive *n* Achievement scores, and also for subjects who had low *n* Achievement scores, presumably a more fearful group.

---

4 I do not mean to exclude the possibility that the very anxious person may suffer a performance decrement due to the arousal of some "task-irrelevant" avoidant responses, as proposed in the interpretation of research which has employed the Mandler-Sarason Measure of Test Anxiety (Mandler & Sarason, 1952).

5 Atkinson, J. W. Towards experimental analysis of human motivation in terms of motives, expectancies, and incentives. To appear in *Motives in fantasy, action, and society.* Princeton: Van Nostrand (in preparation). [Published in 1958—*Editor's note.*]

McClelland[6] has shown the diametrically opposite tendencies in choice of level of aspiration in studies of children in kindergarten and in the third grade. One of the original level-of-aspiration experiments, the ring-toss experiment, was repeated with five-year-olds, and a nonverbal index of the strength of achievement motive was employed. Children who were high in *n* Achievement more frequently set their level of aspiration in the intermediate range of difficulty. They took more shots from a modest distance. Children who were low in *n* Achievement showed a greater preponderance of choices at the extreme levels of difficulty. They more often stood right on top of the peg or stood so far away that success was virtually impossible. The same difference between high and low *n* Achievement groups was observed on another task with children in the third grade. McClelland views these results as consistent with his theoretical argument concerning the role of achievement motivation in entrepreneurship and economic development (1955). He has called attention to the relationship between achievement motivation and an interest in enterprise which requires moderate or calculated risks, rather than very safe or highly speculative undertakings.

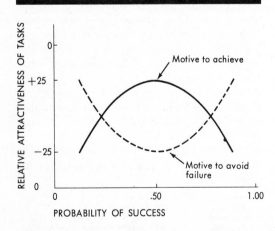

Fig. 2 *Relative attractiveness of tasks which differ in subjective probability of success (i.e., in difficulty). The avoidance curve has been inverted to show that very difficult and very easy tasks arouse less fear of failure and hence are less unattractive than moderately difficult tasks.*

In an experiment designed for another purpose, Clark, Teevan, and Ricciuti (1956) have presented results with college students comparable to those of McClelland. Immediately before a final examination in a college course, students were asked a series of questions pertaining to grade expectations, affective reactions to grades, and the grades they would *settle for* if excused from taking the exam. A number of indices were derived from responses to these questions, by which the students were classified as: *hopeful of success,* i.e., if the *settle-for* grade was near the maximum grade the student thought he could possibly achieve; *fearful of failure,* i.e., if the *settle-for* grade was near the minimum grade the student thought he might possibly drop to; and *intermediate,* i.e., if the *settle-for* grade fell somewhere between these two extremes. Previously obtained *n* Achievement scores were significantly higher for the *intermediate* group than for the two groups who set either extremely high or low levels of aspiration.

In terms of the model presented in Table 1, the two extreme patterns of aspirant behavior which are here designated *hope of success* and *fear of failure* are to be considered two *phenotypically* dissimilar alternatives that are *genotypically* similar. That is, they both function to avoid or reduce anxiety for the person in whom the motive to avoid failure is stronger than the motive to achieve.

A question may arise concerning the legitimacy of inferring relatively stronger motive to avoid failure from a low *n* Achievement score in thematic apperception. The inference seems justified on several counts. First, the kind of learning experience which is thought to contribute to the development of a positive motive to achieve (McClelland et al., 1953; Winterbottom, 1952) seems incompatible with the kind of experience which would contribute to the development of an avoidant motive. In any specific early learning experience in which successful independent accomplishment is encouraged and rewarded, it seems impossible for incompetence, at the same time, to be punished. Second, even if it is assumed that high

6 McClelland, D. C. Risk-taking in children with high and low need for achievement. To appear in *Motives in fantasy, action, and society.* Princeton: Van Nostrand (in preparation). [Published in 1958 — *Editor's note.*]

and low *n* Achievement groups may be equal in the disposition to be fearful of failure, the fact that one group does not show evidence of a strong motive to achieve (the group with low *n* Achievement scores) suggests that fear of failure should be *relatively* stronger in that group than in the group which does show evidence of strong *n* Achievement (high *n* Achievement scores). Finally, Raphelson (1956) has presented evidence that *n* Achievement, as measured in thematic apperception, is *negatively* related to both scores on the Mandler-Sarason Scale of Test Anxiety and a psychogalvanic index of manifest anxiety obtained in a test situation. Test anxiety scores and the psychogalvanic index of manifest anxiety were *positively* correlated, as they should be if each is an effective measure of fear aroused in a competitive situation.

Although a low *n* Achievement score can hardly be viewed as a direct index of the disposition to avoid failure, there seems good presumptive evidence that fear of failure is *relatively* stronger than the achievement motive in such a group. And this presumption is all the theory demands to explain the pattern of goal setting which focuses upon the extremes in the range of difficulty among persons low in *n* Achievement.

The details of the exploratory experiments suggest that one further assumption be made. In both experiments, the high *n* Achievement groups showed evidence of maximum motivation when the observed or stated probability of success was approximately .33. At this point, the high *n* Achievement group showed the highest level of constrained performance. And this point was most favored by the high *n* Achievement group in setting level of aspiration in the McClelland experiment. The assumption to be made seems a reasonable one: the relative strength of a motive influences the subjective probability of the consequence consistent with that motive—i.e., biases it upwards. In other words, the stronger the achievement motive relative to the motive to avoid failure, the higher the subjective probability of success, given stated odds. The stronger the motive to avoid failure relative to the achievement motive, the higher the subjective probability of failure, given stated odds or any other objective basis for inferring the strength of expectancy.

Some evidence from two earlier studies is pertinent. When subjects stated the score that they *expected* to make on a test with very ambiguous or conflicting cues from past performance (McClelland et al., 1953) or when faced with a novel task at which they had no experience (Pottharst, 1956), the stated level of *expectation* was positively related to *n* Achievement. The biasing effect of the motive on subjective probability should diminish with repeated learning experience in the specific situation.

When this assumption is made, the point of maximum motivation to achieve now occurs where the stated (objective) odds are somewhat *lower* than .50; and the point of maximum motivation to avoid failure occurs at a point somewhat higher than stated odds of .50, as shown in Fig. 3. The implications of this assumption for constrained performance in somewhat novel situations are evident in the figure. When the achievement motive is stronger than the motive to avoid failure, there should be a tendency for stronger motivation to be expressed in performance when the objective odds are long, i.e., below .50. When the motive to avoid failure is stronger than the achievement motive, there should be greater motivation expressed when the objective odds are short, i.e., above .50.

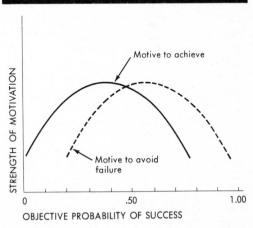

Fig. 3 *Strength of motivation to achieve and to avoid failure as a function of the* objective *probability of success. It is assumed that the subjective probability of the consequence consistent with the stronger motive is biased upwards.*

The effects of success and failure. Let us return to the model and ask, What are the effects of success and failure on the level of motivation? We may refer back to Table 1 to answer this question. First, let us consider the effects of success or failure on the level of motivation in a person whose motive to achieve is stronger than his motive to avoid failure. In the usual level-of-aspiration situation, he should initially set his goal where P_s equals .50. In Table 1, this is Task E. If he succeeds at the task, P_s should increase. And, assuming that the effects of success and failure generalize to similar tasks, the P_s at Task D which was initially .40 should increase toward .50. On the next trial, P_s at Task E is now greater than .50, and P_s at Task D now approaches .50. The result of this change in P_s is diminished motivation to achieve at the old task, E, and increased motivation to achieve at Task D, *an objectively more difficult task.* The observed level of aspiration should increase in a step-like manner following success, because there has been a change in motivation.

A further implication of the change in strength of motivation produced by the experience of success is of great consequence: given a single, very difficult task (e.g., $P_s = .10$), the effect of continued success in repeated trials is first a gradual increase in motivation as P_s increases to .50, followed by a gradual decrease in motivation as P_s increases further to the point of certainty ($P_s = 1.00$). Ultimately, as P_s approaches 1.00, satiation or loss of interest should occur. The task no longer arouses any motivation at all. Why? Because the subjective probability of success is so high that the incentive value is virtually zero. Here is the clue to understanding how the achievement motive can remain insatiable while satiation can occur for a particular line of activity. The strength of motive can remain unchanged, but interest in a particular task can diminish completely. Hence, when free to choose, the person who is stronger in achievement motive should always look for new and more difficult tasks as he masters old problems. If constrained, the person with a strong achievement motive should experience a gradual loss of interest in his work. If the task is of intermediate difficulty to start with ($P_s = .50$), or is definitely easy ($P_s > .50$), his interest should begin to wane after the initial experience of success.

But what of the effect of failure on the person who is more highly motivated to achieve than to avoid failure? Once more we look at the *Approach* column of Table 1. If he has chosen Task E ($P_s = .50$) to start with and fails at it, the P_s is reduced. Continued failure will mean that soon Task F (formerly $P_s = .60$) will have a P_s near .50. He should shift his interest to this task, which was *objectively less difficult* in the initial ordering of tasks. This constitutes what has been called a lowering of the level of aspiration. He has moved to the easier task as a consequence of failure.

What is the effect of continued failure at a single task? If the initial task is one that appeared relatively easy to the subject (e.g., $P_s = .80$) and he fails, his motivation should increase! The P_s will drop toward .70, but the incentive value or attractiveness of the task will increase. Another failure should increase his motivation even more. This will continue until the P_s has dropped to .50. Further failure should then lead to a gradual weakening of motivation as P_s decreases further. In other words, the tendency of persons who are relatively strong in achievement motive to persist at a task in the face of failure is probably attributable to the relatively high subjective probability of success, initially. Hence, failure has the effect of increasing the strength of their motivation, at least for a time. Ultimately, however, interest in the task will diminish if there is continued failure. If the initial task is perceived by the person as very difficult to start with ($P_s < .50$), motivation should begin to diminish with the first failure.

Let us turn now to the effect of success and failure on the motivation of the person who is more strongly disposed to be fearful of failure. If the person in whom the motive to avoid failure is stronger has chosen a very difficult task in setting his level of aspiration (e.g., Task A where $P_s = .10$) and succeeds, P_s increases and his motivation *to avoid* the task is paradoxically increased! It would almost make sense for him deliberately to fail, in order to keep from being faced with a stronger threat on the second trial. If there are more difficult alternatives, he should raise his level of aspiration to avoid anxiety! Fortunately for this person, his strategy (determined by the nature of his motivation) in choosing a very difficult task to start with protects him from this possibility, because P_s is so small that he will seldom face the paradoxical problem just described. If he fails at the most difficult task, as is likely, P_s decreases further, P_f increases further, and the aroused motivation to avoid failure is reduced. By continued failure he further reduces the amount of anxiety about failure that is aroused by this most difficult task. Hence, he should continue to set his level at this point. If he plays the game long enough and fails continuously, the probability of failure increases for all levels of difficulty. Sooner or later the minimal motivation to avoid failure at the most difficult task may be indistinguishable from the motivation to avoid failure at the next most difficult task. This may ultimately allow him to change his level of aspiration to a somewhat less difficult task without acting in gross contradiction to the proposed principle of motivation.

If our fearful subject has initially chosen the easiest task (Task I where $P_s = .90$) and if he fails, P_s decreases toward .80, and his motivation to avoid the task also increases. If there is no easier task, the most difficult task should now appear least *unattractive* to him, and he should jump from the easiest to the most difficult task. In other words, continued failure at a very easy task decreases P_s toward .50; and, as Table 1 shows, a change of this sort is accompanied by increased arousal of avoidant motivation. A wild and apparently irrational jump in level of aspiration from very easy to very difficult tasks, as a consequence of failure, might be mistakenly interpreted as a possible effort on the part of the subject to gain social approval by seeming to set high goals. The present model predicts this kind of activity without appealing to some extrinsic motive. It is part of the strategy of minimizing expected pain of failure after one has failed at the easiest task.

If our fear-disposed subject is successful at the most simple task, his P_s increases, his P_f decreases, and his motivation to avoid this task decreases. The task becomes less and less unpleasant. He should continue playing the game with less anxiety.

Table 1, when taken in its entirety, deals with the special case of the person in whom the two motives are exactly equal in strength.

The implications are clear. In the constrained-performance situation, he should work hardest when the probability of success is .50, because motivation to achieve and motivation to avoid failure will summate in the constrained instrumental act which is at the same time the pathway toward success and away from failure. (This summation should also occur in the cases where one motive is stronger.) But in the level-of-aspiration setting where there is an opportunity for choice among alternatives, the avoidance motivation exactly cancels out the approach motivation. Hence, the resultant motivation for each of the alternatives is zero. His choice of level of aspiration cannot be predicted from variables intrinsic to the achievement-related nature of the task. If there is any orderly pattern in this conflicted person's level of aspiration, the explanation of it must be sought in extrinsic factors, e.g. *the desire to gain social approval.* Such a desire can also be conceptualized in terms of motive, expectancy, and incentive, and the total motivation for a particular task can then be attributed to both achievement-related motives and other kinds of motives engaged by the particular features of the situation.

In recent years there has been something of a rebirth of interest in the problems of level of aspiration, particularly in pathological groups. The tendency for anxious groups to show much greater variability in level of aspiration, setting their goals either very high or very low relative to less anxious persons, was noted in early studies by Sears, Rotter, and others (Lewin et al., 1944). Miller (1951), Himmelweit (1947), and Eysenck and Himmelweit (1946) have produced substantial evidence that persons with affective disorders (neurasthenia or dysthymia) typically set extremely high goals for themselves; hysterics, on the other hand, show a minimal level of aspiration, often setting their future goal even below the level of past performance. In all of these studies, normal control groups have fallen between these two extremes, as might be expected from the present model if *normals* are relatively more positive in their motivation in achievement-related situations.

In the work of Eysenck (1955) and his colleagues, both dysthymics and hysterics show greater *neuroticism* than normal subjects.

Eysenck's interpretation of this factor as autonomic sensitivity is consistent with the implications of the present model, which attributes the setting of extremely high or low levels of aspiration to relatively strong motivation to avoid failure. A second factor, *extraversion-introversion*, discriminates the affective disorders and hysterics where the present model, dealing only with motives intrinsic to the competitive achievement situation, does not. An appeal to some other motivational difference, e.g., in strength of *n* Affiliation, might also predict the difference in pattern of level of aspiration.

Probability Preferences

The present analysis is relevant to another domain of current research interest, that specifically concerned with the measurement of subjective probability and utility. Edwards (1953; 1954), for example, has reported probability preferences among subjects offered alternative bets having the same expected value. We[7] have repeated the Edwards type experiment (e.g., 6/6 of winning 30¢ versus 1/6 of winning $1.80) with subjects having high and low *n* Achievement scores. The results show that persons high in *n* Achievement more often prefer intermediate probabilities (4/6, 3/6, 2/6) to extreme probabilities (6/6, 5/6, 1/6) than do persons low in *n* Achievement. What is more, the same differential preference for intermediate risk was shown by these *same* subjects when they were allowed to choose the distance from the target for their shots in a shuffleboard game. In other words, the incentive values of winning qua winning, and losing qua losing, presumably developed in achievement activities early in life, generalize to the gambling situation in which winning is really *not* contingent upon one's own skill and competence.

Social Mobility Aspirations

Finally, the present model may illuminate a number of interesting research possibilities having to do with social and occupational mobility. The ranking of occupations according to their prestige in Western societies clearly suggests that occupations accorded greater prestige are also more difficult to attain. A serious effort to measure the perceived probability of being able to attain certain levels on the occupational ladder should produce a high negative correlation with the usual ranking on prestige. If so, then the present model for level of aspiration, as well as its implications for persons who differ in achievement-related motives, can be applied to many of the sociological problems of mobility aspirations. A recent paper by Hyman (1953) has laid the groundwork for such an analysis.

SUMMARY

A theoretical model is presented to explain how the motive to achieve and the motive to avoid failure influence behavior in any situation where performance is evaluated against some standard of excellence. A conception of motivation in which strength of motivation is a joint multiplicative function of motive, expectancy (subjective probability), and incentive is offered to account for the selection of one task among alternatives which differ in difficulty (level of aspiration), and also to account for performance level when only one task is presented. It is assumed that the incentive value of success is a positive linear function of difficulty as inferred from the subjective probability of success; and negative incentive value of failure is assumed to be a negative linear function of difficulty. The major implications of the theory are (*a*) that performance level should be greatest when there is greatest uncertainty about the outcome, i.e., when subjective probability of success is .50, whether the motive to achieve or the motive to avoid failure is stronger within an individual; but (*b*) that persons in whom the achievement motive is stronger should prefer intermediate risk, while persons in whom the motive to avoid failure is stronger should avoid intermediate risk, preferring instead either very easy and safe undertakings *or* extremely difficult and speculative undertakings. Results of several experiments are cited, and the implications of the theoretical model for research on probability preferences in gambling and studies of social mobility aspirations are briefly discussed.

---

7 Atkinson, J. W., Bastian, J. R., Earl, R. W., and Litwin, G. H. The achievement motive, goal-setting, and probability preferences (in preparation). [Published in *J. abnorm. soc. Psychol.*, 1960, **60**, 27-36 — *Editor's note.*]

Motivation reconsidered: the concept of competence

ROBERT W. WHITE

When parallel trends can be observed in realms as far apart as animal behavior and psychoanalytic ego psychology, there is reason to suppose that we are witnessing a significant evolution of ideas. In these two realms, as in psychology as a whole, there is evidence of deepening discontent with theories of motivation based upon drives. Despite great differences in the language and concepts used to express this discontent, the theme is everywhere the same: Something important is left out when we make drives the operating forces in animal and human behavior.

The chief theories against which the discontent is directed are those of Hull and of Freud. In their respective realms, drive-reduction theory and psychoanalytic instinct theory, which are basically very much alike, have acquired a considerable air of orthodoxy. Both views have an appealing simplicity, and both have been argued long enough so that their main outlines are generally known. In decided contrast is the position of those who are not satisfied with drives and instincts. They are numerous, and they have developed many pointed criticisms, but what they have to say has not thus far lent itself to a clear and inclusive conceptualization. Apparently there is an enduring difficulty in making these contributions fall into shape.

In this paper I shall attempt a conceptualization which gathers up some of the important things left out by drive theory. To give the concept a name I have chosen the word *competence*, which is intended in a broad biological sense rather than in its narrow everyday meaning. As used here, competence will refer to an organism's capacity to interact effectively with its environment. In organisms capable of but little learning, this capacity might be considered an innate attribute, but in the mammals and especially man, with their highly plastic nervous systems, fitness to interact with the environment is slowly attained through prolonged feats of learning. In view of the directedness and persistence of the behavior that leads to these feats of learning, I consider it necessary to treat competence as having a motivational aspect, and my central argument will be that the motivation needed to attain competence cannot be wholly derived from sources of energy currently conceptualized as drives or instincts. We need a different kind of motivational idea to account fully for the fact that man and the higher mammals develop a competence in dealing with the environment which they certainly do not have at birth and certainly do not arrive at simply through maturation. Such an idea, I believe, is essential for any biologically sound view of human nature.

As a first step, I shall briefly examine the relevant trends of thought in several areas of psychology. From this it will become clear that the ideas advanced in this paper have already been stated, in one way or another, by workers in animal behavior, child development, cognitive psychology, psychoanalytic ego psychology, and the psychology of personality. If there is novelty in this essay, it lies in putting together pieces which are not in themselves new. They already lie before us on the table, and perhaps by looking once more we can see how to fit them into a larger conceptual picture.

THE TREND IN ANIMAL PSYCHOLOGY

One of the most obvious features of animal behavior is the tendency to explore the environment. Cats are reputedly killed by curiosity, dogs characteristically make a thorough search of their surroundings, and monkeys and chimpanzees have always impressed observers as being ceaseless investigators. Even Pavlov,

From *Psychological Review*, 1959, **66**, 297-333.

whose theory of behavior was one of Spartan simplicity, could not do without an investigatory or orientating reflex. Early workers with the obstruction method, such as Dashiell (1925) and Nissen (1930), reported that rats would cross an electrified grid simply for the privilege of exploring new territory. Some theorists reasoned that activity of this kind was always in the service of hunger, thirst, sex, or some other organic need, but this view was at least shaken by the latent learning experiments, which showed that animals learned about their surroundings even when their major needs had been purposely sated. Shortly before 1950 there was a wave of renewed interest not only in exploratory behavior but also in the possibility that activity and manipulation might have to be assigned the status of independent motives.

Exploratory Behavior

In 1953 Butler reported an experiment in which monkeys learned a discrimination problem when the only reward was the opening of a window which permitted them to look out upon the normal comings and goings of the entrance room to the laboratory. The discriminations thus formed proved to be resistant to extinction. In a later study, Butler and Harlow (1957) showed that monkeys could build up a series of four different discriminations solely for the sake of inspecting the entrance room. Butler concluded that "monkeys — and presumably all primates — have a strong motive toward visual exploration of their environment and that learning may be established on the basis of this motive just as it may be established on the basis of any motive that regularly and reliably elicits responses." Montgomery, in 1954, reported a study with rats in which the animals, their major organic needs satiated, learned to avoid the short arm of a Y maze and to take the path which led them into additional maze territory suitable for exploration. Similar findings have been described by Myers and Miller (1954), whose rats learned to press a bar for the sake of poking their heads into a new compartment and sniffing around. Zimbardo and Miller (1958) enlarged upon this study by varying the amount of novelty in the two com-

partments. In their report "the hypothesis advanced is that opportunity to explore a 'novel' environment or to effect a stimulus change in the environment is the reinforcing agent."

These experiments make a strong case for an independent exploratory motive. The nature of this motive can be more fully discerned in situations in which the animals are allowed a varied repertory of behavior. In 1950 Berlyne published a searching paper on curiosity, a theme which he further developed in subsequent years (1955, 1957, 1958). The rats in his experiments were confronted with an unfamiliar space and later with various novel objects placed in it. Approaching, sniffing, and examining were readily elicited by each novelty, were fairly rapidly extinguished, but were restored nearly to original strength when a fresh novelty was added. Exploration on the part of chimpanzees has been studied by Welker (1956), who put various pairs of objects before the animals and observed the course of their interest. The objects were often first approached in a gingerly manner, with signs of uneasiness, then examined and handled quite fully, then discarded. Introducing a new pair of objects promptly reproduced the whole sequence, just as it did with the rats in Berlyne's experiments. Welker used pairs of objects to find out whether or not the chimpanzees would have common preferences. Bigness and brightness evoked more interest, and greater time was spent upon objects which could be moved, changed, or made to emit sounds and light.

Recent reviews by Butler (1958) and Cofer (1959) show that a great deal of similar work is going on in animal laboratories, generally with similar results.

Exploration as a Drive

The designers of these experiments have favored the idea that exploration should be listed as an independent primary drive. In all cases the experimental plan calls for the elimination of other primary drives by satiation. It is recognized, however, that a confirmed advocate of orthodoxy might bring up two objections to the proposed enlargement of the list of primary drives. He might claim that exploratory behavior could be explained as a consequence of secondary reinforcement, or he might contend that it is reinforced by reduction of anxiety.

The first argument meets an immediate difficulty in Butler's finding that discriminations learned on the basis of visual exploration are resistant to extinction. When reinforcement of primary drive never takes place in the experimental situation, it is to be expected that secondary reinforcement will not prevent extinction (Miller, 1951). But even in those cases where extinction is rapid, as it was with Berlyne's rats and Welker's chimpanzees, serious problems are raised by the quick recovery of exploratory behavior when a novel stimulus is introduced (Berlyne, 1950). In order to sustain the idea that secondary reinforcement accounts for this fact, we should have to suppose that primary rewards have often been connected with the exploration of novelties. It would have to be assumed, for instance, that the securing of food by young animals occurred with considerable frequency in connection with the investigation of novel objects. This image may seem to fit mature animals who search the environment for their food, but it certainly cannot apply to young mammals before they are weaned. Here the learning process can do virtually nothing to reinforce an interest in novelties. Gratification comes from following the same old cues to the same old consummatory responses, and the animal whose attention strays to some novel variation of the breast will only find himself frustrated. One can say that the whole mammalian pattern of infancy works in the opposite direction. The mother is more active than the young in providing gratifications, and the babies must be pursued and retrieved if they stray from the scene of her ministry. However one looks at it, the hypothesis of secondary reinforcement seems to me to demand improbable assumptions about the relationship in the lives of young animals between exploration and primary need gratification.

The hypothesis that exploratory behavior is related to fear and receives its reinforcement from the reduction of anxiety is at first glance considerably more plausible. It seems justified by the observation that Welker's chimpanzees showed uneasiness on first contact with novel objects, and it fits the behavior of rats in a new maze, as reported by Whiting and Mowrer (1943), where initial terror gave place to an exploration so feverish that the food reward was not eaten. Montgomery and Monkman (1955) have undertaken to challenge this hypothesis by a direct experimental attack. They showed that fear induced in rats before entering a novel situation did not increase exploratory behavior, and that fear induced within the novel situation decreased exploration to an extent correlated with the intensity of the fear. They find it more reasonable to suppose that fear and exploration are conflicting forms of behavior, and this view can also be defended on purely logical grounds. Fear shows itself in either freezing or avoidance, whereas exploration is clearly an instance of approach. There is hardly a more perfect example of conflict between incompatible responses than that of an animal hesitating between investigation and flight. It is clear that exploration can sometimes serve to reduce anxiety, but the proposition that it comes into existence only for this purpose cannot be so easily accepted.

What assumptions have to be made to support the thesis that exploration is motivated by anxiety reduction? It has to be assumed that certain characteristic stimuli arouse anxiety and that exploration of these stimuli is then found to reduce the anxiety. If the characteristics in question are those of novelty and unfamiliarity, we must heed Berlyne's reminder that for the infant all experience is novel and unfamiliar. Berlyne (1950) proposes that the exploratory reaction "may be one that *all* stimuli originally evoke, but which disappears (becomes habituated) as the organism becomes familiar with them." But if all stimuli at first arouse anxious tension, we would have to deduce that all response would consist of avoidance in the interest of reducing that tension. Approaching a stimulus and taking steps to increase its impact could not occur. An exploratory tendency must be there in the first place before it can achieve the function of reducing anxiety. As Woodworth (1958) expresses it, "if there were no exploratory drive to balance and overbalance the fear drive, an animal would be helpless in a novel situation." I find it hard to believe that creatures so liberally endowed with fear could ever achieve a working mastery of the environment if they were impelled toward it only by the pressure of organic needs.

Both hypotheses thus far examined — secondary reinforcement and anxiety reduction — require us to make improbable assumptions. There remains the possibility that exploration should simply be added to the list of primary drives and otherwise treated in orthodox fashion. Myers and Miller (1954) suggest that this is the appropriate course, provided the new drive shows the same functional properties as those already known. "If an exploratory tendency can produce learning like other drives such as hunger, and also show a similar pattern of satiation and recovery, these functional parallels to already known drives would help to justify its classification in the same category." Logically the problem can be dealt with in this way, but we must consider very carefully what happens to the category of drive if we admit this new applicant to membership.

Using hunger as the chief model, the orthodox conception of drive involves the following characteristics: (a) there is a tissue need or deficit external to the nervous system which acts upon that system as a strong persisting stimulus; (b) this promotes activity which is terminated by a consummatory response with consequent reduction of need; (c) the reduction of need brings about the learning which gradually shapes behavior into an economical pursuit of suitable goal objects. In this scheme the tension of an aroused drive is interpreted as unpleasant, at least in the sense that the animal acts in such a way as to lower the drive and becomes quiescent when it is lowered. There are probably no living champions of so simple an orthodoxy, yet the scheme remains pervasive, and it is therefore worth while to observe that the proposed exploratory drive hardly fits it at all.

In the first place, the exploratory drive appears to bear no relation whatever to a tissue need or deficit external to the nervous system. It is, of course, clearly related to certain characteristics of stimulation from the external environment, a source of motivation which Harlow (1953) would like to see restored to a serious place in contemporary psychology; but it certainly cannot be correlated with a visceral need comparable to hunger, thirst, or sex. Considering the pattern of satiation and recovery shown by Welker's chimpanzees, Woodworth (1958) remarks that "what becomes satiated is not the exploratory tendency in general, but the exploring of a particular place or object." It is possible, as Hebb (1955) has pointed out, that the so-called "reticular activation system" in the brain stem creates a kind of general drive state, and this mechanism might indeed be flexibly responsive to changes in sensory stimulation. This interesting suggestion, however, is still a far cry from viscerogenic drives; it commits us instead to the novel idea of a neurogenic motive, one in which the state of the nervous system and the patterns of external stimulation conspire to produce motivated behavior. There is even a good deal of trouble in supposing that the adequate stimuli for exploration are either strong or persistent. Novelty certainly cannot be equated with strength or persistence, and animals seem readily able to disregard the stimuli to exploration when they are weary.

In the second place, exploratory behavior cannot be regarded as leading to any kind of consummatory response. It is usual for the animal's investigation to subside gradually. If the animal at some point turns away and leaves the once novel object we may say that its curiosity is "satisfied," but we do not mean by this that the equivalent of a consummatory response has just taken place. The sequence suggests rather that curiosity wears out and slowly falls to a level where it no longer guides behavior, at least until a fresh novelty comes into view.

Finally, in the case of exploratory behavior there is real difficulty in identifying reinforcement with need reduction. Montgomery (1954), describing the learning of the Y maze, points out that the short arm, essentially a dead end, would tend to reduce the exploratory drive, whereas the long arm, itself a complex maze, would increase it — but the long arm is chosen. If the long arm functions as a reinforcing agent, "the mechanism underlying this reinforcement is an *increase*, rather than a decrease, in the strength of the exploratory drive." In this experiment, as in their natural habitat, animals do not wait to have novelty thrust upon them, nor do they avoid situations in which novelty may be found. Such behavior can be most readily conceptualized by admitting that under certain circumstances reinforcement can be correlated with an increase in arousal or excitement rather than a decrease. A drive which has no consummatory climax seems almost to require this formulation. It is distinctly implausible to connect reinforcement with the waning of an agreeable interest in the environment or with a general progress from zestful alertness to boredom.

If we admit exploration to the category of drive we are thus committing ourselves to believe that drives need have no extraneural sources in tissue deficits or visceral tensions, that they are not necessarily activated by strong or persistent stimuli, that they do not require consummatory responses, and that drive increase can sometimes be a mechanism of reinforcement.

Activity and Manipulation

Exploration is not the only motive proposed by critics of drive orthodoxy, and novelty is not the only characteristic of the environment which appears to incite motivated behavior. Some workers have suggested a need for activity, which can be strengthened by depriving animals of their normal opportunities for movement. Kagan and Berkun (1954) used running in an activity wheel as the reward for learning and found it "an adequate reinforcement for the instrumental response of bar pressing." Hill (1956) showed that rats will run in an activity wheel to an extent that is correlated with their previous degree of confinement. It is certain that the activity wheel offers no novelty to the animals in these experiments. Nevertheless, they seem to want to run, and they continue to run for such long times that no part of the behavior can readily be singled out as a consummatory response. Perhaps an unpleasant internal state created by inactivity is gradually worked off, but this is certainly accomplished by a tremendous increase of kinaesthetic stimulation and muscular output which would seem to imply increased excitation in the system as a whole.

Harlow and his associates (Harlow, 1953; Harlow, Harlow, & Meyer, 1950) maintain that there is also a manipulative drive. It is aroused by certain patterns of external stimulation and reduced by actively changing the external pattern. The experiments were done with rhesus monkeys, and they involve the solving of a mechanical problem which, however, leads to no further consequences or rewards. The task might be, for instance, to raise a hasp which is kept in place by both a hook and a pin; all that can be accomplished is to raise the hasp, which opens nothing and leads to no fresh discoveries. When the hasp problem is simply installed in the living cages, the monkeys return to it and solve it as many as 7 or 8 times over several days. It seems unlikely that novelty can be postulated as the essential characteristic of the stimulus which evokes this repeated behavior. The simplest interpretation is rather that value lies for the animal in the opportunity, as Zimbardo and Miller (1958) express it, "to effect a stimulus change in the environment." This formulation suggests something like the propensities toward mastery or power that have often been mentioned in discussions of human motivation.

The addition of activity and manipulation to the list of primary drives can only make more serious the difficulties for the orthodox model that resulted from admitting exploration. But recent research with animals has put the orthodox model on the defensive even on its home grounds. It has become increasingly clear that hunger, thirst, and sex cannot be made to fit the simple pattern that seemed so helpful 40 years ago.

Changing Conceptions of Drive

In a brief historical statement, Morgan (1957) has pointed out that the conception of drive as a noxious stimulus began to lose its popularity among research workers shortly after 1940. "On the whole," he says, "the stimulus concept of drive owed more to wishful thinking than to experimental fact." When technical advances in biochemistry and brain physiology made it possible to bring in an array of new facts, there was a rapid shift toward the view that "drives arise largely through the internal environment acting on the central nervous system." One of the most influential discoveries was that animals have as many as a dozen specific hungers for particular kinds of food, instead of the single hunger demanded by Cannon's model of the hunger drive. If an animal's diet becomes deficient in some important element such as salt, sugar, or the vitamin-B complex, foods containing the missing element will be eagerly sought while other foods are passed by, a selectivity that obviously cannot be laid to contractions of the stomach. Similarly, a negative food preference can be produced by loading either the stomach or blood stream with some single element of the normal diet. The early work of Beach (1942) on sexual behavior brought out similar complications in what had for a time been taken as a relatively simple drive. Hormone levels appeared to be considerably more important than peripheral stimulation in the arousal and maintenance of the sex drive. Further work led Beach (1951) to conclude that sexual behavior is "governed by a complex combination of processes." He points out that the patterns of control differ tremendously from one species to another and that within a single species the mechanisms may be quite different for males and females. Like hunger, the sex drive turns out to be no simple thing.

New methods of destroying and of stimulating brain centers in animals have had an equally disastrous effect on the orthodox drive model. The nervous system, and especially the hypothalamus, appears to be deeply implicated in the motivational process. Experimental findings on hypothalamic lesions in animals encourage Stellar (1954) to believe that there are different centers "responsible for the control of different kinds of basic motivation," and that in each case "there is one main excitatory center and one inhibitory center which operates to depress the activity of the excitatory center." As research findings accumulate, this picture may seem to be too cleanly drawn. Concerning sexual behavior, for example, Rosvold (1959) concludes a recent review by rejecting the idea of a single center in the cerebrum; rather, the sex drive "probably has a wide neural representation with a complex interaction between old and new brain structures and between neural and humoral

agents." Nevertheless, Miller's (1958) careful work seems to leave little doubt that motivated behavior in every way similar to normal hunger and normal pain-fear can be elicited by electrical stimulation of quite restricted areas of the hypothalamus. It is clear that we cannot regress to a model of drives that represents the energy as coming from outside the nervous system. Whatever the effects of peripheral stimulation may be, drives also involve neural centers and neural patterns as well as internal biochemical conditions.

What sort of model becomes necessary to entertain these newly discovered facts? In 1938 Lashley expressed the view that motivation should not be equated with disturbance of organic equilibrium but rather with "a partial excitation of a very specific sensorimotor mechanism irradiating to affect other systems of reaction." Beach (1942) postulated that there must be in the nervous system "a condition analogous to Sherrington's central excitatory state." Morgan, in 1943, undertook to capture the facts in a systematic theory which seems to have been well sustained by subsequent research (Morgan, 1957). He distinguished two types of process which he called *humoral motive factors* and *central motive states*. The humoral factors consist of chemical or hormonal constituents of the blood and lymph, and they are conceived to influence behavior chiefly by a direct sensitizing action on neural centers. The central motive states have several properties: They are partly self-maintaining through neural circuits, they tend to increase the organism's general activity, they evoke specific forms of behavior not strongly controlled by the environment, and they prime or prepare consummatory responses which will occur when adequate stimulation is found. This is a far cry from the orthodox model, but we must nowadays admit that the orthodox model is a far cry from the facts.

In view of this radical evolution of the concept of drive, it is not surprising to find the drive reduction hypothesis in serious difficulties. The earlier identification of reinforcement with drive reduction has been directly attacked in a series of experiments designed to show that learning takes place when drive reduction is ruled out.

In 1950 Sheffield and Roby showed that instrumental learning would take place in hungry rats when the reward consisted not of a nutritive substance but of sweet-tasting saccharine in the drinking water. This finding appeared to be "at variance with the molar principle of reinforcement used by Hull, which identifies primary reinforcement with 'need reduction.'" The authors naturally do not question the vital importance of need reduction, but they point out that need-reducing events may accomplish reinforcement through a mechanism more direct and speedy than the reduction of the need itself. They think that "stimulation and performance of a consummatory response appears to be more important to instrumental learning—in a primary, not acquired, way—than the drive satisfaction which the response normally achieves." Their findings are in line with an earlier experiment with chickens by Wolfe and Kaplon (1941), who used different sizes of food pellets so that the number of pecks and the amount of food received could be thrown out of their usual close connection. The chickens, we might say, would rather peck than eat; learning was more strongly reinforced when four pecks were necessary than when one peck was enough to take the same amount of food.

The substitution of the consummatory response for need reduction as the immediate reinforcing mechanism is a step in advance, but it soon turns out that another step is required. Can it be shown that an aroused need which does not reach consummation has a reinforcing effect? To test this possibility Sheffield, Wulff, and Backer (1951) provided male rats with the reward of copulating with a female, but not enough times to produce ejaculation. This reward was favorable to instrumental learning even though there was no need reduction and no performance of the final consummatory act. The results were supported by Kagan (1955), whose animals showed substantial learning under the same conditions, though learning was still faster when ejaculation was permitted. Sheffield, Roby, and Campbell (1954) have proposed a *drive-induction* theory according to which the property of reinforcement is assigned to the excitement of an aroused drive. We have already seen that some such assumption is essential if exploration is to be assigned the

status of a drive. Here it can be added that the whole theory of pregenital sexuality involves motivation without consummatory acts and without any but the most gradual need reduction. And as a final blow to the orthodox hypothesis comes the finding by Olds and Milner (1954) that positive reinforcement can be brought about by direct electrical stimulation of certain areas of the brain. Once again we learn that neural centers are deeply implicated in the plot of motivation. The simple mechanics of need reduction cannot possibly serve as the basis for a theory of learning.

Twenty years of research have thus pretty much destroyed the orthodox drive model. It is no longer appropriate to consider that drives originate solely in tissue deficits external to the nervous system, that consummatory acts are a universal feature and goal of motivated behavior, or that the alleviation of tissue deficits is the necessary condition for instrumental learning. Instead we have a complex picture in which humoral factors and neural centers occupy a prominent position; in which, moreover, the concept of neurogenic motives without consummatory ends appears to be entirely legitimate. Do these changes remove the obstacles to placing exploration, activity, and manipulation in the category of drives?

Perhaps this is no more than a question of words, but I should prefer at this point to call it a problem in conceptual strategy. I shall propose that these three new "drives" have much in common and that it is useful to bring them under the single heading of competence. Even with the loosening and broadening of the concept of drive, they are still in important respects different from hunger, thirst, and sex. In hunger and thirst, tissue deficits, humoral factors, and consummatory responses retain an important position. The mature sex drive depends heavily on hormonal levels and is sharply oriented toward consummation. Tendencies like exploration do not share these characteristics, whatever else they have in common with the better known drives. It is in order to emphasize their intrinsic peculiarities, to get them considered in their own right without a cloud of surplus meanings, that I prefer in this essay to speak of the urge that makes for competence simply as motivation rather than as drive.

THE TREND IN PSYCHOANALYTIC EGO PSYCHOLOGY

Rather an abrupt change of climate may be experienced as we turn from the animal laboratory to the psychoanalytic treatment room, but the trends of thought in the two realms turn out to be remarkably alike. Here the orthodox view of motivation is to be found in Freud's theory of the instincts—they might be known to us as drives if an early translator had been more literal with the German *Trieb*.

Freud's Theories of Instinct and Ego

In his final work, Freud (1949) described instincts as "somatic demands upon mental life" and as "the ultimate cause of all activity." He wrote further:

It is possible to distinguish an indeterminate number of instincts and in common practice this is in fact done. For us, however, the important question arises whether we may not be able to derive all of these instincts from a few fundamental ones. . . . After long doubts and vacillations we have decided to assume the existence of only two basic instincts, *Eros* and the *destructive instinct* (Freud, 1949, p. 20).

The history of Freud's long doubts and vacillations has been lucidly related by Bibring (1941). Up to 1914 Freud used a two-fold classification of sexual instincts and ego instincts. The ego instincts made their appearance in his case histories in a somewhat moral character, being held responsible for the disastrous repression of sexual needs, but in systematic usage they were conceived as serving the goal of self-preservation, and hunger was generally taken as an appropriate model. In 1914, when he evolved the concept of narcissism and saw that it threatened to blur the line between sexual and ego tendencies, Freud (1925b) still expressed himself as unwilling to abandon an idea which followed the popular distinction of love and hunger and which reflected man's dual existence "as reproducer and as one who serves his own ends." Various facts, particularly those of sadism and masochism, served to overcome his reluctance, so that he

finally united self-preservation and preservation of the species under the heading of Eros or life instincts, establishing destructiveness or the death instinct as the great antagonist in a profound biological sense (Freud, 1948). This highly speculative step proved to be too much for some of his otherwise loyal followers, and the earlier orthodoxy did not become entirely extinct.

It is easier to follow Freud's reasoning when we bear in mind the simultaneous development of his ideas about the mental apparatus. Bibring (1941) points out that even in his early thinking a sharp contrast was always drawn between instinct and mental apparatus. Instinct supplied the energy in the form of powerful, persisting internal stimuli; the apparatus guided it into channels which produced organized behavior and eventually put a stop to the persisting stimulation. In 1915 Freud wrote:

The nervous system is an apparatus having the function of abolishing stimuli which reach it or of reducing excitation to the lowest possible level; an apparatus which would even, if this were feasible, maintain itself in an altogether unstimulated condition. . . . The task of the nervous system is—broadly speaking—*to master stimuli* (Freud, 1925c, p. 63).

During the next decade there was a considerable growth in his ideas about the mental apparatus, culminating in the well known division into id, ego, and superego. The activities of the ego now received much fuller recognition. Freud (1927) assigned to it "the task of self-preservation," which it accomplished through its several capacities of perception, memory, flight, defense, and adaptive action. One can see Freud's thought moving from a mechanical analogy—an engine and its fuel—toward a much more adaptational conception of the mental apparatus. Ego instincts did not wholly disappear, but the decline in their systematic importance was compensated by the insight that self-preservative tendencies were to some extent built into the whole living system. It is significant that as he took this course he came to question the earlier tension-reduction theory. In the last year of his life he declared it to be probable "that what is felt as pleasure or unpleasure is not the *absolute* degree of the tensions but something in the rhythm of their changes" (Freud, 1949).

Freud's tendency to revise his thinking makes it difficult to pin down an orthodox doctrine, but most workers will probably agree that his main emphasis was upon somatically based drives, a mental apparatus which received its power from the drives, and, of course, the multitude of ways in which the apparatus controlled, disguised, and transformed these energies. His treatment of the ego was far from complete, and it was not long before voices were raised against the conception that so vital and versatile a part of the personality could be developed solely by libidinal and aggressive energies.

An Instinct to Master

In 1942 Hendrick proposed that this difficulty be met by assuming the existence of an additional major instinct. "The development of ability to master a segment of the environment," he wrote, and the need to exercise such functions, can be conceptualized as an "instinct to master," further characterized as "an inborn drive to do and to learn how to do." The aim of this instinct is "pleasure in exercising a function successfully, regardless of its sensual value." The simpler manifestations are learning to suck, to manipulate, to walk, to speak, to comprehend and to reason; these functions and others eventually become integrated as the ego. "The central nervous system is more than a utility," Hendrick declared. The infant shows an immediate desire to use and perfect each function as it ripens, and the adult secures gratification from an executive function efficiently performed regardless of its service to other instincts.

Hendrick's procedure in this and two supporting papers (1943a, 1943b) is quite similar to that of the animal psychologists who propose listing exploration as an additional primary drive. The instinct to master has an aim—to exercise and develop the ego functions— and it follows hedonic principles by yielding "primary pleasure" when efficient action "enables the individual to control and alter his environ-

ment." It is to this extent analogous to the instincts assumed by Freud. But just as an exploratory drive seemed radically to alter the whole conception of drive, so the instinct to master implied a drastic change in the psychoanalytic idea of instinct. Critics were quick to point out that Freud had always conceived of instincts as having somatic sources external to the ego apparatus, a condition not met by the proposed instinct to master. There was nothing comparable to erogenous zones, to orgasm, or to the sequence of painful tension followed by pleasurable release. Mastery, the critics agreed, could not be an instinct, whatever else it might be.

It is of interest that Fenichel (1945), who definitely rejected Hendrick's proposal, gives us another close parallel to the animal work by attributing mastering behavior to anxiety-reduction. He argued that mastery is "a general aim of every organism but not of a specific instinct." He agreed that there is "a pleasure of enjoying one's abilities," but he related this pleasure to cessation of the anxiety connected with not being able to do things. "Functional pleasure," he wrote, "is pleasure in the fact that the exercise of a function is now possible without anxiety," and he contended that when anxiety is no longer present, when there is full confidence that a given situation can be met, then action is no longer accompanied by functional pleasure. We must certainly agree with Fenichel that anxiety *can* play the part he assigns it, but the proposal that all pleasure in ego functions comes from this source raises the same difficulties we have already considered in connection with exploratory behavior. That we exercise our capacities and explore our surroundings only to reduce our fear of the environment is not, as I have already argued, an assumption that enjoys high probability on biological grounds.

Hartmann on the Ego

A less radical change in the orthodox model is proposed by Hartmann, who, in a series of papers since 1939, often in conjunction with Kris and Loewenstein, has been refining and expanding Freud's views on the ego and the instincts. While the ego is conceived as a "sub-structure" of the personality, this term is somewhat metaphorical because in practice the ego has to be defined by its functions. The list of functions, which includes grasping, crawling, walking, perceiving, remembering, language, thinking, and intention, covers much the same ground that was indicated by Hendrick, but Hartmann does not attribute their growth to an instinct. On the other hand, Hartmann (1950) early came to the conclusion that development could not be explained, as Freud had seemed to conceive it, simply as a consequence of conflict between instinctual needs and frustrating realities. The instincts alone would never guarantee survival; they require mediation by the innate ego apparatus if they are to meet "the average expectable environmental conditions." He therefore proposed that we conceive of an autonomous factor in ego development, an independent maturation of functions taking place in a "conflict-free ego sphere." Functions such as locomotion ripen through maturation and through learning even when they are not caught up in struggles to obtain erotic and aggressive gratification or to avoid anxiety. As Anna Freud (1952) has pointed out, walking becomes independent of instinctual upheavals a few weeks after its beginning; thereafter, it serves the child impartially in situations of conflict and those that are free from conflict.

Hartmann's idea of autonomous ego development has of course been assumed all along by workers in child psychology, but it is an important step to relate it to Freud's disclosures concerning unconscious motivation. In what now looks like an excess of enthusiasm for his own concepts, Freud (1925a) undertook to explain the outgrowing of the pleasure principle and the substituting of the reality principle as a simple and direct consequence of the frustration of instinctual needs. However, the reality principle contained the idea of postponing an immediate gratification in favor of a future one, and Hartmann (1956) properly notes that the capacities for postponement and anticipation cannot be conjured into existence simply by the collision of frustrating reality and ungratified need. Important as frustrations may be, these capacities must already be available, "some preparedness for dealing with

reality" must already exist, before the frustration can produce its momentous educative effect. It can be seen from this example that Hartmann's analysis opens the way for profitable commerce between developmental psychologies inside and outside of psychoanalysis.

Hartmann's emphasis on adaptation permits him to perceive much more that is autonomous about the ego than was ever seriously included in Freud's systematic thought. He allows, for instance, that aims and interests which develop in the beginning as defenses against instincts may later become part of conflict-free spheres of activity—become interests in their own right —and thus achieve "secondary autonomy," a concept very close to Allport's (1937) functional autonomy of motives (Hartmann, 1950). He deals with the possibility that adaptive skills developing in the conflict-free sphere may have a decisive influence on the handling of conflicts. These skills have a history of their own, shaped jointly by the child's abilities and by the responses evoked from parents. As Monroe (1955) has expressed it, they have "a very important role in the development of the conscious and semiconscious psychological self." They may thus have a direct influence upon the outcome when a child becomes involved in conflict. Rapaport (1958) sees Hartmann's ideas on the autonomy of the ego as vital to the proper understanding not only of healthy development but also of psychopathology itself.

In explaining the autonomous growth of the ego, Hartmann makes generous use of the concept of maturation, but he naturally does not exclude learning. Hartmann (1950) entertains the possibility, mentioned casually from time to time by Freud (1916, 1949), that ego functions are supplied with their own sources of energy independent of instincts, and that there is pleasure connected with their mere exercise. However, he makes little systematic use of this idea, relying instead upon a concept more central in Freud's thinking, that of the neutralization of drive energies. Freud (1927) found that he could "make no headway" in accounting for the varied activities of the ego without assuming "a displaceable energy, which is in itself neutral, but is able to join forces either with an erotic or with a destructive impulse, differing qualitatively as they do, and augment its total cathexis." He speculated that the neutral energy came from Eros and could be conceived as desexualized libido. Hartmann, Kris, and Loewenstein (1949) carried the idea forward a logical step by proposing that the energies of aggressive instincts could similarly be neutralized and placed at the disposal of the ego. Neutralized energy contributes to the development of the ego and makes possible a continuing interest in the objects of the environment regardless of their immediate relation to erotic or aggressive needs. Hartmann (1955) finds this concept particularly helpful in unscrambling the confusions that have arisen over the concept of sublimation.

The doctrine of neutralized instinctual energies is a curious one, and we should bear in mind the complex clinical findings that perhaps suggested it. Freud was an unquestioned genius in detecting the subtle operation of erotic urges and aggressive fantasies, along with elaborate mechanisms of defense, behind the seemingly objective or "neutral" activities of everyday life. Remarkable transformations of interest could sometimes be observed in the course of development. For example, a patient's childhood erotic rivalry and aggressive competition with his father might later disappear beneath a strong objective interest in running the family business; then suddenly, on the brink of success, this interest might come to a total halt, paralyzed by anxiety because the underlying instinctual goals came too close to symbolic fulfilment. The reappearance of instinctual preoccupations in such a case lends a certain color to the idea that they have somehow been driving the behavior all the time, even though the daily pursuit of business goals seems utterly remote from instinctual gratifications.

It is worth noticing that Freud's procedure in making the assumption of neutralized instinctual energy is similar to the one followed by orthodox behaviorists in connection with primary drives. These theorists started from the assumption that all behavior was powered by a limited number of organic drives, and then, in order to protect this assumption, they developed further hypotheses, such as secondary reinforcement, to account for motivated behavior that bore no obvious relation to primary goals. At the point where he could "make no headway" without postulating neutralization, Freud could conceivably have made a good deal of headway if he had been willing to assume that neutral energy, neither sexual nor aggressive, was available as a natural endowment in the first place. But he preferred to protect his assumption of two primary drives and to interpret other energies as transformations of these drives. Even so, the concept seems superfluous if we take Freud at his word about the nature of the life instincts. Freud (1949) made it clear that Eros included more than instincts having a sexual aim; its larger goal was "to establish even greater unities and to preserve them thus — in short, to bind together." Under this formula, it would seem possible to include energies inherently directed toward building up the integrated functions of the ego. But Freud did not exploit the full range of his theory of Eros and proposed only that neutral energies should be conceived as desexualized.

The concept of neutralization has in some respects had a good effect on psychoanalytic ego psychology. In Hartmann's writings, as we have seen, and in Rapaport's (1951, 1954) work on thinking, it has encouraged a strong interest in autonomous ego functions and a fresh analysis of their place in personality. Nevertheless, it seems to me an awkward conceptualization, one which in the end is likely to lead, as Colby (1955) has expressed it, to a "metapsychological snarl." The theory requires that instinctual energies can completely change their aims, which makes one wonder what purpose was served in the first place by defining them as having aims. It preserves an image of mobility of energies that seems much out of line with recent research on animal motivation, where energy is being conceived in a constantly closer relation to specific structures. To my mind it thus compares unfavorably with its quite straightforward alternative, which is that the alleged neutralized energies are there in the first place as part of the natural make-up of an adaptive organism. I shall later develop this possibility by means of the concept of competence in its motivational aspect, and I believe that this concept gains support from certain other lines of work in the psychoanalytic tradition.

Motility and a Sense of Industry

The trend away from instinct orthodoxy is illustrated by the work of Kardiner (1947) on what he calls "the development of the effective ego." Kardiner's reflections arose from his work on the traumatic neuroses of war. In these disorders the main threat is to self-preservation, and some of the most important symptoms, such as defensive rituals and paralyses, are lodged in the action systems that normally bring about successful adaptive behavior. It thus becomes pertinent to study the growth of action systems, to discover how they become integrated so as to maintain "controlled contact" with the environment and "controlled exploitation of objects in the outer world," and to work out the conditions which either favor or disrupt this acquired integration. Thinking along these lines, Kardiner is led to conclusions just about the opposite of Freud's: It is the successful and gratifying experiences, not the frustrations, that lead to increasingly integrated action and to the discrimination of self from outer world. Frustration produces chiefly disruptions and inhibitions which are unfavorable to the early growth of the ego. Children are gratified when they discover the connection between a movement executed and the accompanying and subsequent sensations. They are still more gratified when they carry out actions successfully; this "gives rise to the triumphant feeling of making an organ obedient to the will of the ego." Such experiences build up "a definite self- or body-consciousness which becomes the center and the point of reference of all purposeful and coördinated activity." Growth of the ego, in short, depends heavily upon action systems and the consequences of action. The course and vicissitudes of this development have to be studied in their own right, and they' cannot be understood as side effects of the stages of libidinal development.

A similar theme is pursued to even more radical conclusions by Mittelmann (1954) in his paper on motility. Mittelmann regards motility, which manifests itself most typically in skilled motor actions such as posture, locomotion, and manipulation, as an "urge in its own right" in the same sense that one speaks of oral, excretory, or genital urges. From about 10 months of age it has a distinctly "driven" character, and there is restlessness and anger if it is blocked. During the second and third years the motor urge "dominates all other urges," so that it is proper to "consider this period the motor level of ego and libido development." The child makes tremendous efforts to learn to walk, and to walk well, and he exhibits joyous laughter as he attains these ends. Restrictions of motility may occur because the parents are anxious or because the child's assertiveness troubles them, and a lasting injury to the parent-child relationship may result. Clumsiness in motor or manipulative accomplishments may lead to self-hatred and dependence, for "the evolution of self-assertiveness and self-esteem is intimately connected with motor development." Motility is of central importance in many of the most characteristic functions of the ego. Partly by its means the infant differentiates himself from other objects, and the child's knowledge of objects depends on an extensive activity of manipulation and examination. "Thus motility becomes one of the most important aspects of reality testing." Because it is an element in all cognitive behavior, it can also be considered "the dominant integrative function." Mittelmann bases motor development, in short, on an independent urge, and he sees this urge as the really crucial motive behind the development of the ego.

Like Kardiner, Mittelmann does not attempt to formulate in detail the nature of the motility urge. It is likened not to an instinct but to a "partial instinct," and this seems to place it somewhere between Hendrick's instinct to master and Hartmann's dimly sketched independent energies of the ego. This indefiniteness may irk the systematic theorist, but Mittelmann's account of the part played by motility in ego development easily stands as a significant contribution. Even more influential in this respect is the work of Erikson (1953), who has given a highly detailed timetable of ego development. Erikson stays with the libido theory as far as it will go, but he passes beyond its reach in his account of the latency period and some of the later crises of growth. It is clear that something more than the orthodox instincts is involved in the "enormous value" with which the child in the second year "begins to endow his autonomous will." Something more would seem to be implied in the expanding imagination and initiative of the "phallic" child. Certainly more is involved during the school years, when children address themselves to motor, manual, and intellectual achievements and need "a sense of being able to make things and make them well and even perfectly: this is what I call the *sense of industry*." Erikson's (1952) theory of play is also influenced by the idea that learning to deal with the animate and inanimate worlds is an important preoccupation of childhood: "the playing child advances forward to new stages of real mastery." Action systems, motility, and a sense of industry all direct our attention to behavior which can scarcely be contained in the old bottle of instinct theory.

Glancing back over these trends in psychoanalytic ego psychology, we cannot fail to be impressed by striking similarities to the trend in animal work. Using Reik's familiar metaphor, we might say that those who listen with their two ears and those who listen with the third ear have apparently been hearing much the same sounds. In both realms there is discontent with drive orthodoxy. In both there is persistent pointing to kinds of behavior neglected or explained away by drive orthodoxy: exploration, activity, manipulation, and mastery. Similar theories have been proposed to account for the energies in such behavior: (*a*) they are derived or transformed in some way from the primary drives or instincts (secondary reinforcement, neutralization of drive energies); (*b*) they are powered by the need to reduce anxiety; (*c*) they can be accounted for only by postulating a new primary drive (exploratory drive, instinct to master). When these explanations are considered to have failed, the one remaining course is to work out a different idea of motivation. In his study of action systems, Kardiner prefers to leave the question of energy sources unanswered, but Erikson's sense of industry and Mittelmann's motility urge point to a motivational base which is only remotely analogous to primary drives or fundamental instincts. I believe that the difficulties in this undertaking can be greatly reduced by the concept of competence, to which we shall shortly turn.

RELATED DEVELOPMENTS IN GENERAL PSYCHOLOGY

If a systematic survey were in order, it would be easy to show a parallel drift of opinion in other parts of the psychological realm. Among theorists of personality, for example, something like drive orthodoxy is to be found in the work of Dollard and Miller (1950), who have translated the main concepts of Freud's psychoanalysis, including processes such as repression and displacement, into the language of reinforcement theory. With them we might put Mowrer (1950), whose searching analysis of fear as an acquired drive has led him to postulate anxiety-reduction as the master motive behind the development of the ego. Discontent with drive orthodoxy has long been expressed by Allport (1937, 1946), who not only argues for a functional autonomy of motives from their infantile roots in primary drives but also seriously questions the law of effect, the very cornerstone of reinforcement theory. Little comfort for the orthodox can be found in Murray's (1938) detailed taxonomy of needs, especially when it comes to needs such as achievement and construction, which can be tied to primary drives only by conceptual acrobatics. Murray and Kluckhohn (1953), moreover, have made a case for pleasure in activity for its own sake, reviving the *Funktionslust* proposed many years ago by Karl Bühler (1924) and recently developed in some detail by French (1952). They also argue for intrinsic mental needs: "the infant's mind is not acting most of the time as the instrument of some urgent animal drive, but is preoccupied with *gratifying itself*." Murphy (1947) takes the view that all tissues can become seats of tension and thus participants in drive; in addition to visceral drives, he postulates two independent forms, activity drives and sensory drives. Then there are workers such as Goldstein (1939) who approach the whole problem with a holistic philosophy which precludes the dictatorship of any isolated or partial drives. Goldstein (1940) assumes one master tendency, that toward self-actualization, of which the so-called visceral drives are but partial and not really isolated expressions, and which can find expression also in an urge toward perfection — toward completing what is incomplete, whether it be an outside task or the mastery of some function such as walking. It has been shown by the Ansbachers (1956) that Adler, never a friend of instinct orthodoxy, in his later years reached an idea very similar to the urge toward perfection. Maslow (1954, 1955), too, belongs with the heterodox. He insists that we should take account of growth motivation as well as the deficiency motivation implied in the visceral drives, and he offers the valuable idea of a hierarchy of motives, according to which the satisfaction of "lower" needs makes it possible for "higher" needs to emerge and become regnant in behavior.

Mention of these names must suffice here to show that the trends observed in animal psychology and psychoanalytic ego psychology are pervasive in contemporary psychological thought. Doubtless the same controversies and problems could be pointed out in child development, in cognitive psychology, and in other fields. But in order to advance to my main theme, I shall select only certain developments which bear directly on the concept of competence.

Needs for Excitement and Novelty

Human experience provides plentiful evidence of the importance of reducing excessive levels of tension. Men under wartime stress, men under pressure of pain and extreme deprivation, men with excessive work loads or too much exposure to confusing social interactions, all act as if their nervous systems craved that utterly unstimulated condition which Freud once sketched as the epitome of neural bliss. But if these same men be granted their Nirvana they soon become miserable and begin to look around for a little excitement. Human experience testifies that boredom is a bad state of affairs about which something must be done. Hebb (1949) has been particularly insistent in reminding us that many of our activities, such as reading detective stories, skin-diving, or driving cars at high speeds, give clear evidence of a need to raise the level of stimulation and excitement. Men and animals alike seem at times bent on increasing the impact of the environment and even on creating mild degrees of frustration and fear. Hebb and Thompson (1954) reflect upon this as follows:

Such phenomena are, of course, well known in man: in the liking for dangerous sports or roller coasters, where fear is deliberately courted, and in the addiction to bridge or golf or solitaire, vices whose very existence depends upon the level of difficulty of the problems presented and an optimal level of frustration. Once more, when we find such attitudes toward fear and frustration in animals, we have a better basis for supposing that we are dealing with something fundamental if a man prefers skis to the less dangerous snowshoes, or when we observe an unashamed love of work (problem solving and frustration included) in the scientist, or in the business man who cannot retire. Such behavior in man is usually accounted for as a search for prestige, but the animal data make this untenable. It seems much more likely that solving problems and running mild risks are inherently rewarding, or, in more general terms, that the animal will always act so as to produce an optimal level of excitation (Hebb & Thompson, 1954, p. 551).

The concept of optimal stimulation has been developed by Leuba (1955), who sees it as helpful in resolving some of the problems of learning theory. Believing that most theorizing about motivation has been based upon "powerful biological or neurotic drives," Leuba bids us look at the much more common learning situations of nursery, playground, and school, where "actions which increase stimulation and produce excitement are strongly reinforced, sometimes to the dismay of parents and teachers." He proposes that there is an optimal level of stimulation, subject to variation at different times, and that learning is associated with movement toward this optimal level, downward when stimulation is too high and upward when it is too low. A similar idea is expressed by McReynolds (1956) concerning the more restricted concept of "rate of perceptualization." Monotonous conditions provide too low a rate, with boredom; excessive stimulation produces too high a rate, with disruptive excitement; the optimal rate yields the experience of pleasure. These ideas are now amply supported by recent experimental work on sensory deprivation (Lilly, 1956; Hebb, 1958).

In recent papers Young (1949, 1955) has

argued for an hedonic theory of motivation, one in which affective processes "constitute a form of primary motivation." According to Young's theory, "an organism behaves so as to maximize positive affective arousal (delight, enjoyment) and to minimize negative arousal (distress)." McClelland (1953) has offered a version of hedonic theory which is of particular value in understanding the significance of novelty. Affective arousal occurs when a stimulus pattern produces a discrepancy from the existing adaptation level. Small discrepancies produce pleasant affect and a tendency to approach; large ones produce unpleasantness and a tendency toward avoidance. The child at play, like the young chimpanzee and the exploring rat, needs frequent novelty in the stimulus field in order to keep up his interest — in order to maintain pleasant discrepancies from whatever adaptation level he has reached. Hebb's (1949) theory of the neurological correlates of learning also deals with novelty, though in a somewhat different way. He equates sustained interest with a state of neural affairs in which "phase sequences" are relatively complex and are growing, in the sense of establishing new internal relations. Such a state follows most readily from a stimulus field characterized by difference-in-sameness; that is, containing much that is familiar along with certain features that are novel. If the field is entirely familiar, phase sequences run off quickly, are short-circuited, and thus fail to produce sustained interest. Hebb's theory, which has the engaging quality of being able to explain why we enjoy reading a detective story once but not right over again, expresses in a neurological hypothesis the familiar fact that well-learned, habituated processes do not in themselves greatly interest us. Interest seems to require elements of unfamiliarity: of something still to be found out and of learning still to be done.

It seems to me that these contributions, though differing as to details, speak with unanimity on their central theme and would force us, if nothing else did, to reconsider seriously the whole problem of motivation. Boredom, the unpleasantness of monotony, the attraction of novelty, the tendency to vary behavior rather than repeating it rigidly, and the seeking of stimulation and mild excitement

stand as inescapable facts of human experience and clearly have their parallels in animal behavior. We may seek rest and minimal stimulation at the end of the day, but that is not what we are looking for the next morning. Even when its primary needs are satisfied and its homeostatic chores are done, an organism is alive, active, and up to something.

Dealing with the Environment

If we consider things only from the viewpoint of affect, excitement, and novelty, we are apt to overlook another important aspect of behavior, its effect upon the environment. Moving in this direction, Diamond (1939) invites us to consider the motivational properties of the sensorineural system, the apparatus whereby higher animals "maintain their relations to the environment." He conceives of this system as demanding stimulation and as acting in such a manner as to "force the environment to stimulate it." Even if one thinks only of the infant's exploring eyes and hands, it is clear that the main direction of behavior is by no means always that of reducing the impact of stimulation. When the eyes follow a moving object, or when the hand grasps an object which it has touched, the result is to preserve the stimulus and to increase its effect. In more elaborate explorations the consequence of a series of actions may be to vary the manner in which a stimulus acts upon the sense organs. It it apparent that the exploring, manipulating child produces by his actions precisely what Hebb's theory demands as a basis for continuing interest: he produces differences-in-sameness in the stimulus field.

In a critical analysis of Freud's views on the reality principle, Charlotte Bühler (1954) makes a strong case for positive interests in the environment, citing as evidence the responsiveness and adaptiveness of the newborn baby as well as the exploratory tendencies of later months. The problem is worked out in more detail by Schachtel (1954) in a paper on focal attention. Acts of focal attention are characteristically directed at particular objects, and they consist of several sustained approaches "aimed at active mental grasp" while excluding the rest of the field. These qualities can be observed even in the infant's early attempts to follow a moving object with his eyes, and they show more clearly in his later endeavors to learn how objects are related both to himself and to one another. Such behavior bespeaks "a relatively autonomous capacity for object interest." Schachtel makes the proposal that this interest is pursued precisely at those times when major needs are in abeyance. High pressure of need or anxiety is the enemy of exploratory play and is a condition, as every scientist should know, under which we are unlikely to achieve an objective grasp of the environment. Low need pressure is requisite if we are to perceive objects as they are, in their constant character, apart from hopes and fears we may at other times attach to them. Schachtel doubts that "the wish for need-satisfaction alone would ever lead to object perception and to object-oriented thought." Hence an autonomous capacity to be interested in the environment has great value for the survival of a species.

Being interested in the environment implies having some kind of satisfactory interaction with it. Several workers call attention to the possibility that satisfaction might lie in having an effect upon the environment, in dealing with it, and changing it in various ways. Groos (1901), in his classical analysis of play, attached great importance to the child's "joy in being a cause," as shown in making a clatter, "hustling things about," and playing in puddles where large and dramatic effects can be produced. "We demand a knowledge of effects," he wrote, "and to be ourselves the producers of effects." Piaget (1952) remarks upon the child's special interest in objects that are affected by his own movements. This aspect of behavior occupies a central place in the work of Skinner (1953), who describes it as "operant" and who thus "emphasizes the fact that the behavior *operates* upon the environment to generate consequences." These consequences are fed back through the sense organs and may serve to reinforce behavior even when no organic needs are involved. A rat will show an increased tendency to press a bar when this act produces a click or a buzz. A baby will continue to investigate when his efforts produce rattling or tinkling sounds or sparkling reflections from a shiny object. The young chimpanzees in Welker's experiment spent the longest time over objects which could be lighted or made to emit sounds. Skinner finds it "difficult, if not impossible, to trace these reinforcing effects to a history of conditioning." "We may plausibly argue," he continues, "that a capacity to be reinforced by any feedback from the environment would be biologically advantageous, since it would prepare the organism to manipulate the environment successfully before a given state of deprivation developed."

Woodworth's Behavior-Primacy Theory

The most far-reaching attempt to give these aspects of behavior a systematic place in the theory of motivation is contained in Woodworth's recent book, *Dynamics of Behavior* (1958). Woodworth takes his start from the idea that a great deal of human behavior appears to be directed toward producing effects upon the environment without immediate service to any aroused organic need. "Its incentives and rewards are in the field of behavior and not in the field of homeostasis." This is illustrated by exploratory behavior, which is directed outward toward the environment.

Its long-range value as the means of making the child acquainted with the world he has to deal with later, and so equipping him through play for the serious business of life, can scarcely lie within the little child's horizon. His goals are more limited and direct: to see this or that object more closely, to find what is behind an obstacle, to hear the noise an object makes when it strikes the floor, to be told the name of a thing or person (Woodworth, 1958, p. 78).

More complex play, such as building with blocks, illustrates the same outgoing tendency and reveals more plainly the element of finding out what one can and cannot do with objects. Even social play falls into the pattern. Playmates do not chiefly supply affection or satisfy organic needs; rather, they "afford the opportunity to do something interesting in the environment."

Woodworth draws a contrast between *need-primacy* theories of motivation and the *behavior-primacy* theory. The latter holds that "all behavior is directed primarily toward dealing with the environment." It is to be noted that "dealing with the environment" means a good deal more than receiving stimuli and making responses. Stimuli must be taken as indicators of objects in space, and responses must be adapted to produce effects upon these objects. Even the so-called "mental" capacities, such as memory and ideational thinking, become in time high-level methods of dealing with the environment. Woodworth leaves no doubt as to what he considers basic in motivation. "We are making the claim that this direction of receptive and motor activity toward the environment is the fundamental tendency of animal and human behavior and that it is the all-pervasive primary motivation of behavior." Organic drives have to break into this constantly flowing stream of activity and turn it in a special direction. But the goals of drives cannot be achieved without effective action upon one's surroundings. The ever-present, ever-primary feature of motivation is the tendency to deal with the environment.

It may appear to some workers that Woodworth has overshot the mark by making primary what has commonly been regarded as secondary, and by reducing the familiar drives to what sounds a little like a subordinate station. Woodworth's theory, however, like Goldstein's concept of self-actualization, probably should be construed not as an attempt to down-grade the drives but rather as an insistence that they be kept in the context of a whole living organism which during its waking hours is more or less constantly active. Woodworth's emphasis on dealing with the environment makes his theory a point of culmination for many of those driftings away from drive orthodoxy which we have found to be persistent in so many different areas of psychology. It will soon appear that the concept of competence, to which I now turn, represents in many respects a similar way of thinking. It emphasizes dealing with the environment, and it belongs in the trend away from drive *orthodoxy*, but it is not intended to supplant, or even to subsume, such dynamic forces as hunger, sex, aggression, and fear, which everyone knows to be of huge importance in animal and human nature.

COMPETENCE AND THE PLAY OF CONTENTED CHILDREN

A backward glance at our survey shows considerable agreement about the kinds of behavior that are left out or handled poorly by theories of motivation based wholly on organic drives. Repeatedly we find reference to the familiar series of learned skills which starts with sucking, grasping, and visual exploration and continues with crawling and walking, acts of focal attention and perception, memory, language and thinking, anticipation, the exploring of novel places and objects, effecting stimulus changes in the environment, manipulating and exploiting the surroundings, and achieving higher levels of motor and mental coordination. These aspects of behavior have long been the province of child psychology, which has attempted to measure the slow course of their development and has shown how heavily their growth depends upon learning. Collectively they are sometimes referred to as adaptive mechanisms or as ego processes, but on the whole we are not accustomed to cast a single name over the diverse feats whereby we learn to deal with the environment.

I now propose that we gather the various kinds of behavior just mentioned, all of which have to do with effective interaction with the environment, under the general heading of competence. According to Webster, competence means fitness or ability, and the suggested synonyms include capability, capacity, efficiency, proficiency, and skill. It is therefore a suitable word to describe such things as grasping and exploring, crawling and walking, attention and perception, language and thinking, manipulating and changing the surroundings, all of which promote an effective — a competent — interaction with the environment. It is true, of course, that maturation plays a part in all these developments, but this part is heavily overshadowed by learning in all the more complex accomplishments like speech or skilled manipulation. I shall argue that it is necessary to make competence a motivational concept; there is a *competence motivation* as well as competence in its more familiar sense of achieved capacity. The behavior that leads to the building up of effective grasping, handling, and letting go of objects, to take one example, is not random behavior produced by a general overflow of energy. It is directed, selective, and persistent, and it is continued not because it serves primary drives, which indeed it cannot serve until it is almost perfected, but because it satisfies an intrinsic need to deal with the environment.

No doubt it will at first seem arbitrary to propose a single motivational conception in connection with so many and such diverse kinds of behavior. What do we gain by attributing motivational unity to such a large array of activities? We could, of course, say that each developmental sequence, such as learning to grasp or to walk, has its own built-in bit of motivation — its "aliment," as Piaget (1952) has expressed it. We could go further and say that each item of behavior has its intrinsic motive — but this makes the concept of motivation redundant. On the other hand, we might follow the lead of the animal psychologists and postulate a limited number of broader motives under such names as curiosity, manipulation, and mastery. I believe that the idea of a competence motivation is more adequate than any of these alternatives and that it points to very vital common properties which have been lost from view amidst the strongly analytical tendencies that go with detailed research.

In order to make this claim more plausible, I shall now introduce some specimens of playful exploration in early childhood. I hope that these images will serve to fix and dramatize the concept of competence in the same way that other images — the hungry animal solving problems, the child putting his finger in the candle flame, the infant at the breast, the child on the toilet, and the youthful Oedipus caught in a hopeless love triangle — have become memorable focal points for other concepts. For this purpose I turn to Piaget's (1952) studies of the growth of intelligence from its earliest manifestations in his own three children. The examples come from the first year of life, before language and verbal concepts begin to be important. They therefore represent a practical kind of intelligence which may be quite similar to what is developed by the higher animals.

As early as the fourth month, the play of the gifted Piaget children began to be "centered on a result produced in the external environment," and their behavior could be described as rediscovering the movement which by chance exercised an advantageous action upon things" (1952, p. 151). Laurent, lying in his bassinet, learns to shake a suspended rattle

by pulling a string that hangs from it. He discovers this result fortuitously before vision and prehension are fully coordinated. Let us now observe him a little later when he has reached the age of three months and ten days.

I place the string, which is attached to the rattle, in his right hand, merely unrolling it a little so that he may grasp it better. For a moment nothing happens. But at the first shake due to chance movement of his hand, the reaction is immediate: Laurent starts when looking at the rattle and then violently strikes his right hand alone, as if he felt the resistance and the effect. The operation lasts fully a quarter of an hour, during which Laurent emits peals of laughter (Piaget, 1952, p. 162).

Three days later the following behavior is observed.

Laurent, by chance, strikes the chain while sucking his fingers. He grasps it and slowly displaces it while looking at the rattles. He then begins to swing it very gently, which produces a slight movement of the hanging rattles and an as yet faint sound inside them. Laurent then definitely increases by degrees his own movements. He shakes the chain more and more vigorously and laughs uproariously at the result obtained (Piaget, 1952, p. 185).

Very soon it can be observed that procedures are used "to make interesting spectacles last." For instance, Laurent is shown a rubber monkey which he has not seen before. After a moment of surprise, and perhaps even fright, he calms down and makes movements of pulling the string, a procedure which has no effect in this case, but which previously has caused interesting things to happen. It is to be noticed that "interesting spectacles" consist of such things as new toys, a tin box upon which a drumming noise can be made, an unfolded newspaper, or sounds made by the observer such as snapping the fingers. Commonplace as they are to the adult mind, these spectacles enter the infant's experience as novel and apparently challenging events.

Moving ahead to the second half of the first year, we can observe behavior in which the child explores the properties of objects and tries out his repertory of actions upon them. This soon leads to active experimentation in which the child attempts to provoke new results. Again we look in upon Laurent, who has now reached the age of nine months. On different occasions he is shown a variety of new objects.— for instance a notebook, a beaded purse, and a wooden parrot. His carefully observing father detects four stages of response: (*a*) visual exploration, passing the object from hand to hand, folding the purse, *etc.*; (*b*) tactile exploration, passing the hand all over the object, scratching, *etc.*; (*c*) slow moving of the object in space; (*d*) use of the repertory of action: shaking the object, striking it, swinging it, rubbing it against the side of the bassinet, sucking it, *etc.*, "each in turn with a sort of prudence as though studying the effect produced" (1952, p. 255).

Here the child can be described as applying familiar tactics to new situations, but in a short while he will advance to clear patterns of active experimentation. At 10 months and 10 days Laurent, who is unfamiliar with bread as a nutritive substance, is given a piece for examination. He manipulates it, drops it many times, breaks off fragments and lets them fall. He has often done this kind of thing before, but previously his attention has seemed to be centered on the act of letting go. Now "he watches with great interest the body in motion; in particular, he looks at it for a long time when it has fallen, and picks it up when he can." On the following day he resumes his research.

He grasps in succession a celluloid swan, a box, and several other small objects, in each case stretching out his arm and letting them fall. Sometimes he stretches out his arm vertically, sometimes he holds it obliquely in front of or behind his eyes. When the object falls in a new position (for example on his pillow) he lets it fall two or three times more on the same place, as though to study the spatial relation; then he modifies the situation. At a certain moment the swan falls near his mouth; now he does not suck it (even though this object habitually serves this purpose), but drops it three times more while merely making the gesture of opening his mouth (Piaget, 1952, p. 269).

These specimens will furnish us with sufficient images of the infant's use of his spare time. Laurent, of course, was provided by his studious father with a decidedly enriched environment, but no observant parent will question the fact that babies often act this way during those periods of their waking life when hunger, erotic needs, distresses, and anxiety seem to be exerting no particular pressure. If we consider this behavior under the historic headings of psychology we shall see that few processes are missing. The child gives evidence of sensing, perceiving, attending, learning, recognizing, probably recalling, and perhaps thinking in a rudimentary way. Strong emotion is lacking, but the infant's smiles, gurgles, and occasional peals of laughter strongly suggest the presence of pleasant affect. Actions appear in an organized form, particularly in the specimens of active exploration and experimentation. Apparently the child is using with a certain coherence nearly the whole repertory of psychological processes except those that accompany stress. It would be arbitrary indeed to say that one was more important than another.

These specimens have a meaningful unity when seen as transactions between the child and his environment, the child having some influence upon the environment and the environment some influence upon the child. Laurent appears to be concerned about what he can do with the chain and rattles, what he can accomplish by his own effort to reproduce and to vary the entertaining sounds. If his father observed correctly, we must add that Laurent seems to have varied his actions systematically, as if testing the effect of different degrees of effort upon the bit of environment represented by the chain and rattles. Kittens make a similar study of parameters when delicately using their paws to push pencils and other objects ever nearer to the edge of one's desk. In all such examples it is clear that the child or animal is by no means at the mercy of transient stimulus fields. He selects for continuous treatment those aspects of his environment which he finds it possible to affect in some way. His behavior is selective, directed, persistent—in short, motivated.

Motivated toward what goal? In these terms, too, the behavior exhibits a little of everything. Laurent can be seen as appeasing a stimulus hunger, providing his sensorium with an agreeable level of stimulation by eliciting from the environment a series of interesting sounds, feels, and sights. On the other hand we might emphasize a need for activity and see him as trying to reach a pleasurable level of neuromuscular exercise. We can also see another possible goal in the behavior: the child is achieving knowledge, attaining a more differentiated cognitive map of his environment and thus satisfying an exploratory tendency or motive of curiosity. But it is equally possible to discern a theme of mastery, power, or control, perhaps even a bit of primitive self-assertion, in the child's concentration upon those aspects of the environment which respond in some way to his own activity. It looks as if we had found too many goals, and perhaps our first impulse is to search for some key to tell us which one is really important. But this, I think, is a mistake that would be fatal to understanding.

We cannot assign priority to any of these goals without pausing arbitrarily in the cycle of transaction between child and environment and saying, "This is the real point." I propose instead that the real point is the transactions as a whole. If the behavior gives satisfaction, this satisfaction is not associated with a particular moment in the cycle. It does not lie solely in sensory stimulation, in a bettering of the cognitive map, in coordinated action, in motor exercise, in a feeling of effort and of effects produced, or in the appreciation of change brought about in the sensory field. These are all simply aspects of a process which at this stage has to be conceived as a whole. The child appears to be occupied with the agreeable task of developing an effective familiarity with his environment. This involves discovering the effects he can have on the environment and the effects the environment will have on him. To the extent that these results are preserved by learning, they build up an increased competence in dealing with the environment. The child's play can thus be viewed as serious business, though to him it is merely something that is interesting and fun to do.

Bearing in mind these examples, as well as the dealings with environment pointed out by other workers, we must now attempt to describe more fully the possible nature of the motivational aspect of competence. It needs its own name, and in view of the foregoing analysis I propose that this name be *effectance*.

The new freedom produced by two decades of research on animal drives is of great help in this undertaking. We are no longer obliged to look for a source of energy external to the nervous system, for a consummatory climax, or for a fixed connection between reinforcement and tension-reduction. Effectance motivation cannot, of course, be conceived as having a source in tissues external to the nervous system. It is in no sense a deficit motive. We must assume it to be neurogenic, its "energies" being simply those of the living cells that make up the nervous system. External stimuli play an important part, but in terms of "energy" this part is secondary, as one can see most clearly when environmental stimulation is actively sought. Putting it picturesquely, we might say that the effectance urge represents what the neuromuscular system wants to do when it is otherwise unoccupied or is gently stimulated by the environment. Obviously there are no consummatory acts; satisfaction would appear to lie in the arousal and maintaining of activity rather than in its slow decline toward bored passivity. The motive need not be conceived as intense and powerful in the sense that hunger, pain, or fear can be powerful when aroused to high pitch. There are plenty of instances in which children refuse to leave their absorbed play in order to eat or to visit the toilet. Strongly aroused drives, pain, and anxiety, however, can be conceived as overriding the effectance urge and capturing the energies of the neuromuscular system. But effectance motivation is persistent in the sense that it regularly occupies the spare waking time between episodes of homeostatic crisis.

In speculating upon this subject we must bear in mind the continuous nature of behavior. This is easier said then done; habitually we break things down in order to understand them, and such units as the reflex arc, the stimulus-response sequence, and the single transaction with the environment seem like inevitable steps toward clarity. Yet when we apply such an analysis to playful exploration we lose the most essential aspect of the behavior. It is constantly circling from stimulus to perception to action to effect to stimulus to perception, and so on around; or, more properly, these processes are all in continuous action and continuous change. Dealing with the environment means carrying on a continuing transaction which gradually changes one's relation to the environment. Because there is no consummatory climax, satisfaction has to be seen as lying in a considerable series of transactions, in a trend of behavior rather than a goal that is achieved. It is difficult to make the word "satisfaction" have this connotation, and we shall do well to replace it by "feeling of efficacy" when attempting to indicate the subjective and affective side of effectance.

It is useful to recall the findings about novelty: the singular effectiveness of novelty in engaging interest and for a time supporting persistent behavior. We also need to consider the selective continuance of transactions in which the animal or child has a more or less pronounced effect upon the environment—in which something happens as a consequence of his activity. Interest is not aroused and sustained when the stimulus field is so familiar that it gives rise at most to reflex acts or automatized habits. It is not sustained when actions produce no effects or changes in the stimulus field. Our conception must therefore be that effectance motivation is aroused by stimulus conditions which offer, as Hebb (1949) puts it, difference-in-sameness. This leads to variability and novelty of response, and interest is best sustained when the resulting action affects the stimulus so as to produce further difference-in-sameness. Interest wanes when action begins to have less effect; effectance motivation subsides when a situation has been explored to the point that it no longer presents new possibilities.

We have to conceive further that the arousal of playful and exploratory interest means the appearance of organization involving both the cognitive and active aspects of behavior. Change in the stimulus field is not an end in itself, so to speak; it happens when one is passively moved about, and it may happen as a consequence of random movements without becoming focalized and instigating exploration. Similarly, action which has effects is not an end in itself, for if one unintentionally kicks away a branch while walking, or knocks something off a table, these effects by no means necessarily become involved in playful investigation. Schachtel's (1954) emphasis on focal attention becomes helpful at this point. The playful and exploratory behavior shown by Laurent is not random or casual. It involves focal *attention* to some object—the fixing of some aspect of the stimulus field so that it stays relatively constant—and it also involves the focalizing of *action* upon this object. As Diamond (1939) has expressed it, response under these conditions is "relevant to the stimulus," and it is change in the *focalized* stimulus that so strongly affects the level of interest. Dealing with the environment means directing focal attention to some part of it and organizing actions to have some effect on this part.

In our present state of relative ignorance about the workings of the nervous system it is impossible to form a satisfactory idea of the neural basis of effectance motivation, but it should at least be clear that the concept does not refer to any and every kind of neural action. It refers to a particular kind of activity, as inferred from particular kinds of behavior. We can say that it does not include reflexes and other kinds of automatic response. It does not include well-learned, automatized patterns, even those that are complex and highly organized. It does not include behavior in the service of effectively aroused drives. It does not even include activity that is highly random and discontinuous, though such behavior may be its most direct forerunner. The urge toward competence is inferred specifically from behavior that shows a lasting focalization and that has the characteristics of exploration and experimentation, a kind of variation within the focus. When this particular sort of activity is aroused in the nervous system, effectance motivation is being aroused, for it is characteristic of this particular sort of activity that it is selective, directed, and persistent, and that instrumental acts will be learned for the sole reward of engaging in it.

Some objection may be felt to my introducing the word *competence* in connection with behavior that is so often playful. Certainly the playing child is doing things for fun, not because of a desire to improve his competence in dealing with the stern hard world. In order to forestall misunderstanding, it should be pointed out that the usage here is parallel to what we do when we connect sex with its biological goal of reproduction. The sex drive aims for pleasure and gratification, and reproduction is a consequence that is presumably unforeseen by animals and by man at primitive levels of understanding. Effectance motivation similarly aims for the feeling of efficacy, not for the vitally important learnings that come as its consequence. If we consider the part played by competence motivation in adult human life we can observe the same parallel. Sex may now be completely and purposefully divorced from reproduction but nevertheless pursued for the pleasure it can yield. Similarly, effectance motivation may lead to continuing exploratory interests or active adventures when in fact there is no longer any gain in actual competence or any need for it in terms of survival. In both cases the motive is capable of yielding surplus satisfaction well beyond what is necessary to get the biological work done.

In infants and young children it seems to me sensible to conceive of effectance motivation as undifferentiated. Later in life it becomes profitable to distinguish various motives such as cognizance, construction, mastery, and achievement. It is my view that all such motives have a root in effectance motivation. They are differentiated from it through life experiences which emphasize one or another aspect of the cycle of transaction with environment. Of course, the motives of later childhood and of adult life are no longer simple and can almost never be referred to a single root. They can acquire loadings of anxiety, defense, and compensation, they can become fused with unconscious fantasies of a sexual, aggressive, or omnipotent character, and they can gain force because of their service in producing realistic results in the way of income and career. It is not my intention to cast effectance in the star part in adult motivation. The acquisition of motives is a complicated affair in which simple and sovereign theories grow daily more obsolete. Yet it may be that the satisfaction of effectance contributes significantly to those feelings of interest which often sustain us so well in day-to-day actions, particularly when the things we are doing have continuing elements of novelty.

THE BIOLOGICAL SIGNIFICANCE OF COMPETENCE

The conviction was expressed at the beginning of this paper that some such concept as competence, interpreted motivationally, was essential for any biologically sound view of human nature. This necessity emerges when we consider the nature of living systems, particularly when we take a longitudinal view. What an organism does at a given moment does not always give the right clue as to what it does over a period of time. Discussing this problem, Angyal (1941) has proposed that we should look for the general pattern followed by the total organismic process over the course of time. Obviously this makes it necessary to take account of growth. Angyal defines life as "a process of self-expansion"; the living system "expands at the expense of its surroundings," assimilating parts of the environment and transforming them into functioning parts of itself. Organisms differ from other things in nature in that they are "self-governing entities" which are to some extent "autonomous." Internal processes govern them as well as external "heteronomous" forces. In the course of life there is a relative increase in the preponderance of internal over external forces. The living system expands, assimilates more of the environment, transforms its surroundings so as to bring them under greater control. "We may say," Angyal writes, "that the general dynamic trend of the organism is toward an increase of autonomy. . . . The human being has a characteristic tendency toward self-determination, that is, a tendency to resist external influences and to subordinate the heteronomous forces of the physical and social environment to its own sphere of influence." The trend toward increased autonomy is characteristic so long as growth of any kind is going on, though in the end the living system is bound to succumb to the pressure of heteronomous forces.

Of all living creatures, it is man who takes the longest strides toward autonomy. This is not because of any unusual tendency toward bodily expansion at the expense of the environment. It is rather that man, with his mobile hands and abundantly developed brain, attains an extremely high level of competence in his transactions with his surroundings. The building of houses, roads and bridges, the making of tools and instruments, the domestication of plants and animals, all qualify as planful changes made in the environment so that it comes more or less under control and serves our purposes rather than intruding upon them. We meet the fluctuations of outdoor temperature, for example, not only with our bodily homeostatic mechanisms, which alone would be painfully unequal to the task, but also with clothing, buildings, controlled fires, and such complicated devices as self-regulating central heating and air conditioning. Man as a species has developed a tremendous power of bringing the environment into his service, and each individual member of the species must attain what is really quite an impressive level of competence if he is to take part in the life around him.

We are so accustomed to these human accomplishments that it is hard to realize how long an apprenticeship they require. At the outset the human infant is a slow learner in comparison with other animal forms. Hebb (1949) speaks of "the astonishing inefficiency of man's first learning, as far as immediate results are concerned," an inefficiency which he attributes to the large size of the association areas in the brain and the long time needed to bring them under sensory control. The human lack of precocity in learning shows itself even in comparison with one of the next of kin: as Hebb points out, "the human baby takes six months, the chimpanzee four months, before making a clear distinction between friend and enemy." Later in life the slow start will pay dividends. Once the fundamental perceptual elements, simple associations, and conceptual sequences have been established, later learning can proceed with ever increasing swiftness and complexity. In Hebb's words, "learning at maturity concerns patterns and events whose parts at least are familiar and which already have a number of other associations."

This general principle of cumulative learning, starting from slowly acquired rudiments and proceeding thence with increasing efficiency, can be illustrated by such processes as manipulation and locomotion, which may culminate in the acrobat devising new stunts or the dancer working out a new ballet. It is especially vivid in the case of language, where the early mastery of words and pronunciation seems such a far cry from spontaneous adult speech. A strong argument has been made by Hebb (1949) that the learning of visual forms proceeds over a similar course from slowly learned elements to rapidly combined patterns. Circles and squares, for example, cannot be discriminated at a glance without a slow apprenticeship involving eye movements, successive fixations, and recognition of angles. Hebb proposes that the recognition of visual patterns without eye movement "is possible only as the result of an intensive and prolonged visual training that goes on from the moment of birth, during every moment that the eyes are open, with an increase in skill evident over a period of 12 to 16 years at least."

On the motor side there is likewise a lot to be cumulatively learned. The playing, investigating child slowly finds out the relationships between what he does and what he experiences. He finds out, for instance, how hard he must push what in order to produce what effect. Here the S-R formula is particularly misleading. It would come nearer the truth to say that the child is busy learning R-S connections — the effects that are likely to follow upon his own behavior. But even in this reversed form the notion of bonds or connections would still misrepresent the situation, for it is only a rare specimen of behavior that can properly be conceived as determined by fixed neural channels and a fixed motor response. As Hebb has pointed out, discussing the phenomenon of "motor equivalence" named by Lashley (1942), a rat which has been trained to press a lever will press it with the left forepaw, the right forepaw, by climbing upon it, or by biting it; a monkey will open the lid of a food box with either hand, with a foot, or even with a stick; and we might add that a good baseball player can catch a fly ball while running in almost any direction and while in almost any posture, including leaping in the air and plunging forward to the ground. All of these feats are possible because of a history of learnings in which the main lesson has been the effects of actions upon the stimulus fields that represent the environment. What has been learned is not a fixed connection but a flexible relationship between stimulus fields and the effects that can be produced in them by various kinds of action.

One additional example, drawn this time from Piaget (1952), is particularly worth mentioning because of its importance in theories of development. Piaget points out that a great deal of mental development depends upon the idea that the world is made up of objects having substance and permanence. Without such an "object concept" it would be impossible to build up the ideas of space and causality and to arrive at the fundamental distinction between self and external world. Observation shows that the object concept, "far from being innate or ready-made in experience, is constructed little by little." Up to 7 and 8 months the Piaget children searched for vanished objects only in the sense of trying to continue the actions, such as sucking or grasping, in which the objects had played a part. When an object was really out of sight or touch, even if only because it was covered by a cloth, the infants undertook no further exploration. Only gradually, after some study of the displacement of objects by moving, swinging, and dropping them, does the child begin to make an active search for a vanished object, and only still more gradually does he learn, at 12 months or more, to make allowance for the object's sequential displacements and thus to seek it where it has gone rather than where it was last in sight. Thus it is only through cumulative learning that the child arrives at the idea of permanent substantial objects.

The infant's play is indeed serious business. If he did not while away his time pulling strings, shaking rattles, examining wooden parrots, dropping pieces of bread and celluloid swans, when would he learn to discriminate visual patterns, to catch and throw, and to build up his concept of the object? When would he acquire the many other foundation stones necessary for cumulative learning? The more closely we analyze the behavior of the human infant, the more clearly do we realize that infancy is not simply a time when the nervous system matures and the muscles grow stronger. It is a time of active and continuous learning, during which the basis is laid for all those processes, cognitive and motor, whereby the child becomes able to establish effective transactions with his environment and move toward a greater degree of autonomy. Helpless as he may seem until he begins to toddle, he has by that time already made substantial gains in the achievement of competence.

Under primitive conditions survival must depend quite heavily upon achieved competence. We should expect to find things so arranged as to favor and maximize this achievement. Particularly in the case of man, where so little is provided innately and so much has to be learned through experience, we should expect to find highly advantageous arrangements for securing a steady cumulative learning about the properties of the environment and the extent of possible transactions. Under these circumstances we might expect to find a very powerful drive operating to insure progress toward competence, just as the vital goals of nutrition and reproduction are secured by powerful drives, and it might therefore seem paradoxical that the interests of competence should be so much entrusted to times of play and leisurely exploration. There is good reason to suppose, however, that a strong drive would be precisely the wrong arrangement to secure a flexible, knowledgeable power of transaction with the environment. Strong drives cause us to learn certain lessons well, but they do not create maximum familiarity with our surroundings.

This point was demonstrated half a century ago in some experiments by Yerkes and Dodson (1908). They showed that maximum motivation did not lead to the most rapid solving of problems, especially if the problems were complex. For each problem there was an optimum level of motivation, neither the highest nor the lowest, and the optimum was lower for more complex tasks. The same problem has been discussed more recently by Tolman (1948) in his paper on cognitive maps. A cognitive map can be narrow or broad, depending upon the range of cues picked up in the course of learning. Tolman suggests that one of the conditions which tend to narrow the range of cues is a high level of motivation. In everyday terms, a man hurrying to an important business conference is likely to perceive only the cues that help him to get there faster, whereas a man taking a stroll after lunch is likely to pick up a substantial amount of casual information about his environment. The latent learning experiments with animals, and experiments such as those of Johnson (1953) in which drive level has been systematically varied in a situation permitting incidental learning, give strong support to this general idea. In a recent contribution, Bruner, Matter, and Papanek (1955) make a strong case for the concept of breadth of learning and provide additional evidence that it is favored by moderate and hampered by strong motivation. The latter "has the effect of speeding up learning at the cost of narrowing it." Attention is concentrated upon the task at hand and little that is extraneous to this task is learned for future use.

These facts enable us to see the biological appropriateness of an arrangement which uses periods of less intense motivation for the development of competence. This is not to say that the narrower but efficient learnings that go with the reduction of strong drives make no contribution to general effectiveness. They are certainly an important element in capacity to deal with the environment, but a much greater effectiveness results from having this capacity fed also from learnings that take place in quieter times. It is then that the infant can attend to matters of lesser urgency, exploring the properties of things he does not fear and does not need to eat, learning to gauge the force of his string-pulling when the only penalty for failure is silence on the part of the attached rattles, and generally accumulating for himself a broad knowledge and a broad skill in dealing with his surroundings.

The concept of competence can be most easily discussed by choosing, as we have done, examples of interaction with the inanimate environment. It applies equally well, however, to transactions with animals and with other human beings, where the child has the same problem of finding out what effects he can have upon the environment and what effects it can have upon him. The earliest interactions with members of the family may involve needs so strong that they obscure the part played by effectance motivation, but perhaps the example of the well fed baby diligently exploring the several features of his mother's face will serve as a reminder that here, too, there are less urgent moments when learning for its own sake can be given free rein.

In this closing section I have brought together several ideas which bear on the evolutionary significance of competence and of its motivation. I have sought in this way to deepen the biological roots of the concept and thus help it to attain the stature in the theory of behavior which has not been reached by similar concepts in the past. To me it seems that the most important proving ground for this concept is the effect it may have on our understanding of the development of personality. Does it assist our grasp of early object relations, the reality principle, and the first steps in the development of the ego? Can it be of service in distinguishing the kinds of defense available at different ages and in providing clues to the replacement of primitive defenses by successful adaptive maneuvers? Can it help fill the yawning gap known as the latency period, a time when the mastery of school subjects and other accomplishments claim so large a share of time and energy? Does it bear upon the self and the vicissitudes of self-esteem, and can it enlighten the origins of psychological disorder? Can it make adult motives and interests more intelligible and enable us to rescue the concept of sublimation from the difficulties which even its best friends have recognized? I believe it can be shown that existing explanations of development are not satisfactory and that the addition of the concept of competence cuts certain knots in personality theory. But this is not the subject of the present communication, where the concept is offered much more on the strength of its logical and biological probability.

SUMMARY

The main theme of this paper is introduced by showing that there is widespread discontent with theories of motivation built upon primary drives. Signs of this discontent are found in realms as far apart as animal psychology and psychoanalytic ego psychology. In the former, the commonly recognized primary drives have proved to be inadequate in explaining exploratory behavior, manipulation, and general activity. In the latter, the theory of basic instincts has shown serious shortcomings when it is stretched to account for the development of the effective ego. Workers with animals have attempted to meet their problem by invoking secondary reinforcement and anxiety reduction, or by adding exploration and manipulation to the roster of primary drives. In parallel fashion, psychoanalytic workers have relied upon the concept of neutralization of instinctual energies, have seen anxiety reduction as the central motive in ego development, or have hypothesized new instincts such as mastery. It is argued here that these several explanations are not satisfactory and that a better conceptualization is possible, indeed that it has already been all but made.

In trying to form this conceptualization, it is first pointed out that many of the earlier tenets of primary drive theory have been discredited by recent experimental work. There is no longer any compelling reason to identify either pleasure or reinforcement with drive reduction, or to think of motivation as requiring a source of energy external to the nervous system. This opens the way for considering in their own right those aspects of animal and human behavior in which stimulation and contact with the environment seem to be sought and welcomed, in which raised tension and even mild excitement seem to be cherished, and in which novelty and variety seem to be enjoyed for their own sake. Several reports are cited which bear upon interest in the environment and the rewarding effects of environmental feedback. The latest contribution is that of Woodworth (1958), who makes dealing with the environment the most fundamental element in motivation.

The survey indicates a certain unanimity as to the kinds of behavior that cannot be successfully conceptualized in terms of primary drives. This behavior includes visual exploration, grasping, crawling and walking, attention and perception, language and thinking, exploring novel objects and places, manipulating the surroundings, and producing effective changes in the environment. The thesis is then proposed that all of these behaviors have a common biological significance: they all form part of the process whereby the animal or child learns to interact effectively with his environment. The word *competence* is chosen as suitable to indicate this common property. Further, it is maintained that competence cannot be fully acquired simply through behavior instigated by drives. It receives substantial contributions from activities which, though playful and exploratory in character, at the same time show direction, selectivity, and persistence in interacting with the environment. Such activities in the ultimate service of competence must therefore be conceived to be motivated in their own right. It is proposed to designate this motivation by the term effectance, and to characterize the experience produced as a *feeling of efficacy.*

In spite of its sober biological purpose, effectance motivation shows itself most unambiguously in the playful and investigatory behavior of young animals and children. Specimens of such behavior, drawn from Piaget (1952), are analyzed in order to demonstrate their constantly transactional nature. Typically they involve continuous chains of events which include stimulation, cognition, action, effect on the environment, new stimulation, *etc.* They are carried on with considerable persistence and with selective emphasis on parts of the environment which provide changing and interesting feedback in connection with effort expended. Their significance is destroyed if we try to break into the circle arbitrarily and declare that one part of it, such as cognition alone or active effort alone, is the real point, the goal, or the special seat of satisfaction. Effectance motivation must be conceived to involve satisfaction— a feeling of efficacy—in transactions in which behavior has an exploratory, varying, experimental character and produces changes in the stimulus field. Having this character, the behavior leads the organism to find out how the environment can be changed and what consequences flow from these changes.

In higher animals and especially in man, where so little is innately provided and so much has to be learned about dealing with the environment, effectance motivation independent of primary drives can be seen as an arrangement having high adaptive value. Considering the slow rate of learning in infancy and the vast amount that has to be learned before there can be an effective level of interaction with surroundings, young animals and children would simply not learn enough unless they worked pretty steadily at the task between episodes of homeostatic crisis. The association of interest with this "work," making it play and fun, is thus somewhat comparable to the association of sexual pleasure with the biological goal of reproduction. Effectance motivation need not be conceived as strong in the sense that sex, hunger, and fear are strong when violently aroused. It is moderate but persistent, and in this, too, we can discern a feature that is favorable for adaptation. Strong motivation reinforces learning in a narrow sphere, whereas moderate motivation is more conducive to an exploratory and experimental attitude which leads to competent interactions in general, without reference to an immediate pressing need. Man's huge cortical association areas might have been a suicidal piece of specialization if they had come without a steady, persistent inclination toward interacting with the environment.

The drive-reducing function of fantasy behavior[1] [2]

SEYMOUR FESHBACH

The primary object of this research is to investigate the hypothesis that fantasy will reduce the strength of a motive by means of symbolic satisfaction. Current interest in fantasy as a form of behavior stems primarily from: (a) the emphasis placed by psychoanalysis on the role of fantasy in human adjustment, (b) the widespread use of the Thematic Apperception Test as a diagnostic instrument, and (c) recent studies exploring the effects of experimentally induced drives upon various cognitive processes including fantasy. These latter investigations have in general confirmed the assumption that ungratified needs are reflected in fantasy. However an unresolved and neglected problem is whether fantasy behavior to any degree satisfies these needs.

Psychoanalysts have long maintained that fantasies including dreams, daydreams, myths, and artistic productions represent wish fulfillment. According to Freud, "unsatisfied wishes are the driving power behind phantasies; every separate phantasy contains the fulfillment of a wish, and improves on unsatisfactory reality" (1949, p. 176). More recently Symonds (1946), writing from the psychoanalytic standpoint, clearly suggests that goal responses expressed in fantasy may be drive reducing. The latter hypothesis is compatible with a behavior theory which holds that self-initiated verbal responses may have secondary reward value and thus reinforce the tendency to repeat those responses when stimulated by the drive which had originally occasioned them. Some such hypothesis is suggested by a reinforcement theory in explaining the persistence of certain forms of fantasy behavior as, for example, that found in obsessional neurosis.

Although the hypothesis that fantasy behavior has a substitute or compensatory function is widely entertained (Allport, 1937; A. Freud, 1946; Tomkins, 1947), it is by no means universally accepted. McClelland et al. (Atkinson & McClelland, 1948; McClelland, Clark, Roby, & Atkinson, 1949) have explicitly doubted its validity on the basis of indirect inference from the content of TAT-type fantasies. A study by Wittenborn and Eron (1951), also based on TAT fantasies, finds some substantiation for a drive-reduction hypothesis in the pattern of intercorrelations among certain features of TAT responses. However, positive or negative evidence directly bearing upon the hypothesis is lacking.

Experimental studies of substitute behavior, conducted chiefly by Lewin and his students, have touched upon this problem (Dembo, 1940; Escalona, 1943; Lewin, 1935; Mahler, 1940). Some of their results suggest that, with the

From the *Journal of Abnormal and Social Psychology*, 1955, **50**, 3-11.

1 The study was carried out while the author was a United States Public Health Service Research Fellow.

2 The present study was undertaken as a doctoral dissertation in the Department of Psychology at Yale University. The author wishes to express his appreciation to Professors Child, Janis, and Sarason of Yale University for their interest and assistance.

exception of "play" situations, fantasy completion of interrupted or insoluble tasks has little, if any, substitute value. However, the exclusive use of the resumption technique as a measure of drive strength and of the interrupted-task technique as the primary method of inducing motivation (in addition to inadequate experimental procedures) greatly limits the generality of their findings. An experimental approach using more sensitive and direct measures of drive strength, and inducing drives with possibly wider theoretical and practical implications, seems necessary.

In addition, in order to demonstrate the phenomenon of drive reduction as an effect of fantasy behavior, it seems desirable to use a drive which by reason of theory and experience seems likely to be measurably reduced by fantasy; i.e., a psychogenic as contrasted to a physiologically rooted drive. With these considerations in mind, the present research is designed to test the following hypothesis: Fantasy expression of hostility will partially reduce situationally induced aggression. Ideally, this hypothesis might be tested by inducing aggressive drive, measuring the strength of the drive induced and, after an interpolated fantasy activity, measuring the strength of aggressive drive a second time. The decrement in aggression from the first occasion to the second would provide the most direct test of the hypothesis. There are practical difficulties in carrying out this design. For one thing, it is difficult to find measures of aggression that can be meaningfully applied twice within a short period of time. Secondly, in preliminary work, the subjects (Ss) would not accept the situation when the measures of aggression were given directly after aggression was aroused.

For these reasons the drive-reduction hypothesis is to be tested by comparing the strength of aggressive drive (at the end of the experimental session) in two groups, one of which receives the opportunity to express hostile fantasy while the other engages in nonfantasy or control activities. The actual test is then simply a measure of the subsequent difference in aggression between these two groups. The specific prediction is that the fantasy group will be less aggressive than the control group. The predicted difference is just as pertinent to the drive-reduction hypothesis

as the ideal test previously described, even though the measure is one of end effect and relative difference rather than of absolute change in each group.

METHOD

The Ss were all members of introductory psychology classes at a large metropolitan college. Classes were randomly assigned to one of three experimental treatments: (a) arousal of aggression and interpolation of fantasy activity (Insult Fantasy group); (b) arousal of aggression and interpolation of nonfantasy activities (Insult Control group); (c) nonarousal of aggression and interpolation of fantasy activities (Noninsult Fantasy group). The Insult Fantasy group consisted of 123 Ss (five classes), the Insult Control group of 56 Ss (three classes), and the Noninsult Fantasy group of 78 Ss (three classes).[3] In the total group there were approximately twice as many men as women. However, the sex ratio from class to class varied considerably.

Aggression was aroused by the experimenter (E), who assumed an insulting attitude toward a class of college students. The interpolated activities provided one group of insulted Ss the opportunity to express their hostility in fantasy (Insult Fantasy group), whereas the activities in which a comparable group of insulted Ss were engaged permitted little or no opportunity for fantasy (Insult Control group). These two groups were then compared on subsequent measures of hostility toward E and the experiment to determine if the fantasy experience resulted in less aggression than did the nonfantasy activity.

The Noninsult Fantasy group engaged in the same fantasy activity as did the Insult Fantasy group and received the same measures of aggression as did the two Insult groups. Comparison between the Noninsult and Insult groups on these measures would indicate whether E's insulting attitude actually did arouse aggression in the insulted groups and at the same time would establish the validity and usefulness of the measures of

_____

3 These are the Ss who remained after eliminating from all Insult groups 23 Ss who in class discussions held several days after the experiment said they knew the insulting attitude of E was feigned. Because of administrative limitations, classes, not Ss, were assigned at random to the various experimental treatments.

aggression with respect to the principal comparison between the Insult Fantasy and Insult Control groups.

Procedure. Two *Es* were used in carrying out the study. The individual who acted as the principal *E*[4] was carefully selected for his ability to arouse the hostility of *Ss* in the Insult groups without their realizing that his remarks were deliberately intended to achieve that end. The writer acted as his assistant in each of the 11 classes which participated in the study.

The *E* was briefly introduced to the class by its instructor, who left the classroom and did not return until near the end of the period. Administration of the experimental procedures consumed one 50-minute class period and all the classes were seen within a four-day period.

After the instructor left the classroom, *E*, in an authoritarian, arrogant manner, made several derogatory remarks about the motivation, ability, and level of maturity of the student body of the college. For example, he made such comments as "Now I realize that you — — — College students, or should I say — — — College grinds have few academic interests outside of your concern for grades . . . if you will try to look beyond your limited horizons, your cooperation will be useful. In other words, I'd like you to act like adults rather than adolescents."[5] The Noninsult classes received a friendly introduction designed to gain their cooperation.

Fantasy-nonfantasy variable. The *E* who acted as insulter did not know whether the insulted class was to be in the Fantasy or Control group until after he made his insulting comments. After making his introductory remarks, he opened a folder from which he read the instructions for the particular activity to be given. This procedure was followed so as to eliminate the possibility that *E*'s behavior could be biased by foreknowledge of whether the class was to be in the Fantasy or Control group.

Four TAT pictures (Dollard & Miller, 1950, 18GF, 7BM, and 12M) were presented by means of a slide projector to the Noninsult Fantasy and Insult Fantasy groups. The order in which the pictures were given was systematically varied. The instructions and procedure for administration of the group TAT followed those used by McClelland, Clark, et al.; these instructions present the TAT as an achievement task which involves the construction of an interesting and dramatic story under specific time limitation. The TAT was given as a test of ability, and in this respect is like the nonfantasy activities administered to the Control group.

The Insult Control classes received tests which offered little, if any, opportunity for fantasy. Each class was given a different nonfantasy activity which consumed the same amount of time as the TAT procedure. The nonfantasy activity was varied in an attempt to control for possible differences in preference for the fantasy vs. the nonfantasy activity. Had only one nonfantasy activity been used in all three classes in the Control group, then one might argue that if the Fantasy group subsequently displayed less aggression than the Control group, the difference could be due to the negative characteristics of the nonfantasy activity. Two of the Control classes were given standard tests; one Series AA of the Revised Minnesota Paper Form Board Test, and the second, Parts 1 through 4 of the General Clerical Aptitude Test. The instructions for the tests were abridged so as to correspond in length with those given for the TAT. The remaining class was given a "picture description test" which required a one-sentence description of each of a series of slides projected on a screen. These slides consisted of scenic photographs and paintings in which architectural forms predominated.

Measures of aggression. Subsequent to the interpolated activity all groups were administered a slightly modified version of the Rotter-Willerman (1947) form of the Sentence Completion Test. The instructor then returned, and the *Es* left the classroom. The instructor informed the class that the faculty was interested in reactions of the students to having research take up class time. He then administered to the class a questionnaire consisting of eight items dealing with attitudes toward the experimenter, experiment, and psychological research.

---

4 The writer is very much indebted to John Dickinson, at the time a graduate law student, whose caustic skills and courtroom demeanor were very effective in antagonizing the students and at the same time restraining them from overt aggressive behavior.

5 A full account of all procedures including measures of aggression has been deposited with the American Documentation Institute. Order Document No. 4244 from the ADI Auxiliary Publications Project, Photoduplication Service, Library of Congress, Washington 25, D. C., remitting in advance $2.50 for 6×8 in. photoprints or $1.75 for 35 mm. microfilm. Make checks payable to Chief, Photoduplication Service, Library of Congress.

Table 1 *Percentage of subjects in each group giving extreme aggressive responses on the attitude questionnaire*

Question	Response	Non-insult Fantasy (N = 78)	Insult Fantasy (N = 107)	Insult Control (N = 56)	Diff. IC-IF	t	p
1. How much did you like participating in the study just recently conducted?	very irritated and extremely irritated	0	9.3	25.0	15.7	2.7	<.004
2. How worth while was it to participate in the study just recently conducted?	considerable complete waste of time	6.4	15.9	19.7	3.8	0.62	<.27
3. If you were asked by the Experimenter to volunteer for another study he was conducting, would you volunteer?	probably not, definitely not	6.4	32.7	50.0	17.3	2.15	<.02
4. In your opinion, how much of a contribution will this study make to the field of psychology?	very little, none	11.5	26.1	30.4	4.3	0.63	<.27
5. In your opinion, how competent was the psychologist who conducted the experiment in which you participated?	very incompetent and extremely incompetent	3.8	21.5	35.7	14.2	1.95	<.03
6. What is your reaction now to the psychologist who conducted this experiment? How much do you like or dislike him?	dislike very much	0	42.0	57.2	15.2	1.85	<.04
7. Is there anything you disliked about the experiment?	yes	42.0	73.0	82.0	9.0	1.3	<.10
8. Several experiments are going to be conducted by the psychology department. Are you willing to volunteer?	no	56.0	56.0	66.0	10.0	1.2	<.12

RESULTS

Effects of the Insulting Behavior of E

The attitude questionnaire. The attitude questionnaire administered by the instructor at the close of the class hour is the most explicit and direct measure of aggression toward E. If the insulting attitude assumed by E had the intended effect of arousing hostility toward him, then this effect should be reflected by the responses of the insulted Ss on the questionnaire.

The Insult and Noninsult groups[6] were initially compared on each question separately. For the first six items, each of which had six alternatives, comparisons are based on the proportion of Ss selecting the most aggressive alternatives, points 5 and 6 on the six-point scale. Preliminary experiments had indicated that the best discrimination between insulted and noninsulted groups would probably be obtained in this way. For the remaining questions, which had only two possible answers, "yes" and "no," the differences are based on the proportion of people who gave the more aggressive of the two answers. The Insult groups display considerably more aggression on the questionnaire than the Noninsult group. The differences between the Noninsult and Insult Fantasy groups are significant for five of the eight questions, and differences between the Noninsult and Insult Control groups are significant for seven of the eight questions.

In addition to the item analysis, a more general measure of aggression was obtained based on the first six items by assigning scores to each response, the least aggressive choice receiving a score of 1 and the most aggressive choice receiving a score of 6. A second measure was based only on the three questions dealing with attitudes toward E (items 3, 5, and 6). The third measure was based on the two questions concerning evaluation of the experiment (items 2 and 4).[7] On all three of these measures there are highly significant differences between the Insult groups and the Noninsult group.

The results of both the item comparisons and the over-all scores confirm the existence of the intended effect of the insult variable. As anticipated, the insulted Ss are much more critical of the study and much more hostile toward E than Ss who were not insulted.

The Sentence Completion Test. The responses to this test were scored for aggression according to a detailed scoring scheme[8] based primarily on distinctions according to the object of aggression and the form in which the aggression was expressed. The most important categories were: (*a*) aggression toward E; (*b*) aggression expressed toward possible substitutes for E (teachers, research workers); (*c*) aggression toward the test situation; (*d*) aggression expressed toward possible substitutes for the test situation (tests in general, experiments, college); (*e*) general aggression (agression toward people, institutions, or practices). Within each of the above categories a distinction was made between emotional and objective aggression. The former was denoted by such terms as hate, dislike, detest, while the latter referred to criticism of the objects specified in each category. Emotional aggression was conceived to be a more direct expression of hostility than objective aggression.

An analysis was made of the percentage of Ss having one or more responses in each scoring category.[9] Only three categories yielded differences in aggression between the Noninsult group and either of the Insult groups significant at the .05 level or above.[10] These categories — 1, 2Em, and 3 — deal, respectively, with aggression toward E, emotional aggression toward possible substitutes for E, and aggression toward the test. There is no significant difference in category 5 which represents aggression toward individuals who do not show

---

6 In order to avoid repetition of tables, the Noninsult Fantasy group data are presented in the section of the results concerned with differences between the Insult Fantasy and Insult Control groups. For those interested in the specific numerical results pertinent to the responses of the Noninsult Fantasy group on the questionnaire, reference can be made to Tables 1 and 2.

7 Question 1 was omitted from these two more specific measures because it could not be unambiguously assigned to either one.

8 A study of the reliability of the scoring categories based on 30 Ss selected at random was carried out with another psychologist. The tests were independently scored. There was disagreement in scoring of only seven sentences.

9 Due to lack of time, one class in the Noninsult Fantasy group and one class in the Insult Fantasy group failed to complete the test. These classes are not included in the analysis of the results for the Sentence Completion Test. A second class in the Insult Fantasy group was eliminated from this analysis in order to equate the proportion of the two sexes in each experimental group.

10 The data are presented in Table 4. Yates's correction for continuity was used in all chi-square tests of independence.

Table 2 *Mean aggression scores of each group on the attitude questionnaire*

Group	Total aggression (all 6 items)	Personal aggression toward E (items 3, 5, 6)	Aggressive evaluation of the experiment (items 2 and 4)
Noninsult Fantasy (N = 78)	14.92	7.04	5.96
Insult Fantasy (N = 107)	21.17	11.47	7.03
Insult Control (N = 56)	23.09	12.88	7.23
Difference (IC − IF)	1.92	1.41	.20
t	2.02	2.49	.56
p	<.025	<.01	<.29

any manifest similarity to E. The results provide tentative evidence of a gradient of generalization—aggression toward objects being a decreasing function of their similarity to the original instigator of the aggression in this situation.

The analysis of the attitude questionnaire and the Sentence Completion Test has demonstrated that both are sensitive to the arousal of aggression by the insulting comments of E and can therefore be used to test differences in aggression between the Insult Fantasy and Insult Control groups.

Effect of Fantasy

The attitude questionnaire. The results of the item analysis of the attitude questionnaire are presented in Table 1. Inspection of the table reveals that on every item the Insult Control group is more aggressive than the Fantasy group.[11] The smallest differences, not statistically significant, are on questions which deal with attitudes toward the study. The differences on questions which deal explicitly with attitudes toward E are much larger and are also statistically significant.[12] The consistently lower amount of aggression displayed by the Insult Fantasy group is in accord with the hypothesis that aggression expressed

The means of the Insult Fantasy and Insult Control groups on the more general measures based on the attitude questionnaire are given in Table 2. The differences between the two insulted groups indicated by the item comparisons are borne out by this method of analysis. The over-all aggression scores of the Insult Control group are significantly higher than those of the Insult Fantasy group. For the measure reflecting only aggression toward E this difference is significant at the .01 level. For the measure based on the criticism of the experiment, the difference is in the same direction but is small and not statistically significant.

The conclusions stated thus far about the statistical significance of the results have been reached by treating each individual as an independent case. However, it is possible that differences in E's behavior, in the several classes in which he tried to keep his behavior constant, may have caused all the members of one class to vary from the others uniformly. To control for this possibility, another significance test of the difference between the two Insult groups was made using only the class means to constitute the sample. The comparison was based on the class means of the men only because of the varying proportions of women in different classes, and their tendency to have lower aggression scores than the men. The results of this analysis are presented in Table 3. All differences are in the predicted direction, thus confirming the findings reported above. The differences in over-all aggression between the Insult Fantasy and Insult Control groups approaches significance, while the difference based on attitudes toward E is

---

11 The number of women in the Insult Fantasy group was reduced in order to equate the proportion of the two sexes in each experimental group. Since the women displayed less aggression than the men, a higher proportion of women in the Insult Fantasy group would tend to lower the mean aggression scores of that group. Cases to be eliminated were selected by use of a table of random numbers.

12 The *p* values reported in this paper, with the exception of the Sentence Completion Test analysis, are based on a one-tailed test of significance. The one-tailed test is used where specific predictions of the directions of the anticipated difference were made. In the case of the Sentence Completion Test, the predictions were not specific enough to indicate on which of the scoring categories the Fantasy group would show less aggression than the Nonfantasy group.

Table 3 *Mean aggression scores on the attitude questionnaire of men in each class in the Insult groups*

Group	Total aggression (all 6 items)	Personal aggression toward E (items 3, 5, 6)	Aggressive evaluation of the experiment (items 2 and 4)
Insult Fantasy			
Class D	23.04	11.83	7.15
Class E	21.95	11.81	7.00
Class F	20.14	11.00	6.85
Class G	22.19	12.62	7.06
Class H	18.10	9.60	6.70
Mean	21.08	11.37	6.95
Insult Control			
Class J	23.13	12.47	7.33
Class K	23.13	12.88	7.25
Class L	23.80	13.40	7.50
Mean of classes	23.35	12.92	7.36
Difference between mean of classes	2.27	1.55	0.41
t	1.91	2.01	3.37
p	<.06	<.05	<.01

significant at the .05 level of confidence. Also, the difference based on evaluation of the study is significant at the .01 level.

The Sentence Completion Test. The results of a chi-square analysis of the percentage of Ss having one or more responses in each of the aggression categories are reported in Table 4. The most relevant measures for comparing the two Insult groups are categories 1, 2Em, and 3, which, since they discriminate between the Insult and Noninsult groups, are the most indicative of aggression. On each of these three measures, the Insult Control group displays more hostility than the Insult Fantasy Ss. The difference is significant at the .05 level for category 2Em and is not statistically significant for the other categories. If one computes for

each individual the number of aggressive responses based on all three categories, the differences between the Insult Control and Insult Fantasy groups are considerably enhanced. The results of this comparison are presented in Table 5 and show the Insult Fantasy group to have significantly less hostility than the Insult Control group. Thus the differences in aggression found between the two groups on the attitude questionnaire are confirmed by the Sentence Completion Test.

Fantasy Data

The effect of the insults upon the fantasy responses. The TAT stories were coded to conceal identity of Ss and the experimental treatment and then

Table 4 *Percentage of subjects in each group having one or more aggressive responses in each scoring category on the Sentence Completion Test*

Scoring category	Non insult Fantasy (N = 51)	Insult Fantasy (N = 76)	Insult Control (N = 55)	x^2 (IF, IC)	p^*
1. Aggression toward E					
Emotional	2	13	24		
Objective	0	3	2		
Combined	2	13	25	2.46	>.13
2. Aggression toward E substitute					
Emotional	4	5	18	4.31	>.05
Objective	18	18	7	2.47	>.13
Combined	21	23	25		
3. Aggression toward test					
Emotional	0	8	11		
Objective	4	13	18		
Combined	4	17	25	.95	>.35
4. Aggression toward test substitute					
Emotional	6	5	4		
Objective	24	32	16	3.13	>.09
Combined	26	32	20		
5. Aggression toward individuals other than those included under categories 1 and 2					
Emotional	21	24	24		
Objective	16	22	15		
Combined	28	34	36		

*The p values are based on two-tailed tests of significance.

rated on a five-point rating scale of aggression, a rating of five being given to the most aggressive fantasy. The results of the ratings are presented in Table 6. The stories of the Insult Fantasy group are consistently more aggressive than those of the Noninsult Fantasy group. However, the differences are small and only for Card 18 GF is the mean difference significant. The difference between the two groups in total mean aggression scores based on all four cards is also small but is statistically significant.

The insulted Ss did then express more hostility in fantasy than the noninsulted Ss. This difference is consistent with an interpretation of the main findings, reported in the previous section, as due to reduction of aggressive drive by aggressive fantasy.

The relationship between aggression in fantasy and aggression toward E. A negative correlation between aggression in fantasy and subsequent aggression toward E would tend to support the major hypothesis but is not a critical test. A Pearson r was calculated between over-all aggression on the attitude questionnaire and aggression as rated from the TAT fantasies. The correlation for the Insult Fantasy group is $-.25$ and is significant at the .01 level of confidence. The corresponding correlation for the Noninsult Fantasy group is $-.15$ which is not significantly greater than zero. The two correlations are not, however, significantly different from each other.

The relationship between aggression in fantasy and subsequent aggression toward E is in a direction, then, which tends to support the hypothesis of a drive-reducing effect of fantasy.

DISCUSSION

The experimental findings confirm the major prediction based on the drive-reduction hypothesis, namely, that those Ss who were insulted by an E and were given the opportunity to express their aggression in fantasy would subsequently display less hostility toward E than a comparable insulted group which engaged in nonfantasy activities. The fact that two different and independent measures of drive strength, the attitude questionnaire and the Sentence Completion Test, yielded similar results increases confidence in the genuineness of the phenomenon. These measures are different in

Table 5 *Percentage frequency distributions of Insult groups for scores based on categories 1, 2E, and 3 on Sentence Completion Test*

Aggression score	Insult Fantasy (N = 76)	Insult Control (N = 55)
0	71	45
1	17	22
2	5	15
>2	7	18

Note: Dichotomizing between 0 and 1, $x^2 = 7.7$; $p < .01$; dichotomizing between 1 and 2, $x^2 = 7.3$; $p < .01$.

Table 6 *Comparisons between Insult Fantasy and Noninsult Fantasy groups on mean aggression ratings on the TAT stories*

Picture	Non-insult Fantasy	Insult Fantasy	t	p
4	2.07	2.23	1.0	<.17
18GF	2.09	2.44	2.2	<.02
7BM	1.72	1.89	1.3	<.10
12M	1.95	2.06	0.7	<.25
Total (all 4 pictures)	7.83	8.62	2.1	<.02

several important respects. The expression of aggression on the attitude questionnaire was sanctioned for all groups by the instructor, who encouraged the students to reveal their feelings about experiments in which they had been participants. In addition, the range of alternatives to each question gave tacit sanction to the holding of extreme attitudes about E. On the other hand, the Sentence Completion Test involved the spontaneous expression of aggressive feelings toward E despite the knowledge that the test responses would be available to him.

The question arises as to possible alternative explanations of the difference in hostility between the two insulted groups. One might argue that the difference is a result of an increment in hostility in the Control group rather than a decrement in the Fantasy group. Such an increment could conceivably arise from differences in the frustrating qualities of the control and fantasy activities, the former supposedly being more frustrating. An effort was made to control this factor in the experimental design by varying the nature of the nonfantasy task. There is no a priori reason for assuming that the control activities are any more or less demanding than the activity of constructing TAT stories which is presented as an achievement task. Moreover, because the variation of class means in the Insult Control group is very small and the statistical analysis based on class means takes account of the effect of possible differences in the frustrating character of the particular task used in each class, the obtained difference cannot be attributed to an assumed frustrating quality of just one or two of the control tasks.

Any obvious frustration produced by the control activities should be reflected on the measures of aggression. In response to a question on the attitude questionnaire requesting the students to indicate if there was anything about the experiment they disliked, 82 per cent of the Insult Control group and 73 per cent of the Insult Fantasy group expressed dislike of some aspect of the experiment including the E. An analysis of these spontaneous comments revealed that, of those who expressed some criticism, 16 per cent of the Insult Fantasy group criticized the fantasy activity while only 11 per cent of the Insult Control group criticized the control activities.[13] Thus, in addition to the a priori argument, there is no empirical evidence to indicate that the control tasks are more frustrating than the fantasy task.

One must look then to the fantasy activity as the cause of the significant difference in aggression between the Fantasy and Control groups. The most direct explanation of this difference is the reduction of hostility by means of aggressive fantasy. A possible alternative to the drive-reduction hypothesis is one that assumes that guilt and not drive reduction is the primary mechanism responsible for the lowered aggression in the fantasy group. Here it would be supposed that the evocation of aggressive fantasy aroused guilt responses which generalized to subsequent expressions of hostility on the tests of aggression and tended to inhibit aggressive responses on those tests.

The experimental data provide some basis for rejecting the assumption that guilt is the important mediating mechanism. If guilt were the crucial factor, then one would expect the increase in hostile fantasy in the Insult group to be associated with an increase in expression of guilt. The TAT stories were analyzed for indications of guilt in regard to aggressive expression. The difference in expression of guilt between the Insult Fantasy and Noninsult Fantasy groups was slight and insignificant. In addition, the Sentence Completion Test was scored for self-aggressive responses, which might be taken as an index of guilt. The frequency of such responses was very low in all experimental groups, and the small differences among the groups were insignificant.

The drive-reduction hypothesis seems the simplest and also the most suited to account for the differences between the Fantasy and Control groups. A basic assumption underlying this hypothesis is that fantasy expression is a form of behavior that follows the same behavioral principles that have been derived from motor phenomena. Fantasy or imaginative behavior, like other forms of behavior, can serve as a substitute goal response when the most adequate goal response cannot be made. In the present experiment, Ss could not give vent to their hostility directly because of social inhibiting factors, fear of possible punishment from an authority figure, or lack of adequate opportunity. The Fantasy group Ss, however, were given an opportunity for indirect expression of hostility in their fantasy constructions.

Fantasy responses may acquire reward value, i.e., become drive reducing in at least two ways: (a) through response generalization from direct, overt aggression or (b) through a gradient of reward; if in the past covert aggressive thoughts and wishes preceded and/or accompanied overt aggressive responses which were reinforced, these preceding covert verbal responses may acquire secondary reinforcing properties.

This interpretation is compatible with a more general hypothesis relating verbal behavior and drive reduction which has been developed by Dollard and Miller (1950). In explaining various abnormal phenomena such as delusional fantasies, these authors emphasize the reduction of anxiety as the primary reinforcement of the delusional responses. The results of

13 Even in the Noninsult Fantasy group, 14 per cent of Ss (33 per cent of those who expressed some dislike of the experiment) criticized the fantasy task. They complained of insufficient time in which to complete the stories and of having to do too much writing.

the present study suggest that these delusional responses may also reduce the drive, e.g., aggression, which is eliciting anxiety.

As viewed here, fantasy behavior is an adjustment mechanism which can serve to reduce tensions and provide substitute goal satisfactions. It may function as an outlet for socially unacceptable motives and frustrated achievement strivings. The effects of fantasy are likely to depend on a number of factors such as the particular drive, the type of fantasy, and individual predisposition. For example, one might expect that fantasy behavior would be less effective in reducing such primary drives as pain, hunger, and thirst. Spontaneous fantasy, as in daydreams, may be more effective than induced fantasy, as represented by TAT stories, in reducing motivation. This might occur because, in the former case, the fantasy responses are more similar to those present in the real-life situation. Finally, in some individuals fantasy might conceivably increase rather than decrease drive. Thus rehearsal of undisguised aggressive thoughts might augment the aggressive motives of people who characteristically express their hostility in direct, overt behavior and consequently have not learned to use fantasy as a means of discharging their aggression. The extent of drive reduction produced by fantasy under various circumstances is a problem to be solved by future research.

SUMMARY AND CONCLUSIONS

The purpose of this study was to investigate the hypothesis that the expression of aggression in fantasy will serve to partially reduce aggressive drive.

This hypothesis was tested by experimentally inducing aggression by insulting a group of students, interpolating a fantasy or nonfantasy activity, and subsequently measuring the strength of the aggressive drive. Another group was not insulted but was administered the fantasy activity and the subsequent tests of aggression in order to provide a means of validating the measures of aggression used.

The results are consistent with the drive-reduction hypothesis:

1. The insulted group which had an opportunity to express aggression in fantasy subsequently displayed significantly less aggression toward E than did the control group which engaged in nonfantasy activities. This difference was found with two independent and valid measures of aggression.

2. A significant negative correlation was found between the amount of aggression expressed in fantasy and subsequent aggression toward E for the insulted group which had engaged in fantasy.

3. The insulted Ss expressed significantly more aggression in their fantasies than did the noninsulted Ss.

A personality scale of manifest anxiety

JANET A. TAYLOR

A series of recent studies (Lucas, 1952; Peck, 1950; Spence & Taylor, 1951; Taylor, 1951; Taylor, 1952; Wenar, 1950; Wesley, 1950) has shown that performance in a number of experimental situations, ranging from simple conditioning and reaction time to a "therapy" situation involving experimentally induced stress, is related to the level of anxiety as revealed on a test of manifest anxiety. Most of these investigations were concerned with the role of drive or motivation in performance,

drive level being varied by means of selection of subjects on the basis of extreme scores made on an anxiety scale rather than by experimental manipulation (e.g., electric shock, stress-producing instructions, etc.). The use of the anxiety scale in this connection was based on two assumptions: first, that variation in drive level of the individual is related to the level of internal anxiety or emotionality, and second,

From the *Journal of Abnormal and Social Psychology,* 1953, **48**, 285-290.

Table 1 *Items included on the Manifest Anxiety Scale and responses scored as "anxious" items are numbered as they appear in the complete Biographical Inventory.*

4. I do not tire quickly. (False)

5. I am troubled by attacks of nausea.* (True)

7. I believe I am no more nervous than most others.* (False)

11. I have very few headaches. (False)

13. I work under a great deal of tension.* (True)

14. I cannot keep my mind on one thing. (True)

16. I worry over money and business. (True)

18. I frequently notice my hand shakes when I try to do something. (True)

24. I blush no more often than others.* (False)

25. I have diarrhea once a month or more.* (True)

26. I worry quite a bit over possible misfortunes.* (True)

27. I practically never blush. (False)

33. I am often afraid that I am going to blush. (True)

35. I have nightmares every few nights. (True)

36. My hands and feet are usually warm enough. (False)

37. I sweat very easily even on cool days. (True)

38. Sometimes when embarrassed, I break out in a sweat which annoys me greatly.* (True)

41. I hardly ever notice my heart pounding and I am seldom short of breath.* (False)

43. I feel hungry almost all the time. (True)

44. I am very seldom troubled by constipation.* (False)

48. I have a great deal of stomach trouble. (True)

51. I have had periods in which I lost sleep over worry.* (True)

54. My sleep is fitful and disturbed.* (True)

56. I dream frequently about things that are best kept to myself.* (True)

66. I am easily embarrassed. (True)

67. I am more sensitive than most other people.* (True)

77. I frequently find myself worrying about something.* (True)

82. I wish I could be as happy as others seem to be.* (True)

83. I am usually calm and not easily upset. (False)

86. I cry easily. (True)

87. I feel anxiety about something or someone almost all the time.* (True)

94. I am happy most of the time. (False)

99. It makes me nervous to have to wait. (True)

100. I have periods of such great restlessness that I cannot sit long in a chair.* (True)

103. Sometimes I become so excited that I find it hard to get to sleep. (True)

107. I have sometimes felt that difficulties were piling up so high that I could not overcome them.* (True)

112. I must admit that I have at times been worried beyond reason over something that really did not matter.* (True)

117. I have very few fears compared to my friends.* (False)

123. I have been afraid of things or people that I know could not hurt me. (True)

136. I certainly feel useless at times. (True)

138. I find it hard to keep my mind on a task or job. (True)

145. I am unusually self-conscious.* (True)

152. I am inclined to take things hard.* (True)

153. I am a high-strung person.* (True)

163. Life is a strain for me much of the time.* (True)

164. At times I think I am no good at all. (True)

168. I am certainly lacking in self-confidence.* (True)

183. I sometimes feel that I am about to go to pieces.* (True)

187. I shrink from facing a crisis or difficulty.* (True)

190. I am entirely self-confident.* (False)

*Statements rewritten for subsequent revision.

that the intensity of this anxiety could be ascertained by a paper and pencil test consisting of items describing what have been called overt or manifest symptoms of this state.

Since the scale has proved to be such a useful device in the selection of subjects for experimental purposes, a description of the construction of the test and the normative data that have been accumulated in connection with it may be of interest to other investigators in the field of human motivation.

DEVELOPMENT OF THE SCALE

The manifest anxiety scale was originally constructed by Taylor (1951) for use in a study of eyelid conditioning. Approximately 200 items from the Minnesota Multiphasic Personality Inventory were submitted to five clinicians, along with a definition of manifest anxiety that followed Cameron's (1947) description of chronic anxiety reactions. The judges were asked to designate the items indicative of manifest anxiety according to the definition. Sixty-five items on which there was 80 per cent agreement or better were selected for the anxiety scale. The 65 statements, supplemented by 135 additional "buffer" items uniformly classified by the judges as non-indicative of anxiety, were administered in group form to 352 students in a course in introductory psychology. The measures ranged from a low anxiety score of one to a high score of 36, with a median of approximately 14. The form of the distribution was slightly skewed in the direction of high anxiety.

Subsequently, the scale went through several modifications.[1] At present it consists of 50 of the original 65 items that showed a high correlation with the total anxiety scores in the original group tested. Furthermore, the buffer items have been changed so that the total test, which has been lengthened from 200 to 225 items, includes most of the items from the L, K, and F scales of the MMPI and 41 items that represent a rigidity scale developed by Wesley (1950). The 50 anxiety items are reproduced in Table I, along with the responses to these items considered as "anxious" and the ordinal numbers of the statements as they appear in the present form of the test.

Normative data. Under the innocuous title of *Biographical Inventory,* the test in its present form has been administered to a total of 1971 students in introductory psychology at the State University of Iowa during five successive semesters from September, 1948 to June, 1951. The distribution for this sample is presented in Fig. I. As can be seen by inspection, the distribution shows a slight positive skew, as did the original scale. The fiftieth percentile falls at about 13, the eightieth at about 21, and the twentieth at about 7. The mean of the distribution is 14.56.

Sex differences. A comparison of the scores of males and females in this total sample revealed that the mean score of the women was somewhat higher. The difference between the two means however was not statistically significant. For this reason, both sexes have been included in a single distribution.

Different populations. Scores on the scale are also available for samples drawn from somewhat different populations. Distributions for 683 airmen tested at the beginning of basic training at Lackland Air Force Base and for 201 Northwestern University night-school students of introductory psychology show essentially the same form as the group reported above, while the quartiles are in close agreement.

Consistency of scores. In order to determine the stability of the anxiety scores over time, groups of individuals have been retested on the scale after various intervals. In one instance, the results of retesting 59 students in introductory psychology after a lapse of three weeks yielded a Pearson product-moment coefficient of .89. In a second test-retest study,[2] the scale was given to 163 students in an advanced undergraduate psychology course who had previously taken the test as introductory students. For 113 of these cases 5 months had elapsed since the first testing, while an interval of 9-17 months had intervened for the remaining 50.

---

1 Hedlund, J. L., Farber, I. E., & Bechtoldt, H. P. Normative characteristics of the Manifest Anxiety Scale. Unpublished paper. The statistical analysis, along with most of the data collected with the scale, was carried out under the direction of H. P. Bechtoldt at the State University of Iowa.
2 See footnote 1.

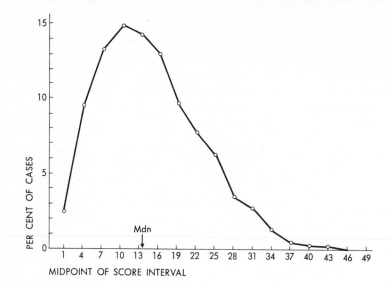

Fig. 1 *Frequency polygon showing per cent of the 1971 university students receiving the indicated scores on the Manifest Anxiety Scale.*

The test-retest coefficient was found to be .82 over 5 months and .81 for the longer period. Furthermore, no systematic change, upwards or downwards, was found in these distributions, i.e., the means of each of the three sets of scores remained essentially the same after retesting. Thus, for all groups tested, both the relative position of the individual in the group and his absolute score tended to remain constant over relatively long periods of time.

Relationship of the Biographical Inventory to the MMPI. Since it might be desired to obtain anxiety scores for individuals who have been given the complete MMPI rather than the Biographical Inventory, it is necessary to consider the effects of the different sets of filler items on the 50 anxiety statements. There is some evidence[3] to suggest that the distribution of anxiety scores given in the form of the MMPI will differ significantly from that obtained from the Biographical Inventory. The Biographical Inventory was administered to 282 freshmen males, and approximately 18 weeks later the group MMPI was given to the same students. The correlation between the two sets of measures, obtained by determining the scores on the 50 anxiety items on each test, was .68. This, it will be noted, is a slightly lower figure

than that obtained by test-retest on the Inventory after a comparable length of time. In addition, the forms of the distributions were statistically different, as indicated by a chi-square test of homogeneity. Since the initial scores of this group, obtained from the Biographical Inventory, were similar to those found with other groups, the discrepancy of the results between the Inventory and the MMPI suggests that the radical change in filler items may exert a definite influence on the anxiety scores. Before anxiety scores obtained from the MMPI can be evaluated it would appear to be necessary to have more normative data concerning the scale scores obtained from this form.

REVISION OF THE SCALE

A further revision of the scale is now being carried out by the writer. This variation represents an attempt to simplify the vocabulary and sentence structure of some of the anxiety items that appear to be difficult to comprehend, especially for a noncollege population. Toward this end, the 50 anxiety items were first submitted to 15 judges who were instructed to

---

3 See footnote 1.

Table 2 *The 28 items rewritten for the revised form of the Manifest Anxiety Scale and responses scored as "anxious"*

(Items are numbered as they appear in the Biographical Inventory.)

5. I am often sick to my stomach. (True)

7. I am about as nervous as other people. (False)

13. I work under a great deal of strain. (True)

24. I blush as often as others. (False)

25. I have diarrhea ("the runs") once a month or more. (True)

26. I worry quite a bit over possible troubles (True)

38. When embarrassed I often break out in a sweat which is very annoying. (True)

41. I do not often notice my heart pounding and I am seldom short of breath. (False)

44. Often my bowels don't move for several days at a time. (True)

51. At times I lose sleep over worry. (True)

54. My sleep is restless and disturbed. (True)

56. I often dream about things I don't like to tell other people. (True)

67. My feelings are hurt easier than most people. (True)

77. I often find myself worrying about something. (True)

82. I wish I could be as happy as others. (True)

87. I feel anxious about something or someone almost all of the time. (True)

100. At times I am so restless that I cannot sit in a chair for very long. (True)

107. I have often felt that I faced so many difficulties I could not overcome them. (True)

112. At times I have been worried beyond reason about something that really did not matter. (True)

117. I do not have as many fears as my friends. (False)

145. I am more self-conscious than most people. (True)

152. I am the kind of person who takes things hard. (True)

153. I am a very nervous person. (True)

163. Life is often a strain for me. (True)

168. I am not at all confident of myself. (True)

183. At times I feel that I am going to crack up. (True)

187. I don't like to face a difficulty or make an important decision. (True)

190. I am very confident of myself. (False)

---

sort them into four piles according to comprehensibility, the first position representing the simplest to understand and the fourth the most difficult. It was found that 28 of the items had a mean scale value of 2.00 or more. These 28 items were selected for revision and rewritten in at least two alternate forms.[4] Each set of alternatives was then ranked by a different set of 18 judges, first for ease of understanding and then for faithfulness of meaning to the original statement. For most of the items, the alternative judged to be simplest was also chosen as being closest in meaning to the original item and was therefore selected for the new scale. For those items in which a discrepancy occurred, faithfulness of meaning was chosen over simplicity. However, in every case, the new statement selected for inclusion on the scale was judged simpler than the original. These 28 rewritten items are shown in Table 2.

Relationship between the old and new versions of the scale. To demonstrate the relationship between the old and new versions of the test, both forms were administered to students in introductory psychology at Northwestern University College. A sample was selected from the college population for this purpose since it was thought that this group would show the least confusion in interpreting the original versions of the difficult items and, therefore, better demonstrate the comparability of the two forms than less verbally sophisticated individuals. Scores obtained from 59 students showed a Pearson product-moment correlation of .85 between the old and new versions, the latter being administered three weeks after the initial testing. This figure is quite comparable to the

4 In rewriting the items, the Thorndike word count (Thorndike & Lorge, 1941) was consulted. These counts primarily determined substitution of words within an item whenever this was done.

test-retest coefficient found for the previous form of the scale after a similar time interval. Considering only the 28 rewritten items, the correlation becomes .80.

While the correlation coefficient shows the high degree of relationship between the old and revised forms, the question still remains as to whether rewriting the 28 items has reduced the difficulty level of these statements so as to minimize confusion and misinterpretation. In an attempt to determine this, the scores of the 59 students given both versions were analyzed into two components: that for the 28 difficult items and that for the 22 items left intact. For each form, scores on the 28 items were correlated with the remaining 22. It was reasoned that if the original forms of the 28 items were confusing, then the rewritten items, if attempts to simplify were successful, would show a higher correlation with the 22 items left intact than would the original statements. The actual correlations obtained in this manner were .81 for the old version and .83 for the new. Although the difference between the coefficients was in the desired direction, a *t* test indicated that it was statistically insignificant. However, a significant difference in correlations might be obtained with subjects of lesser educational attainment since misinterpretation of the 28 original items would be more likely to occur with such a group.

Normative characteristic of the new scale. To determine further characteristics of the distribution of scores on the new version, 229 students in introductory psychology were given only the revised form of the scale (Ahana, 1952). It was found that the shape of the distribution and the values of the quartiles did not differ significantly from those obtained with the previous form.

Retest scores are also available for 179 individuals from the sample described above. A product-moment correlation of .88 was found after an intertest interval of four weeks. However, while the position of the individuals in the group tended to remain the same, a downward shift in the absolute scores of the entire distribution was noted from test to retest. The difference between means (14.94 vs. 12.92) was significant at the .01 level of confidence, as indicated by a *t* test.

RELATIONSHIP OF THE ANXIETY SCALE TO OTHER MEASURES

The anxiety scale was developed for, and has been used exclusively as, a device for selecting experimental subjects, without regard to the relationship of the scores to more common clinical definitions (e.g., clinical observation).

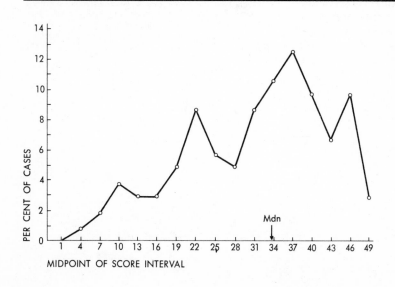

Fig. 2 *Graph of the frequency distribution of Manifest Anxiety scores received by 103 psychiatric patients.*

While defining degree of anxiety in terms of the anxiety-scale scores is a perfectly legitimate operational procedure, determining the relationship between this definition and clinical judgments might extend the applicability of both the scale and the experimental results found in the studies utilizing the scale.

In order to determine the relationship between the scale and clinical judgments, it would be necessary to have ratings made by trained observers for a large, randomly selected group of individuals and to correlate these with the anxiety-scale scores. Such an investigation has not yet been carried out. However, some indirect evidence on this point is provided by the anxiety scores of patients undergoing psychiatric treatments.[5] The anxiety scale used with these patients is essentially the same as the unrevised Biographical Inventory except that it is being administered in an individual form.

Anxiety scores are available for 103 neurotic and psychotic individuals, drawn from both an in- and outpatient population. As can be seen from Fig. 2, the distribution of scores is highly skewed toward the low anxiety end of the scale. The median score is approximately 34, a score equivalent to the 98.8 percentile of the normal subjects shown in Fig. 1. Thus the distributions of scores for the patient and the normal group are markedly different.

On the assumption that psychiatric patients will tend to exhibit more manifest anxiety symptoms (as determined by direct observation) than do normal individuals, this difference between the two groups appears to indicate that there is some relationship between the anxiety-scale scores and clinical observation of manifest anxiety.

SUMMARY

A manifest anxiety scale, consisting of items drawn from the Minnesota Multiphasic Personality Inventory judged by clinicians to be indicative of manifest anxiety, was developed as a device for selecting subjects for experiments in human motivation.

After statistical analysis the original 65-item scale was reduced to the 50 most discriminating statements. These items, supplemented by 225 statements nonindicative of anxiety, are given under the title of the Biographical Inventory. Normative data and test-retest correlations found with scale scores taken from the Biographical Inventory are presented.

A further revision of the scale was undertaken in which certain items were rewritten in an attempt to simplify their vocabulary and sentence structure. Characteristics of the scores obtained from this revised version were found to be similar to those of the previous form.

In an attempt to determine the relationship between the anxiety-scale scores and manifest anxiety as defined and observed by the clinician, the anxiety scores for groups of normal individuals and psychiatric patients were compared.

5 These data are obtained from a study currently being conducted by the writer and K. W. Spence investigating the role of anxiety in neurotic and psychotic disorders by means of an eyelid conditioning technique. [Conditioning level in the behavior disorders. *J. abnorm. soc. Psychol.*, 1954, **41**, 363-365 — Editor's note.]

part 3

LEARNING PERSONALITY TRAITS

When we think of learning, most of us tend to think of schools and the acquisition of skill in spelling or arithmetic. True enough, the ability to write *mischievous* correctly or to solve a problem in long division is a product of learning, but so are many other classes of behavior. For psychologists, *learning* is a term applied to any change in behavior as a function of experience. It follows that probably most of the traits which define our unique personalities are learned — that is, are products of our experience built into distinctive regularities in our conduct.

The present section comprises two empirical studies and a theoretical analysis, each concerned with a different substantive problem and a different method of studying the conditions under which personality traits are learned. Farber, for example, investigates the ways in which emotionally stressful conditions influence a characteristic response pattern, using albino rats as his subjects. Because of the ethical restrictions on experimentation with people, the method of the animal analogue is popular among psychologists, and it is surprising how much we can learn about ourselves from the systematic observation of lower organisms in situations contrived to be generally representative of those in which human beings often find themselves.

McArthur, on the other hand, is concerned with a very different determiner of personality, studied by a very different method. According to various principles of learning, we acquire many of our personality traits from the social groups of which we are members. One of the most important of these groups, in America at least, is our social class. Using a picture-story technique, McArthur examines the differences in the values and the personal traits most characteristic of (a) members of the middle-class "core culture" and (b) representatives of one major segment of the American upper class.

Finally, Adams and Romney devote their attention to the crucially important matter of how the authority of one person affects the behavior of another — an issue that bears on such relationships as that of parent to child, teacher to student, supervisor to employee, etc. Their "functional analysis" is an excellent example of the application of B. F. Skinner's brand of behaviorism to such problems. An interesting exercise is to take their behavioral examples and apply a different theoretical formulation—for example, a psychoanalytic interpretation—to them. Do very different understandings of authority emerge, suggesting predictions that are at variance with each other; or does an analysis of the same situations in different terms lead to very similar inferences about the effects of authority on the acquisition of behavioral regularities? How much of a difference to our comprehension do our theoretical preferences make?

The utility of these articles can be considerably enhanced if they are carefully read against two sets of questions. One set begins with the query: Do they apply to me and the people I know? To the extent that they do not, what changes in the formulations or the methods of inquiry would make them more pertinent? The other set is concerned with the differences in approach. To what extent are the problems studied in the domain of personality essentially set by the psychologists' preferences for particular theoretical ideas and particular methods of observation and experiment, and to what extent are the problems derived from direct experience of the human puzzle? After all, the personality and background of the psychologist, who is also a person, are not entirely irrelevant to the substantive issues he is interested in and the methods he regards as most congenial. Science, it must be remembered, is a very *human* enterprise.

Response fixation under anxiety and non-anxiety conditions[1]

I. E. FARBER

INTRODUCTION

A number of experimental studies with rats have revealed that responses which occur in close temporal contiguity with shock may acquire unusual strength, tending to persist with little variability even though they do not lead to a goal and are therefore no longer adaptive. Such persistent non-adaptive behavior has been termed 'fixation,' and has been found to occur under a variety of conditions.

Among the most frequently investigated of these have been shock situations designed to produce in rats a phenomenon comparable to that of regression in human Ss. The relationship of fixation to regression has been indicated by Hamilton and Krechevsky, who define regression as "a reversion to an earlier, well-established mode of behavior, and persistence in that mode despite the relative inefficiency of that behavior in solving the problem . . ." (1933, p. 238). Thus defined, regression

becomes merely a special case of fixation. In the typical regression experiment an animal is trained to select one of two or more alternative approaches to a goal; this habit is then weakened by failure or by delay of reward and a second habit is established. Shock is then introduced into the situation; if the animal reverts to its first habit, it is said to have regressed.

The experimental investigations concerned with this problem have not shown unequivocally that regression occurs under these conditions (Everall, 1935; Hamilton & Krechevsky, 1933; Kleemeier, 1942; Martin, 1940; Mowrer, 1940a; O'Kelly, 1940a; Sanders, 1937). The weight of the evidence indicates, rather, that

From the *Journal of Experimental Psychology*, 1948, **38**, 111-131.
1 This article is based on a dissertation submitted to the faculty of the Department of Psychology of the State University of Iowa in partial fulfillment of the requirements for the Ph.D. degree. The writer is greatly indebted to Professor Kenneth W. Spence for his advice and assistance during the course of this study.

the occurrence of regression is a direct function of the relative strength of previously established habits and an inverse function of the relative strength of on-going responses. The results with reference to fixation, however, have been consistent. Whatever its effect upon the direction of response, shock tends to constrict behavior. The initial response or responses elicited by shock serve as the behavior which is fixated, whether it be a previously made response, the ongoing response, or a response never before made by the animal in that situation.

The major findings with respect to the variables influencing fixation have been reviewed by Everall (1935), Kleemeier (1942), Mowrer (1940a), and Sears (1943). The following discussion is therefore concerned only with a brief analysis of certain methodological considerations in the study of fixation as a function of shock.

Much of the evidence for fixation derives from situations in which an animal shows little variability of performance *during shock trials*, while taking the spatially or temporally longer of two or more possible paths to a goal (Hamilton & Krechevsky, 1933; Kleemeier, 1942; Martin, 1940; Sanders, 1937).[2] Thus, Hamilton and Krechevsky (1933) found, during 100 trials in a simple maze involving a long and a short path to food, that animals subjected to shock showed only about one-ninth as much variability of performance as non-shock animals. Increased resistance to extinction of a response maintained under shock conditions has also been demonstrated. In Everall's experiment (1935), when a previously established maze habit was no longer rewarded, animals shocked during the extinction period shifted to the correct response far more slowly than did non-shock control animals.

Kleemeier (1942) has reported similar results using a four-choice maze. After successively establishing two different habits, both affording immediate access to food, 16 out of 20 of his animals persisted in their second habit during 30 or more shock trials (or reverted to it after first selecting another alley pointed in the same general direction). When a delay was introduced in the selected alley during an additional 20 to 30 shock trials, 96 percent of the runs were perseverative. When the locus of

the shock was shifted to a point after choice during yet another 20 to 30 trials, only one animal showed any decided shift in preference, 93 percent of the group's runs continuing as before.

As Kleemeier has observed, these results demonstrate only that "it is more difficult to effect a change in preference while the animal is being shocked . . . than when the animal is not given such a shock" (1942, p. 5); he prefers, therefore, to reserve the term fixation for persistence in a response "when shock [is] no longer given and the demands of the new situation [are] such that the mode of response adopted to shock [is] made inadequate" (1942, p. 5). O'Kelly (1940a), using rats in an open-field situation, has demonstrated this sort of fixation; five of seven of his shock animals persisted in a previously established response for 16 to 29 trials after shock was removed. His control animals required an average of only 6.8 trials to shift to the correct response. The two shock animals which learned the new response required 12 and 15 trials respectively. Kleemeier (1942), in a second experiment, established two successive responses in 60 rats in his four-choice maze, and then gave 50 shock trials. The mean number of runs of these animals to the particular alley selected by each during the shock trials was 44.5, a score identical with that made by a control group of 10 non-shock animals. However, when shock was then removed and a delay of reward introduced for the ongoing response, the group which had been shocked averaged 29 perseverative responses whereas the non-shock group averaged only five. Nine of the shock animals persisted in their fixated response during the entire 50 trials.

Despite some lack of uniformity in the application of criteria to a definition of fixation, the experimental results clearly indicate that behavior under shock conditions may become highly rigid and resistant to extinction, even though alternative responses are made to have greater value in terms of reward or length of delay. This kind of behavior has been subjected

2 Perhaps Everall's study (1935) should also be included among these. Although she gave no reward in the longer alley, her discussion does not clearly indicate whether a correction procedure was used. If it was, the longer path involved merely a delay of reward rather than an absence of reward.

to two sharply conflicting interpretations. One interpretation considers it to be a learning phenomenon, whereas the other regards it as abnormal — qualitatively different from learned behavior and explicable only in terms quite independent of those applied to learning phenomena.

The former interpretation of fixation has been best formulated by Sears (1943, pp. 76 ff.), who identifies it with the concept of habit strength. Noting that experimental investigations have typically been concerned with instrumental act fixation rather than with the object or drive fixations so widely dealt with by Freud, he observes:

As habit strength is customarily measured, it is equivalent to strength of instrumental act, and this latter is the quantitative continuum at one end of which lies what Freud called fixation, i.e., great strength.

The chief measure of instrumental act strength is *degree of resistance to change* either by extinction (nonreward) or by retraining (reward of an incompatible habit). This is essentially the criterion of fixation used in the clinical situation . . . (Sears, 1943, p. 81).

Sears has listed a number of different factors which have been shown to influence the strength of instrumental acts in white rats; in his summary, punishment by means of shock is included among such other factors as amount of reinforcement and interval between instrumental act and goal response.

That fixation is a phenomenon which may be subsumed under the concept of habit strength has also been suggested by Mowrer, who has observed that in humans the habits that are acquired at successive stages of development necessarily have certain strengths, "and it is the varying strength of such habits that determines the extent to which *relative* fixation may be said to have occurred at any given point" (1940a, p. 58).

Certain of the experimental evidence strongly favors the notion that fixations which occur under shock conditions are merely relative and differ only in degree of strength from other habits. Animals subjected to shock do not by any means fall into two distinct groups — those which fixate and those which do not. The curves indicating degree of resistance to extinction of a response in shock animals are continuous, and in fact, typically overlap those for animals not subjected to punishment. Everall (1935), for instance, found that shock animals had fewer hypotheses and maintained them for a longer period than did non-shock animals, but nevertheless observed that there was great variability in this respect, some animals tending to fixate regardless of the conditions under which they were run.

In sharp opposition to this point of view is that of Maier and his colleagues (Klee, 1944; Kleemeier, 1942; Maier, 1939; Maier, Glaser, & Klee, 1940; Maier & Klee, 1943). Maier (1939) has suggested that what is conventionally called the 'learning function' actually often involves processes other than learning. Such extraneous processes, including the "tendency to persist in an acquired mode of behavior after it ceases to be adaptive" (1939, p. 250), should properly, according to his view, be studied as a problem independent of learning.[3]

Martin has differentiated fixation from learning on the grounds that fixation or "habit stability" is "determined primarily by factors of frequency, recency, and intensity," whereas "learning . . . seems to be primarily purposive and adjustive . . ." (1940, p. 13). It is somewhat surprising to find here the suggestion that a phenomenon be distinguished from learning because it appears to be influenced by the very factors which are regarded by most learning theorists as determinants of habit strength. However, Tolman (1942, pp. 59 ff.), has urged a distinction between learning and the 'psychological dynamisms' on somewhat similar grounds. He states:

---

3 Much of the discussion relevant to these differing interpretations has been concerned with the fixations which occur in animals in situations involving insoluble problems rather than noxious stimulation. However, proponents of the view that fixation involves a mechanism other than learning have explicitly included both under the rubric of abnormal phenomena (Klee, 1944; Kleemeier, 1942; Maier, Glaser & Klee, 1940). It is interesting to note in this connection the frequent use of air-blast in the insoluble problem situation. When Klee (1944) eliminated air-blast as a factor under one experimental condition, he obtained fixation in only two out of 12 animals in an insoluble problem situation, whereas with air-blast nine out of 12 animals fixated. It is not suggested, however, that resistance to extinction in such situations is entirely a function of punishment; data from other sources (Mowrer & Jones, 1945) indicate that the pattern of reinforcement may be an important factor.

Learning is . . . a 'reasonable' activity which tends to keep the individual well adjusted to the actual environmental realities. . . . The dynamisms are, however, far less 'reasonable' than learning. . . . Learning corrects itself when the environmental relationships change. The dynamisms, on the other hand, tend to persist in hardened and blind form (pp. 60-61).

We shall understand by fixation the tendency, after an auxiliary response or technique has been learned (because of its instrumental value), for such response or technique to become relatively fixed and permanent—even though conditions may change so that it no longer has this original auxiliary value. This is the type of process for which Allport has coined the term 'functional autonomy' (pp. 61-62).

In opposition to this view McClelland has pointed out the gratuitousness of the assumption that certain acts must be performed for their own sake if they continue for an extended period after the conditions which originally instigated or maintained them have apparently been removed. As he puts it, "If it can be shown that there are good reasons why the act should continue, there will be no need to postulate a force within the act that keeps it going" (1942, p. 275).

Following out this general line of thought, it might be assumed, for instance, that some form of secondary motivation and secondary reward could operate to produce such behavior phenomena. Thus, in the case of shock-produced fixation it would not seem unreasonable to suppose that the maintenance of the response is a consequence of secondary reinforcement due to the reduction of anxiety which has been conditioned to the stimulus cues at the locus of the shock.

This conception of anxiety reduction as a secondary reinforcing state has been elaborated in a number of papers by Mowrer (1939; 1940b; 1941) and by Miller and Dollard (1941, p. 57 ff.). It assumes, in brief, that intense stimuli such as shock evoke in the organism certain responses, mediated largely by the sympathetic division of the autonomic nervous system, which produce an internal drive state. External cues (as well as internal cues) occurring at the time of shock acquire the capacity to evoke these visceral responses and thereby

the drive, which, when thus elicited, is termed 'anxiety.'

A response which removes these conditioned cues would reduce the anxiety aroused by them and so strengthen the connection between these cues and any response which occurs in temporal contiguity with them, in accordance with the principle of reinforcement. According to this schema, the occurrence of the goal response (escape from pain or anxiety) strengthens first of all the tendency for the drive state to elicit the responses leading to the drive reduction. It also strengthens the connections between the cues present at the time of shock and the responses producing the drive state, between the cues and the escape response, and under certain conditions,[4] between the cues and the response actually leading to the noxious stimulus.

A hungry animal which escapes shock by entering a goal box in which it also obtains food is in effect being doubly reinforced. If the food is removed but the shock continued, there is no reason why, apart from the possible disruptive effect of the changed goal situation, the response leading to escape should not continue. Indeed, its strength should continue to increase, though perhaps by smaller increments. More notably, even if the shock also is discontinued, the response would still receive secondary reinforcement due to the reduction of anxiety following escape from the cues associated with the shock. It is apparent then that if the mechanisms of secondary motivation and reinforcement are operative, the extinction of responses as a result of failure of food reinforcement should by no means proceed as rapidly in shock animals as in non-shock animals.

---

4 Ordinarily, any increment of strength in the response to approach a noxious stimulus will not suffice to overcome the much greater increment in strength of the response which escapes it; when these two responses are incompatible, the escape response will almost invariably dominate. However, under at least two circumstances the approach responses may actually gain in relative strength: (a) if the situation is such that punishment is unavoidable, so that the only possible mode of escape is by way of an initial approach response; or (b) if the approach response already has considerable strength at the time punishment is introduced, so that it actually occurs a number of times, followed by escape from the punishment. Under these conditions, the complete sequence CUE→APPROACH→ANXIETY→ESCAPE may become very strong.

STATEMENT OF PROBLEM

Among the implications of the theory that the fixation of non-adaptive responses in a shock situation may be the result of uncontrolled secondary reinforcement resulting from anxiety reduction is the following: if the anxiety were eliminated, by one means or another, the possibility of the maintenance of such responses by secondary reinforcement would be precluded. For instance, feeding in a situation in which anxiety has developed might remove the anxiety state, thereby eliminating the operation of secondary reinforcement and so decreasing the resistance to extinction of any non-adaptive response.

The present study compared the resistance to extinction of responses in a single-unit T-maze in two groups which had been subjected to shock, one of which had then been fed at the locus of shock, and the second of which had not. As a control for the possibility that the feeding activity competed with the responses directly rather than by way of reducing anxiety, a similar comparison was made between the resistance to extinction in two groups of animals not subjected to shock, but otherwise trained under conditions identical with those for the two shock groups.

The rationale of this study may be summarized as follows: when, under shock conditions, fixation of a response could be expected to occur, any diminution in the strength of that fixation as a result of feeding at the locus of shock could be ascribed either to direct interference with the fixated habit or to interference with some process maintaining it. If it were shown that feeding did not interfere directly with the habit, the hypothesis that its effectiveness in reducing fixation was the result of interference with or elimination of a maintaining mechanism (secondary reinforcement resulting from anxiety reduction) would be supported.

EXPERIMENTAL PROCEDURE

Subjects. The Ss were 96 naive male rats obtained from three colonies maintained at the State University of Iowa, as follows: 28 hooded and 28 albino rats—Psychology Department; 16 hooded

rats—Anatomy Department; 24 albino rats—Pharmacology Department. The ages of the animals ranged from 57 to 75 days at the beginning of the experiment. An equal number of animals from each colony and strain was assigned at random to each experimental condition.

Apparatus. The apparatus was a single-unit T-maze constructed of unpainted white pine. Its sides were $3\frac{1}{2}$ in. high; its floor plan and other dimensions were as indicated in Fig. 1. The roof of the starting box, through which animals were placed in the maze, was of colorless plexiglas, as were the roofs of the stem and the choice point. The remainder of the maze was covered with $\frac{1}{4}$ in. wire mesh. The doors were of plywood (with the exception of a plexiglas door dividing the choice point from the stem), and were operated vertically by E from behind a one-way screen situated in front of the apparatus. Black cloth curtains placed in front of the doors to the goal boxes prevented the Ss from noting the presence or absence of food in the goal boxes prior to their choice.

The starting box contained an end wall which could be pushed forward to move animals into the stem; a single continuous grid covered the floor of the stem and the choice point; separate grids covered the floors of the arms from the choice point up to either goal box. Each grid consisted of two separate lengths of no. 20 copper wire wound in alternate turns $\frac{1}{4}$ in. apart about a piece of $\frac{1}{4}$ in. bakelite. The floor and walls of the left goal box were covered with fine wire screening; the right goal box was lined with cork matting. Use of

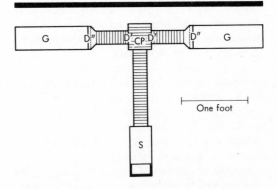

Fig. 1 *Floor plan of maze. S—starting box; CP—choice point; G—goal box; D—door; dotted line in front of door—curtain; shaded area—grid.*

these different cues was designed to accelerate learning by decreasing the generalization of reinforcement from one side of the maze to the other.

Shock was produced by means of a direct current, the source of which was a type 6C6 pentode vacuum tube provided with a plate voltage of 650 volts. The magnitude of the current was adjusted by means of a variable bias voltage from a battery and its associated potentiometer. The grids could be independently activated by means of three single-throw knife switches. Variations in the bodily resistance of animals in series with this circuit produced no measurable change in the current.

Preliminary training. Prior to training all animals were given five days of habituation to the feeding regimen of the experiment; each received eight gm. of Purina Dog Chow in individual feeding cages once daily at the hour in the afternoon at which they were to be run. Three days of preliminary training were then given as follows:

Day 1 — Four trials in a straight alley (38 in. long and built of unpainted white pine) to food, consisting of a single small pellet (approximately .10 gm.) of dog chow.

Day 2 — Fifteen min. of exploration in the T-maze in groups of two or three, followed by four trials in the straightaway, through a black cloth curtain, to food.

Day 3 — Four non-reinforced trials in the T-maze, consisting of two runs to the right and two to the left. The first two runs were free; runs on trials 3 and 4 were forced when necessary. This procedure was followed in order to reduce to some extent any strong position preferences.

Method in learning series. Beginning on day 4 all animals were given 10 trials a day for the remainder of the experiment. At the beginning of each day's runs the animals were under a 20 to 21-hour hunger drive. The inter-trial interval was always at least 10 min. and the modal interval 15 min. On trial 1 of the learning series food was present in both goal boxes. An animal's choice on this trial was assumed to define its preference and thereafter food was presented only on that side. Neither correct nor incorrect responses involved any delay; runs to the incorrect side were unreinforced either by the presence of food or by the presence of the food-container (a metal tray two inches square). Correction, i.e., retracing after an incorrect response, was not allowed.

After 40 trials Ss were assigned at random to two experimental groups and to two control groups, and were then run for an additional 60 trials. The control animals continued under the same conditions as before; but the experimental animals, though continuing to receive food on their preferred side, were now administered a shock after choice[5] by means of the grids located in the arms of the maze. The grids on both sides were activated, so that these animals were shocked whether or not they continued their old response, i.e., the shock could not be avoided merely by a reversal of choice. On the first three trials shock was administered just as the animals were leaving the grid and entering the goal box; thereafter they were shocked as soon as they touched the grid. The shock was progressively increased during the shock trials from an initial intensity of 50 microamperes to a final intensity of 140 microamperes.

Since the experimental animals soon refused to approach the shock grid it was necessary to administer an occasional shock in the stem of the maze. The time allowed for a choice before shock was given in the stem was progressively reduced during the course of the shock trials from 10 to three sec. This served roughly to equate the running times of the experimental and control animals and possibly influenced the strength of habits in the experimental group.

During the shock trials the end wall of the starting box was moved forward at the beginning of each trial (for the control as well as for the experimental groups). Consequently, the shock could not be avoided by refusal to leave the starting box nor escaped by running back into it.

Maze-feeding procedure. As indicated above, both the experimental and control animals were divided into two groups. Half of the experimental

---

5 In order to investigate the effectiveness of anxiety elimination as a means of preventing fixation, it was first necessary, of course, to determine the specific conditions under which fixation could be clearly established. The use of shock after choice as well as a number of other procedures described in this section was decided upon only after rather extensive preliminary investigation. It is by no means believed that the finally-adopted procedure is the one calculated to produce the greatest possible degree of fixation under shock conditions. This procedure, however, proved effective. The fact that certain other procedures, some of which have been favorably reported elsewhere, proved less effective emphasizes the necessity for systematic investigations designed to determine the specific variable of which strength of fixation under shock conditions is a function.

Table 1 *Mean number of correct responses in four groups during the first 40 trials (food reinforcement only) of the learning series (N = 24 in each group)*

	Experimental group		Control group	
	S	SF	NS	NSF
M	38.50	38.71	39.08	38.25
SD	2.08	1.72	1.25	2.83

Table 2 *Mean number of correct responses in four groups during the last 60 (shock) trials of the learning series (N = 24 in each group)*

	Experimental group		Control group	
	S	SF	NS	NSF
M	58.29	58.54	58.71	58.38
SD	3.15	1.80	1.57	1.73

animals and half of the control animals were fed in the maze immediately after the last trial of the learning series; the other half of these groups were not given this experience. The feeding procedure was as follows: the door separating stem from choice point, the door (D') leading to the incorrect alley and the door (D") leading to the correct goal box were closed. The area thus circumscribed consisted of the choice point (4 in. × 4½ in.) and the arm leading to the correct goal box (approximately 2 in. × 7½ in.). Two grams of food were scattered on the grid, the roof above the choice point was removed, the animal was placed directly on the grid facing in the direction of the goal, and the roof was then replaced. The animal was allowed to feed for 10 min. and was then removed. Two such feeding sessions about 1½ hours apart were given. The maze was then carefully cleaned in order to eliminate any traces of food.

At the end of this time the animals not fed in the maze were given their usual daily food ration and the others received an amount which, added to the food eaten in the maze, equalled their daily ration.

The four subgroups will be designated as follows: SF, shock animals fed in the maze before extinction; S, shock animals not fed in the maze; NSF, non-shock animals fed in the maze before extinction; NS, non-shock animals not fed in the maze. The shock animals when considered as a group will be referred to as the experimental group and the non-shock animals as the control group.

Method in extinction series. On the following day, approximately 21 hours after the last trial of the learning series, extinction was begun. The food reward was shifted to the non-preferred side for each animal, and no shock was administered. All animals were run 10 trials a day under relatively distributed practice conditions (10 min. or more between trials) to a criterion of two successive responses to the non-preferred side, which now led to food.

RESULTS

Learning Series

Learning scores for the initial 40 trials of the learning series are presented in Table 1. Examination of these data reveals that the differences among the four subgroups during these trials were negligible.

During the last 60 trials of the learning series, the experimental groups (S and SF) were shocked whereas the control groups (NS and NSF) were not. The mean number of correct responses made by each subgroup during these trials are presented in Table 2. As in the first 40 trials the mean total scores show no significant differences among the subgroups (the between-groups variance being smaller than that within groups).

However, when comparisons were made

between the experimental and control groups during shock trials on a day by day basis instead of on the basis of total correct score, a somewhat different picture was presented. The results of such a comparison are shown in Fig. 2, which gives the percentage of errors made each day by the experimental and control Ss throughout the learning series.

It may be seen from these curves that during the period in which both groups were treated identically (first 4 days) their percentages of errors were highly similar from day to day. However, during the shock period (last six days) the error curves differed considerably. Introduction of shock on day 5 for the experimental group was accompanied by a sharp increase in errors for that group;[6] after 20 shock trials this curve drops to a point somewhat below that of the control group.

These results appear to be of some interest in relation to both regression theory and to fixation as defined in terms of response consistency. It is seen that although the error curve of the experimental group rose sharply when shock was introduced, the disruption of the on-going responses in these Ss was only temporary. In three animals whose results are not included in the present discussion shock effected a more permanent disruption of the on-going responses, so that these animals continued to run incorrectly throughout the shock trials.[7] Since the very large majority (48) of

the shock animals showed no such disruption of behavior, previous findings with respect to the strong perseverative tendencies of strong habits even when shock is introduced are strongly supported. The additional fact that the mean number of errors during the shock trials was so similar in the experimental and control groups indicates that fixation defined in terms of response persistence may be an insensitive measure of habit strength when frequency of response nears 100 percent. In the present experiment the on-going habit represented an initially preferred response which was further reinforced by food for 40 trials. It was scarcely to be expected that the two groups would exhibit wide differences in variability thereafter. The inadequacy of response consistency as a differential measure of fixation in this instance does not, of course, invalidate its use under other conditions.

6 An increase in errors for the control group along with some variability from day to day during the shock trials should be noted. These phenomena do not ordinarily occur under non-shock conditions in this type of learning situation. In this instance it is probably attributable to the fact the control and experimental Ss were run concurrently. Cleaning of the grids following the occasional urination of the shock animals was observed to disrupt to some extent the behavior of the non-shock animals subsequently run in the maze.
7 The subsequent behavior of these animals during the extinction series is believed to have important implications for a general theory of fixation. However, since the present study is concerned only with the behavior of the animals which continued to run correctly, the data for these Ss have been omitted.

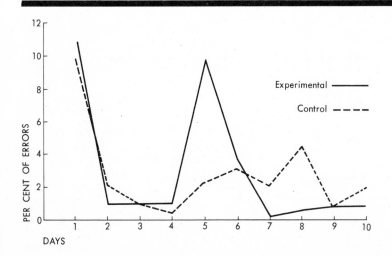

PER CENT OF ERRORS

DAYS

Experimental ———

Control – – – –

Fig. **2** *Percentage of errors made on successive days of learning series by experimental and control groups (N = 48 for each group). Days 1-4 involved identical treatments for both groups; days 5-10 involved shock for the experimental group, no shock for the control group.*

Table 3 *Number of trials to extinction for all Ss in four sub-groups (N = 24 in each group)*

	S	SF	NS	NSF
Psychology hooded	11	17	8	10
	14	15	17	6
	12	3	7	12
	8	7	17	8
	57	7	5	10
	41	10	8	7
	48	4	7	5
Psychology albino	19	10	6	7
	25	5	9	13
	63	26	6	19
	14	16	8	6
	24	21	10	8
	27	4	11	9
	33	4	8	4
Pharmacology albino	255*	19	5	7
	263*	3	15	2
	15	6	6	3
	57	33	17	5
	33	3	17	9
	163	98	11	6
Anatomy albino	36	10	11	17
	193	3	8	28
	10	10	7	17
	46	27	11	10
Mdn.	33	10	8	8
M	61.12	15.04	9.71	9.50
SD	74.09	19.24	3.83	5.75

*These two animals refused to extinguish at all under the ordinary extinction procedure. After 25 days during which they ran 250 trials without a single reversal of their original habit their inter-trial interval was reduced to two min. Under this relatively massed condition, they reached the criterion within a short time.

Extinction Series

The speed with which the original habit was extinguished under the four conditions is revealed in Table 3, which gives the number of trials required by each S to reach the criterion of two reversals and the medians, means and SD's of the extinction scores for each group.

In order to test the hypothesis that response fixation, defined in terms of relative resistance to extinction, may result from the reduction of anxiety, it was first necessary to demonstrate that under shock there was greater fixation than under the non-shock condition. Examination of the data in Table 3 shows that this condition was satisfied. The S animals, it will be seen, required on the average many more trials to reach the extinction criterion than did the NS animals. The extent of the difference is indicated not only by the measures of central tendency but also by the relatively small amount of overlapping between the two distributions. Thus, the largest score (17) for the NS group was below the 30th percentile score for the group S, while the lowest score for the latter was at the median of the NS group. There can be little doubt that shock, as compared with absence of shock, was effective in fixating the originally learned response.

If our major hypothesis with respect to the relationship of anxiety to fixation was correct, the elimination of the anxiety should have reduced the tendency to fixation. It was supposed that the feeding of the Ss in the anxiety-arousing situation would have this effect. We therefore turn to a comparison of the extinction scores of the experimental animals which were subjected to this 'therapeutic' treatment (feeding in the maze) with those which were not.

Perhaps the most convincing proof that feeding at the locus of shock did reduce fixation, i.e., decrease resistance to extinction, is furnished by examination of the individual scores. Thus, it is seen that only two of the 24 members of the SF group had as large a score as the median animal in the S group; and conversely, only two members of the S group had as small a score as the median animal in the SF group. The differences between the measures of central tendency were strikingly large—almost as large, in fact, as those between the S and NS groups.

A t-test of the significance of the difference between the means of groups S and SF was not possible, since their variances differed greatly and the distributions departed markedly from normality. However, a number of other types of tests of significance were applicable.

Chi-square was employed in testing the hypothesis that the two groups were homogeneous with respect to the number of responses required for extinction. Classifying the number of animals in each group into those which required less than 15 trials to extinguish and those which required 15 or more trials, the following contingency table was obtained:[8]

No. Trials to Extinction	S	SF
Below 15	6	15
15 or above	18	9

The χ^2 value for these data is found to be 6.86, which, for one degree of freedom, is significant beyond the one percent level of confidence.

If the results are analyzed by means of a technique suggested by Festinger (1945) for determining the significance between means of samples drawn from positively skewed populations, it is found that the ratio between the means yields an F-value of 4.53, which for the degrees of freedom involved (33 and 29), is significant well beyond the one percent level.

A further test of the mean difference between these groups was obtained by first transforming the original extinction scores into log log scores. This transformation satisfied the requirements of normality and equality of variances in the two sets of scores and thus permitted the use of the t-test. The resulting t is 4.87, which, for 46 d.f., is well above the value required for significance at the one percent level of confidence.

The agreement among the results of these tests of significance afforded a very sound basis for rejecting the null hypothesis (that the groups did not differ in their extinction scores) and presented a convincing verification of our prediction that feeding at the locus of shock would reduce the tendency to fixation. There was reason to believe, in fact, that the feeding procedure not only reduced the degree of fixation in the SF group but *on the average* prevented fixation entirely. When the extreme score (98) in the SF group was omitted so that the conditions for the application of the t-test could be met, no basis was found for rejecting the hypothesis that the SF group did not differ from the two non-shock groups. Failure to obtain such a difference is believed to lend even

8 The value 15 represents the mean number of trials to criterion for SF animals. Other bases for dividing the groups might have been used. The distributions overlap so little, however, that it is difficult to find a score for this purpose which has some ordinary statistical significance and also permits conformity to the stricture that the theoretical frequency in each cell be greater than ten. For instance, use of the median of either group as the point of division results in higher values of χ^2, but does not allow a test involving theoretical frequencies greater than 10.

Table 4 *Means and SD's of psychology and non-psychology animals for four experimental conditions*

	Psychology animals (N = 14 for each condition)		Pharmacology and anatomy animals (N = 10 for each condition)	
	M	SD	M	SD
S	28.29	17.11	117.10	92.82
SF	10.64	6.98	21.20	27.48
NS	9.07	3.58	10.80	4.17
NSF	8.86	3.73	10.40	7.64

stronger support to the interpretation that fixation is, in the present experiment at least, closely related to secondary drive and its associated reinforcing mechanism.

It has been proposed that this prevention of response fixation in the SF group was the result of interference with the mechanism of anxiety reduction which maintained the response, rather than the result of direct interference with the original response. This latter alternative was tested by comparing the resistance to extinction of the NS and NSF animals. If the procedure of feeding in the maze directly affected the original response, weakening it in some manner, the means of these two groups should have differed. A *t*-test of the difference between the means yields a value of .15, which for 46 d.f. would be obtained by chance 80 to 90 percent of the time. The results therefore failed to support this alternative hypothesis and thus added credibility to our supposition that the decreased resistance to extinction of the SF group is to be attributed primarily to the elimination of anxiety through feeding.

Influence of Colony Differences on Fixation

Among the important variables found to be related to the strength of fixation of shock animals was the particular colony from which they were obtained. Examination of the individual scores in Table III reveals that there were large differences between the animals bred in the Psychology laboratory and those obtained from the Anatomy and Pharmacology laboratories.

Table 4 presents the means and SD's of the distributions of scores in the four sub-groups for the Psychology and non-Psychology animals separately. The differences between the hooded and albino strains in the Psychology group were negligible, and the relatively small N's for each of the other groups did not warrant their separation for purposes of statistical analysis. Consequently, all Psychology animals were combined into one group, while all others were combined into the second.

It is apparent that the most strong fixated animals were those from Pharmacology and Anatomy. It might then be questioned whether the difference obtained between the total S and SF groups was actually restricted to the non-Psychology animals and not found in the Psychology Ss. The *t*-test applied on the hypothesis that there was no difference between the S and SF animals from Psychology yields a value of 3.44, which, at 26 d.f., is well beyond the one percent level. Thus it is seen that a significant difference in the fixation of the S and SF groups was obtained in this more limited group of Ss.[9]

The fact that the average strength of fixation in the non-Psychology Ss far exceeded that of the Psychology animals may be of no little significance for our theory. It will be recalled that our major hypothesis states that when fixation occurs as a result of shock, it is due to the reinforcing effect of anxiety reduction. Presumably, therefore, the degree of fixation is a function of the strength of the anxiety drive. Since anxiety is thought to be essentially a visceral

[9] The difference of 95.90 between the means for the S and SF groups in the other animals was found, as might be expected, to be highly significant by the Festinger test.

response, the general emotionality of individual animals might be taken as an index of the amount of anxiety they would show in a given situation and consequently of the extent to which they would be likely to maintain non-adaptive responses in that situation.

Note was made on alternate days of the learning series of all animals that defecated during the experimental period. Inasmuch as defecation is commonly regarded as a sign of emotionality, the number of Psychology and non-Psychology Ss respectively that defecated during the experiment (particularly during the initial learning series, which involved only a routine learning situation) could be taken as a rough measure of the anxiety level of the two groups.

The data showed that defecation occurred in 20 of the 56 Psychology animals and in 33 of the 40 non-Psychology animals. The χ^2 test of homogeneity based on these frequencies yields a value of 20.6, which, for one d.f., is significant well beyond the one percent level. If defecation is accepted as a valid measure of emotionality, one may conclude that the non-Psychology Ss were more emotional than those from Psychology.

There is considerable reason to believe that the Psychology animals represented a population which has resulted from selective breeding for non-emotionality. Animals in psychological research that are difficult to handle, which refuse to run and which cannot learn maze and discrimination problems are usually discarded. Those used as breeding stock, therefore, are precisely the ones which make a more rapid adjustment to new situations, i.e., are less emotional. This is presumably not the case with animals bred in laboratories in which behavior problems are not studied. In consequence, it was not surprising that Psychology animals showed less anxiety and therefore fewer fixation tendencies than other animals, under the conditions of the present experiment.

DISCUSSION

One of the bases for the belief that fixation is not to be explained in terms of learning principles appears to be the fact that *any* response elicited by shock tends to be fixated, *regardless of its strength prior to the time shock is introduced.* It is not difficult, certainly, from the point of view of learning theory, to explain why any response, *once it has occurred,* might persist during shock trials. Despite the fact that it may never have been previously reinforced, or may not currently represent an efficient habit as far as immediate access to food is concerned, the fact that it leads to escape from shock would nevertheless be an adequate basis for predicting its continuance. We should, however, examine more carefully the grounds for the claim that the likelihood of evocation of a particular response by shock is independent of its relative strength during the pre-shock period.

Among the results tending to support this conclusion are data reported by Everall (1935). She found that only one animal in ten shifted to a new response during shock trials after having learned a previous response to a criterion of 38 correct out of 40 trials, whereas two animals in ten shifted after having learned a previous response to a criterion of 111 out of 120 trials. In this instance it appears likely that the strength of responses learned to the lesser criterion generally sufficed to preclude successful competition of another response. It was not to be expected, therefore, that further training on these responses should make an appreciable difference.

It is of interest in this connection to compare the results obtained by Everall with her 40-trial food-reinforcement group with those of the present experiment, which also involved 40 food-reinforced trials in the pre-shock period. Despite certain procedural differences which tended to minimize response shifting in our experiment, the percentages of animals showing disruption of response with shock were very similar, being 10 and six percent respectively, in the two experiments. It may be concluded that in these situations the tendency to disruption of response (shifting to a response not previously reinforced) was slight indeed. Everall herself decided on the basis of additional studies that "when shock was administered before a choice point, the majority of animals reacted in the direction they had selected most frequently in the past" (1935, p. 357).

The results of a number of other experiments indicate that the relative strengths of habits have a decided influence on the tendency for those responses to be elicited in a shock situation. Thus, Mowrer (1940a) and O'Kelly (1940b) found that animals continued their correct response when shock was introduced *if no other response had been previously learned,* whereas animals which had previously learned a different response tended to revert to it. Martin found that the greater the relative amount of training on an earlier habit, the less the tendency to persevere in a later habit during shock; he concluded that "other things being equal the amount of training on the responses involved will be the decisive factor in the occurrence of regression, and that native or unlearned preferences have no effects that cannot be counter-balanced by training" (1940, p. 13). Kleemeier (1942), who does not favor the view that the relative strengths of habits are an important factor in determining response to shock, nevertheless found that a much larger proportion of animals responded to shock by running to an alley which had been previously learned than by running to an alley which had not been previously learned. The weight of the evidence thus offers little support to the interpretation that the factors operating to produce responses under shock conditions are independent of those which determine responses in other ordinary learning situations.

A second basis for the belief that fixation may represent an abnormal phenomenon has been the observation that fixated animals may show considerable constriction of behavior. Thus, in Kleemeier's investigation it was found that when their fixated response was blocked, a great many animals refused to run altogether. This behavior, according to Kleemeier, is not to be explained on the asumption that shock choices are determined by their relative habit strengths. He writes: "If this were the determining factor then elimination of [the alley with] the highest excitatory value should merely cause a shift in behavior toward the alley with the next highest value" (1942, p. 32).

If the word 'response' had been substituted for the word 'alley' in this quotation, the position of the proponents of a learning interpretation would have been fairly stated. If one examines the conditions under which ten out of 16 animals in Kleemeier's first experiment finally refused to run, one finds that this re-sponse was actually fairly low in the response hierarchy. It was elicited in these animals only after a long sequence (varying somewhat for two sub-groups) which included, during some 200 trials, the following order of events: (1) training in two different habits; (2) shock at the choice point; (3) blocking of any new responses elicited by the shock; (4) introduction of delay of reward for the resulting habit; (5) removal of shock; (6) introduction of shock after choice; and finally (7) blocking of the then on-going habit. It is noteworthy that during this somewhat elaborate series of conditions, seven of the 16 animals experienced blocking of the alley to which they had initially responded when shocked and all animals experienced blocking of the alley which they eventually fixated. It is scarcely remarkable, under these circumstances, that 10 of the 16 Ss should have refused to enter any other alley. From the point of view of learning theory, one would have to consider the effects of such blocking, particularly the likelihood of their generalization to the other alleys in the maze. Such generalized extinction effects might be expected[10] to produce just such failure of response as Kleemeier found.

A final basis for the belief that fixation represents a non-learning phenomenon is its apparently unusual (abnormal?) strength. Thus animals may persevere in a response elicited under shock conditions for what may appear to be an 'unreasonable' length of time. For instance, in Kleemeier's study, a comparison of the effect upon resistance to extinction of 50 food reinforced trials with that of a like number of shock trials revealed a truly impressive difference. Whereas no animal in his non-shock group required more than 12 trials in which to discard a non-adaptive response (involving delay of reward), 15 percent of his shock Ss failed to discard the response in 50 trials.

Comparable results were obtained in the present study. When the on-going response was made incorrect (no longer leading to food) none of the non-shock animals required more than 28 trials to reverse this response, despite

---

10 Cf. Hull (1937), who deduces that "in certain situations the organism will give up seeking, i.e., cease making attempts, and thus fail to perform the correct reaction even when it possesses in its repertoire a perfectly correct excitatory tendency" (p. 13).

the fact that it had been initially preferred and had been further reinforced for 100 trials by food reward. In the shock (S) group on the other hand, 29 percent of the animals persisted in the response for as many as 50 trials and 17 percent for as many as 150 trials, during which they went entirely unrewarded as far as food was concerned.

It is this phenomenon of persistence of response in the absence of any apparent reward (goal) which seems most contrary to learning theory. Learned behavior, according to the widely accepted view, is goal directed, whereas fixated behavior appears to be merely repetitious. It seems to continue without rhyme or reason, despite the fact that it may no longer be effective in escaping shock or reaching food or, in fact, achieving any apparent goal.

We have proposed to explain such fixation in terms of principles derived from ordinary learning experiments. Assuming that the pain response (anxiety) may be conditioned to the cues contiguous with the noxious stimulus and that escape from this anxiety constitutes a reinforcing state of affairs, it is possible to explain many of the findings with respect to response fixation under shock conditions.

It is important to note that the present treatment *supplements* an explanation of fixation in terms of habit strength alone. Although it is believed that escape from shock ordinarily constitutes a very strong reinforcement and probably results in habits of great strength, it would be possible under the present set of postulates to conceive of the fixation of a relatively weak habit so long as a *maintaining mechanism* resulting from anxiety reduction were operating. This view appears to be most consistent with the common clinical observation that mal-adaptive habits may be readily extinguished *if the anxiety aroused by the situations in which they occur is eliminated first.*

In view of the successful prediction of the results of the present study on the basis of the assumption of secondary reinforcement (and the likelihood that the same mechanism has operated as an uncontrolled variable in a number of studies relevant to this problem), it would seem appropriate to conclude that the continuation of acts under conditions which might be expected to result in their extinction is, in fact, due to factors operating in ordinary learning

situations. This possibility must be given serious consideration before the view is accepted that fixation is not explicable in terms of learning concepts and principles.

SUMMARY

The present study was concerned with the problem of the extent to which the persistence of a non-adaptive response in a shock situation may be the result of uncontrolled secondary reinforcement resulting from anxiety reduction. The anxiety reduction hypothesis involves the following assumptions:

1. Intense stimuli such as shock evoke in the organism certain responses, mediated largely by the sympathetic division of the autonomic nervous system, which produce an internal drive state.

2. External cues present at the time of shock acquire the capacity to evoke these visceral responses and thereby the drive, which, when elicited in this manner, is termed 'anxiety.'

3. Removal of these cues reduces the anxiety and therefore constitutes a reinforcing state of affairs.

It follows from these assumptions that even after shock has been removed, the secondary reinforcement resulting from the reduction of anxiety following escape from the cues eliciting it may materially retard the extinction of any response closely associated with these cues.

Among the implications of this theory is the consideration that the elimination of the anxiety in this situation should preclude the possibility of maintenance by means of secondary reinforcement alone of responses which are no longer adaptive. It was hypothesized that feeding in a situation in which anxiety had been developed would be adequate to remove the anxiety state, thus eliminating this source of secondary reinforcement and decreasing the resistance to extinction of any non-adaptive response.

To test these implications, two groups of 24 rats were given 100 trials in a single-unit T-maze, with food reward in the goal box on their preferred side. During the last 60 trials these animals where shocked immediately after the choice point in the maze. At the completion of this training, one group was fed in the maze at the locus of shock for two ten-minute periods. On the day following this 100-trial learning series, the food reward was shifted to the goal box on the non-preferred side for each animal, and no shock was administered. All animals were run until their original response was extinguished, and the number of trials to extinction for the shock (S) animals and for the shock-fed (SF) animals were compared.

As a control for the possibility that the feeding activity affected the original responses directly rather than by way of anxiety elimination, two additional groups of 24 Ss each were trained under the conditions indicated above, but were not shocked. As in the case of the shock animals, one group (NSF) was fed in the arm of the maze immediately after the choice point, while the other group (NS) was not. These groups were then compared on the basis of the number of trials required to extinguish the original response.

The following results were obtained:

1. Responses of the S animals showed great resistance to extinction as compared with those of the NS animals.

2. Responses of the S animals were signifi-cantly more resistant to extinction than those of the SF animals.

3. There was no significant difference in resistance to extinction between the responses of the SF animals and those of the two control groups.

4. There was no significant difference in resistance to extinction between the responses of the two control groups.

It was concluded that:

1. The experimental conditions were adequate to effect fixation in the animals run under shock conditions.

2. The feeding procedure was 'therapeutic' in that it prevented fixation in the average SF animal.

3. The prevention of fixation in the SF group was the result of interference with some mechanism maintaining the fixated responses rather than the result of direct interference with the responses themselves.

On the basis of these considerations, the inference has been drawn that fixation resulting from shock may be the result of the operation of secondary reinforcement resulting from anxiety reduction, and therefore due to factors operating in ordinary learning situations.

Personality differences between middle and upper classes[1]

CHARLES McARTHUR

The empirical question in this experiment is whether middle- and upper-class students tell different Thematic Apperception Test stories and whether the differences that occur are predictable from theories held by cultural anthropologists. It may be too much to attempt to generalize the findings as a fresh demonstration of the relation between "culture" and "personality." Yet some interest attaches to demonstrating that consistent results may be obtained from the operations of an anthropologist, who infers the values of a group by observing typical modes of behavior, and from the operations of a clinical psychologist, who infers the more emotionally involved concerns and wishes of an individual by observing responses to a projective test.

A few psychologists (Henry, 1947; Milner, 1949; Mitchell, 1951) have reported culturally explicable differences in responses to the TAT. What is new here is the examination of psychological differences between the American middle-class "core culture" and one subculture within the Eastern upper class. These groups seemed a happy choice for investigation for two reasons. First, little has been done to investigate subcultural effects on personality (Sargent, 1949). Second, while there exist many studies (Davis, 1943; Davis, 1948; Davis,

From the *Journal of Abnormal and Social Psychology,* 1955, **50,** 247-254.

1 This paper is derived from a thesis submitted in partial fulfillment of the requirements for the Ph.D. in the Department of Social Relations, Harvard University. Revision was made possible by the Study of Adult Development.

1949; Davis & Havighurst, 1949; Ericson, 1947; Hollingshead, 1949; Kluckhohn & Kluckhohn, 1947) contrasting the American middle and lower classes, the sparse literature on the upper class is mostly literary (Marquand, 1937; Marquand, 1949; Morley, 1944). No psychological examination of American upper-class personality seems to exist.

DOMINANT VS. ALTERNATIVE OPERATIONS

The theory that seems most useful for formulating American subcultural personalities has been proposed by Kluckhohn (1950) who starts by assuming that:

The five human problems which are tentatively singled out as those of key importance can be started quite directly in the form of questions: (1) What are the innate predispositions of men? (2) What is the relation of man to nature? (3) What is the significant time dimension? (4) What type of personality is to be most valued? (5) What is the dominant modality of the relationship of man to other men? (p. 378)

These five problems, she argues, are everywhere immanent in the human situation.

Solutions to these problems are limited. If one's phrasing is general enough, one can state three logically possible answers to each. The innate predisposition of man may be good, it may be evil, or it may be a mixture of the two. Man's relation to nature may be dominating, or submissive, or simply one of being "in" the natural world. The important temporal emphasis may be on past, present, or future. Man may emphasize his ties to his predecessors (and be said to possess a "Lineal" orientation), or he may emphasize his bonds with his contemporaries ("Collateral" orientation), or he may emphasize the importance of the single person (and so be said to possess an "Individualistic" orientation). As to the preferred types of personalities, people may value a man for what he can accomplish ("Doing" orientation), for what he already is ("Being" orientation), or for what he may, e.g., through spiritual growth, become ("Being-in-Becoming" orientation). There may be other possibilities, Kluckhohn realizes, but these sets of three offer "at least a testable con-

ceptualization" of the range. A summary of the above paragraph is shown in Table 1.

The dominant American orientation (the well-known middle-class value system often called "the American success culture") has the profile shown in Table 2. Doing orientation is most commonly viewed as the core of this value system, and related to the predominant economic institutions and to the importance of the male wage earner in the household. Future orientation comes next; the wage earner must plan to "get ahead." Individualistic orientation is strong; one "looks out for Number One." There is, however, secondary emphasis

Table 1 *Possible answers to basic human problems*

Problem	Range of answers		
Innate predispositions	Evil	Mixed or neither	Good
Man-Nature relation	Man subjugated to Nature	Man in Nature	Man vs. or over Nature
Time dimensions	Past	Present	Future
Preferred personality	Being	Being-in-Becoming	Doing
Modality of human relations	Lineal	Collateral	Individualistic

Table 2 *The dominant american "profile" and an upper-class variant*

Dimension	Dominant profile	Variant profile
Relational	I / \ C L	L / \ C I
Personality	Doing Being Being-in-Becoming	Being - Being-in-Becoming Doing
Time	Future	Past
Discipline	Lenient	Strict
Man-Nature	Man-over-Nature	?

on the Collateral. One is loyal to one's peers, but rarely to other generations. Doers regard nature as something to conquer, valuing Man's potential position "over nature." These values are all facets of the dominant culture profile in America.

But "let a person or group of persons shift on any single variable and we no longer have the ideal typical American achievement pattern."[2] Shifts on several variables occur in some members of the Eastern upper class.

We have at the upper-class level some persons who in the relational configuration they follow clearly emphasize the Lineal of the family or extended group. In some cases there is no attempt at all to adjust to the dominant occupational sphere in terms of the dominant profile. Although we do not have in our occupational system specific careers and jobs which belong by definition to upper-class persons, some try to create roles for themselves. For example, the man who spends his time, the time that others spend in a definite job, on the management of family business affairs; or the man who links a strong "C" with the "L" and occupies himself with philanthropy. . . .[3]

The rest of the dominant profile may also change. A logical corollary of Lineal values is emphasis on Past Time. Upper-class Past orientation has been described by Warner (Warner & Lunt, 1941) in Newburyport and by Davis and Gardner (1949) in the *Deep South*. Other shifts follow. The purest contrast between middle-class, dominant orientation and this upper-class alternative is stated in Table 2.

The presumption seems to be that this particular alternative is not very common and is concentrated in the upper-upper class (especially in New England) though it still does not entirely disappear as one moves down through the upper-middle class. The inverse presumption would be that the dominant profile pervades the middle class but gives way increasingly to the alternative orientation as one moves up the social scale. There are no grounds for stating what the exact frequencies might be.

THE EXPERIMENTAL DATA

The experimental groups are two samples of Harvard freshmen who attended, respectively, public and private secondary schools. We assume the public school group to be heavily saturated with middle-class members while the private school group, though more heterogeneous, includes nearly all the boys from upper-class families. That assumption would not apply in many universities but is accepted as "common knowledge" about Harvard. It can be justified from income and occupational data. It follows that more public school boys than private school boys possess the middle-class dominant orientation while the upper-class alternative orientation must be commoner among private school people.

The dependent variables in this experiment were provided by stories written in Part II of the Visual Impressions Test. This instrument was developed at Harvard's Office of Tests. Part I consists of ten ink-blots. Part II contains five of the standard TAT pictures:

#1   The "violin picture,"
#4   Young couple and "pin-up,"
#6BM Old woman and young man,
#14   Lone silhouette,
#7BM Old man and young man,

together with printed instructions for group or self-administration.

The stories so called had been scored by the writer on nine variables before the beginning of the present experiment. These variables referred to unequivocal aspects of the manifest tale, so that "scoring" merely consisted of answering these concrete questons:

1. Are any parents "introduced" into the plot who are not represented in the picture? If so, are they fathers, mothers, or both? How do they interact with the hero?

2. Is an exemplar present in the plot?

3. Does the hero do any work (including studying), or does he do merely "token work" in order to conform with the letter but not the spirit of his assigned chores, or does he do no work at all?

4. What is the emotional "meaning" of work to the hero, as *stated* in the story? (Cite the phrase.)

5. Is school cited in the story? If so, what is its "meaning" to the hero, as stated in the tale? (Cite the phrase.)

6. Does aggression occur in the story?

7. Who are the objects of the hero's aggressive acts or feelings?

2 Kluckhohn, Florence. Dominant and variant and deviant American value orientations. Unpublished manuscript.
3 Kluckhohn, Florence. Some variant orientations. Unpublished manuscript.

8. Is the story outcome, in Rosenzweig's (1934) sense, intropunitive, impunitive, or extrapunitive?

9. Which of several popular "themes" occurs in this tale? (These themes will be described when they enter our results.)

Scoring was done under supervised "blind" conditions, in connection with another experiment. At the time that he formulated predictions about subcultural differences in these scores, the writer had no knowledge of who had written the tests, except that they were a sample (with turnout losses) of their Harvard class. The author did know, obviously, which responses had occurred with enough frequency to be worth hypothesizing about. His problem was to predict which of these frequent responses would show significant differences between subcultures, and to predict the direction of these differences.

DERIVING THE HYPOTHESES

Between the abstractions about "orientation" and predictions of the relative frequency of certain TAT stories, there are two kinds of intermediate premises.

First, there are certain premises about what typical family patterns each orientation produces. These premises can be stated as pure deductions from the cultural profile, but the fact is that they have already been given (Gorer, 1949; Mead, 1942; Mead, 1949) some empirical support.

The Future, Doing-oriented family must produce sons reared in the "achievement mores," taught to look forward to by-passing or surpassing their father's occupational roles. Even when the father is himself successful, the son is likely to "detour" him as a model, perhaps choosing an alternate profession. It is the hopes of the mother that these sons must realize in order to feel successful. They will have been drawn close to their mother, who so assiduously "brought them up," and they will have introjected her precepts. It is these boys who will, after college, be expected to leave the family and "make their own way," establishing a new small, mobile family unit like the one from which they came. These experiences and expectations ought to underlie their TAT stories.

Families possessing the alternative cultural orientation create none of these situations. Past, Lineal orientation suggests that the son accept his father as a model. So does the Being orientation: fashions in gentlemen are slow to change. Nor does such a culture exert pressure on the boy to achieve autonomy, at least in the sense of founding a mobile, independent family unit. Nor can he gain autonomy by achieving success; if he dreams of running off, he dreams of running off to be happy (Being) or to find spiritual (Being-in-Becoming) fulfillment, rather than to make his fortune. To dream of surpassing his father is likely to be quite meaningless.

The second kind of intermediate premise concerns the way the content of TAT stories is related to the characteristics of the narrator. Traditionally, these premises are:

1. That the TAT works by "direct projection." That is, the things that the story heroes do are the things the narrator has done or wishes to do. Furthermore, he selects as story topics those deeds or wishes in which he has large emotional involvement. A traditional way of stating this is that "the narrator identifies with the hero."

Similarly, what is done to the hero is something that the narrator perceives as having been done to him or wishes to have done to him. (All these statements are true only at a suitable level of abstraction like that represented by Murray's [1938] need and press categories. The stories are not necessarily autobiographical.)

2. That the TAT contains thematic projections. The sequences of events in the stories parallel sequences of events that the narrator has experienced or expects or wishes to experience. It is therefore possible to make statements about what the narrator regards as necessary prerequisites to certain events—the "conditions for" these events, as Tomkins (1947) has phrased it.

It is also possible to make statements about what the narrator regards as a likely or desirable goal of certain actions. Murray has spoken of the "subsidiation" of one need to another. Tomkins speaks of "the meaning of" certain acts.

3. That departure from the given picture is a sign of strong affect. In particular, what is added to the picture or "introduced" into the

story is probably something about which the narrator feels strongly. What is omitted or distorted may also be strongly affect-laden.

THE HYPOTHESES

The first scoring question was, "Are any parents 'introduced' into the stories who do not appear in the picture?" The answer is "yes" most often in stories about picture 1. According to our third premise about the TAT, the "introduced" parent should be the one who is more emotionally significant to the narrator. In discussing dominantly-oriented families, we pointed out that mothers may assume special importance to their sons, while alternatively-oriented families may rear sons who give more significance to their fathers. Testing this, we formulate:

Hypothesis 1. *Private school boys will tell more stories to picture 1 in which the father is the "introduced" parent.* The second half of the same scoring question reads, "Name the introduced parents' relation to the hero and summarize their part in the story." Two relationships are frequent in the stories. The parent either serves as a model for the hero or gives orders to the hero. We have seen that in Past, Lineal-oriented families, a parent is more likely to find acceptance as a model. To produce a Doing, Future-oriented child, the parent indoctrinates, desiring the child to obey rather than emulate him. We would expect Future, Doing-oriented children to project this situation, creating heroes who experience parental "press Dominance." Such tales being frequently told to the violin picture, we guess that:

Hypothesis 2. *More public school boys will tell stories to picture 1 in which the parent dominates the child.* The next scoring question is, "Is an exemplar present?" Past, Lineal orientation gives special relevance to exemplars, so we may expect the alternatively-oriented boys to project the importance of models into their stories.

Hypothesis 3. *Private school boys will more often tell stories involving an exemplar.* We have no reason to state Hypothesis 3 as "only private school boys will tell stories about exemplars." Therefore, we are free to speculate about a cluster of stories in which models are selected

for the heroes by their mothers. This sounds very like what was earlier described as an important pressure placed on sons of middle-class families: to make them like someone other than their father, the mother must hold other standards before them. We have assumed that this pressure was constant enough to become an emotionally significant and therefore projectable portion of the son's experience.

Hypothesis 4. *More public school boys will tell stories in which the mother holds up a model before her son.* The next scoring question asks if heroes do any work. Work and models are linked in some plots in this way: the hero finds some excuse to reject a model and then feels free to do no more work. While the rejection of models might be expected from Future orientations, the rest of this plot seems to be a projective statement of the conditions (experienced or wished for) under which this narrator could feel justified in dropping work. Obviously, Past, Lineal orientations might lend to exemplars such critical importance. Future orientation provides other spurs, in the exemplar's absence.

Hypothesis 5. *More private school boys will tell stories in which the rejection of a model is a condition for lack of effort by the hero.* In another group of plots, the exemplar's merits are so great that the hero feels inferior. Again, Past orientation might lead to such overrating of an older model. It is also true that alternatively-oriented boys are more likely to have upper-class models who, like the exemplars over whom Henry Adams once spent a lifetime of conflict, are in reality unsurpassable.

Hypothesis 6. *More private school boys will tell stories in which the presence of a model leads to the hero's feeling inferior.* The third scoring question leads to two kinds of positive instances of "work." A strategy is to test the single phenomenon of work's total absence. There were, in fact, tests in which no mention was made of work. On our premise that emotionally significant topics are the ones projected into the TAT and our further premise that Doing is the core of the dominant value system, it seems unlikely that many middle-class boys would go through a whole test without somewhere projecting their concern with the question of work. On the other hand, a Being orientation permits one to remain uninvolved.

Hypothesis 7. *Private school boys should more often write tests in which no hero works at all.* The Being or Being-in-Becoming orientation also implies that, when work does get mention, it will probably be a means to other goals. The empirical fact is that heroes worked for three reasons: ambition, desire for independence, and desire for self-realization. Self-realization is one aspect of Being-in-Becoming. Operationally, these stories had been scored in terms of Murray's need Sentience, that may include an interest in good taste, in all-round well-being, or any way of getting to feel in top mental, spiritual, and/or aesthetic form.

Hypothesis 8. *More private school boys will tell stories in which the "meaning of work" is need Sentience.* The Future-oriented hero should project his concern about other goals. One of these is need Autonomy. Not only may he wish to escape the dominance of his middle-class parents, but he also should have introjected their demand that he equip himself to leave home to "go to work" and to establish a new family unit. In our tests, there were many stories to card 6BM in which the hero was just at the moment of leaving home to go away and take his first job. This scene usually involved a conflict over leaving the mother and the comforting implication that the step being taken was socially normal. For most freshmen, this great day has not been experienced; the tales are to be taken as wishful or as concrete statements of an inner conflict that has been felt in a more general way. The theme of guilty but justifiable autonomy through work seems a projection of feelings more likely to be aroused in middle-class sons.

Hypothesis 9. *More public school boys will tell stories to picture 6BM in which the "meaning of work" is need Autonomy.* Another justifiable use of work to gratify need Autonomy is the process of by-passing the father. The dominantly-oriented family will usually have taught its sons to seek extra-familial goals. Often, these goals will be defined in terms of some abstract standard of success rather than of the father or any family exemplar. Picture 7BM was almost always structured as a father and son or some

thinly disguised surrogate pair. Work often occurs in stories to this card. We expect this work to be unrelated to the father primarily in stories from dominantly-oriented boys.

Hypothesis 10. *Public school boys will more often tell stories to picture 7BM in which the "meaning of work" is an impersonal social lure external to the family: an ideal, glory, or fortune.* One less obvious corollary of middle-class family life is a danger that the son may doubt his own manhood. This "sissy complex" has been noted, usually with surprise, by foreign (Gorer, 1948) observers. Presumably one reason this possibility is left open is that the family and the subculture have so consistently devalued the father, who is to be by-passed. A male identification becomes that much more difficult. Then, too, the mother, in her role (Gorer, 1948; Kluckhohn, 1950) as "culture-bearer" makes demands on the son that increase his difficulty with learning to be a male. It happens that picture 1 evokes stories about a stereotyped crisis: the music lesson. We assume that such stories project the conflict over the definition of male role that has been observed in the dominant orientation.

Hypothesis 11. *More public school boys should tell stories to picture 1 in which the "meaning of work" is that the violin is "sissy."* The next scoring question reads, "Is college or school cited? What does it mean to the hero?" All we have said points to the overwhelming necessity for the dominantly-oriented student to perceive college as a road to success. His Doing orientation, the need to surpass his father, the common circumstance that, at Harvard as well as elsewhere, he may be attending a "better" college than that of his father, his Future orientation, and more contribute to his feeling that college is or ought to be an opportunity. For the alternatively-oriented boy Harvard, like most colleges he is likely to attend, offers many chances to express Being orientation: the Club, the "gentleman's C," the irrelevance of college grades to future career. If both groups project what they want from college:

Hypothesis 12. *More public school boys will tell stories in which attending college is an expression of need Achievement.* There seems to be no theoretical basis for predicting relative frequencies of answers to the next scoring question, "Is aggression present?" The further question about who becomes the object of the hero's aggression is empirically answered, in both subcultures, to be "the mother!" If we invoke customary psychodynamic theories about the handling of dangerous emotions, we may wonder if the dominantly-oriented boy will not be forced to inhibit some of his hostility because his mother has become too essential a person and her standards have been too completely introjected. The alternative orientation permits much more cathection of the father, so that aggression against the mother may not be so likely to bring about total destruction of one's private world. All of this is relevant to the next scoring question, which asks, "Is the outcome of aggressive stories (in Rosenzweig's terms) extrapunitive, intropunitive, or impunitive?" We know, empirically, that the dominantly-oriented boy expresses much aggression toward his mother, usually, as the picture offers the chance, in stories to card 6BM. (We might have expected him not to do so; however, he does.) If this aggression of his is as dangerous as the middle-class family situation ought to make it, he may still prevent catastrophe by letting his impulse fall short of its goal. In other words, if his heroes are direct projections of himself, their aggression to the mother ought to remain goal-inhibited.

Hypothesis 13. *More public school boys will tell stories to picture 6BM involving aggression but leading to an impunitive ending.* The next question is, "What common themes are present?" One of the commonest is the Token Work theme, a story in which the hero explicitly does what is required, and no more, because his heart isn't in it. This story is usually told to the violin picture. Even though such slighting of work might be taken as an expression of lack of Doing values, our first premise about the TAT requires that such a plot be the projection of a conflict over work, told by a narrator to whom the question of moral obligation to work was important and ambivalent. (The story assumes, after all, that work is required.) So we guess that this is a Doing, not a Being, plot.

Hypothesis 14. *More public school boys will tell Token Work stories to picture 1. The Way of All Flesh* theme is an interesting story in which the

hero is a victim of an "impossible" parent, usually a father, usually crusty and insensitive to the boy's needs. After swearing for years that he will never behave so odiously, the hero reaches middle age and subjects his own son to the same shabby treatment. Psychologically, this is a story projecting weaning conflict and ambivalence toward or devaluation of the father as a model. Presumably, these are issues that are ego-involved for the boys raised in dominantly-oriented families.

Hypothesis 15. *More public school boys will tell stories containing the* Way of All Flesh *theme.* These fifteen hypotheses were derived in about the above-stated manner. It is difficult to state all of the logic so briefly, especially when the only alternative is to spell out at great length what seems so obvious to the author. Each hypothesis can, if necessary, be stated as a consequence of a syllogism that begins with the known fact that a given plot had been seen in the tests with some frequency and goes on to use the stated premises about subcultural values, resulting family patterns, and the nature of the TAT as a test of direct projection. The usual concepts of psychodynamics are, of course, the framework that was always present, though seldom explicitly invoked.

TESTING THE HYPOTHESES

Each null hypothesis ought to be stated, to be technically correct, in the form: "That this story property is related to public or private school background only by chance." If we reject this hypothesis at a decent confidence level, we imply the presence of some relation between the projective test stories and social background and that this relation runs in the predicted direction. We shall use as our statistic Fisher's "p," both because of its exactness (Fisher, 1941) and because we hope for zero cells, which would prevent the use of chi square (Edwards, 1950; Lewis & Burke, 1949). It is also true that the predictive task was like that measured by "p." The marginal frequencies (number private and public, number of tests containing and not containing the plot) were already known when the prediction was made.

It happens that our 201 cases were not all collected the same year. Invitations went to two

Table 3 *Number of tests in which a father is "introduced" into story 1*

	R	U	Total
Father introduced	18	7	25
No father introduced	72	104	176
Total	90	111	201

Note.— $p < .01$

batches of freshmen two years apart. We may compute "p" separately for Sample A and Sample B to obtain some clue about the reliability of our hypotheses.

For Hypothesis 1, out of 25 records containing introduced fathers, 18 were from private school boys and seven from public (see Table 3). If we compute "p" separately for the two samples, both are in the expected direction and reach creditable significances (.04 and .08), but the numbers in the most important cells are small. Such breakdowns

Table 4 *Validity of the hypotheses*

Hypothesis	U:R	p^*
1. Father "introduced"	7:18	.01
2. Parent dominates	60:32	.05
3. Exemplar present	19:25	.05
4. Exemplar held up by mother	12:3	.05
5. Exemplar rejected; work rejected	5:13	.01
6. Exemplar causes inferiority	5:12	.05
7. No work in stories	2:8	.05
8. Work for n Sentience	3:11	.06
9. Work for n Autonomy	11:3	.06
10. Work for glory, money, or ideal	31:5	.05
11. Work is sissy	7:0	.01
12. College for n Achievement	10:1	.01
13. Unable to "hurt" mother	28:14	.08
14. Token Work theme	21:7	.05
15. *Way of All Flesh* theme	12:2	.01
N	111:90	

*Fisher's exact value of p.

have been made for all fifteen hypotheses. In no case does the predicted direction reverse between samples: most single samples are significant at the .15 level. The trends reported here have, therefore, proven reasonably reliable between our samples.

The empirical tests of the 15 hypotheses are summarized in Table 4. All are confirmed and for all but three the confirmation reaches a customary level of confidence and these three approach it. Since only one other hypothesis was tested, the very consistency of the items suggests greater validity than is implied by the small numbers involved in any of them. The abandoned hypothesis, that Future-oriented boys from public schools would tell more stories in which the hero had already graduated, turned out to be valid but correlated with Hypothesis 12, so that both could not be independently tested. All 15 hypotheses included in Table 4 are independent of each other. The statements about the role of exemplars in stories (Hypotheses 4, 5, and 6) obviously depend on the presence of an exemplar (Hypothesis 3), but they can be established as quite valid ($p \sim .08$) when only stories containing exemplars are used. The "work-is-sissy" stories (Hypothesis 11) all occurred within the plots that contained dominant parents (Hypothesis 2). If we pull out the seven "sissy" stories, however, the dominance hypothesis still stands. The remaining hypotheses do not correlate with each other.

DISCUSSION

The most important thing to say about these findings is that they are based on small numbers. In spite of the consistency and the satisfactory levels of confidence, one is less than sure that the results could be reproduced on a third sample.

If the empirical results are valid, what theoretical importance have they? Perhaps the broadest claim that can be made is the one stated in the opening paragraph. More specifically, one could claim that these facts in some small way buttress the theories of the anthropologists about American culture, especially the excellent formulation given by Florence Kluckhohn. As a concrete addition to descriptive science, there may be some interest in the way these data depict the upper-class personality.

How are the findings to be systematized? One way would be to assume that TAT stories merely reflect the narrator's premises about life. It would then be no more than a semantic statement to relate "subcultural values" to "individual attitudes." Little more would have been accomplished than to reaffirm the definition that values are attitudes shared by groups. One fact suggests such an interpretation: not all of the TAT material could be used. The observation was simply that, of the themes occurring often, some could be predicted to occur with different frequencies in the two subcultures. No basis could be found for making predictions about many themes. Since we have long known that parts of the TAT material are "dynamically superficial," we could infer that it was only these superficial themes that we were able to predict.

Is there any evidence that the two subcultures differ in psychodynamic variables that cannot be reduced to mere premises or values? That may be an operationally meaningless question. Wishes, for example, are in the last analysis based upon values. The same may be said of inner conflicts. Even implied differences in "infantile complexes," e.g., Oedipal themes, may be reduced to statements about "the more enduring assumptions" that undergird a man's expectations about life. Perhaps differences in "choice of defense" or "choice of symptom" would have been less reducible, but such

differences were not observed in these data. Other observers might well seek out such very "deep" differences, however.

CONCLUSIONS

The conclusions to be drawn are conservative. It has been shown, at least for two samples of Harvard classes, that differences in the frequency of certain Thematic Apperception Test responses given by members of the American core culture and members of an upper-class alternative subculture could be predicted. A formulation of the value profiles of these two groups by Florence Kluckhohn turned out to be an excellent predictive device. Evidently, conclusions of an anthropologist could be matched to conclusions of a psychologist, despite the different operations employed in these two disciplines.

An implication of the findings is that there can be detected a psychologically distinct "upper-class personality." What distribution this personality type may have remains unclear. Nor is it demonstrable that this finding is semantically distinct from the more obvious statement that there is a distinct upper-class value system. Nonetheless, it is interesting to be able to extend the description of American social class personalities and values from the well-known comparisons between middle and lower classes to include a contrast between middle and upper classes.

A functional analysis of authority[1]

J. STACY ADAMS and A. KIMBALL ROMNEY

An important segment of social interaction that requires systematic analysis is the behavioral control of one person over another: in other words, authority. The purpose of this paper is to analyze this type of interaction for the dyad, showing of what variables it is a function.

Authority, as defined below, is seen as a special case of verbal behavior as analyzed by

Skinner (1957), and is consonant with his definition of the "mand." Thus, the analysis of authority will make fundamental use of the

From *Psychological Review*, 1959, **66**, 234-251.

1 This paper was written at the Interdisciplinary Program in the Behavioral Sciences at the University of New Mexico, Summer, 1958, sponsored by the Behavioral Sciences Division, Air Force Office of Scientific Research, under Contract AF 49 (638)-33. We gratefully acknowledge their support.

concept of the reciprocal reinforcement of behavior. The general aim is to carry through an analysis of the dyadic situation, and simple extensions of it, that specifies the conditions that are relevant to the occurrence of "authority behavior" and the variables of which such behavior is a function.

We begin with a definition of authority. A basic paradigm of an authority sequence will then be given and the variables of which such an authority sequence is a function will be discussed in detail. Finally, functional relationships between authority sequences will be analyzed.

DEFINITION OF AUTHORITY

We define authority as follows: Person A has authority over Person B, in a given situation, when a response of A, under the control of deprivation or aversive stimulation and specifying its own reinforcement, is reinforced by B.

This definition implies that authority is a social relation under the dual or reciprocal control of both A and B. It is social in the sense that it requires behavior on the part of both A and B and that the behavior of A constitutes a stimulus for B and vice versa. For the relation to be maintained, B's behavior must be reinforcing for A and A's behavior must be reinforcing for B. As will be discussed later, the controlling relation of A over B may be enduring or temporary, and it may extend over a large or small range of B's responses.

The relation of authority is asymmetrical in that A's initial response (such as a command, request, suggestion, etc.) specifies its own reinforcement, whereas B's does not. The reinforcement is provided by B's response, if the response reduces the state of deprivation or withdraws aversive stimuli for A. For the maintenance of the relationship B's response must be likewise reinforced by A, but the reinforcement is not specified as in the case of A.

The phrase, "in a given situation," indicates that the authority relation is not assumed to be a general one between individuals regardless of time and place. Authority is learned in specific situations, although it may later be transferred to other situations by such processes as stimulus induction. The phrase also implies the reversi-

bility of the relation from one situation to another. This reversibility may violate the usual definition of and feeling for "authority." For example, one readily accepts the notion of a father's authority over his son, while one would balk at a statement of a child's "authority" over his father. Yet, precisely the same functional relationships may hold in both cases, as we shall demonstrate. It is, therefore, both rigorous and useful to speak of a person's having "authority" over another whenever the same relationships are found, even though this practice might do violence to everyday usage.

The clause, "under the control of deprivation or aversive stimulation," indicates that it is not sufficient to know only the topography of the response of A, but that it is also necessary to specify the controlling variables of the response of A. For example, if A says, "Water, please," in the presence of B, we must know whether the controlling variable of that response is water deprivation or some other deprivation, or whether it is aversive stimulation.

When it is said that the response of A specifies its own reinforcement, we assume that there is "communication" between A and B. Not only does the presence of B, in part, set the occasion for the response of A, but the reinforcement of A's response is contingent upon a response by B. Thus authority behavior is necessarily verbal behavior as defined by Skinner (1957), i.e., behavior the reinforcement of which is contingent upon stimulation of and response by another individual. The definitions of all other terms used in the analysis closely follow the behavioral, empirical definitions given by Verplanck (1957).

BASIC PARADIGM OF AN AUTHORITY SEQUENCE

The central idea in authority relations is that of the reciprocal control and reinforcement of behavior of two persons. Basically, the paradigm is that a response of one person, A, is reinforced by another person, B, and that, in turn, the reinforcing response of B is, itself, reinforced by A. Such an interaction will be called an *authority sequence*. An example is the situation in which Person A asks B for water and B complies by giving A water. Figure 1 gives an illustration of the process. The figure is divided into two parts, the top half representing stimuli and responses directly related to Person A, while the lower half pertains to Person B. The interaction between A and B begins at the far left of the figure with A in a state of deprivation and in the presence of a discriminative stimulus, S_d and S_B^D. These stimuli set the occasion for the response R_{A1}, "Give me water." S_d is the stimulus, presumably physiological in the example, that results from water deprivation. S_B^D is the discriminative stimulus resulting from B's presence in A's environment. S_B^D is a discriminative stimulus with respect to R_{A1} in this illustration by virtue of previous conditioning. The response, "Give me water," would not occur unless A were thirsty; nor would it occur unless someone were present to give A water. In some sense, R_{A1} is "appropriate" only in the presence of S_d and S_B^D, and these stimuli may therefore be viewed as "setting the occasion for" and as having control over R_{A1}. As will be seen, this control is not exclusive, however, for it is the reinforcement of R_{A1} in the presence of the two stimuli that is crucial for the demonstration of authority.

Once the verbal command, "Give me water," has been emitted, it is a stimulus to B. Specifically, it is a discriminative stimulus, S_{A1}^D, in that it sets the occasion for a response by B that is later reinforced. The major characteristic of R_{A1} is that it specifies how B can reinforce it. B is in fact "told" that the response, "Give me water," will be reinforced by giving water

to A. When B gives water to A, his response, R_{B1}, constitutes the reinforcement, S_{B1}^R of response R_{A1}. In addition, R_{B1} is also a discriminative stimulus, S_{B1}^D, that sets the occasion for a further response by A. The response in this example is, "Thank you," R_{A2}. In turn, R_{A2}, a generalized reinforcer, constitutes a reinforcement of R_{B1}. Although the reciprocal reinforcement of responses on that part of A and B is terminated arbitrarily in the present example, R_{A2} itself would need to be reinforced by a further response of B, perhaps the verbal response, "You're welcome," or a nod or smile. As the dots to the far right of Fig. 1 suggest, the sequence is theoretically infinite, though in practice it is finite.

The use of only one discriminative stimulus (S_B^D) is greatly simplifying a situation encountered in "real life." The essence of the model is in no way affected by this simplification, however. Quite complex stimuli could be made discriminative – i.e., given "sign" status – in an experimental situation, and an authority sequence from "real life" could be replicated.

In the illustrative sequence of behavior presented, it is important to note that if the sequence is interrupted at any point, predictable consequences follow. Assume, for example, that B does not give water to A, after A has said, "Give me water." This might be because R_{A1} did not result in a discriminate stimulus for B, i.e., it had no "meaning" for B because of lack of previous learning. Or it may be that R_{A1} resulted in a discriminative stimulus that

Fig. 1   *Authority sequence with initial response under control of deprivation.*

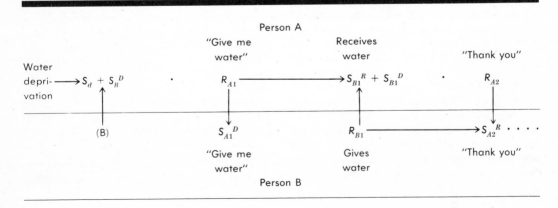

Fig. 2 *Authority sequence with initial response under control of aversive stimulation.*

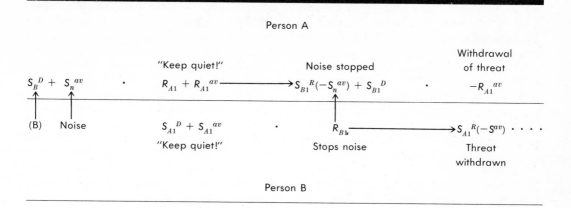

Person A

$S_B^D + S_n^{av}$ ·   "Keep quiet!"

$R_{A1} + R_{A1}^{av}$ ⟶ Noise stopped $S_{B1}^R(-S_n^{av}) + S_{B1}^D$ ·   Withdrawal of threat $-R_{A1}^{av}$

(B)   Noise $S_{A1}^D + S_{A1}^{av}$ · R_{B1} ⟶ $S_{A1}^R(-S^{av})$ · · · ·

"Keep quiet!"   Stops noise   Threat withdrawn

Person B

set the occasion for a response other than giving water, perhaps telling A to get his own
water. Whatever the reason for not giving
water to A, the consequence would be for R_{A1}
to undergo some extinction. Similarly, if the
sequence were interrupted by A's not emitting
R_{A2}, B's response, R_{B1}, giving water, would
undergo some extinction, with the result that
the probability of R_{A1}'s being reinforced would
be decreased. As before, the probability of A's
emitting R_{A1} would then be smaller. In both
instances where the sequence is interrupted,
it is evident that A's authority over B is decreased, at least in this particular situation. It
is interesting to note that in the first instance
the decrease in A's authority is primarily "because of a failure attributable to B. In the second instance, however, A's authority is affected
"because" of his failure to reinforce B's response, R_{B1}. The use of "because" here is very
loose, of course; no attribution of causality to
A and B as persons is intended. Their responses are completely determined, except
on their very first occurrence, by their previous
reinforcement history and by antecedent stimulus conditions.

In Fig. 1, A's initial response was partly
under the control of deprivation. Instead it
could have been under the partial control of
aversive stimulation. For example, B might
have been making some disturbing noise and
this aversive stimulus might have set the occasion for the response, "Keep quiet!" It is also

true that B's response, R_{B1}, need not necessarily
be reinforced by the presentation of a positive
reinforcing stimulus. It could have been reinforced by the withdrawal of an aversive stimulus or conditioned aversive stimulus. Figure 2
shows how aversive stimuli might exercise control in an authority interaction.

An aversive noise stimulus, S_n^{av}, and a discriminative stimulus, S_B^D, set the occasion for
the responses R_{A1} and R_{A1}^{av}, constituted by the
verbal response, "Keep quiet!" and an implied
threat carried by the accentuation and intona-
tion of the verbal response. Thus B is presented
with a discriminative verbal stimulus, S_{A1}^D, and
a conditioned aversive stimulus, S_{A1}^{av}. These
stimuli set the occasion for stopping the noise,
indicated in the figure as R_{B1}. This response
consists of the withdrawal of the aversive noise
stimulus, S_n^{av}, and constitutes a negative reinforcing stimulus for A, as well as a discriminative stimulus, S_{B1}^D, setting the occasion for a
further response. The response, in this example, is the withdrawal of implicit threat and
is labelled, $-R_{A1}^{av}$. This, in turn, is an appropriate negative reinforcing stimulus for B's
response, R_{B1}. As in the previous example, the
sequence of behavior is stopped at this point.
Thus, we have here an interesting case of
escape conditioning, with an implied threat as
a conditioned aversive stimulus, as well as one
of avoidance conditioning with respect to the
negative reinforcing stimulus inferred from the
threat.

In a manner analogous to that presented earlier, interruption of the behavioral sequence has implications for the authority A has over B. If B, for example, does not stop making noise (perhaps because of the inadequate control of S_{A1}^D and S_{A1}^{av}), A's response, "Keep quiet!" will undergo some extinction and A's authority over B will be weakened under the particular circumstances described. However, B's lack of compliance may of itself constitute additional aversive stimulation for A and thus set the occasion for a new response, perhaps, "If you don't stop that noise, you'll suffer the consequences," which may generate enough additional aversive stimulation for B to make him stop the noise. If this occurred, A would maintain his authority over B, though at some additional expense. A could, of course, alternatively "leave the field," in which case there would be no question of authority over B.

The sequence in Fig. 2 would also be interrupted if A did not withdraw aversive stimulation after B had complied with his command. The consequence would be that R_{B1} would have less likelihood of occurring in the future, a fact which would tend to reduce the probability of occurrence of R_{A1} and R_{A1}^{av} and, therefore, would tend to reduce A's authority over B in this illustrative situation. As was pointed out before, the resulting loss of control of A over B might set the occasion for new responses by A.

In both the illustrations given thus far, certain assumptions have been made which need to be made explicit before the implications of the paradigm are further explored. Some of the assumptions concern the discriminative status of stimuli. For example, it is assumed in Fig. 1 that B is a discriminative stimulus (S_B^D) setting the occasion for the response, "Give me water." But by definition a discriminative stimulus is one in the presence of which a response is reinforced and in the absence of which it is unreinforced. Since A's response, R_{A1}, is not reinforced until some time later, B cannot initially be a discriminative stimulus in the sense of setting the occasion for R_{A1}. What is assumed, then, is some previous learning, i.e., some previous temporal contiguity of response (R_{A1}) and reinforcing stimulus (S_{B1}^R) in the presence of B. The assumption is, however, only one of convenience, and what has been said applies to the free operant situation as well. If A had merely emitted spontaneously the response, "Give me water," in the presence of B (and in the context of deprivation), and if B had responded appropriately to reinforce A's response, the behavioral consequences would have been the same as previously discussed. The only difference is that B would have been a mere stimulus without discriminative properties. However, on *subsequent* occasions B would have discriminative characteristics, assuming further that A's responses had been unreinforced on some occasion when B was absent. The same line of reasoning applies to other stimuli which appear as discriminative stimuli in the figures.

Another assumption is that the reciprocal reinforcement of behavior is a finite sequence. It was stated earlier that the reciprocal reinforcement sequence in the authority relation may be theoretically infinite but that we assumed it was finite in practice. The assumption is difficult to substantiate even though everyday observation suggests that persons in an authority relation do not reinforce each other's responses ad infinitum. There are, of course, cases where reinforcement continues for considerable lengths of time, for example the endless exchange of bows that occurs when a Westerner visits a Japanese home. Nevertheless, the fact is that in our culture the interaction usually stops at approximately the point indicated in Figs. 1 and 2, and that extinction is not a consequence. The reason for this may be that terminating an interaction sequence at a certain point is of itself reinforcing in that it avoids aversive consequences which would be forthcoming were the sequence not terminated. Thus, for example, in our own culture there are conventions about the termination of an interaction sequence beyond which further responding is punished by the use of conditioned aversive stimuli. As an illustration, it is commonly observed that after compliance with a request, anything beyond a "Thank you" and "You're welcome" results in raised eyebrows, a sardonic smile, or a look of impatience, which may be discriminative stimuli for stopping the interaction. When the stimuli for stopping are not known to one of the parties in the interaction (i.e., are not discriminative), responding may continue for some time, as in the bowing example above. In some situations responding beyond a given point may have the aspect of impertinence and have appropriate aversive results. Alternatively, responding beyond a certain point is unreinforced by society, and an agreed-upon sequence of reciprocal reinforcement becomes a discriminative stimulus for stopping to respond further.

CONTROLLING VARIABLES

Thus far it has been shown how an authority relation between two persons can evolve and either be maintained or be destroyed. The external events (independent variables) of which responses (dependent variables) in an authority interaction are a function will now be discussed. This will be done by grouping variables into general classes and discussing instances under class headings. The basic A-B interaction paradigm will be used throughout.

Reinforcing Stimulus Variables

Stimulus events that have the property of increasing the probability of recurrence of a preceding response are fundamental controlling variables. B's giving water to A and A's saying "Thank you" in Fig. 1 are such events in that they increase the probability of A's again asking B for water when he is later water-deprived, and of B's giving A water, respectively, other variables remaining constant. In other words, certain responses such as "Give me water" have consequences which empirically increase their probability of recurrence and thus in part determine the authority A has over B.

The importance of reinforcing stimuli is more pervasive than has been suggested above, however. The discriminative character of other stimuli is dependent upon their being paired with reinforcement. Thus, for example, in Fig. 1, B's presence would not constitute a discriminative stimulus for A's demanding water, unless it had been temporally contiguous with the reinforcement of A's response. Nor, in Fig. 2, would A's verbal command "Keep quiet!" be a discriminative stimulus for B's stopping noisiness, unless stopping to make noise had

been reinforced following the occurrence of the stimulus resulting from A's response. It can therefore be seen that a reinforcing contingency is *necessary* before a stimulus can acquire discriminative properties. This is, of course, not a *sufficient* characteristic: It is also required that the absence of a stimulus be associated with nonreinforcement before it can be a discriminative stimulus. For example, with respect to Fig. 1, it would be necessary that A's response, "Give me water," be unreinforced in the absence of B.

The withholding of reinforcing stimuli following a response is the operation resulting in experimental extinction and, as an observable consequence, produces a decreased probability of response. Illustrations of this have been given previously.

The general properties and the importance of reinforcing stimuli having been pointed out, A and B as the agents or mediators of reinforcement must now be considered.

A as a reinforcer. A can act as a direct mediator of reinforcement or as a conditioned reinforcer. As a direct mediator he can both present positive reinforcers (or conditioned reinforcers) and withdraw negative reinforcers (or conditioned negative reinforcers). A father can reinforce his child for obeying a command by giving it candy. The business executive can reinforce his secretary's compliance with an order by withdrawing an implied threat, much as in the example of Fig. 2. In a similar fashion the traffic policeman reinforces stopping at his gestured command by lowering his arm and, hence, removing conditioned negative reinforcers.

It is evident that, as a direct mediator of reinforcement, A can exercise considerable control over B's behavior. But it is also true that, indirectly, he exercises control over his *own* responses, for the probability of recurrence of his own responses is in part a function of the extent to which he is successful in reinforcing B's responses. Other things being equal, then, A is in some sense the master of his own authority over B. This notion is not a new one, but in the present case it has the advantage of being systematically derivable from the basic model.

A further derivation is that A's probability of successfully developing or maintaining an authority relation over B will in part be a function of the amount and variety or range of reinforcers he has available. The person who can mediate reinforcements appropriate to several states of deprivation can exercise more authority than one who can, say, provide only food (e.g., a parent versus a neighbor). The person who has access to a large range of aversive stimuli can have more authority than one who has not (e.g., a company commander versus a corporal). From a similar consideration it also follows that the greater the amount and range of reinforcers available to A, the greater the range of B's responses he can control, other variables remaining constant. Thus a parent can have wider authority than an older sister who can mete out limited punishment only and who has no money for material rewards.

As a conditioned reinforcer, either positive or negative, A may also exercise control over B's behavior, as well as indirectly over his own. Before he can act as a conditioned reinforcer, however, it is necessary that he have acted on previous occasions as a direct mediator of reinforcement, or, at least, that he be similar to someone who acted as a reinforcer. The important thing to consider is that the mere presence of A can reinforce some of B's responses, no direct reinforcement being given. For example, using the illustration of Fig. 1, it is possible for A to omit saying, "Thank you," and for B's response to remain at considerable strength, provided stimulus attributes of A have become conditioned or generalized reinforcers by virtue of A's having previously, and frequently, reinforced B's responses. However, in order for the attributes of A to remain effective conditioned reinforcers (and discriminative stimuli as well), it is necessary that on occasion A mediate direct reinforcement; otherwise B's operant will undergo extinction. The same applies to A qua A as a negative conditioned reinforcer.

B as a reinforcer. The distinguishing characteristic of B as a reinforcer is that his reinforcing response has no, or only a few, degrees of freedom, as contrasted with A as a reinforcer. His reinforcing response is specified by A, by definition. To be sure, the discrete topography of his response may vary, but its net effect on A is specified. Thus, for example, B may get and

bring water to A in a variety of ways, but the giving of water is the essential property of the response that will reinforce A's request and, therefore, establish or maintain the authority relation.

In a manner similar to A, B may also act as a conditioned reinforcer or negative conditioned reinforcer, in that the authority relation between the two will be maintained or strengthened. This presumes, of course, that B, or someone similar to B, will have appropriately reinforced A's behavior in the past under similar circumstances.

Generalization of A and B as conditioned reinforcers. It has been pointed out that A and B may exercise control over each other's behavior, and thus maintain or strengthen an authority relation, in their capacities as conditioned reinforcers. It is also true that conditioned reinforcement may be effected by individuals other than A and B who have physical properties similar to A and B. Thus, an officer never before encountered may act as a conditioned reinforcer of an enlisted man's compliance with an order, by virtue of the fact that he has properties similar to those of other officers who have reinforced the same response. The dimensions of similarity in this example might be the uniform and emblems of office; or the relevant dimension might be physical characteristics of verbal operants, e.g., "'ten shun!" Similarly, the authority of policemen is partially maintained, even though never before seen personally, through stimulus induction. How often has one slowed down at the sight of an unknown policeman whose back was turned?

Deprivation and Aversive Stimulus Variables Affecting A

As stated in the definition of authority, A's initial response (order, command, request, demand, etc.) is partially under the control of deprivation or aversive stimulation, other control being exercised by discriminative stimuli (e.g., the presence of a B). This results from the fact that certain responses of the human organism are typically followed by specific consequences under certain conditions agreed upon by the social community, and that when this occurs the probability of occurrence of these responses will be a function of the deprivation of aversive stimulation paired with the reinforcing consequences. Thus the response, "Give me water," has a greater probability of occurrence under water deprivation than under satiation because other organisms are more likely to have provided water when A emitted this response and was thirsty. It should be noted that deprivation and aversive stimulation do not *necessarily* exercise control over the response. The control results from the fact that other organisms are predisposed by "societal consensus," so to speak, to respond in certain characteristic ways. This predisposition of other organisms is analogous to certain automatic consequences of the nonanimal environment. For example, picking and eating an apple is automatically reinforcing when the organism is food-deprived, though not if he is satiated. Thus, food deprivation would come to control picking and eating an apple. A similar line of reasoning applies to aversive stimulation, though in this case reinforcement consists in the withdrawal of an aversive stimulus.

The relations holding between deprivation (or aversive stimulation), response topography of A, and reinforcing response by B are stated in idealized terms. This is especially true with regard to A's response topography "specifying" its reinforcement. It is conceivable, for example, that the response, "Give me water," specified not a state of water deprivation which could be reinforced by water but rather a demand for submissiveness on the part of B, the state of deprivation being for something other than water. In such a case the content of A's response does not clearly specify the appropriate reinforcing stimulus—at least the words used do not clearly convey the state of A's deprivation. However, other aspects of the verbal response than the words may serve as appropriate discriminative stimuli for submissiveness (i.e., sheer compliance). The imperative mood of the response, for example, may serve this function. Whether it does this effectively on a particular occasion is, of course, a function of appropriate previous differential reinforcement. To put it somewhat loosely, it is a function of whether B has learned that use of the imperative mood is a "sign" for compliance regardless of the specific content of A's response.

Discriminative Stimulus Variables

In the discussion of Figs. 1 and 2 the role of discriminative stimuli was made explicit. We wish to expand the discussion at this point and focus specifically on the discriminative stimuli that control A's initial response. The discriminative stimulus characteristics of responses by A and B will be omitted, as they are evident.

Two general groups of discriminative stimulus variables controlling A's initial response may be considered, stimulus characteristics of B and situational stimuli, excluding B. A general characteristic of B that may serve as a discriminative stimulus is his being an organism with the potentiality of responding. Without another person's being present, a response by A cannot be reinforced, and A cannot exercise any authority. There are, however, other relevant aspects of B. One is B as a particular individual, i.e., the stimulus characteristics of a B who has previously reinforced A's response, as opposed to a B who has not. A second is B as the incumbent in a particular role, as an office boy or corporal, for example. In this instance characteristics of B serve as discriminative stimuli for a comparatively narrow range of responses by A. In other instances characteristics of B may set the occasion for one class of responses only; for example, the elevator boy is a discriminative stimulus for the response, "Take me to the sixth," only. Thus we may think of B as having discriminative stimulus characteristics that excercise control over A's responses with different degrees of specificity. The specificity of control exercised is a function of the extent of differential reinforcement carried out in the presence of particular characteristics.

The second group of discriminative stimulus variables are situational variables. They include virtually all relevant stimuli not directly pertaining to B. Some situational variables are part of the purely physical environment. Thus, the request, "Take me to the sixth," has a low probability of being reinforced in the absence of an elevator. Similarly, "Give me water," will usually have a low probability of occurring

Fig. 3 *Response-related authority sequences.*

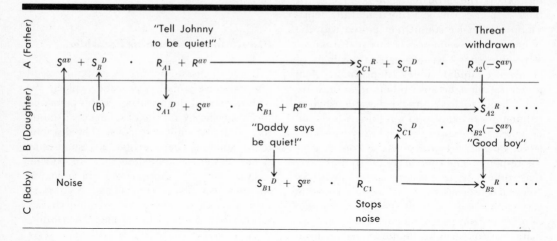

without a source of water in the immediate environment. However, in an instance of this sort, deprivation may become so severe that it exercises almost exclusive control. The "Water, water!" of the wounded soldier on the deserted battlefield is an example. Other situational variables are of a more "social" character in that the presence of other persons, or of persons having particular types of interaction, has a controlling discriminative stimulus function. Certain kinds of commands or requests are not issued to one's wife at home in the context of a cocktail party (and would go unreinforced, if issued), though they are issued and reinforced when just family members are present. Orders may be successfully given to an employee at the office, though not at the country club.

Whether discriminative stimulus control is exercised by B proper or by situational variables, it will be achieved only after differential reinforcement. The controlling stimulus variables may, of course, be of great complexity and require considerable training. For example, an authority response, R_{A1}, will be reinforced only if Stimuli I, J, . . . , or N are present, *and* if Stimuli B and C are present, *and* if Stimulus R is absent. The situation is analogous to those encountered in concept formation studies (e.g., Bruner, Goodnow, & Austin, 1956). In the present instance a response is reinforced only in the presence of particular stimuli, whereas in concept formation studies a response is said to be "correct" in the presence of some stimulus combinations and "incorrect" in the presence of other combinations.

Since complex stimulus control of this type requires considerable training with differential reinforcement, it follows that in early stages of training control will be imperfect. Some variables, in the absence of others which are necessary for reinforcement, will exercise some control over a response, even though it will not be reinforced. It is also possible that during the course of differential training "irrelevant" variables would exercise some control over an authority response. This inappropriate control of stimuli results when a response is reinforced in the presence of both appropriate discriminative stimuli and irrelevant other stimuli. These stimuli then acquire some discriminative stimulus capacity. Their control is eventually weakened and abolished during further differential training.

THE FUNCTIONAL INTERRELATION OF AUTHORITY SEQUENCES

The classes of variables of which authority is a function have been specified for a two-person situation. In large groups new problems arise with respect to the arrangement of authority sequences within the group. The problems associated with relating authority sequences arise from the basic characteristics of authority and the presence of more than two persons in the total situation. This section is addressed to these problems and consists of an analysis of the ways in which authority sequences are patterned within the limitations imposed by the assumptions of authority as outlined in the preceding section.

In order for two authority sequences to be functionally related, one of the following conditions must be met: (a) authority sequence, K, or some part of it, controls authority sequence, L, or some part of it; (b) all or some part of authority sequences, K and L, are under the control of a common (or similar) variable (variables); and (c) two simultaneous initial responses are made that specify incompatible reinforcement responses by B.

For purposes of exposition, these will be regarded as distinct cases of authority sequence interrelationships and will be discussed separately.

Case I:
One Sequence Exercises Functional Control Over Another

There are a number of ways in which an authority sequence exercises control over a succeeding sequence, but it is important to note that an all-or-none relationship of control is not implied. The whole or any part of an authority sequence may control a succeeding sequence. This control may be either partial or complete and affect all or part of the succeeding sequence. Discussion will be limited to two basic ways in which two sequences may be functionally related.

Situation where a response in Sequence K controls a response in Sequence L. Authority sequences are frequently related by virtue of the fact that a response in the first sequence controls a response in the second. Generally speaking, with exceptions to be noted, the response by B in the first sequence is the initial response in the second sequence. For example, when a father orders his daughter to tell baby to be quiet, the response of daughter saying "quiet" to baby is B's response in the sequence father-daughter,

and also the initial response in the sequence involving daughter-baby. Figure 3 gives an illustration of how the process might operate.

A's response, "Tell Johnny to be quiet," is under the control of aversive stimuli from noise being made by the baby and of B as a discriminative stimulus. B's response of going and telling baby, "Daddy says, 'be quiet,'" is under the control of the stimuli of A's initial response, i.e., of a discriminative stimulus ($S_{A1}{}^D$) and of a conditioned aversive stimulus (S^{av}) consisting of an implied threat of punishment for noncompliance. B's response, R_{B1}, unlike responses in the dyadic situation, does not directly reinforce A's initial response, R_{A1}. Rather, it constitutes stimuli for C to stop making noise, R_{C1}. It is C's response, R_{C1}, that reinforces the original response of A, i.e., R_{A1}. This in turn sets the occasion for A to make a response that reinforces B's response; i.e., $R_{A2}(-S^{av})$ constitutes reinforcement for R_{B1}. The form of this response might be the removal of the implied threat. In order for the behavior to be maintained, C's response, R_{C1}, must also be reinforced. In the figure this response is a discriminative stimulus for B, who makes a response something like "Good boy," R_{B2}, which reinforces the response of stopping noise, R_{C1}, by removing an aversive stimulus.

Functionally related series of this general sort take many different forms. For example, in Fig. 3, it would be possible for the second response of the father, $R_{A2}(-S^{av})$, to take the form "Thank you, children" and constitute reinforcement for not only the response of the daughter, R_{B1}, but also for the response of the baby, R_{C1}. In such an event it would be unnecessary for the daughter to reinforce the baby. Another very common situation in command chains arises when, for example, the president of a company asks the vice-president for a report, and the vice-president asks a department head for the report. In this case the department head gives the report to the vice-president, who in turn gives it to the president. Here the action of the department head, C, does not directly reinforce any response by the president, but rather of the vice-president.

An inherent characteristic of situations involving a chain of command is that there is some delay in the reinforcement of A's initial response. This delay in reinforcement has implications for the readiness with which such responses are conditioned. Generally, conditioning of the response is a decreasing function of the delay between response and reinforcement. In practical situations there are techniques available to "help A across" such a time lag by presenting conditioned reinforcers during the delay period. For example, B can supply comments such as, "The report will be ready at three," "Yes, sir," "Right away, sir," "I'll attend to it immediately," and so on. Periodic "progress reports," frequent personal communications, and verbal reassurances are probably manifestations of the utility of supplying some supplementary conditioned reinforcement to A where the situation involves a long delay in reinforcement. This is in accord with the findings of Perin (1943a, 1943b) and Grice (1948) on the effects of removing conditioned reinforcers upon the delay of reinforcement gradient.

Situation where a response in Sequence K is under control of Sequence L. In this situation the whole of one sequence constitutes part of the situation for a second sequence. When the second sequence can be shown to be, at least in part, under the control of the first sequence, then the two sequences are functionally related. Consideration is limited here to the situation in which no individuals who are in the first sequence are also in the second.

An authority sequence frequently controls a response in another sequence either through "imitative" mechanisms—that is to say, by serving as a discriminative stimulus—or by increasing deprivation or aversive stimulation. Consider, for example, a group of mothers and children, where the children are playing in the mud. The first mother tells her child to stop playing in the mud. The child complies and is rewarded. This authority sequence may constitute a conditioned aversive stimulus for the second mother. The aversive stimulus may be social disapproval of not following the first mother's "example." The first sequence may also be a discriminative stimulus setting the occasion for the second mother's telling her child to stop playing in the mud. If the child complies, the aversive disapproval (perhaps only implied) of the first mother is withdrawn, and the second mother's behavior is reinforced.

Case II:
A Common Variable Exercises Functional Control over Two or More Sequences

Probably the simplest manner in which authority sequences are functionally related is by sharing a common controlling variable. Sequences interrelated in this way are found most commonly in large groupings of face-to-face interactions where more complex ways of

Fig. 4 *One-to-many authority sequences.*

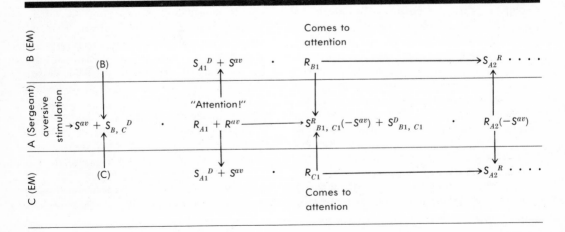

Fig. 5 *Many-to-one authority sequences.*

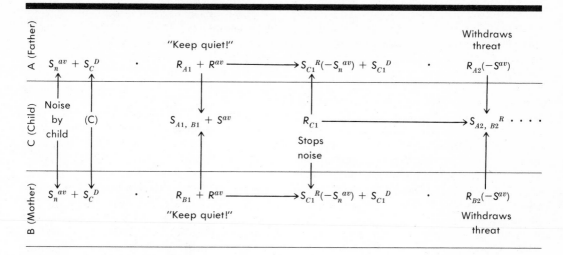

arranging authority sequences becomes unwieldy. Two types may be considered: (*a*) where an initial response by A specifies the behavior of several people, and (*b*) where two or more initial responses specify a single reinforcing response on the part of one person.

Situation where an initial response specifies behavior of several individuals. The situation in which one individual, A, directs a response to a large number of individuals, B, C, ... , N, is a common one. The authority sequences in such an event are all under the control of the variables affecting the initial response of A. For example, when a drill sergeant calls a company of soldiers to attention we have a situation where the response, "Attention!" specifies as its reinforcement the behavior of several individuals. Each pair formed by the sergeant and an individual soldier may be thought of as an authority sequence, assuming, of course, that they all come to attention and are reinforced by some behavior of the sergeant. These authority sequences are functionally related by the fact that they are all under the control of whatever variables determine the response of the sergeant, namely, calling the company to attention. The situation is illustrated in abbreviated form in Fig. 4. An interesting implication of this type of authority situation is that the authority response of A is likely to remain in

considerable strength and to be very resistant to extinction by virtue of the fact that the more other persons his response is addressed to, the more likelihood there is for some compliance and, hence, the more likely he is to get some reinforcement. In some limiting cases, of course, it is possible that the compliance of *all* Bs is the sole effective reinforcement for A. In such cases, the Bs can be treated as a single entity. It could be predicted, then, that certain military men, certain types of supervisors and foremen, teachers, housewives with large families, etc., would on the average have greater strength of authority responses in these situations than others, because there is a greater probability of their being reinforced. These are in fact persons who are often labeled "bossy."

Situations where two or more initial responses specify a single reinforcing response. Under certain circumstances to be specified below, two or more individuals may simultaneously initiate an authority sequence (give a command, request, suggest, etc.) with a third party, in which both of their responses specify the same behavior on the part of the third party as reinforcement. The example of a father and mother both saying, "Keep quiet" to their noisy child at the same time is diagramed in Fig. 5.

The sequences are here functionally related

by the fact that R_{C1} is part of both sequences. Since every response in a sequence exercises some control over the sequence, these sequences are under the control of the common variables related to the common response. The sequences are also related by the fact that the aversive stimulation in partial control of R_{A1} and R_{B1} is from the same source.

This type of relation between authority sequences is subject to more restrictions than any of those previously discussed. The most important restriction is that the two initial responses by A and B must specify a response on the part of C that will reinforce both initial responses. A and B, of course, need not specify an identical response, though in practice this may often be the case. It is only necessary that the responses specified be equivalent in their effects. Figure 5 illustrates a common way in which this arises, namely, A and B are under the control of a common aversive stimulus, the noise of a child. Under other circumstances A and B could be under the control of a common deprivation. Other more complex and subtle relations are not uncommon. For example, an audience in the presence of a good performer may be under the control of common stimuli so that they all applaud and shout "Bis!" and the performer complies with an encore. Here the exact specification of the controlling variables for the audience is somewhat difficult, and there may be a variety of variables operating on different members of the audience.

Other things being equal, C is under more aversive stimulation than in the simple authority sequence by virtue of the fact that he is under multiple aversive stimulation, as shown in Fig. 5 by the two implied threats symbolized by $S_{A1}{}^{av}$ and $S_{B1}{}^{av}$. Making the assumption that degree of control and amount of aversive stimulation (or of deprivation), up to a limit, are positively correlated, it follows that compliance will be an increasing function of aversive stimulation (or of deprivation).

Another feature to note in these types of relationships between sequences is that A and B may be viewed as a "coalition" under the control of common deprivation or aversive stimulation. When they do not act as a coalition, i.e., when they are not under common deprivation or aversive stimulation so that the initial

responses specify incompatible responses on the part of C, the total relation becomes impossible to complete. That is to say, contradictory behavior may be required of C such that it is impossible for him to reinforce the responses of A and B simultaneously. We call such a situation one of *authority conflict.*

Case III:
Authority Conflict

Two or more authority sequences may be functionally related in that one sequence is associated with the interruption of another or that the sequences mutually preclude the completion of each other. Specifically, sequences interfere with terminal reinforcements. In such cases there exists *authority conflict.*

Figure 6 provides an illustration. The situation is that of two bosses descending simultaneously upon their joint secretary late in the day with rush jobs. The typing jobs are of such a nature that only one can be completed. The two bosses, A and C, issue requests, R_{A1} and R_{C1}, with implied threats for noncompliance. These, let us assume, constitute discriminative stimuli plus aversive stimulation for the secretary, B. (The consequences to be discussed do not require this assumption, but it is made for the sake of reality.) Since B can comply with only one of the requests, there exist for her two incompatible (conflicting) response tendencies. These response possibilities exist for her: (a) she can comply with A's request and thus reinforce his response; (b) she can comply with C's request and thus reinforce his response; or (c) she can comply with neither request and therefore reinforce neither A's nor C's response. The consequences of the first two possibilities are analogous, while those of the third are different.

If B complies with A's request and therefore reinforces his initial response, A's response will have an increased probability of recurrence in the future under similar circumstances and C's response will tend to undergo extinction. If we now assume further that when C alone — that is, in the absence of A — makes a request of B, she complies and his behavior is reinforced, it follows that A will become a negative discriminative stimulus for C. In sum, if B reinforces C in the absence of A and does not reinforce him in the presence of A, C will "learn" to make his requests in the absence of A. In practice, this may lead to a scheduling of authority responses, as when Boss 1 directs the secretary mornings and Boss 2 directs her afternoons.

The factors which result in B's reinforcing A's behavior in preference to C's are of interest. One factor is that A may have reinforced B more frequently than had C in the past for the same or similar responses, with the result that A's response exercised greater control over B. Another possibility is that A, perhaps because of powers associated with his rank or position, could give B greater reinforcement than could C, frequency of reinforcement by A and C being equal. It might also be that, even though having reinforcing powers equal to those of C, A made greater (and "better") use of generalized reinforcers. His expression of thanks, for example, might generally be more reinforcing (it might be less perfunctory). Another factor may be that A, as opposed to C, has acquired conditioned reinforcing properties under circumstances quite different from the boss-secretary relation. Finally, if we assume a completely free operant situation and no previous learning histories, it could be that B's response to A merely has a higher operant level than the conflicting response to C.

The second case to consider is when B complies with and reinforces neither A's nor C's request. In such an instance it is clear that both A's and C's initial authority responses will undergo extinction. However, it is clearly possible for the secretary's inactivity to set the occasion for new responses on the part of A or C or both which will be reinforced. Thus, A and C might say, "Type A's paper now and C's tomorrow." Furthermore, it is possible that, if A and C, when interacting alone with B, are reinforced in their requests, they will come to make their requests only in the absence of the other. This follows from the operation of differential reinforcement and of the resultant control exercised by a negative discriminative stimulus.

What the antecedents are for nonresponse on the part of B are many and need not be enumerated. Generally, however, the situation is that both A's and C's responses and situational stimuli exercise the same degree of control over B's responses. To use a vector analogy, the vectors representing B's two response tendencies are of equal length and at 180 degrees to each other.

In the discussion of authority conflict, attention has thus far been limited to the consequences of B's responses upon the behavior of A and C. It is evident, however, that the types of conflict envisaged will have effects upon the behavior of B. One effect is that, when B reinforces the behavior of A in preference to C's

Fig. 6 *Authority conflict situation.*

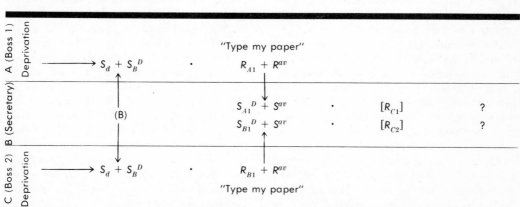

and is in turn reinforced by A, her response to A will have an increased probability of recurrence, whereas any response tendency toward compliance with C's request will be weakened under similar circumstances. When B responds neither to A nor C, whatever response tendencies exited at the time will undergo extinction since they will not be reinforced. In both of these cases it is interesting to note that the conflict of responses on the part of B is self-reducing, in one case because one of the two response tendencies is weakened and in the other because both are weakened. However, the existence of conflict may have other side-effects.

If it is assumed that being in conflict results in aversive stimulation, certain consequences can be predicted. Under this assumption the secretary in the illustration will be subjected to aversive stimulation. Furthermore, this aversive stimulation will be contingent upon her responding or tending to respond to A and C. That is to say, the conflict and consequent aversive stimulation exist solely *because* of her competing responses (of course, phenomenally, B may perceive A and C as being instrumental in her conflict). It follows, then, that A and C, as well as other aspects of the total situation, will become conditioned negative reinforcers and that B will tend to *avoid* them. Making the further assumption that degree of conflict and resulting aversive stimulation are positively correlated, it also follows that the strength of B's avoidance response will increase with increasing degree of conflict. Since degree of conflict will be a function of the strength similarity of B's two incompatible response tendencies, it may be concluded that the more nearly equal the response tendencies, the greater will be the avoidance of A and C.

The preceding analysis of authority conflict has dealt exclusively with the case in which only one of two (or more) incompatible responses can be emitted by B. It can, however, also happen that one response will be emitted first and that a second will subsequently be emitted upon the completion of the first. Thus, the fictional secretary could have typed A's letter first and, upon completion of that job, could have typed C's. In such a case both A's and C's authority responses will be reinforced. However, it is evident that some delay is entailed in the rein-

forcement of C's responses. The consequence of this will be to weaken the effect of the reinforcement, the magnitude of the net effect being inversely proportional to the amount of delay.

SUMMARY

We have suggested the following definition of authority: A person A has authority over B, in a given situation, when a response of A, under the control of deprivation or aversive stimulation and specifying its own reinforcement, is reinforced by B. Authority, so defined, has been analyzed as a function of the following variables:

1. Reinforcing stimulus variables
   (a) A as a reinforcer
   (b) B as a reinforcer
   (c) Generalization of A and B as conditioned reinforcers
2. Deprivation and aversive stimulus variables affecting A
3. Discriminative stimulus variables.

A paradigm of an authority sequence was analyzed in terms of these variables. Series of functionally related sequences were defined as sequences under the control of one another or of common variables. Three classes of functionally related sequences were analyzed:

1. Where one sequence exercises functional control over another
2. Where a common variable exercises functional control over two or more sequences
3. Authority conflict.

The functional analysis of authority that has been presented places primary emphasis upon the reciprocal nature of authority interactions and, by so doing, suggests how authority evolves, is maintained, and may be weakened.

As the analysis suggests, it is actually improper to speak of the locus of authority, except perhaps for "short-hand" purposes. Authority is behavior and is a function of certain operationally defined variables. By adopting this functional approach, it should be possible not only to account for observations that have been made about authority, but to deduce systematically the consequences of manipulating variables in specified ways.

part 4

THE PROGRAMING OF HUMAN LEARNING

One of the liveliest debates in psychology, which holds important implications for education, has to do with so-called teaching machines and the "programed" learning materials that can be used either with the machines or in connection with other methods of presentation. The two articles in this section are representative of the two sides of this debate.

The primary idea of programing is that if a learner is led through the material to be learned in a step-by-step fashion such that he never progresses to a more advanced level until he has mastered the information, skills, and concepts of earlier levels, then his learning will be more efficient and his ultimate achievement will be greater. Perhaps the strongest proponent of programed learning is B. F. Skinner, who regards it as a direct translation into an educational technology of his conception of learning generally.

Opposed to Skinner is Sidney L. Pressey, who, in spite of building some thirty-five years ago what was probably the first teaching machine, finds serious flaws not only in the technology of programing but in the whole complex of theoretical ideas on which it is based. In reading these selections, it will be important to identify with precision the issues joined between these two men and to evaluate the evidence relevant to their very different points of view.

Within the last five years, the literature on programed learning has become large and, for the most part, partisan. These two articles will serve as a good beginning for a critical appraisal of one of the newest and most vigorously argued developments in psychology.

Teaching machines

B. F. SKINNER

There are more people in the world than ever before, and a far greater part of them want an education. The demand cannot be met simply by building more schools and training more teachers. Education must become more efficient. To this end curricula must be revised and simplified, and textbooks and classroom techniques improved. In any other field a demand for increased production would have led at once to the invention of labor-saving capital equipment. Education has reached this stage very late, possibly through a misconception of its task. Thanks to the advent of television, however, the so-called audio-visual aids are being reexamined. Film projectors, television sets, phonographs, and tape recorders are finding their way into American schools and colleges.

Audio-visual aids supplement and may even supplant lectures, demonstrations, and textbooks. In doing so they serve one function of the teacher: they present material to the student and, when successful, make it so clear and interesting that the student learns. There is another function to which they contribute little or nothing. It is best seen in the productive interchange between teacher and student in the small classroom or tutorial situation. Much of that interchange has already been sacrificed in American education in order to teach large numbers of students. There is a real danger that it will be wholly obscured if use of equipment designed simply to *present* material becomes widespread. The student is becoming more and more a mere passive receiver of instruction.

PRESSEY'S TEACHING MACHINES

There is another kind of capital equipment which will encourage the student to take an active role in the instructional process. The possibility was recognized in the 1920's, when Sidney L. Pressey designed several machines for the automatic testing of intelligence and information. . . . In using [one such machine, for example] the student refers to a numbered item in a multiple-choice test. He presses the button corresponding to his first choice of answer. If he is right, the device moves on to the next item; if he is wrong, the error is tallied, and he must continue to make choices until he is right[1]. Such machines, Pressey pointed out (1926), could not only test and score, they could *teach*. When an examination is corrected and returned after a delay of many hours or days, the student's behavior is not appreciably modified. The immediate report supplied by a self-scoring device, however, can have an important instructional effect. Pressey also pointed out that such machines would increase efficiency in another way. Even in a small classroom the teacher usually knows that he is moving too slowly for some students and too fast for others. Those who could go faster are penalized, and those who should go slower are poorly taught and unnecessarily punished by criticism and failure. Machine instruction would permit each student to proceed at his own rate.

The "industrial revolution in education" which Pressey envisioned stubbornly refused to come about. In 1932 he expressed his disappointment (1932). "The problems of invention are relatively simple," he wrote. "With a little money and engineering resource, a great deal could easily be done. The writer has found from bitter experience that one person alone can accomplish relatively little and he is regretfully dropping further work on these problems. But he hopes that enough may have

From *Science*, October 24, 1958, **128**, 969-977.

1 The Navy's "Self-Rater" is a larger version of Pressey's machine. The items are printed on code-punched plastic cards fed by the machine. The time required to answer is taken into account in scoring.

been done to stimulate other workers, that this fascinating field may be developed."

Pressey's machines succumbed in part to cultural inertia; the world of education was not ready for them. But they also had limitations which probably contributed to their failure. Pressey was working against a background of psychological theory which had not come to grips with the learning process. The study of human learning was dominated by the "memory drum" and similar devices originally designed to study forgetting. Rate of learning was observed, but little was done to change it. Why the subject of such an experiment bothered to learn at all was of little interest. "Frequency" and "recency" theories of learning, and principles of "massed and spaced practice," concerned the conditions under which responses were remembered.

Pressey's machines were designed against this theoretical background. As versions of the memory drum, they were primarily testing devices. They were to be used after some amount of learning had already taken place elsewhere. By confirming correct responses and by weakening responses which should not have been acquired, a self-testing machine does, indeed, teach; but it is not designed primarily for that purpose. Nevertheless, Pressey seems to have been the first to emphasize the importance of immediate feedback in education and to propose a system in which each student could move at his own pace. He saw the need for capital equipment in realizing these objectives. Above all he conceived of a machine which (in contrast with the audio-visual aids which were beginning to be developed) permitted the student to play an active role.

ANOTHER KIND OF MACHINE

The learning process is now much better understood. Much of what we know has come from studying the behavior of lower organisms, but the results hold surprisingly well for human subjects. The emphasis in this research has not been on proving or disproving theories but on discovering and controlling the variables of which learning is a function. This practical orientation has paid off, for a surprising degree of control has been achieved. By arranging appropriate "contingencies of reinforcement," specific forms of behavior can be set up and brought under the control of specific classes of stimuli. The resulting behavior can be maintained in strength for long periods of time. A technology based on this work has already been put to use in neurology, pharmacology, nutrition, psychophysics, psychiatry, and elsewhere (Skinner, 1957a).

The analysis is also relevant to education. A student is "taught" in the sense that he is induced to engage in new forms of behavior and in specific forms upon specific occasions. It is not merely a matter of teaching him *what* to do; we are as much concerned with the probability that appropriate behavior will, indeed, appear at the proper time—an issue which would be classed traditionally under motivation. In education the behavior to be shaped and maintained is usually verbal, and it is to be brought under the control of both verbal and nonverbal stimuli. Fortunately, the special problems raised by verbal behavior can be submitted to a similar analysis (Skinner, 1957b).

If our current knowledge of the acquisition and maintenance of verbal behavior is to be applied to education, some sort of teaching machine is needed. Contingencies of reinforcement which change the behavior of lower organisms often cannot be arranged by hand; rather elaborate apparatus is needed. The human organism requires even more subtle instrumentation. An appropriate teaching machine will have several important features. The student must *compose* his response rather than select it from a set of alternatives, as in a multiple-choice self-rater. One reason for this is that we want him to recall rather than recognize—to make a response as well as see that it is right. Another reason is that effective multiple-choice material must contain plausible wrong responses, which are out of place in the delicate process of "shaping" behavior because they strengthen unwanted forms. Although it is much easier to build a machine to score multiple-choice answers than to evaluate a composed response, the technical advantage is outweighed by these and other considerations.

A second requirement of a minimal teaching machine also distinguishes it from earlier versions. In acquiring complex behavior the student must pass through a carefully designed sequence of steps, often of considerable length. Each step must be so small that it can always be taken, yet in taking it the student moves somewhat closer to fully competent behavior. The machine must make sure that these steps are taken in a carefully prescribed order.

Several machines with the required characteristics have been built and tested. Sets of separate presentations or "frames" of visual material are stored on disks, cards, or tapes. One frame is presented at a time, adjacent frames being out of sight. In one type of machine the student composes a response by moving printed figures on letters (Skinner, 1954). His setting is compared by the machine with a coded response. If the two correspond, the machine automatically presents the next frame. If they do not, the response is cleared, and another must be composed. The student cannot proceed to a second step until the first has been taken. A machine of this kind is being tested in teaching spelling, arithmetic, and other subjects in the lower grades.

For more advanced students—from junior high school, say, through college—a machine which senses an arrangement of letters or figures is unnecessarily rigid in specifying form of response. Fortunately, such students may be asked to compare their responses with printed material revealed by the machine. . . . [M]aterial is printed in 30 radial frames on a 12-inch disk. The student inserts the disk and closes the machine. He cannot proceed until the machine has been locked, and, once he has begun, the machine cannot be unlocked. All but a corner of one frame is visible through a window. The student writes his response on a paper strip exposed through a second opening. By lifting a lever on the front of the machine, he moves what he has written under a transparent cover and uncovers the correct response in the remaining corner of the frame. If the two responses correspond, he moves the lever horizontally. This movement punches a hole in the paper opposite his response, recording the fact that he called it correct, and alters the machine so that the frame will not appear again when the student works around the disk a second time. Whether the response was correct or not, a second frame appears when the lever is returned to its starting position. The student proceeds in this way until he has

responded to all frames. He then works around the disk a second time, but only those frames appear to which he has not correctly responded. When the disk revolves without stopping, the assignment is finished. (The student is asked to repeat each frame until a correct response is made to allow for the fact that, in telling him that a response is wrong, such a machine tells him what is right.)

The machine itself, of course, does not teach. It simply brings the student into contact with the person who composed the material it presents. It is a labor-saving device because it can bring one programmer into contact with an indefinite number of students. This may suggest mass production, but the effect upon each student is surprisingly like that of a private tutor. The comparison holds in several respects. (i) There is a constant interchange between program and student. Unlike lectures, textbooks, and the usual audio-visual aids, the machine induces sustained activity. The student is always alert and busy. (ii) Like a good tutor, the machine insists that a given point be thoroughly understood, either frame by frame or set by set, before the student moves on. Lectures, textbooks, and their mechanized equivalents, on the other hand, proceed without making sure that the student understands and easily leave him behind. (iii) Like a good tutor the machine presents just that material for which the student is ready. It asks him to take only that step which he is at the moment best equipped and most likely to take. (iv) Like a skillful tutor the machine helps the student to come up with the right answer. It does this in part through the orderly construction of the program and in part with techniques of hinting, prompting, suggesting, and so on, derived from an analysis of verbal behavior (Skinner, 1957b). (v) Lastly, of course, the machine, like the private tutor, reinforces the student for every correct response, using this immediate feedback not only to shape his behavior most efficiently but to maintain it in strength in a manner which the layman would describe as "holding the student's interest."

PROGRAMMING MATERIAL

The success of such a machine depends on the material used in it. The task of programming a

Table 1. *A set of frames designed to teach a third- or fourth-grade pupil to spell the word* manufacture.

1. **Manufacture** means to make or build. *Chair factories manufacture chairs.* Copy the word here:

   □□□□□□□□□□□

2. Part of the word is like part of the word **factory**. Both parts come from an old word meaning *make or build*.

   manu□□□□**ure**

3. Part of the word is like part of the word **manual**. Both parts come from an old word for *hand*. Many things used to be made by hand.

   □□□□**facture**

4. The same letter goes in both spaces:

   m□**nuf**□**cture**

5. The same letter goes in both spaces:

   man□**fact**□**re**

6. **Chair factories** □□□□□□□□□□□ **chairs.**

---

given subject is at first sight rather formidable. Many helpful techniques can be derived from a general analysis of the relevant behavioral processes, verbal and nonverbal. Specific forms of behavior are to be evoked and, through differential reinforcement, brought under the control of specific stimuli.

This is not the place for a systematic review of available techniques, or of the kind of research which may be expected to discover others. However, the machines themselves cannot be adequately described without giving a few examples of programs. We may begin with a set of frames (see Table 1) designed to teach a third- or fourth-grade pupil to spell the word *manufacture*. The six frames are presented in the order shown, and the pupil moves sliders to expose letters in the open squares.

The word to be learned appears in bold face in frame 1, with an example and a simple definition. The pupil's first task is simply to copy it. When he does so correctly, frame 2 appears. He must now copy selectively: he must identify "fact" as the common part of "manufacture" and "factory." This helps him to spell the word and also to acquire a separable

"atomic" verbal operant (Skinner, 1957b). In frame 3 another root must be copied selectively from "manual." In frame 4 the pupil must for the first time insert letters without copying. Since he is asked to insert the same letter in two places, a wrong response will be doubly conspicuous, and the chance of failure is thereby minimized. The same principle governs frame 5. In frame 6 the pupil spells the word to complete the sentence used as an example in frame 1. Even a poor student is likely to do this correctly because he has just composed or completed the word five times, has made two important root-responses, and has learned that two letters occur in the word twice. He has probably learned to spell the word without having made a mistake.

Teaching spelling is mainly a process of shaping complex forms of behavior. In other subjects — for example, arithmetic — responses must be brought under the control of appropriate stimuli. Unfortunately the material which has been prepared for teaching arithmetic[2] does not lend itself to excerpting. The numbers 0 through 9 are generated in relation

2 This material was prepared with the assistance of Susan R. Meyer.

to objects, quantities, and scales. The operations of addition, subtraction, multiplication, and division are thoroughly developed before the number 10 is reached. In the course of this the pupil composes equations and expressions in a great variety of alternative forms. He completes not only $5 + 4 = \square$, but $\square + 4 = 9$, $5 \square 4 = 9$, and so on, aided in most cases by illustrative materials. No appeal is made to rote memorizing, even in the later acquisition of the tables. The student is expected to arrive at $9 \times 7 = 63$, not by memorizing it as he would memorize a line of poetry, but by putting into practice such principles as that nine times a number is the same as ten times the number minus the number (both of these being "obvious" or already well learned), that the digits in a multiple of nine add to nine, that in composing successive multiples of nine one counts backwards (*nine, eighteen*, twenty-*seven*, thirty-*six*, and so on), that nine times a single digit is a number beginning with one less than the digit (nine times *six* is *fifty* something), and possibly even that the product of two numbers separated by only one number is equal to the square of the separating number minus one (the square of eight already being familiar from a special series of frames concerned with squares).

Programs of this sort run to great length. At five or six frames per word, four grades of spelling may require 20,000 or 25,000 frames, and three or four grades of arithmetic, as many again. If these figures seem large, it is only because we are thinking of the normal contact between teacher and pupil. Admittedly, a teacher cannot supervise 10,000 or 15,000 responses made by each pupil per year. But the pupil's time is not so limited. In any case, surprisingly little time is needed. Fifteen minutes per day on a machine should suffice for each of these programs, the machines being free for other students for the rest of each day. (It is probably because traditional methods are so inefficient that we have been led to suppose that education requires such a prodigious part of a young person's day.)

A simple technique used in programming material at the high-school or college level . . . is exemplified in teaching a student to recite a poem. The first line is presented with several unimportant letters omitted. The student must read the line "meaningfully" and supply the missing letters. The second, third, and fourth frames present succeeding lines in the same way. In the fifth frame the first line reappears with other letters also missing. Since the student has recently read the line, he can complete it correctly. He does the same for the second, third, and fourth lines. Subsequent frames are increasingly incomplete, and eventually—say, after 20 or 24 frames—the student reproduces all four lines without external help, and quite possibly without having made a wrong response. The technique is similar to that used in teaching spelling: responses are first controlled by a text, but this is slowly reduced (colloquially, "vanished") until the responses can be emitted without a text, each member in a series of responses being now under the "intraverbal" control of other members.

"Vanishing" can be used in teaching other types of verbal behavior. When a student describes the geography of part of the world or the anatomy of part of the body, or names plants and animals from specimens or pictures, verbal responses are controlled by nonverbal stimuli. In setting up such behavior the student is first asked to report features of a fully labeled map, picture, or object, and the labels are then vanished. In teaching a map, for example, the machine asks the student to describe spatial relations among cities, countries, rivers, and so on, as shown on a fully labeled map. He is then asked to do the same with a map in which the names are incomplete or, possibly, lacking. Eventually he is asked to report the same relations with no map at all. If the material has been well programmed, he can do so correctly. Instruction is sometimes concerned not so much with imparting a new repertoire of verbal responses as with getting the student to describe something accurately in any available terms. The machine can "make sure the student understands" a graph, diagram, chart, or picture by asking him to identify and explain its features—correcting him, of course, whenever he is wrong.

In addition to charts, maps, graphs, models, and so on, the student may have access to auditory material. In learning to take dictation in a foreign language, for example, he selects a short passage on an indexing phonograph according to instructions given by the machine.

He listens to the passage as often as necessary and then transcribes it. The machine then reveals the correct text. The student may listen to the passage again to discover the sources of any error. The indexing phonograph may also be used with the machine to teach other language skills, as well as telegraphic code, music, speech, parts of literary and dramatic appreciation, and other subjects.

A typical program combines many of these functions. The set of frames shown in Table 2 is designed to induce the student of high-school physics to talk intelligently, and to some extent technically, about the emission of light from an incandescent source. In using the machine the student will write a word or phrase to complete a given item and then uncover the corresponding word or phrase shown here in the column at the right. The reader who wishes to get the "feel" of the material should cover the right-hand column with a card, uncovering each line only after he has completed the corresponding item.

Several programming techniques are exemplified by the set of frames in Table 2. Technical terms are introduced slowly. For example, the familiar term "fine wire" in frame 2 is followed by a definition of the technical term "filament" in frame 4; "filament" is then asked for in the presence of the nonscientific synonym in frame 5 and without the synonym in frame 9. In the same way "glow," "give off light," and "send out light" in early frames are followed by a definition of "emit" with a synonym in frame 7. Various inflected forms of "emit" then follow, and "emit" itself is asked for with a synonym in frame 16. It is asked for without a synonym but in a helpful phrase in frame 30, and "emitted" and "emission" are asked for without help in frames 33 and 34. The relation between temperature and amount and color of light is developed in several frames before a formal statement using the word "temperature" is asked for in frame 12. "Incandescent" is defined and used in frame 13, is used again in frame 14, and is asked for in frame 15, the student receiving a thematic prompt from the recurring phrase "incandescent source of light." A formal prompt is supplied by "candle." In frame 25 the new response "energy" is easily evoked by the words "form of . . . ." because the expression "form of energy" is used earlier in the frame. "Energy" appears again in the next two frames and is finally asked for, without aid, in frame 28. Frames 30 through 35 discuss the limiting temperatures of incandescent objects, while reviewing several kinds of sources. The figure 800 is used in three frames. Two intervening frames then permit some time to pass before the response "800" is asked for.

Unwanted responses are eliminated with special techniques. If, for example, the second sentence in frame 24 were simply "It is a(n) — — source of light," the two "very's" would frequently lead the student to fill the blank with "strong" or a synonym thereof. This is prevented by inserting the word "powerful" to make a synonym redundant. Similarly, in frame 3 the words "heat and" preempt the response "heat," which would otherwise correctly fill the blank.

The net effect of such material is more than the acquisition of facts and terms. Beginning with a largely unverbalized acquaintance with flashlights, candles, and so on, the student is induced to talk about familiar events, together with a few new facts, with a fairly technical vocabulary. He applies the same terms to facts which he may never before have seen to be similar. The emission of light from an incandescent source takes shape as a topic or field of inquiry. An understanding of the subject emerges which is often quite surprising in view of the fragmentation required in item building.

It is not easy to construct such a program. Where a confusing or elliptical passage in a textbook is forgivable because it can be clarified by the teacher, machine material must be self-contained and wholly adequate. There are other reasons why textbooks, lecture outlines, and film scripts are of little help in preparing a program. They are usually not logical or developmental arrangements of material but strategems which the authors have found successful under existing classroom conditions. The examples they give are more often chosen to hold the student's interest than to clarify terms and principles. In composing material for the machine, the programmer may go directly to the point.

A first step is to define the field. A second is to collect technical terms, facts, laws, prin-

Table 2. *Part of a program in high-school physics. The machine presents one item at a time. The student completes the item and then uncovers the corresponding word or phrase shown at the right.*

Sentence to be completed	Word to be supplied
1. The important parts of a flashlight are the battery and the bulb. When we "turn on" a flashlight, we close a switch which connects the battery with the ——.	bulb
2. When we turn on a flashlight, an electric current flows through the fine wire in the —— and causes it to grow hot.	bulb
3. When the hot wire glows brightly, we say that it gives off or sends out heat and ——.	light
4. The fine wire in the bulb is called a filament. The bulb "lights up" when the filament is heated by the passage of a(n) —— current.	electric
5. When a weak battery produces little current, the fine wire, or ——, does not get very hot.	filament
6. A filament which is *less* hot sends out or gives off —— light.	less
7. "Emit" means "send out." The amount of light sent out, or "emitted," by a filament depends on how —— the filament is.	hot
8. The higher the temperature of the filament the —— the light emitted by it.	brighter, stronger
9. If a flashlight battery is weak, the —— in the bulb may still glow, but with only a dull red color.	filament
10. The light from a very hot filament is colored yellow or white. The light from a filament which is not very hot is colored ——.	red
11. A blacksmith or other metal worker sometimes makes sure that a bar of iron is heated to a "cherry red" before hammering it into shape. He uses the —— of the light emitted by the bar to tell how hot it is.	color
12. Both the color and the amount of light depend on the —— of the emitting filament or bar.	temperature
13. An object which emits light because it is hot is called "incandescent." A flashlight bulb is an incandescent source of ——.	light
14. A neon tube emits light but remains cool. It is, therefore, not an incandescent —— of light.	source
15. A candle flame is hot. It is a(n) —— source of light.	incandescent
16. The hot wick of a candle gives off small pieces or particles of carbon which burn in the flame. Before or while burning, the hot particles send out, or ——, light.	emit
17. A long candlewick produces a flame in which oxygen does not reach all the carbon	

particles. Without oxygen the particles cannot burn. Particles which do not burn
rise above the flame as ____.

smoke

18. We can show that there are particles of carbon in a candle flame, even when it is
not smoking, by holding a piece of metal in the flame. The metal cools some of the
particles before they burn, and the unburned carbon ____ collect on the metal as
soot.

particles

19. The particles of carbon in soot or smoke no longer emit light because they are ____
than when they were in the flame.

cooler, colder

20. The reddish part of a candle flame has the same color as the filament in a flashlight with a weak battery. We might guess that the yellow or white parts of a candle
flame are ____ than the reddish part.

hotter

21. "Putting out" an incandescent electric light means turning off the current so that the
filament grows too ____ to emit light.

cold, cool

22. Setting fire to the wick of an oil lamp is called ____ the lamp.

lighting

23. The sun is our principal ____ of light, as well as of heat.

source

24. The sun is not only very bright but very hot. It is a powerful ____ source of light.

incandescent

25. Light is a form of energy. In "emitting light" an object changes, or "converts," one
form of ____ into another.

energy

26. The electrical energy supplied by the battery in a flashlight is converted to ____ and
____.

heat, light;
light, heat

27. If we leave a flashlight on, all the energy stored in the battery will finally be
changed or ____ into heat and light.

converted

28. The light from a candle flame comes from the ____ released by chemical changes
as the candle burns.

energy

29. A nearly "dead" battery may make a flashlight bulb warm to the touch, but the
filament may still not be hot enough to emit light — in other words, the filament
will not be ____ at that temperature.

incandescent

30. Objects, such as a filament, carbon particles, or iron bars, become incandescent
when heated to about 800 degrees Celsius. At that temperature they begin to ____
____.

emit light

31. When raised to any temperature above 800 degrees Celsius, an object such as an
iron bar will emit light. Although the bar may melt or vaporize, its particles will
be ____ no matter how hot they get.

incandescent

32. About 800 degrees Celsius is the lower limit of the temperature at which particles
emit light. There is no upper limit of the ____ at which emission of light occurs.

temperature

33. Sunlight is ____ by very hot gases near the surface of the sun.

emitted

34. Complex changes similar to an atomic explosion generate the great heat which
explains the ____ of light by the sun.

emission

35. Below about ____ degrees Celsius an object is not an incandescent source of light.

800

ciples, and cases. These must then be arranged in a plausible developmental order—linear if possible, branching if necessary. A mechanical arrangement, such as a card filing system, helps. The material is distributed among the frames of a program to achieve an arbitrary density. In the final composition of an item, techniques for strengthening asked-for responses and for transferring control from one variable to another are chosen from a list according to a given schedule in order to prevent the establishment of irrelevant verbal tendencies appropriate to a single technique. When one set of frames has been composed, its terms and facts are seeded mechanically among succeeding sets, where they will again be referred to in composing later items to make sure that the earlier repertoire remains active. Thus, the technical terms, facts, and examples in Table 2 have been distributed for reuse in succeeding sets on reflection, absorption, and transmission, where they are incorporated into items dealing mainly with other matters. Sets of frames for explicit review can, of course, be constructed. Further research will presumably discover other, possibly more effective, techniques. Meanwhile, it must be admitted that a considerable measure of art is needed in composing a successful program.

Whether good programming is to remain an art or to become a scientific technology, it is reassuring to know that there is a final authority —the student. An unexpected advantage of machine instruction has proved to be the feedback to the *programmer*. In the elementary school machine, provision is made for discovering which frames commonly yield wrong responses, and in the high-school and college machine the paper strips bearing written answers are available for analysis. A trial run of the first version of a program quickly reveals frames which need to be altered, or sequences which need to be lengthened. One or two revisions in the light of a few dozen responses work a great improvement. No comparable feedback is available to the lecturer, textbook writer, or maker of films. Although one text or film may seem to be better than another, it is usually impossible to say, for example, that a given sentence on a given page or a particular sequence in a film is causing trouble.

Difficult as programming is, it has its compensations. It is a salutary thing to try to guarantee a right response at every step in the presentation of a subject matter. The programmer will usually find that he has been accustomed to leave much to the student— that he has frequently omitted essential steps and neglected to invoke relevant points. The responses made to his material may reveal surprising ambiguities. Unless he is lucky, he may find that he still has something to learn about his subject. He will almost certainly find that he needs to learn a great deal more about the behavioral changes he is trying to induce in the student. This effect of the machine in confronting the programmer with the full scope of his task may in itself produce a considerable improvement in education.

Composing a set of frames can be an exciting exercise in the analysis of knowledge. The enterprise has obvious bearings on scientific methodology. There are hopeful signs that the epistemological implications will induce experts to help in composing programs. The expert may be interested for another reason. We can scarcely ask a topflight mathematician to write a primer in second-grade arithmetic if it is to be used by the average teacher in the average classroom. But a carefully controlled machine presentation and the resulting immediacy of contact between programmer and student offer a very different prospect, which may be enough to induce those who know most about the subject to give some thought to the nature of arithmetical behavior and to the various forms in which such behavior should be set up and tested.

CAN MATERIAL BE TOO EASY?

The traditional teacher may view these programs with concern. He may be particularly alarmed by the effort to maximize success and minimize failure. He has found that students do not pay attention unless they are worried about the consequences of their work. The customary procedure has been to maintain the necessary anxiety by inducing errors. In recitation, the student who obviously knows the answer is not too often asked; a test item which is correctly answered by everyone is discarded as nondiscriminating; problems at the end of a section in a textbook in a mathematics generally include one or two very difficult items; and so on. (The teacher-turned-programmer may be surprised to find this attitude affecting the construction of items. For example, he may find it difficult to allow an item to stand which "gives the point away." Yet if we can solve the motivational problem with other means, what is more effective than giving a point away?) Making sure that the student knows he doesn't know is a technique concerned with motivation, not with the learning process. Machines solve the problem of motivation in other ways. There is no evidence that what is easily learned is more readily forgotten. If this should prove to be the case, retention may be guaranteed by subsequent material constructed for an equally painless review.

The standard defense of "hard" material is that we want to teach more than subject matter. The student is to be challenged and taught to "think." The argument is sometimes little more than a rationalization for a confusing presentation, but it is doubtless true that lectures and texts are often inadequate and misleading by design. But to what end? What sort of "thinking" does the student learn in struggling through difficult material? It is true that those who learn under difficult conditions are better students, but are they better because they have surmounted difficulties or do they surmount them because they are better? In the guise of teaching thinking we set difficult and confusing situations and claim credit for the students who deal with them successfully.

The trouble with deliberately making education difficult in order to teach thinking is (i) that we must remain content with the students thus selected, even though we know that they are only a small part of the potential supply of thinkers, and (ii) that we must continue to sacrifice the teaching of subject matter by renouncing effective but "easier" methods. A more sensible program is to analyze the behavior called "thinking" and produce it according to specifications. A program specifically concerned with such behavior could be composed of material already available in logic, mathematics, scientific method, and psychology. Much would doubtless be added in completing an effective program. The machine has already yielded

important relevant by-products. Immediate feedback encourages a more careful reading of programmed material than is the case in studying a text, where the consequences of attention or inattention are so long deferred that they have little effect on reading skills. The behavior involved in observing or attending to detail—as in inspecting charts and models or listening closely to recorded speech—is efficiently shaped by the contingencies arranged by the machine. And when an immediate result is in the balance, a student will be more likely to learn how to marshal relevant material, to concentrate on specific features of a presentation, to reject irrelevant materials, to refuse the easy but wrong solution, and to tolerate indecision, all of which are involved in effective thinking.

Part of the objection to easy material is that the student will come to depend on the machine and will be less able than ever to cope with the inefficient presentations of lectures, textbooks, films, and "real life." This is indeed a problem. All good teachers must "wean" their students, and the machine is no exception. The better the teacher, the more explicit must the weaning process be. The final stages of a program must be so designed that the student no longer requires the helpful conditions arranged by the machine. This can be done in many ways —among others by using the machine to discuss material which has been studied in other forms. These are questions which can be adequately answered only by further research.

No large-scale "evaluation" of machine teaching has yet been attempted. We have so far been concerned mainly with practical problems in the design and use of machines, and with testing and revising sample programs. . . .[3]

3 Dr. [Lloyd E.] Homme prepared sets of frames for teaching part of college physics (kinematics), and Mrs. [Susan R.] Meyer has prepared and informally tested material in remedial reading and vocabulary building at the junior high school level. Others who have contributed to the development of teaching machines should be mentioned. Nathan H. Azrin cooperated with me in testing a version of a machine to teach arithmetic. C. B. Ferster and Stanley M. Sapon used a simple "machine" to teach German [see "An application of recent developments in psychology to the teaching of German," *Harvard Educational Rev.* **28**, 1 (1958)]. Douglas Porter, of the Graduate School of Education at Harvard, has made an independent schoolroom test of machine instruction in spelling [see "Teaching machines," *Harvard Graduate School of Educ. Assoc. Bull.* **3**, 1 (1958)]. Devra Cooper has experimented with the teaching of English composition for freshmen at the

[Under a grant from the Fund for the Advancement of Education, a self-instruction room containing ten machines] was recently used to teach part of a course in human behavior to Harvard and Radcliffe undergraduates. Nearly 200 students completed 48 disks (about 1400 frames) prepared with the collaboration of [James G.] Holland. The factual core of the course was covered, corresponding to about 200 pages of the text (Skinner, 1953). The median time required to finish 48 disks was $14\frac{1}{2}$ hours. The students were not examined on the material but were responsible for the text which overlapped it. Their reactions to the material and to self-instruction in general have been studied through interviews and questionnaires. Both the machines and the material are now being modified in the light of this experience, and a more explicit evaluation will then be made.

Meanwhile, it can be said that the expected advantages of machine instruction were generously confirmed. Unsuspected possibilities were revealed which are now undergoing further exploration. Although it is less convenient to report to a self-instruction room than to pick up a textbook in one's room or elsewhere, most students felt that they had much to gain in studying by machine. Most of them worked for an hour or more with little effort, although they often felt tired afterwards, and they reported that they learned much more in less time and with less effort than in conventional ways. No attempt was made to point out the relevance of the material to crucial issues, personal or otherwise, but the students remained interested. (Indeed, one change in the reinforcing contingencies suggested by the experiment is intended to *reduce* the motivational level.) An important advantage proved to be that the student always knew where he stood, without waiting for an hour test or final examination.

SOME QUESTIONS

Several questions are commonly asked when teaching machines are discussed. Cannot the results of laboratory research on learning be used in education without machines? Of course they can. They should lead to improvements in textbooks, films, and other teaching materials. Moreover, the teacher who really understands the conditions under which learning takes place will be more effective, not only in teaching subject matter but in managing the class. Nevertheless, some sort of device is necessary to arrange the subtle contingencies of reinforcement required for optimal learning if each student is to have individual attention. In nonverbal skills this is usually obvious; texts and instructor can guide the learner but they cannot arrange the final contingencies which set up skilled behavior. It is true that the verbal skills at issue here are especially dependent upon social reinforcement, but it must not be forgotten that the machine simply mediates an *essentially verbal* relation. In shaping and maintaining verbal knowledge we are not committed to the contingencies arranged through immediate personal contact.

Machines may still seem unnecessarily complex compared with other mediators such as workbooks or self-scoring test forms. Unfortunately, these alternatives are not acceptable. When material is adequately programmed, adjacent steps are often so similar that one frame reveals the response to another. Only some sort of mechanical presentation will make successive frames independent of each other. Moreover, in self-instruction an automatic record of the student's behavior is especially desirable, and for many purposes it should be foolproof. Simplified versions of the present machines have been found useful—for example, in the work of Ferster and Sapon, of Porter, and of Gilbert[4] —but the mechanical and economic problems are so easily solved that a machine with greater capabilities is fully warranted.

Will machines replace teachers? On the contrary, they are capital equipment to be used by teachers to save time and labor. In assigning certain mechanizable functions to machines, the teacher emerges in his proper role as an indispensable human being. He may teach more students than heretofore—this is probably inevitable if the world-wide demand for education is to be satisfied—but he will do so in

University of Kentucky. Thomas F. Gilbert, of the University of Georgia, has compared standard and machine instruction in an introductory course in psychology, and with the collaboration of J. E. Jewett has prepared material in algebra. The U. S. Naval Training Devices Center has recently contracted with the University of Pennsylvania for a study of programs relating to the machine instruction of servicemen, under the direction of Eugene H. Galanter.
4 See footnote 3.

fewer hours and with fewer burdensome chores. In return for his greater productivity he can ask society to improve his economic condition.

The role of the teacher may well be changed, for machine instruction will affect several traditional practices. Students may continue to be grouped in "grades" or "classes," but it will be possible for each to proceed at his own level, advancing as rapidly as he can. The other kind of "grade" will also change its meaning. In traditional practice a *C* means that a student has a smattering of a whole course. But if machine instruction assures mastery at every stage, a grade will be useful only in showing *how far* a student has gone. *C* might mean that he is halfway through a course. Given enough time he will be able to get an *A*; and since *A* is no longer a motivating device, this is fair enough. The quick student will meanwhile have picked up *A*'s in other subjects.

Differences in ability raise other questions. A program designed for the slowest student in the school system will probably not seriously delay the fast student, who will be free to progress at his own speed. (He may profit from the full coverage by filling in unsuspected gaps in his repertoire.) If this does not prove to be the case, programs can be constructed at two or more levels, and students can be shifted from one to the other as performances dictate. If there are also differences in "types of thinking," the extra time available for machine instruction may be used to present a subject in ways appropriate to many types. Each student will presumably retain and use those ways which he finds most useful. The kind of individual difference which arises simply because a student has missed part of an essential sequence (compare the child who has no "mathematical ability" because he was out with the measles when fractions were first taken up) will simply be eliminated.

OTHER USES

Self-instruction by machine has many special advantages apart from educational institutions. Home study is an obvious case. In industrial and military training it is often inconvenient to schedule students in groups, and individual instruction by machine should be a feasible alternative. Programs can also be constructed in subjects for which teachers are not available — for example, when new kinds of equipment must be explained to operators and repairmen, or where a sweeping change in method finds teachers unprepared (Menger, 1958). Education sometimes fails because students have handicaps which make a normal relationship with a teacher difficult or impossible. (Many blind children are treated today as feebleminded because no one has had the time or patience to make contact with them. Deafmutes, spastics, and others suffer similar handicaps.) A teaching machine can be adapted to special kinds of communication — as, for example, Braille — and, above all, it has infinite patience.

CONCLUSION

An analysis of education within the framework of a science of behavior has broad implications. Our schools, in particular our "progressive" schools, are often held responsible for many current problems — including juvenile delinquency and the threat of a more powerful foreign technology. One remedy frequently suggested is a return to older techniques, especially to a greater "discipline" in schools. Presumably this is to be obtained with some form of punishment, to be administered either with certain classical instruments of physical injury — the dried bullock's tail of the Greek teacher or the cane of the English schoolmaster — or as disapproval or failure, the frequency of which is to be increased by "raising standards." This is probably not a feasible solution. Not only education but Western culture as a whole is moving away from aversive practices. We cannot prepare young people for one kind of life in institutions organized on quite different principles. The discipline of the birch rod may facilitate learning, but we must remember that it also breeds followers of dictators and revolutionists.

In the light of our present knowledge a school system must be called a failure if it cannot induce students to learn except by threatening them for not learning. That this has always been the standard pattern simply emphasizes the importance of modern techniques. John Dewey was speaking for his culture and his time when he attacked aversive educational practices and appealed to teachers to turn to positive and humane methods. What he threw out should have been thrown out. Unfortunately he had too little to put in its place. Progressive education has been a temporizing measure which can now be effectively supplemented. Aversive practices can not only be replaced, they can be replaced with far more powerful techniques. The possibilities should be thoroughly explored if we are to build an educational system which will meet the present demand without sacrificing democratic principles.

Teaching machine (and learning theory) crisis [1]

SIDNEY L. PRESSEY

For several years now, all over the country, learning theorists have been programing books and other matter into numerous little "frames" each consisting of a very easy question or statement with space for writing a one or two word "constructed" response, to be verified by turning a page or turning up a "teaching machine" roll. One learned by responding (the theory was) and the more responding the more adequate the learning. In preparing each question the effort was not so much to contribute to a larger meaning as to assure that the student "emitted" the desired response, on the ground that he learned by making correct responses and an error would tend to recur. Multiple-choice questions are not used, because they involve the presentation of wrong alternatives, and also call merely for discrimination. All this has seemed plausible theoretically, and hopes have been high for extraordinary educational advances.

NOT GAIN BUT CONFUSION

Instead, evidence has been accumulating that the above hypotheses on which the programing was being based were, *for human learning of meaningful matter,* not so! Such learners dealing with such materials may profit by seeing not only what a thing is but what it is not, may profit by mistakes, may learn to recall from learning to discriminate. Further, some half-dozen investigators have reported that as much may be learned in a given time simply by reading, as by reading *and* responding (Pressey, 1962; Silberman, 1962). In short, these theorists have independently discovered what educators have known about and been investigating for over 40 years—silent reading! Further, as programed matter has been used over a period of time, it has been realized that for skimming for main ideas, for review—for any use except that initial go-through—the programed book is almost impossible and the teaching-machine roll entirely so. Mostly, even for the first go-through, they are unsatisfactory, because most important matter to be learned has structure, which the programing destroys except the serial order, and most important learning is integrative and judgmental, so requires a looking about in what is being studied; for all such purposes a teaching machine seems about as hampering as a scanning device which required that one look at a picture only 1 square inch at a time, in a set order. Much seems very wrong about current attempts at autoinstruction.

A possible basic factor is suggested by Hilgard (1956) when he questions.

the generalization from comparative studies that there are no differences, except quantitative ones, between the learning of lower mammals and man. . . . It is strange that the opposite point of view is not more often made explicit—that at the human level there have emerged capacities not approached by the lower animals, including other primates. . . . Language in man is perhaps the clearest of the emergents which carries with it a forward surge in what may be learned. . . . There are probably a number of different kinds of learning, following different laws. [Further, in man] the ceiling of ability itself may be modified by training.

From the *Journal of Applied Psychology,* 1963, **47,** 1-6.

1 This paper was presented in modified form at the St. Louis meetings of the American Psychological Association, August 31, 1962.

[Thus after acquiring] appropriate linguistic or mathematical tools [he can solve problems previously impossible] (pp. 460-461).

Surely that now taken-for-granted but really marvelous skill, silent assimilative reading, is such a tool. Also more important than often recognized are a variety of skills and strategies in learning usually grouped together as methods of study.

With Hilgard's position the writer would agree. He would say that the learning theorists have with notable vigor and consistency applied "generalizations from comparative studies" to problems of learning in school, and that the results have shown, more adequately than ever before, the unsatisfactoriness of those generalizations for that purpose. For a learner with reading-study skills, conventional textual matter orders and structures its contents in paragraphs and sections and chapters, exhibits that structure in headings and table of contents, makes all readily available in index with page headings and numbers. The learner thus has multiple aids to the development and structuring of his understanding. If need be he can, with a flick of the finger, move about in the material; he can skip the already known, turn back as a result of a later felt need, review selectively. As a way to present matter to be learned, the average textbook may not be best. But thousands of frames on a teaching-machine roll or strung through a programed book would seem close to the worst. To make a very bad pun, the programers have "framed" the textbook. Instead of trying to improve their programs, they might better consider very broadly how best to present matter for learning. The opinion is ventured that the best will be found closer to texts than to their programs.

But did not Socrates so teach the slave boy? The boy could not read. What about the often-cited skillful tutor? He assumed that the student had done some reading. However, both Socrates and the tutor did further learning by asking questions. The writer would contend that neither simply presented an idea and then reinforced it. Brownell's (1928) early research regarding primary school children's learning of arithmetic here seems relevant. Simply telling them that $2 \times 3 = 6$ did *not* bring about real learning of that number combina-

tion. These sturdy little empiricists had not merely to be *told;* they had to be *shown,* as by putting out two sets each of three pennies and demonstrating that they did indeed count to six. They had similarly to verify, and to differentiate, that $2 + 3$ was 5 and $3 - 2$ was only 1. As Piaget (1954) and others have described, children gradually develop a number system, also cognitive schema as of space, causality; and they do this not by so crude a rote process as the accretion of bit learnings stuck on by reinforcements, but by progressive processes of cognitive integration and clarification.

Moreover, such clarification is commonly by differentiation, and multiple-choice items involve just such processes. The three-choice question $2 \times 3 = 1$, 5, or 6 differentiates the correct answer from answers got by wrongly subtracting or adding. In this one concise little item are thus packed three arithmetic processes and three number combinations, and study of the item might well involve all six issues, with autoinstructional dealing with the item clarifying of all. The point will be returned to.

But first a brief summary of the position so far. The past decade has seen an extraordinary "boom" in autoinstruction; most of this work has been dominated by concepts of operant conditioning deriving directly from animal experimentation and has become stylized in terms of initial presentation of tasks in numerous frames with immediate constructed response. Because thus so special in origin and nature, as well as yielding often question raising results, a basic critical review of current autoinstructional concepts seemed called for. Doubts have been raised as to whether human learning of meaningful material can be adequately accounted for by animal based theory, programed matter is satisfactory for such learning, and reinforcement adequately accounts for the process (Gagné, 1962).

BUT WHERE FROM HERE?

When in doubt about such a theory-dominated situation, it is sometimes well to pull back and see whether a very practical analysis may helpfully reconstrue issues. If this be done, an obvious early question is this: what is the best way *initially* to present matter to be learned? The programers have been cutting it into little pieces each responded to, but now recognize that one may learn from reading without responding. Then how big may the piece be? The writer has stressed that the bigger piece may have structure which should be made evident, and that first consideration as well as review or selective use may make it desirable that the learner can move about freely in the material. Perhaps it would be granted that a questioner who interrupted the reading of this paper should be asked to wait until it was all before him—that it would be then that the discussion could be most profitable. Surely it will be granted that the paper can best be understood if seen in print so that one can glance about and see headings; rather than if heard, when one cannot thus study—as one cannot study a teaching-machine roll. So the suggestion is: that the initial presentation might most often best be a very well organized and well written substantial statement much like a chapter in a good textbook! And the autoinstruction should follow and should be like a series of questions in a very good discussion of such a chapter.

Some "autopresentation" might be helpful: a teaching-machine roll might picture two groups each of three pennies and then six and so make clear to the child mind that 2×3 does make six. *After* his number system has been somewhat established, there may be automatized drill. The printed word "house" may be thus associated with a picture of one. Sundry sorts of detail-learning and of drill may be dealt with piecemeal. But mostly (the writer believes) initial presentation of what is to be learned will be in field trip, demonstration or experiment, or most commonly a substantial unit like an incisive textbook chapter, *not* all mixed up with autoinstruction. The "autodiscussion" would follow, and its function would be (to paraphrase a statement in Ausubel's 1961 review) to enhance the clarity and stability of cognitive structure by correcting misconceptions, and deferring the instruction of new matter until there had been such clarification and elucidation.

In difficult matter such as a science text or industrial or military training manual, bits of autoinstruction may be needed more frequently; each step in the solution of a difficult problem may need such autoelucidation. But the manual or text need not be fragmented into thousands of frames. Problems may be explicated in autoinstructional matter supplementary to the text; and there, or perhaps every 3 or 4 pages in the book, clusters of autoexplicating queries may keep check on understanding. But a book's structured coherence and orderliness of presentation and its convenience for overview, review, and reference, can be kept.

If the autoinstruction is thus to *follow* presentation of what is to be learned, then (like a good tutor or teacher) it will deal only with issues which need further clarification or emphasis. Such adjunct autoelucidation will *not* cover everything, may jump from one point to another or even back and forth. It will be very much shorter than present "programs," which attempt both to present matter to be learned and autoinstruct about it in the same aggregate. Being so different, such supplemental autoinstruction might well be given a different name, as autoelucidation or explication.

But how would matter for adjunct autoinstruction or explication be selected? Experienced teachers would have many suggestions as to points needing special elucidation. They would be indicated in published research regarding pupils' learning of and difficulties in spelling, arithmetic, algebra, composition, science, and history. Additional research, for development and trial of such elucidative material, would suggest more items and better ways of presenting them. Some could be cleared up by making the initial presentation more lucid. But some students would still have difficulty with some items; perhaps those troubling 10% of the pupils or more would be dealt with in the adjunct autoinstruction.

The items should usually there appear (the writer is convinced) as multiple-choice questions with only such wrong alternatives as express common misunderstandings and a right answer notably clear. There is evidence that, contrary to theoretical inference, students do, after autoinstruction with such items, *less* often make the so-labeled mistakes, more often get things right, and transfer or generalize so that the gains appear on recall and yet other types of end tests (see for instance Jones, 1954; Lumsdaine & Glaser, 1960, pp. 52-93). Only half the students in a class may get such an item right on a pretest, but almost all of them do so on an end test a month later. In striking contrast, the perverse requirements of the orthodox programer make any such effectiveness impossible: the item is initially supposed to be so easy that at least 95% pass it, errors cannot be identified as such because they must not be shown, and right statements are limited to such as the student can be maneuvered into hastily formulating himself. And orthodox improvement consists of making the items yet easier! In contrast, improvement of such an item as here urged would involve making wrong alternates clearer expressions of common misconceptions and the right more clearly right so that gains would be yet greater. In addition, the ease of checking objective items, with immediate indication of correctness (as by instant change of color of the check mark on a "chemo-card" or turn to next question on a key machine) makes possible going through many more items in a given time—so presumably more learning.

RANGE OF EVALUATIONS

But what of the argument that orthodox programs have been found greatly to save time, so that for instance a college course was finished in the first 2 months of a semester, or an industrial training course similarly shortened? Independent study plans have made possible marked reduction of time in class without any such programs (Baskin, 1960). The average class and the average business training session may be very time wasting and otherwise inefficient, and a number of alternatives may be shown to be better. In a college or secondary school course with several sections, it should be feasible to have one or more taught in conventional fashion, one or more use an orthodox program, a similar number try what the writer has called adjunct autoinstruction, another venture a planned independent study procedure, and outcomes on a carefully made final examination compared. If so made, such examinations can yield some analysis of outcomes: does one method or another bring more recall, transfer, application? Experiments of this type under the writer's direction have shown adjunct autoinstruction superior to conventional classes in all these respects.

These experiments also showed the adjunct materials very useful in planned independent study: in a room set aside for such use and having all the readings, laboratory material, and adjunct autoinstructional sheets available but looked after by an assistant, the students came in and worked when they wished, in small groups or individually, consulting the assistant when they so desired. All finished the 11-week course within 6 weeks. All did well on midterm and final examinations. But informal reports and interviews indicated yet other values, as gains in ability to work independently—though the students became better acquainted than in formal classes! The opportunity to save time was motivating. Several of these students took another course by independent study during the second half of the quarter.

More broadly, appraising experiments involving considerable numbers of students with different instructors over considerable periods of time—preferably a whole school or business training course—have yet other values. Methods have to be tolerable in long continued and routine, not simply brief and special, use. In the work just described, the best all-purpose "teaching machine" was judged to be a 3 × 5 chemo-card having 30 lines each of four squares: on this answer card the student checked his choice of answer to each of 30 four-choice questions on a teach-test sheet, using a special red ink which instantly turned black when he marked in the right answer-box (because of an invisible chemical printed there). The student kept trying on each question until this color-change feedback told him he had the correct answer. For remedial review he had only to note where his red marks were, the sum of them was his error-score; the instructor had only to note where he saw most red on the cards for a given day to see where some corrective discussion might be desirable, and for both him and the students the cards were a compact easily-filed record.[2] In the writer's adjunct autoinstructional procedure, everything except the cards could be used over and over again, easily returned to again as for review. For long-continuing flexible use

2 Yet more convenient autoinstructional cards are possible. Instead of a pen with special ink, only a pencil may be needed; a mark with it, or a stroke of its eraser, breaks through an overprint to reveal a "c" underneath when the right answer is found. For 30-item 3-choice teach tests, a device little larger than a stop watch, and less complicated, may both teach and keep score. An apparatus little larger than an electric desk clock may both teach and provide selective review.

and re-use, it seemed apparent that a text or business manual plus perhaps 50 adjunct auto-instructional sheets (and some chemo-cards) was far more practicable than that manual or text cut up into 3,000 frames on a teaching-machine roll (with the machines) or strung through a programed book.

RESUME AND RECOMMENDATIONS

Teaching machines and programed materials are now being used all over the country in schools and colleges and in industrial and military training. Manufacture and sale of such products are a major enterprise of many publishers and equipment makers. Ambitious young people are embarking on careers in such work. The whole subject has become an accepted topic of everyday talk. However, there is disturbing evidence that current auto-instruction is *not* up to the claims made for it, that the current "boom" might be followed by a "bust" unfortunate for those involved — and for psychology. This paper is first of all a plea that to guard against such a danger the whole situation be soon given close critical inspection, and not merely to assure (as is now being attempted) that programs are good; but critically to consider whether the whole current concept of programing may be at fault, and an almost totally different approach than now orthodox to all ideas about autoinstruction be called for.

The archvillain, leading so many people astray, is declared to be learning theory! No less a charge is made than that the whole trend of American research and theory as regards learning has been based on a false premise — that the important features of human learning are to be found in animals. Instead, the all-important fact is that human has transcended animal learning.[3] Language, number, such skills as silent reading, make possible facilitations of learning, and kinds of learning, impossible even for the apes. Autoinstruction should enhance such potentials. Instead, current animal derived procedures in autoinstruction destroy meaningful structure to present fragments serially in programs, and replace processes of cognitive clarification with largely rote reinforcings of bit learnings.

An "adjunct autoinstruction" is urged which keeps, makes use of, and enhances meaningful structure, the autoinstruction serving to clarify and extend meaningfulness. Texts, manuals, laboratory exercises, instructional moving pictures and television would be kept (though often improved), and the autoinstruction would aid in their use and increase their value. The materials would be perhaps only a tenth as bulky as present programs; and being objective, their use could be greatly facilitated by auto-mating devices.

Evaluations should not merely (as is now projected) compare the merits of various "orthodox" programs. Those should be compared with such adjunct autoinstructional materials as here advocated. Adaptability should be compared for use with other media as books and movies and other methods as guided independent study. Convenience and cost for continuing general use should be hard-headedly appraised. The prediction is ventured that in all respects adjunct autoinstruction will be found far superior: time and work saving will be great yet more will be accomplished — courses often completed in half the usual time, years saved but nevertheless more accomplished in school and college, industrial and military training tasks reduced perhaps a third in length and all with great time and trouble saved instructional staffs. Then at long last the "industrial revolution" in education may come about which the writer predicted (Pressey, 1932) just 30 years ago. Further, somewhat as the practical testing movement from the first world war on greatly stimulated and aided research and theorizing regarding abilities, so autoinstruction may get research on learning out from under its long dominance by comparative psychology and confinement in the laboratory and evolve vigorous new theory.

---

3 For this conclusion there is no less evidence than the whole history of civilization! Basically more significant than Skinner's brilliant research regarding animal learning may well be the almost forgotten finding of Kellogg and of Cathy Hayes that even if an ape be raised in a home like a child, it can never learn to talk. Far more remarkable than Skinner's pigeons playing ping pong is the average human scanning a newspaper — glancing about to find matter of interest to him, judging, generalizing, reconstruing, all in silent reading without overt respondings or reinforcings. Most remarkable of all is it to see learning theorists, hypnotized by the plausibilities of a neat theory, trying to teach that human as if he were a pigeon — confining his glance to the rigid slow serial peep show viewing of innumerable "frames" each demanding that he respond and be reinforced.

part **5**

THE ASSESSMENT OF BEHAVIOR

That men make daily judgments of each other, attempting to "size each other up," is a commonplace observation and a fact of human life. Some of us believe we do the job rather well; others of us are less sure of our perceptiveness.

Viewed psychologically, the process of one man's making assessments of another is complex and not too well understood. This is true in spite of the fact that one group of psychological specialists, clinical psychologists (along with psychiatrists), are professionally charged with the responsibility of assessing the patients who consult them. Paul Meehl, in attempting to throw some light on both the clinical process of assessment and the success with which it is carried out, takes us behind the scenes to observe how clinicians obtain what they think is relevant data and then draw inferences from them in order to arrive at professional judgments. The results are likely to raise some productive questions about the validity and usefulness of most of the judgments that we make about each other, often on brief and superficial acquaintance.

J. McV. Hunt, on the other hand, while not directly concerned with the assessment problem, offers a radical reinterpretation of recent evidence that is relevant to the question of how one person can make adequate judgments about another. Hunt's argument is that traditional conceptions of motivation can lead us seriously astray. What we need to know in order to assess another individual is the way he has processed the "information" provided by his past experience. That is, we need to know something about his concept of himself, his expectations, his aspirations, and the meanings he has assigned to various aspects of his environment. If we are then told something of the circumstances he is likely to face — for example, the duties entailed by a new job for which he is being considered — we can make judgments about the extent to which the new situation will be congruent or dissonant to his private store of meanings, the interpretations made on the basis of his history.

In both Meehl's and Hunt's papers, we are concerned less with the technology of assessment — questionnaires, projective tests, interview schedules, etc. — than with the process itself and the ideas underlying it. When these two papers have been read, it will be a fruitful exercise to try two different enterprises. One is to devise some method of observation or inferences that, by hypotheses drawn from these analyses, would improve the assessment procedure. The second is to keep a record of one's own assessments of his acquaintances for a period of two weeks, making as specific predictions about their behavior as possible, and at the end of the fortnight, to make an accurate tally of the proportion of times the predictions have been correct as against the proportion of errors.

The cognitive activity of the clinician

PAUL E. MEEHL

Somebody has described psychotherapy as "the art of applying a science which does not yet exist." Those of us who try to help people with their troubles by means of that special kind of conversation are uncomfortably aware of the serious truth behind this facetious remark. The clinical psychologist has been able to assuage some of his therapeutic anxiety, and to refurbish his sometimes battered self-image, by keeping one foot planted on what seemed like comparatively solid ground, namely, psychodiagnosis. In recent years, some clinicians have been making a determined effort to assess the validity of our currently fashionable diagnostic instruments, and the findings are not very impressive. The cumulative impact of validation studies is reflected, for example, in Garfield's excellent textbook (1957), where one does not need a highly sensitive third eye to discern a note of caution (or even pessimism?). F. L. Kelly finds that 40% of young clinicians state that they would not go into clinical psychology if they had it to do over again. One suspects that at least part of this professional disillusionment springs either from awareness of the weaknesses in our psychodiagnostic methods or from the chronic intrapsychic (and interprofessional!) strain exacted of those who ward off such a confrontation. Who, for example, would *not* react with discouragement upon reading the recent monograph by Little and Shneidman (1959) where, in an unbiased and well-designed study, we find a very low congruency among interpretation of psychological test data, the test interpreters having been chosen as "experts" on four widely used

instruments? Any tendency I felt to rejoice at the slight superiority of the MMPI over the three projective techniques with which it was competing was counteracted by the finding that my favorite test, like the others, does not do at all well when judged in absolute terms.

The cognitive activity of the clinician can be separated into several functions, which I have discussed in a recent paper (Meehl, 1959a). Setting aside for the moment that special kind of cognitive activity which goes on within the therapeutic interview, we can distinguish three classes of functions performed by the psychodiagnostician: *formal diagnosis* (the attachment of a nosological label); *prognosis* (including "spontaneous" recoverability, therapy-stayability, recidivism, response to therapy, indications for differential treatment); and *personality assessment* other than diagnosis or prognosis. This last may be divided, somewhat arbitrarily, into *phenotypic* and *genotypic:* the former being the descriptive or surface features of the patient's behavior, including his social impact; the latter covering personality structure and dynamics, and basic parameters of a constitutional sort.

Quite apart from the validity of current techniques for performing these various cognitive functions, their pragmatic value is open to question. It is commonly believed that an accurate pretreatment personality assessment of his patient is of great value to the psychotherapist. It is not known to what extent, if at all, this is true. However, what do psycho-

From the *American Psychologist*, 1960, **15**, 19-27.

therapists themselves have to say about it? Bernard C. Glueck, Jr. and I have recently collected responses from 168 psychotherapists (both medical and nonmedical, and representing a wide spectrum of orientations: e.g., Freudian, neo-Freudian, Radovian, Sullivanian, Rogerian, eclectic, "mixed") to a questionnaire dealing with 132 aspects of therapeutic technique. One of our items reads: "It greatly speeds therapy if the therapist has prior knowledge of the client's dynamics and content from such devices as the Rorschach and TAT." While the self-styled groups differ significantly in their response to this item (ranging from a unanimous negative among Rogerians to a two-thirds affirmative among George Kelly disciples), all groups except the last tend to respond negatively. The overall percentage who believe that such prior knowledge of the client's personality greatly speeds therapy is only 17%. This low figure, taken together with the fashionable de-emphasis upon nosology and the feebleness of most prognostic studies, at least raises doubts about the practical value of our diagnostic contribution.

Although they do not bear directly upon this question, we have some other interesting results which suggest considerable skepticism among therapists as to the significance of causal understanding itself in the treatment process. For example, 43% state that "Warmth and real sympathy are much more important than an accurate causal understanding of the client's difficulty." Over one-third believe that "Literary, dramatic, aesthetic, or mystical people are likely to be better therapists than people of a primarily scientific, logical, or mathematical bent." Four out of five believe that "The personality of the therapist is more important than the theory of personality he holds." About half believe that "Interpretation as a tool is greatly overrated at present." Two out of five go as far as to say that "Under proper conditions, an incorrect interpretation, not even near to the actual facts, can have a real and long-lasting therapeutic effect." Time does not permit me to read other examples of items which, in the aggregate, suggest minimization of the importance of the therapist's forming a "correct" picture of the client's psyche.

Setting aside the pragmatic question of the therapeutic value of assessment, let us look briefly at the inductive structure of the assessment process. The epistemological rock bottom in a single, concrete, dated slice or interval in the behavior flux, an "episode," identified by certain physical or social properties. Having observed one or more episodes of a given kind, we make an inductive inference as to the strength of low order *dispositions* which these episodes exemplify. Such dispositions are grouped into families, the justification for this grouping being, as Cattell (1946, 1950) has emphasized, some kind of covariation (although not necessarily of Type R) among the members of the disposition-family. It is perhaps possible to formulate the clinician's decision making behavior entirely in terms of such disposition-classes. In such a formulation, clinical inference involves probabilistic transition from episodes to dispositions, followed by the attribution of further dispositions, as yet unobserved. Ideally, such inferences would be based upon an extensive actuarial experience providing objective probability statements. Given a particular configuration of dispositions present in a patient, the statistical frequencies for all other dispositions of practical import would be known within the limits of observational and sampling errors. In practice, of course, this ideal is rarely achieved, the conditional probabilities being subjectively judged from clinical experience without the benefit of an actual tallying and accumulation of observations, and the probabilities being expressed in rough verbal form, such as "frequently" and "likely," rather than as numerical values.

I am still of the opinion (McArthur, Meehl, & Tiedeman, 1956; Meehl, 1954, 1956, 1957) that the practical utility of this approach has been insufficiently explored, and I think that many clinicians are unaware of the extent to which their daily decision making behavior departs from such a model not by being qualitatively different but mainly by being less explicit and, therefore, less exact. However, we must recognize that a purely dispositional approach is not the *only* way of proceeding. An alternative, more exciting (and more congenial to the clinician's self-concept) is to view the clinician's cognitive activity as aiming at the assessment of hypothetical inner states, struc-

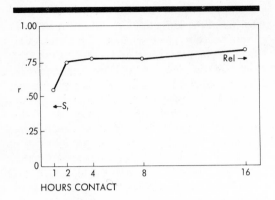

Fig. 1 *Q correlations between therapist's sort at 24 contacts and earlier sorts. (Phenotypic pool; N = 182 items; Stopol)*

tures, or events which cannot be reduced to dispositions but which belong to the domain of theoretical entities, crude though the theory may be. Episodes and dispositions are here treated as "signs" or "indicators" of the postulated internal states. These states should not be spoken of as "operationally defined" in terms of the dispositions, because the logical relationship between propositions concerning theoretical entities and those describing dispositions is not one of equivalence, but merely one of degrees of confirmation. The inference *from* dispositions *to* states of theoretical variables is again only probabilistic, partly because statistical concepts occur within the causal model itself (i.e., probability appears, as in the other sciences, in the object-language) and partly because the theoretical network is incomplete and imperfectly confirmed.

A fundamental contribution to the methodology of inference from multiple indicators is the "multitrait-multimethod matrix" of Campbell and Fiske (1959). These authors show that in order to support a claim of construct validity, we must take into account more kinds of correlational data than have been traditionally provided and that it is just as important for some correlations to be low as it is for others to be high. Consider two or more traits (e.g., dominance and sociability), each of which is allegedly measured by two or more methods (e.g., MMPI scores and peer group ratings). Computing all possible intercorrela-

tions, we construct a multitrait-multimethod matrix. The relationships within this matrix may or may not lend support to the claim of construct validity. The monotrait-hetero-method coefficients should be not only statistically significant and respectable in size, but should exceed both the heterotrait-heteromethod and heterotrait-monomethod coefficients. For example, if MMPI dominance and sociability correlate higher than does MMPI dominance with peer group dominance or than MMPI sociability with peer group sociability, we ought to be nervous about the relative contribution of methods factors versus traits under study. Campbell and Fiske point out that the individual differences literature is very weak in this respect, usually failing to provide the necessary data and, when it does, usually showing unimpressive results.

An interesting adaptation of the Campbell-Fiske technique arises if we substitute "persons" for "traits" and deal with Q correlations rather than R correlations. Suppose that a therapist provides us with Q sort descriptions of two patients. From the MMPI profiles these patients are then Q sorted independently by two interpreters. This set up generates a modified Campbell-Fiske matrix of 15 Q correlations, in which the validity diagonals (i.e., hetero-method-mono*patient* coefficients) represent how similarly the same patient is perceived by the therapist and the two MMPI readers; the monomethod-heteropatient and hetero-method-heteropatient values reflect the projections, stereotypes, and other idiosyncratic sorting biases of the therapist and of the two interpreters, the extent to which such stereotypes are shared by all three, and the unknown true resemblance of the particular patient pair. Robert Wirt and I have been running a series of such matrices, and thus far our results are as unencouraging as those of the Little and Shneidman study. I have decided to spare you the slides, faintly hoping that the pairs thus far completed will turn out to be atypically bad.

The situation is not much improved by selecting a small subset of "high confidence" items before Q correlating. One disadvantage of Q sort is that it requires the clinician to record a judgment about every trait in the deck. The technique has the advantage that it presents the judge with a standard set of dispositions and constructs and therefore gets judgments which he is able to make but would often fail to make in producing a spontaneous description. But, for this advantage in coverage we have to pay a price. Such a situation is clinically unrealistic: whether we are starting with test data, history, or interview impressions, the particular facets which stand out (whether high or low) will not be the same for different patients. It may be that the meager results of recent validation studies are attributable in part to the calculation of hit frequencies or Q correlations over the entire range of traits, only a minority of which, variable in composition, would willingly be judged by the clinician on any one patient.

I cited earlier the statistic that only one psychotherapist in six believes that he is greatly helped in the treatment process by having advance knowledge of the patient's psychodynamics. One relevant consideration here is the rate at which the psychotherapist's image of his patient converges to a stable picture. John Drevdahl, Shirley Mink, Sherman Nelson, Murray Stopol, and I have been looking into this question. So far, it seems that the therapist's image of his patient crystallizes quite rapidly, so that somewhere between the second and fourth therapeutic hour it has stabilized approximately to the degree permitted by the terminal sort-resort reliabilities. Let me show you a couple of typical results. Figure 1 shows the Q correla-

tions between Stopol's phenotypic sort after the twenty-fourth hour and his successive sorts after the first, second, fourth, eighth, and sixteenth hours. "S," indicates correlation of his stereotype with twenty-fourth-hour sort. "Rel" is sort-resort reliability. (The phenotypic and genotypic ratings are made separately.) Figure 2 shows results for the genotypic pool. I do not mean to suggest that the therapist's perception at the end of 24 hours is "the criterion," which would involve a concept of validation that I reject (Cronbach and Meehl, 1955, pp. 284-285, 292-294). But presumably his perception after 24 contacts is more trustworthy than after only one. Or, if we (a) assume that some information gained early is subsequently lost by forgetting, erroneous revisions, and the like; (b) take as our standard of comparison the average value of ratings over all six sortings; and (c) treat this as a kind of "best combined image," the essential character of the situation remains as shown.

Now this state of affairs presents any psychological test with a difficult task. If, after two to four hours of therapeutic interviewing, the therapist tends to arrive at a stable image of the patient which is not very different from the one he will have after 24 contacts, and if that final image is pretty accurate, the test would need to have very high validity before we could justify the expenditure of skilled psychological time in giving, scoring, interpreting, and communicating it.

When we first began this convergence study, our primary interest was in the pragmatic utility of the MMPI. One way to consider validity (which makes more practical sense than the conventional validation study) is to ask: "How long does it take the psychotherapist to find out what the test would have told him in the first place?" We were interested in plotting the Q correlation between a blind MMPI description of the patient and the successive sorts done by the therapist as he gathered more extensive samples of the latter's behavior during treatment, hoping to find that, as the therapist gets "wised up" by further interviews, he learns what the MMPI would have told him all along. This pleasant fantasy was disturbed by the rapidity with which the therapist's image of the patient converges, even before the Campbell-Fiske correlations were run. It is of some

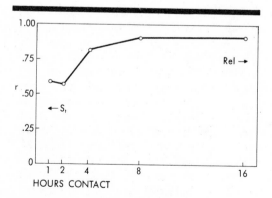

Fig. 2 *Q correlations between therapist's sort at 24 contacts and earlier sorts. (Genotypic pool; N = 113 items; Stopol)*

interest to plot the curve of Q correlation between a "good" blind MMPI description of the patient and the successive descriptions by the therapist (Figure 3). These results are surely nothing to write home about!

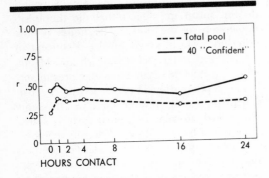

Fig. 3 *Q correlations between MMPI reader's sort and successive sorts by therapist. (Phenotypic pool; Meehl and Stopol)*

In recent paper reporting on an empirical study of MMPI sorting behavior (Meehl 1959b) I listed six factors or circumstances which might be expected theoretically to favor the clinician's brain as a cognizing and decision making instrument in competition with the traditional statistical methods of combining data. Among these six factors is one in which I have a particular interest, I suppose partly because it lends itself more readily to quantitative study than do some of the others. This factor is the presumed ability of the clinician to react on the basis of higher order configural relations (Meehl 1954, pp. 130-134; Horst 1954) by virtue of the fact that a system of variables can be graphically represented as a profile; and thereafter, given extensive clinical experience with a particular instrument, the clinician can respond to the visual gestalt. This he could do by *exemplifying* a complex mathematical function which neither he nor anyone else had as yet succeeded in *formulating*. The search for that function could take place in the context of studying the generalization and discrimination of complex visual forms. I recommend to your attention the recent work of Paul J. Hoffman on this

subject, some of which has been reported (1958a, 1958b, 1959). Hoffman has undertaken a mathematical analysis of the rating behavior of judges who are presented with multivariable profiles, and the application of his formulas should teach us a great deal about the clinician's cognitive activity.

Comparing the impressionistic judgment of a group of Minnesota clinicians as to the amount of "psychotic tendency" revealed by MMPI profiles with six statistical methods of treating the profiles, I found that the pooled judgment of 21 clinicians was significantly better (against the diagnostic criterion) than the linear discriminant function. In fact, there was a significant tendency (although slight) for even the *individual* clinicians to do a better job than the linear discriminant function. However, the best cross-validative results displayed by any method of sorting these profiles thus far tried utilizes a very complex set of configural rules developed by Grant Dahlstrom and myself (Meehl & Dahlstrom, 1960). Table 1 shows the results of applying these rules to almost a thousand cases from eight clinics over the United States. These rules were concocted by a combination of clinical experience with statistical checking; and, while relatively crude and surely failing to extract all of the profile information, they are more efficient at this than a linear combination of scores, the pooled

Table 1 *Concurrent validity of Meehl-Dahlstrom rules in eight cross-validation samples*

Sample	N	H%	M%	I%	$\frac{H}{H+M}$	P
A*	92	55	16	28	.77	<.001
B*	77	45	29	26	.61	<.05
C	103	49	16	35	.75	<.001
D	42	40	21	38	.65	nonsig.
E*	181	45	18	36	.71	<.001
F	166	47	20	33	.70	<.001
G	273	63	12.	25	.84	<.001
K*	54	78	5	17	.93	no test
Total	988	53	17	30	.76	.001

*Essentially uncontaminated samples.

judgments of 29 MMPI readers, or the judgment of the best of 29. Without knowing the form and constants of the mathematical function relating probability of psychosis to the MMPI variables, we cannot answer the question: "How much of the information contained in the profile is extracted by the clinician?" One may plot probability of psychosis as a function of the clinicians' placement of profiles on an 11-step subjective scale of degree (or confidence) of psychoticism. Figure 4 shows probability of psychosis as a function of impressionistic profile placement by the best and worst clinician, and the pooled judgment of a group of 29. Figure 5 shows hit rate (whether neurotic or psychotic) as a function of the amount of consensus among 29 judges.

While our data do indicate that the clinician's judging behavior with respect to the psychoticism variable is significantly configural, the *amount* of departure from a linear, additive model does not appear to be very great. For many years, skeptical statisticians have been pointing out to us clinicians that there is more conversation about nonlinear functions than there is actual demonstration of such and, anyway, that the value of departures from linearity and additivity involved in clinical judgments is likely to be attenuated, if not completely washed out, by the clinician's assignment of nonoptimal weights and the unreliability invariably involved in the impressionistic use of multivariate data.

Lykken, Hoffman, and I plan to utilize some of the MMPI psychoticism data for the kinds of analysis the latter has suggested, but in the meantime I have applied one of Hoffman's formulas to a portion of these data. He suggests that, if we treat the clinician's quantitative sorting as the dependent variable, the multiple R of this variable upon the profile scores should differ from unity only because of the clinician's unreliability, provided his sorting behavior follows a linear model. The multiple R of the 11-step psychoticism ratings for my four best clinicians, when divided by the square root of their reliabilities (Hoffman's "complexity" formula), varies from .871 to .975, with a mean of .942, indicating that the departure of their judging behavior from a linear model is small. It is also interesting that the *inter*sorter reliability (Horst's generalized coefficient) reaches

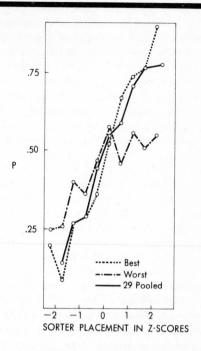

Fig. 4 *Probability of psychosis as function of MMPI profile placement by sorters.*

.994 for the four best sorters and .987 for the four worst. Whatever these MMPI readers are doing when asked to judge psychoticism from the profile, they seem to be doing it in very much the same way.

Let me turn next to a brief account of an exploratory study which was a dismal failure and which I am still trying to figure out. All told, there now exist almost 200 different scoring keys for the MMPI item pool, ranging all the way from "dependency" to "baseball talent" and derived by a variety of methods (including factor analysis, face validity, and criterion keying). I thought it might be interesting to treat the patient's MMPI behavior more like the psychoanalyst than like the factor analyst: namely, to overdetermine the psychology of the patient by scoring him on a large number of these scales, in spite of their redundancy. Imagine two patients who produce identical profiles when scored on a very large number of partially overlapping but distinguishable variables. One might hope, except for the intrinsic defects of *coverage* in the MMPI item pool, that such a pair of individuals would be, so to speak, pinpointed in personality space as very close together. In practice it is impossible to find identical (or even nearly identical) profiles as the number of scored dimensions is increased, but perhaps one could get an estimate of this extreme by extrapolating interpatient similarities from lesser degrees of profile resemblance.

Selecting a sample of 20 female outpatients rated by staff psychiatrists or psychologists in connection with a study on the new ataraxic Mellaril (Fleeson, Glueck, Heistad, King, Lykken, Meehl, & Mena, 1958), we calculated the interviewer rating Q correlations for all possible pairs, thus generating an interpatient resemblance matrix of 190 elements. Turning then to the MMPI (by which the clinical raters were, of course, uncontaminated) and eliminating scales of fewer than 10 or more than 80 items, we set up random sets of 10 scales after defining the first set of 10 as the basic profile of clinical scales commonly used. The Cronbach-Gleser distance measure was then computed on the MMPI profiles for the same 190 pairs. Thus we had a matrix of interpatient resemblances as clinically described by skilled interviewers through Q sorts and a corresponding matrix of MMPI profile similarity indices. A *series* of matrices of this latter kind was then generated by progressively extending the profile, adding successive blocks of 10 randomly chosen scales. Thus, the first MMPI matrix was based upon the interpatient distance measures for the usual 10 scores, the second one upon 20 scores (the usual 10 plus 10 randomly chosen), the third one on 30 scores, and so forth up to a profile of 160 variables! The idea, of course, was that through this procedure we would be squeezing all of the blood out of the psychometric turnip and that a second order correlation (apologies to the statisticians) between the corresponding elements of the two matrices would show a steady rise.

It would have been very nice had the asymptote of this intermatrix coefficient, when plotted as a function of the number of MMPI variables entering into the distance measure, approached a very high value. That is, if you measure — however unreliably and redundantly — a huge mass of variables (schizoid trend, recidivism, dominance, defensiveness, baseball

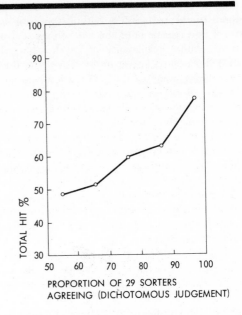

Fig. 5 *Hit rate as function of MMPI sorter consensus. (neurosis-psychosis)*

talent, dependency, control, ego strength, use of repression, tendency to homesickness, academic potential, etc.), then the psychological resemblance between two patients will be closely related to their profile similarity on this extended list of MMPI scores. It turned out that there was no problem of curve fitting, for the simple reason that the intermatrix resemblances began at zero for the first 10 scales and remained at zero, without the slightest tendency to increase as we included further blocks of scales in computing the distance measures. We know from a good deal of evidence that neither the MMPI nor the clinical Q sorts are quite *that* bad, and I am at a loss to understand these results. My suspicion is that they arise from inadequacies of the distance measure itself, and further analysis of the data is being undertaken with this hypothesis in mind. I still think that it was an interesting idea.

Leaving profile pattern interpretation, I should like to consider one more topic briefly. One of the most important problems in clinical psychology is deciding what kind of language communicates the largest amount of information about a patient. Most clinical practice today is predicated upon the assumption that useful statements about the patient can best be formulated (or at least inferentially mediated) by a theoretical language. The power of theoretical discourse in the other sciences makes this predilection understandable, and the characteristic Allport-Vernon-Lindzey profiles of clinical psychologists reflect strong theoretical interest. However, we learn in undergraduate physics that in order to apply theoretical constructs to the solution of practical problems (specifically, to predict the subsequent course of a particular physical system), one must fulfill two conditions. First, he must possess a reasonably well developed theory. That is, he must know the laws that systems of the given kind obey. Secondly, he must have a technology, a set of measuring instruments, for determining the initial and boundary conditions of the particular system under study. To the extent that either, or both, of these conditions are not fulfilled, predictions arrived at by theoretical inference will be untrustworthy. I do not see how anyone taking an objective view of the enterprise could claim that we fulfill *either*, let alone both, of these conditions in clinical psychology today. For this reason, in spite of my own personal interest in theoretical questions, I remain among that minority who persist in skepticism as to the pragmatic utility of theoretical constructions in daily clinical decision making.

Suppose, however, that some kind of theoretical discourse is to be used; which of the several kinds of theoretical sublanguages is most economical? As a pilot study in connection with a Ford Foundation project now going on at Minnesota, I collected some preliminary data which you may find of interest. Twenty psychotherapists were asked to describe a patient whom they had had in treatment for at least 25 hours, using the 182-item phenotypic pool which generated the curves previously shown. They also described the patient in terms of the 113-item genotypic pool. Although the latter pool was not constructed in any systematic way with respect to theoretical orientation, having been built for a different purpose, one can identify five relatively homogeneous subsets of genotypic items as follows: 25 Murray needs, 14 areas of conflict, 13 mechanisms of defense,

10 value-orientation components, and 7 items referring to dimensions of psychiatric nosology. After calculating the 190 interpatient Q correlations based upon each of these subpools, we may ask how well the pattern of interpatient resemblances in the phenotype is reproduced by the genotypic matrix. Unfortunately, I have not been able to find a statistician who will tell me how to do a significance test on such data, but the coefficients obtained are shown in Table 2. It is remarkable, I think, that the 13 defense mechanisms do about as well in reproducing the 182-item phenotypic matrix as does the entire genotypic pool consisting of almost 10 times as many items. We hope that with a more systematic coverage of the domain the Ford project will give us some definite information about this question.

Table 2 *Correlations between interpatient* P *matrix and* G *matrices based on various subpools*

Variables	r
P (182 items) vs. entire G pool (113 items)	.59
P vs. 13 defense mechanisms	.52
P vs. 25 Murray needs	.22
P vs. 7 nosological components	.22
P vs. 10 value dimensions	.03
P vs. 14 conflict areas	−.03
P vs. all 69 G items in above subpools	.45

Note. — $_{20}C_2$ patients rated; $N = 190$ coefficients.

I have presented some samples of research currently in progress at Minnesota which, while somewhat heterogeneous and difficult to pull together, all treat of what we see as pragmatically important aspects of the clinician's cognitive activity. In order to place any confidence in either the theoretical constructs we employ in discussing patients, or in the instrument-interpreter combinations we use to assess them, studies of convergent and discriminative validity must be carried out. The Campbell-Fiske multitrait-multimethod matrix, or the multiperson-multimethod variant of it, should be useful for this purpose. It seems obvious that even adequate and sophisticated studies of construct validity must be supplemented by data upon the *rate* at which the clinician acquires information from various sources. Since the commonest justification for expenditure of psychometric time is the utility to the therapist of "advance knowledge" (expecially of the genotype), the skepticism expressed by our sample of psychotherapists, taken in combination with the convergence curves for the therapist's perception of his patient, put this widely held belief badly in need of experimental support. An important aspect of such data, presumably rather specific to various populations and clinical instruments, is that of differential convergence rates among items. There are probably certain attributes for which a test's validity is insufficient to justify a marked departure from the base rates or mean rating of the given clinical population, and others for which the therapist tends to be in error early in the game and to converge to the truth rather slowly in contrast to the test. I would predict that an example of this is MMPI Scale 6, which is a rather weak scale when used as an exclusion test, but which, when elevated, turns out almost invariably to be right. I have had patients in treatment whose paranoid potential did not manifest itself until 50 or 75 sessions, by which time I had concluded (erroneously) that the MMPI was giving me a false positive.

As has been pointed out by many clinicians, lacking adequate clinical cookbooks (Meehl 1956) we have in practice to treat our instruments as instrument-interpreter combinations. I believe we can say upon present evidence that no one interpreter succeeds in extracting all of the information contained in a profile and that the development of objective configural methods of profile analysis (of which the Meehl-Dahlstrom rules are a primitive example) is a task of great importance. David Lykken and I are currently engaged in a study comparing more complex functions—such as a second degree polynomial having squares and cross-products—with clinical judgment and the Meehl-Dahlstrom Rules. I am betting on the last-named, because—while nonoptimally weighted—they do at least tap configural effects involving interactions up to the sixth order.

Finally, the question of what is the most economical language to employ in describing a patient remains open, although it appears that there are many practitioners who are not sufficiently aware that this problem exists.

I look forward to the next decade of research in clinical psychology with a certain ambivalence. We are asking more sensible questions and being more critical of our procedures; and several research techniques are now available, and in wide use, which should give us some pretty clear answers. The reason for my ambivalence (and I regret that in the role of prophet I have to sound like Jeremiah) is that the evidence already available suggests that the outcomes will look pretty gloomy. My advice to fledgling clinical psychologists is to construct their self-concept mainly around "I am a researcher" or "I am a psychotherapist," because one whose self-concept is mainly "I am a (test oriented) psychodiagnostician" may have to maintain his professional security over the next few years by not reading the research literature, a maneuver which has apparently proved quite successful already for some clinicians. Personally, I find the cultural lag between what the published research shows and what clinicians persist in claiming to do with their favorite devices even more disheartening than the adverse evidence itself.

Psychologists cannot administer shock treatment or pass out tranquilizers, and I do not know of any evidence that we are better psychotherapists than our psychiatric colleagues. If there is anything that justifies our existence — other than the fact that we come cheaper — it is that we think scientifically about human behavior and that we come from a long tradition, going way back to the very origins of experimental psychology in the study of human error, of being critical of ourselves as cognizing organisms and of applying quantitative methods to the outcomes of our cognitive activity. If this methodological commitment is not strong enough to compete with the commitments clinicians have to particular diagnostic instruments, the unique contribution of our discipline will have been lost. I can mobilize some enthusiasm for the next 10 years within the field: while I expect discouraging findings at the level of practice, from the standpoint of the sociology of professions and the history of ideas, the developments should be very interesting to watch.

Experience and the development of motivation: some reinterpretations[1]

J. McV. HUNT

A recent issue of the *Saturday Evening Post* carried a cartoon that some of you may have noted. It depicts a boy entering his house, perhaps from school, where his father is sitting with his paper. The boy appears to be fixing his father with an accusing glare. The punchline reads, "Somebody goofed. I'm improperly motivated."

This cartoon depicts the vantage point from which I have been examining what we think we know about the relation between experience and motivation. When a child's behavior fails to fit the standards somebody in our society holds for him, it is pretty well agreed among us who are supposed to be experts on human nature that "somebody goofed." And that somebody is usually considered to be a parent.

The question is: what is the proper formula? If one examines the accruing evidence relevant to what has been the dominant conception of the experiential sources of motivation, one can hardly escape the conclusion that this conceptual scheme needs some revisions. If we based our childrearing entirely on our dominant theory of motivational development, we would probably goof as often and as badly as run-of-the-mill parents.

Today I wish, first, to remind you of three of the most basic and general of the propositions in that theory of motivation which has been dominant for the past 30 to 40 years. These are propositions which, although stated in somewhat varied forms, have been shared by both psychoanalysts and academic behavior theorists. Secondly, I wish to cite evidence which calls these propositions into question, and thirdly, to suggest tentatively three new interpretative principles which appear to me to be congruent with a large number of facts and which have interesting implications.

Our conceptions of motivation have traditionally been concerned with three large questions. (a) Why does an organism or person become active? (b) Why does the organism or person act one way rather than another? and (c) How do you get the organism or person to change his behavior to something conceived to be more desirable or appropriate?

THE DOMINANT THEORY

Drive

According to our dominant theory, it is claimed, first of all, that "all behavior is motivated," and that the aim or function of every instinct, defense, action, or habit is to reduce or eliminate stimulation or excitation within the nervous system. It is not easy to state when this view was first presented. Signs of it appear in the seventh chapter of Freud's *Interpretation of Dreams* (1938a) in 1900, and the idea is fullblown in his paper entitled *Instincts and Their Vicissitudes* (1950) in 1915. The idea also appears in Woodworth's *Dynamic Psychology* (1918), published in 1918, where the term *drive* was first introduced into the glossary of American psychology. The idea was full-blown in Dashiell's *Fundamentals of Objective Psychology* (1928) in 1928.

Although Freud (1950) believed that the source of motivation lay outside the domain of psychology in physiology, American psychologists, untroubled by such limits to their domain, have gone on to answer the first question concerning what motivates organisms to become

From *Child Development*, 1960, **31**, 489-504.

1 Earlier versions of this paper were read at the Eleventh Annual Institute in Psychiatry and Neurology of the Veterans Administration Hospital at North Little Rock, Arkansas, 27 February 1959, and at colloquia of the Department of Psychology at Vanderbilt University and of the Department of Psychiatry at the Medical School of Colorado. The paper was prepared in connection with a survey of the implications of the work in behavioral science for childrearing which has been supported by the Russell Sage Foundation.

active by saying that they are *driven*. Organisms have been conceived to be driven, first, by those so-called primary, inner stimuli which arise from homeostatic inbalances or needs. With no shame whatsoever, psychologists have long cited the evidence from the work of such physiologists as Claude Bernard (1859) and his successors, and especially of Walter B. Cannon (1915), and also of the psychologist Curt Richter (1927) to document this answer. Organisms are driven, second, by various forms of intense and painful external stimulation. It has been assumed that these two forms of stimulation arouse an inner state of excitement which has usually been called *drive*.

It is also assumed, as the proposition that "all behavior is motivated" implies, that the organism would be inactive unless driven by either inner or outer stimuli. Freud (1950) has been highly explicit about this assumption, and the assumption lies implicitly behind the notion of conditioned or learned drive in behavior theory and behind the traumatic notion of anxiety in psychoanalysis. It is sometimes obvious, of course, that animals and people are sometimes active when it is hard to see how either homeostatic drive or painful external stimulation could be operative. It is then assumed that some of the weak, innocuous stimuli present must have been associated in the past with either painful stimuli or homeostatic needs. In such a way the weak stimuli which are present must have acquired the capacity to arouse the drive, often now called anxiety by psychologists as well as psychoanalysts, and it is such acquired or conditioned drive that is conceived to activate the organism.

Such conditioned drive or anxiety has been well demonstrated in the laboratory. Before World War II, Miller (1941; 1948) at Yale showed that rats which had been repeatedly shocked in a white box would, when later returned to the white box, make an effort to escape. Moreover, in the course of these efforts, they could be got to learn new skills such as that of turning a wheel to open a door. Rats which had not been shocked in the white box made no such efforts to escape. In another demonstration Solomon and Wynne (1953) have shown that dogs which have experienced a tone or a buzzer paired a few times with a subtetanizing shock will run away from that

tone or buzzer for hundreds of trials, with the average reaction time of starting continuing to decrease through 600 such trials. In my own work (Hunt, 1941) rats fed irregularly in infancy ate more and sometimes (Hunt, 1947) hoarded more than their litter-mate controls in adulthood after a period without food. Here, as I conceived it, the cues of hunger were conditioned to intense hunger excitement during the infantile experience. In adulthood the conditioned hunger drive facilitated the rate of eating and, sometimes, hoarding.

Such work has demonstrated that this notion of conditioned drive or anxiety, which goes back to the work of Bechterev (1913) and Watson and Raynor (1920), has a solid basis in reality. But in what has been the dominant theory of motivation, as epitomized by Freud's (1936) later traumatic theory of anxiety and by the Hull (1943) and Dollard-Miller (Dollard & Miller, 1950; Miller & Dollard, 1941) theory of acquired drives, conditioning is conceived to be the only way in which an organism can become fearful of innocuous stimuli.

Habit

Habit has been the answer to the second question concerned with why an animal or person acts one way rather than another. The organism is controlled by the habits which have served to reduce drive in the past when that organism was in the presence of the inner and outer drive stimuli and the cue stimuli impinging upon him at any given now. Under the term *habit*, I am including psychoanalytic modes, which have supposedly been fixated during infancy in the course of either too much gratification or too much frustration, and I am including also ego-defenses, or anxiety equivalents, and cathexes, as well as the instrumental responses and traits commonly investigated in psychological laboratories.

Changing behavior has been conceived to be a matter of motivating the organism with either punishment or homeostatic need to make the desired behavior which can then be reinforced by arranging for it to reduce the drive aroused by the punishment or the need. Although the conditions and conceptions of psychotherapy in the clinic differ considerably from the conditions and conceptions of the behavior theorist investigating learning in laboratory animals, in either case it is conceived that motivation is a necessity, and motivation means changing the emotional or drive conditions which are quite extrinsic to either the instrumental behavior or the cognitive, informational processes concerned.

This dominant theory has been a conceptual edifice of large dimensions and of considerable detail. It has provided a plausible account of both personality development and social motives. The experimental facts of homeostasis and of conditioned drive and fear are sound. Nevertheless, it has become more and more evident in the past 10 years that some of the basic assumptions of this dominant theoretical scheme and some of the explanatory extrapolations contradict facts and call for reinterpretation.

REINTERPRETATIONS

Is All Behavior Motivated?

The first of the assumptions to be called into question is the one that *all behavior is motivated* and that *organisms become inactive unless stimulated* by homeostatic need or painful stimulation or conditional stimuli for these. A large variety of observations contradict this assumption and imply spontaneous molar activity. Beach (1945) has reviewed the observations of play in the young to show that playful activities are most likely to occur when either young animals or children are homeostatically satisfied and also comfortably warm. The very occurrence of either homeostatic need or strong external stimulation stops play and turns the young animal or child to activities calculated to relieve such stimulation. Berlyne (1950; 1955) has shown that well-fed and watered rats will explore areas new to them if given only the opportunity. Montgomery (1953), moreover, has shown that hunger and thirst tend to limit the exploratory behavior of rats rather than facilitate it, and Montgomery and Monkman (1955), as well as others, have shown that conditioned fear inhibits exploration. Harlow, Harlow, and Meyer (1950) have demonstrated that well-fed monkeys will learn to unassemble a three-

device puzzle with no other drive and "no other reward than the privilege of unassembling it." In another study Harlow (1950) found two well-fed and well-watered monkeys worked repeatedly at unassembling a six-device puzzle for 10 continuous hours, and they were still showing what he characterized as enthusiasm for their work on the tenth hour of testing. From his observations of the human child, moreover, Piaget (1952) remarks repeatedly on the enthusiastic and repeated performance of such emerging skills as the release of a toy, sitting up, standing, etc.

Such evidences of spontaneous behavior, which is unmotivated in the traditional sense, have led to the naming of such new motives as a curiosity drive by Berlyne (1955), an exploratory drive by Montgomery (1951), and exteroceptive and curiosity drives by Harlow (1953). I would like to object that merely naming such drives explains nothing. If we continue, we shall be revisiting McDougall's (1915) practice of postulating a separate drive for almost every variety of activities. Let us stop with noting that such observations do contradict our assumption that organisms will become inactive unless driven by homeostatic needs and painful stimuli and give up this ancient Greek notion that living matter is inert substance to which motion must be imparted by extrinsic forces. We can then embrace the thermodynamic conception of living things as open systems of energy exchange which exhibit activity intrinsically and upon which stimuli have a modulating effect, but not an initiating effect.

This notion of activity being intrinsic in living tissue is receiving support from studies of organ systems as well as studies of molar organisms. The EEG, for example, shows that brain cells are continuously active (Jasper, 1937; Prosser, 1934). In sleep the slow waves of large amplitude are taken to imply that large numbers of cells are firing synchronously, and the effect of waking and stimulation and exciting the brain-stem-reticular formation is to asynchronize this firing which shows in rapid waves of low magnitude (Lindsley, 1957).

Granit (1955) points out that the spontaneous firing of retinal cells increases with dark adaptation and thereby functions to prevent the deafferentization of visual contex with darkness. Twenty years ago, this spontaneous firing was considered, at worst, to be due to some failure of experimental control, or at best, noise in the channel of information. Recently, the Laceys (1958) have found spontaneous fluctuations of sudomotor activity and cardiac activity which they also see as functioning in the control of the organism's relations with its environment. Especially intriguing is their notion that the carotid sinus mechanism functions as a feedback loop which participates in the directing of attention inward or outward by inhibiting or facilitating receptor inputs. But the point of mentioning these evidences of spontaneous activities of organ systems here is merely to help inter for good the notion that activity of living systems requires homeostatic need or painful external stimulation and to foster the idea that to live means to be active in some degree.

Reinforcement

This idea of activity being intrinsic in living organisms has implications for our conception of reinforcement. It makes it unnecessary to see all activity as a matter of either reducing or avoiding stimulation which is implied in the assumption that organisms become inactive unless stimulated. This is a second fundamental assumption of the dominant theory which has been shared by psychoanalysts and behavior theorists alike.

On the one hand, there is still a place for drive reduction. It is clear that under conditions of homeostatic need and painful stimulation, and perhaps under circumstances when the conditions of stimulation are changing with too great rapidity, both animals and persons learn techniques and strategies leading to gratification or reduction in external stimulation. The evidence that led Thorndike to formulate the "law of effect" is as convincing as ever. Moreover, in association with reductions of homeostatic need, animals and men may also learn cathexes or emotional attachments. The facts referred to are those highly familiar in secondary reinforcement (Hull, 1943; Pavlov, 1927).

On the other hand, the facts implying that organisms show spontaneous molar activity also imply that, when animals and human

beings have been living under conditions of low and unchanging stimulation for a time, increases of stimulation become reinforcing. Butler has shown that rhesus monkeys will learn quite complex discriminations with the only reward being a peek through a glass window (1953) at the things in the next room or a few seconds of auditory experience (1957). Berlyne (1950) has shown that, the greater the variety of stimulation in an area which rats are permitted to explore, the longer they continue their explorations.

Especially important in this connection are the studies of human behavior under conditions of minimal variation in stimulation. I refer to the studies of perceptual isolation by Bexton, Heron, and Scott (1954) at McGill and also the work of Lilly (1956). At McGill, college students were paid 20 dollars a day to do nothing. They lay for 24 hours a day on a comfortable bed. The temperature was optimal and constant. Eyes, ears, and hands were shielded to minimize stimulus variation. Few subjects could endure more than two or three days of such conditions. They developed a desire for variation which was almost overwhelming.

While interpreting such facts in terms of a multiple set of drives for curiosity, exploration, or stimulation will get us only to a redescription of them, Hebb's (1955) notion of an optimal level of activation—and, I would like to add, stimulus variation below which *increases* are reinforcing and above which *decreases* are reinforcing—is an integrative conception of fair magnitude. Moreover, the drive-reduction principle of reinforcement may be seen to be but half of this more general curvilinear principle.

But this is probably not the whole story. It looks as if there were natively both positive and negative forms of exciting stimulation. Sheffield, Roby, and Campbell (1954) have argued that the reinforcing effect of eating is not a matter of reduction of the hunger drive but rather a matter of the positive value of the consummatory act of eating. Moreover, Sheffield, Wulff, and Backer (1951) have shown that male rats will learn mazes to get to females in heat even when they are allowed only intromission but not allowed to continue coitus to the point of drive-reducing ejaculation. From the fact that Davis (Davis & Buchwald, 1957) and his collaborators at Indiana have shown that showing pictures of nude women to college males increases excitement as shown by increased palmar conductance and the arrest of EEG-alpha, it is clear that such stimulation is exciting rather than excitement-reducing. Young (1955) has long emphasized the importance of the hedonic quality of experience for reinforcement, and he has shown that speed of running in rat subjects increases with the concentration of sucrose in the incentive drink.

The suggestion that the two forms of excitation, one positive and one negative, are built into organisms comes also from the work of Olds and Milner (1954). Electrical stimulation of the septal area is positively reinforcing, but electrical stimulation of the brain-stem reticular formation is negatively reinforcing. Perhaps, it is not without significance that the septal area is part of the old olfactory brain which has been considered to have an especially important part in the mediation of sexual and consummatory behavior in mammals. At any rate, it looks as though certain types of stimulation may be positively reinforcing even though they be intense and exciting. This may mean that the curvilinear principle may be limited in its domain to strong stimulation via the exteroceptors when homeostatic needs are minimized.

The suggestion of innate, positive, and negative exteroceptive stimulation comes secondly from recent work by Harlow (1958). It has been customary to see an infant's cathexis or love for its mother developing as secondary reinforcement largely out of its feeding experiences. Freud (1938b), of course, contended that the pleasure from stimulation of the oral erogenous zone furnished the experiential basis for both pleasure-sucking and maternal attachment, a contention which contradicted his most definitive formulations of drive theory (1950). The fact than an infant must suck for its nourishment, according to libido theory (Freud, 1938b, p. 587), merely guaranteed discovery of the pleasures of oral stimulation. Behavior theorists have seen both sucking and love of mother as forms of secondary reinforcement deriving from the fact that the child satisfies its hunger by means of sucking the mother's breasts (Mussen & Conger, 1956, pp. 137ff.). Harlow (1958), however, has recently compared the degree of attachment of young monkeys to a wire mother-surrogate on which they nursed at a bottle with attachment to a padded and cloth-covered mother-surrogate on which they received nothing but the feel of the softness. In terms of the amount of time spent on each of the two mother-surrogates, the monkeys showed more than 10 times the attachment to the soft-padded surrogate as to the wire surrogate. When various fear-evoking stimuli were presented to the baby monkeys in their cages, it was to the padded and cloth-covered surrogate that the frightened, infant monkey turned, not to the wire surrogate on which it had been nursed. Harlow argues from these findings that it is the sensory quality of softness which gives the reinforcement. His study suggests, moreover, that it is important to investigate the capacity for various kinds of stimuli for positive and negative reinforcement in the very young. Pratt (1954) cites a monograph by Canestrini (1913) on the sensory life of the newborn for an observation that certain stimuli are associated with decreases in the rate of the heart rate, and are therefore pleasant, while others are associated with increases in heart rate and are unpleasant.[2] In view of the finding by Davis (Davis & Buchwald, 1957) and his collaborators that seeing a picture of a nude female results in reduction in the heart rate of male college students, it is possible that this physiological indicator may provide a technique for determining the direction of the reinforcing effect of stimuli in the newborn. At any rate, what is suggested is that McDougall's (1915) old notion of natively positive and negative values for receptors inputs be reexamined.

Conditioned Fear and Anxiety

The third assumption that I wish to examine in the light of empirical evidence is the notion that fear and anxiety are *always* inculcated as a consequence of traumatic experiences of help-

2 An examination of Canestrini (1913) monograph shows that Pratt was mistaken in stating that Canestrini remarked upon decreases in heart rate being associated with pleasure, but some of his published kymograph records do indicate decreases in heart rate. It may well be that heart rate could serve as an indicator of the emotional value of various sensory inputs, and these might be tested for their reinforcement values. I am indebted to Dr. William Gerler for reading this monograph carefully to check my own impressions of Canestrini's text.

lessness in the face of homeostatic need or painful external stimulation. Note that I am not denying that such conditioned fears do exist. I am only questioning the word *always* . . . are always inculcated as a consequence of traumatic experiences.

The first relevant studies go way back to the 1920's. Harold and Mary Cover Jones (1928) attempted to test the claims of Watson (1928) and Watson and Raynor (1920) concerning conditioned fears. They exposed their subjects of various ages, ranging from early infancy to adult, to a large but sluggish and harmless bull-snake. Fear of the snake was exceedingly common among adults, teenagers, and latency-age children, but it was absent in children below three years of age. It began to appear among children older than three and was typical of children six and older. From the fact that the fear appeared at a younger age in those of higher intelligence than those of lower intelligence, the Joneses argued that fear of snakes is a response which comes automatically into the developing child's repertoire through maturation. This remains as an alternative hypothesis to that of conditioned fear.

A study by Frances Holmes (1935), which is seldom cited, calls both of these interpretations into question. Holmes compared the fearfulness of the children of lower-class background, who were attending a day nursery, with the fearfulness of children of upper-class background, who were attending a private nursery school. She got her fear scores by indicating that the child could get some attractive toys with which to play by going into the dark room adjacent to the examining room, or by taking them off a chair situated beside that of a strange woman dressed in a large floppy black hat and a long gray coat, or by climbing along a plank some three feet off the floor. If the child started immediately for the toys, he got a score of one for that item. If he hesitated but ultimately went ahead on his own, he got a score of two. If he would go only if accompanied by the examiner, the score was three. If he refused to go at all, the score was four. There were seven such situations. The results show that the fear scores of the lower-class children averaged only about half the size of those for the upper-class children, and the fear scores for boys were lower than those for girls. Yet it would be the lower-class children who had experienced the more homeostatic need and painfully rough treatment than the upper-class children, and the boys had probably experienced more painful experiences than the little girls. That intelligence is not the factor is shown by the fact that the fear scores showed a correlation of only about +.2 with mental age, and the differences were still significant when intelligence was partialed out. Something besides either conditioned fear or the correlation between fear and intelligence is required to make these results comprehensible.

Recently evidence even more contradictory to the notion of conditioned fears has been coming from the work of Seymour Levine. Levine, Chevalier, and Korchin (1956) have compared the adult behavior of rats shocked and rats petted daily from birth to their 20th day with the adult behavior of rats left continuously in their nests with their mothers. When he started this work, Levine expected to find that the shocked animals would show traumatic effects of their shock experiences in heightened emotionality and damaged capacity to learn adaptive responses. On the contrary, the shocked animals, along with the handled animals, gained weight faster than those left in the nest (Levine, 1957a; Levine, 1957b; Levine, 1958; Levine, Chevalier, & Korchin, 1956). Byron Lindholm, working with the writer, has repeated and confirmed this finding. Moreover, Levine's shocked and handled animals both showed less emotionality than those left continuously in the nest with their mothers, i.e., less emotionality in the sense that they defecated and urinated less frequently when placed in a strange situation. Finally, the shocked and handled animals, which have appeared alike in all of these experiments, learned an avoidance response more rapidly and drank more readily after 18 hours without water than did the rats left in the nest with their mother.

Clearly these results on both human children and rats imply that fear and anxiety must sometimes have some other basis than that of being associated with painful stimulation. As many of you know, Hebb (1946; 1949) has formulated a radically different explanation of fear which may be termed either an incongruity or a dissonance theory.

The facts which suggested Hebb's conception came largely from observing chimpanzees being raised under controlled conditions at the Yerkes Laboratory. Fear, defined as withdrawal behavior in response to the appearance of some object, does not appear in young chimpanzees until they are approximately four months old. Then, the objects feared are familiar objects in unfamiliar guise. Fear of strangers is an example. This appears spontaneously to the first stranger seen, so it cannot be based on associating strangers with painful stimulation. Fear of strangers does not appear in chimpanzees—or in children, I might add—who have always been exposed to a large number of persons. While the avoidance response is unlearned, the familiar, expected aspects of objects must be learned. The young animal must have established as residues of his experience cortical firing patterns (or cognitive structures—whichever term you like) from which new receptor inputs can be incongruous. Consider the kinds of objects regularly feared. They are, for instance, the familiar keeper or experimenter in strange clothes, the experimenter in a Hallowe'en mask, a plaster cast of a chimpanzee head (which lacks, of course, the familiarly attached body), an anesthetized chimpanzee infant (from which the familiar patterns of motion are absent). On the other hand, objects which have never entered into the young chimpanzee's life may be strange without evoking withdrawal. In other words, the feared object is one which excites receptors in a fashion which is incongruous with the central, sequential pattern of neural firing which has accrued as a residue of the chimpanzee or human infant's past experience. Until the central pattern has been learned, incongruous stimulation is impossible.

Such a conception can well account for Holmes' findings that lower-class children are less fearful than higher-class children and that boys are less fearful than girls even though both lower-class children and boys of nursery school age are likely to have had the wider experience with the sorts of situations used by Holmes to evoke fear. It may well be that being shocked and handled provides a variety of experience which leaves the rat pups which have been subjected to it less disturbed by such things as open fields and 18 hours without water, but these effects may ultimately be found to be a matter of still another mechanism. It is too early to say.

Taking seriously this incongruity-dissonance conception of the genesis of fear leads to interesting reinterpretations of a great many of the motivational phenomena of child development. Consider these few. In considering separation anxiety, the incongruity principle makes it unnecessary to puzzle about how the absence of mother could be the conditional stimulus for the traumatizing and helpless distress that has been supposed to have occurred in her absence. In considering fear of the dark, it also becomes unnecessary to puzzle about how the absence of light stimulation could so widely have been associated with painful stimulation. Multiple mothering need not be seen as a traumatizing experience in the light of this conception, but rather as an inoculation against social shyness and fear. The timidity of the overprotected child and the social shyness of the rural mountain people get an explanation which has been difficult in terms of the theory of conditioned fear.

MOTIVATION IN TERMS OF THE INCONGRUITY-DISSONANCE PRINCIPLE

This introduction of the incongruity-dissonance principle concludes the three reinterpretations I wish to present today, but I do wish to call your attention to the pervasive character of this incongruity-dissonance principle. It appears to have great explanation power which figures, in one guise or another, in several systematic theories, besides that of Hebb, all of which have been characterized as nondynamic.

Hebb's (1949) theorizing is physiological, at least in a verbal sense, in that he conceives the residues of past inputs to be stored in semi-autonomous, reverberating cerebral circuits which he terms *cell assemblies*. These cell assemblies are the neural analogue of concepts, and they get sequentially integrated into what he calls *phase sequences*. The sequential organization in time provides for the subjective phenomenon of expectation. When markedly incongruous receptor inputs disrupt this sequential organization, behavior is changed and the process is felt as unpleasant emotion. Slight degrees of incongruity, which can readily be accommodated, lend interest and may provide attractive problems, but the larger ones are repelling and perhaps even devastating.

Piaget (1952; 1954) utilizes very much the same incongruity notion to account for the development of intelligence and concepts in human children. In his system, the child comes at birth with certain sensory-motor coordinations which he terms *schemata*. Variation in stimulus situations call for adaptive *accommodations* or changes in these schemata, which changes are *assimilated* or stored as residues. Piaget also finds limited incongruities between central schemata and receptor inputs to be interesting and facilitative of growth, but incongruities which extend beyond the child's capacity for accommodation instigate withdrawal or fear and even terror. In Piaget's theory the child's gestalt-like conceptions of reality (space, time, and number) are schemata which develop through a continuous process of accommodations and assimilations and become fixed or static only when the child's schemata come to correspond so well with reality that no further accommodations are required. Here agreement among people is dictated by reality.

Helson (1947; 1948) has called the residues of immediate past experience in the typical psychophysical experiment an *adaptation level*. Both he and McClelland (McClelland, Atkinson, Clark, & Lowell, 1953) have seen affective arousal to be a matter of the size of the discrepancy between receptor inputs and the adaptation level. Small discrepancies may be attractively pleasant, large ones repellingly unpleasant. As an example, some of you will readily recall having experienced the affective startle that comes when you have been set to pick up what you thought was a full pail, only to find it empty.

Festinger (1957) has recently written a book entitled *A Theory of Cognitive Dissonance* in which he shows that a discrepancy between belief about a situation and perception of that situation acts like a drive. The subject acts to reduce the *dissonance* by either withdrawing from the incredible situation or by changing his beliefs, and, not incidentally, he finds the dissonance highly unpleasant.

Rogers (1951) has described the basis for anxiety as discrepancy between the "phenomenological field" and the perceived reality as represented by his two circles. Rogers' phenomenological field, however, is not the perceptually-given phenomenal field of such German phenomenologists as Delthei and Husserl. It is rather the inferred storehouse of past experience and represented in the present by expectations, aspirations, self-concept, and the like. Thus, his conceptual scheme appears to fall within the domain of the incongruity-dissonance principle.

Kelly's (1955) *Psychology of Personal Constructs* also makes central use of this principle. The term *personal constructs* refers to the ways in which individuals construe and anticipate events. These each person derives from the way in which he has experienced such events in the past. When a person's constructions fail to predict events, this is disturbing, even anxiety-producing, and it motivates some kind of change, but the change may take place in defenses against such change of constructs or in avoiding such events, or in the constructs themselves.

Perhaps, it is worth noting in closing that this incongruity-dissonance principle makes both motivation and reinforcement intrinsic to the organism's relations with its environment, intrinsic, if you will, to the organism's information-processing. It is as if the organism operated like an error-actuated, feedback system where the error is derived from discrepancy between receptor-inputs of the present and the residues of past experience which serve as the basis for anticipating the future. The dominant view of the past half century has seen both motivation and reinforcement as extrinsic to the information-processing. This has put a tremendous burden of responsibility for the management of affective motivation on parents, teachers, and all those in positions of authority and control. Visions of man completely controlled, as exemplified by George Orwell's *1984,* are conceivable only by assuming that the extrinsic motivating forces of homeostatic need and painful stimulation are completely dominant. In this light the terror of the baby chimp at seeing his keeper in a Hallowe'en mask and the irritation of the believer when his beliefs are disconfirmed are perhaps symbols of hope. They may justify Abraham Lincoln's well-known dictum that "you can fool some of the people all the time, and all the people some of the time, but you cannot fool all the people all the time."

To return to the cartoon of the lad who was improperly motivated: Perhaps, the task of developing proper motivation is best seen, at least in nutshell form, as limiting the manipulation of extrinsic factors to that minimum of keeping homeostatic need and exteroceptive drive low, in favor of facilitating basic information-processing to maximize accurate anticipation of reality.

part **6**

TWO ROUTES OF SCIENCE

One of the purposes of this book has been to illustrate the diversity of approach, both in method and in ideas, that is part of the strength of psychology as a way of attacking the human puzzle. The eminent physicist-philosopher Percival W. Bridgeman once insisted that science was fundamentally a matter of "doing one's damnedest with one's eyes and one's hands"; and in the study of behavior, it seems clear that there is ample room for many ways of "doing one's damnedest" to make systematic observation further our understanding.

At the same time, diversity is not the same thing as chaos. Many psychological approaches to the conduct of organisms are or can be related to each other, and the clarification of such relationships often leads to greater power—an increase in our ability to make observations that lead to sharper insights into the mystery of man. "The Two Disciplines of Scientific Psychology," the paper by Lee J. Cronbach which closes this volume, is a case in point.

Cronbach's article identifies points of articulation between two long-standing traditions of psychological investigation. One is the tradition of measurement and correlations. Within this psychometric discipline, psychologists investigate the interrelationships among test scores, demographic data, and such indices as ratings on personality or performance dimensions, showing by statistical analyses the patterns of covariation among variables. In other words, observations are reduced through technical procedures to numbers, and the relationships among the resulting quantities are the direct objects of study. The second tradition is the rather different one of experiment. The experimental discipline requires that controls be imposed on the observational process itself and that the variables under consideration be actually manipulated rather than simply measured. In consequence, the direct object of study is behavior (not simply numerical indices) as affected by different conditions which are controlled by the investigator.

An example may shed some light on the difference between the two approaches. If we are interested in the effects of caffein (the stimulant in coffee) on learning, we can attack our problem by ringing various changes on two broad themes. One theme is a psychometric one. We can choose two groups of college students, essentially equal on a measure of academic aptitude but very different in their reports of how much coffee they drink—one group made up of people who drink ten or more cups per day and the other of people who drink three cups or less per day. We can then compare the performance of these two groups, presumably similar in intellectual competence but different in their indices of caffein intake, on an achievement test to see whether one has learned more information than the other. Our second theme, however, is the experimental one. Here we can present a group of subjects with a learning task under conditions where they have had no coffee for a period of twenty-four hours. Observing their performance under this condition, we can then administer a standard dose of caffein to the same people and have them undertake a learning task that has been carefully developed as equivalent to the initial one. Our comparison is then with how well they learned when deprived of caffein and how well they learned when given it. The variations on our psychometric and experimental themes can be quite elaborate, and both can be highly useful. The main point here is that in one case, we are concerned with observations made under naturalistic conditions and reduced to measurements which we then study by means of statistical devices; in the other case, we are concerned with observations made under controlled conditions which permit our direct manipulation of the circumstances that we think may affect some form of behavior.

Cronbach's "Two Disciplines," in demonstrating ways in which the psychometric and the experimental approaches can supplement and strengthen each other, tells its own interesting story. In suggesting one of the ways in which psychological approaches can be fruitfully combined without minimizing the diversity of avenues that lead to a heightened comprehension of the human puzzle, this article provides a fitting conclusion to our brief sampling of how psychologists may contribute to our deeper understanding of ourselves and our fellows.

The two disciplines of scientific psychology [1]

LEE J. CRONBACH

No man can be acquainted with all of psychology today, as our convention program proves. The scene resembles that of a circus, but a circus grander and more bustling than any Barnum ever envisioned—a veritable week-long diet of excitement and pink lemonade. Three days of smartly paced performance are required just to display the new tricks the animal trainers have taught their charges. We admire the agile paper-readers swinging high above us in the theoretical blue, saved from disaster by only a few gossamer threads of fact, and we gasp as one symposiast thrusts his head bravely between another's sharp toothed jaws.

This 18-ring display of energies and talents gives plentiful evidence that psychology is going places. But whither?

In the simpler days of psychology, the presidential address provided a summing-up and a statement of destination. The President called the roll of the branches of psychology—praising the growth of some youngsters, tut-tutting patriarchally over the delinquent tendencies of others—and showed each to his

From the *American Psychologist*, 1957, **12**, 671-684.
1 Address of the President at the Sixty-Fifth Annual Convention of the American Psychological Association, New York, New York, September 2, 1957.

proper place at the family table. My own title is reminiscent of those grand surveys, but the last speaker who could securely bring the whole of psychology within one perspective was Dashiell, with his 1938 address on "Rapprochements in Contemporary Psychology" (1939). My scope must be far more restricted.

I shall discuss the past and future place within psychology of two historic streams of method, thought, and affiliation which run through the last century of our science. One stream is *experimental psychology;* the other, *correlational psychology.* Dashiell optimistically forecast a confluence of these two streams, but that confluence is still in the making. Psychology continues to this day to be limited by the dedication of its investigators to one or the other method of inquiry rather than to scientific psychology as a whole.

A stream of thought is identified by many features: philosophical underpinnings, methods of inquiry, topical interests, and loci of application. The experimental and correlational streams have all these aspects, but I am concerned with them as disciplines within scientific psychology. The job of science is to ask questions of Nature. A discipline is a method of asking questions and of testing answers to determine whether they are sound. Scientific psychology is still young, and there is rapid turnover in our interests, our experimental apparatus and our tests, and our theoretical concepts. But our methods of inquiry have become increasingly stable, and it is these methods which qualify us as scientists rather than philosophers or artists.

THE SEPARATION OF THE DISCIPLINES

The experimental method — where the scientist changes conditions in order to observe their consequences — is much the more coherent of our two disciplines. Everyone knows what experimental psychology is and who the experimental psychologists are. Correlational psychology, though fully as old as experimentation, was slower to mature. It qualifies equally as a discipline, however, because it asks a distinctive type of question and has technical methods of examining whether the question has been

properly put and the data properly interpreted.

In contrast to the Tight Little Island of the experimental discipline, correlational psychology is a sort of Holy Roman Empire whose citizens identify mainly with their own principalities. The discipline, the common service in which the principalities are united, is the study of correlations presented by Nature. While the experimenter is interested only in the variation he himself creates, the correlator finds his interest in the already existing variation between individuals, social groups, and species. By "correlational psychology" I do not refer to studies which rely on one statistical procedure. Factor analysis is correlational, to be sure, but so is the study of Ford and Beach (1952) relating sexual behavior to differences along the phylogenetic scale and across the cultural spectrum.

The well-known virtue of the experimental method is that it brings situational variables under tight control. It thus permits rigorous tests of hypotheses and confident statements about causation. The correlational method, for its part, can study what man has not learned to control or can never hope to control. Nature has been experimenting since the beginning of time, with a boldness and complexity far beyond the resources of science. The correlator's mission is to observe and organize the data from Nature's experiments. As a minimum outcome, such correlations improve immediate decisions and guide experimentation. At the best, a Newton, a Lyell, or a Darwin can align the correlations into a substantial theory.

During our century of scientific psychology, the correlators have marched under many flags. In perhaps the first modern discussion of scientific method in psychology (1874), Wundt (1904) showed how "experimental psychology" and "ethnic psychology" (i.e., cross-cultural correlations) supplement each other. In one of the most recent (1953), Bindra and Scheier (1954) speak of the interplay of "experimental" and "psychometric" method. At the turn of the century, the brand names were "experimental" and "genetic" psychology, although experimenters were also beginning to contrast their "general psychology" with the "individual psychology" of Stern and Binet.

In 1913, Yerkes made the fundamental point that all the correlational psychologies are one.

His name for this branch was "comparative psychology."

Although comparative psychology in its completeness necessarily deals with the materials of the psychology of infant, child, adult, whether the being be human or infra-human; of animal or plant [!]—of normal and abnormal individuals; of social groups and of civilizations, there is no reason why specialists in the use of the comparative method should not be so distinguished, and, if it seems necessary, labelled (1913).

Even in advocating research on animals (1914), Yerkes is emphatic in defining the goal as correlation across species. In France, *la psychologie comparée* continues to include all of differential psychology; but in America, as Beach (1950) has lamented, comparative psychology degenerated into the experimental psychology of the white rat and thereby lost the power of the correlational discipline.

Except for the defection of animal psychologists, the correlational psychologists have remained loosely federated. Developmental psychologists, personality psychologists, and differential psychologists have been well acquainted both personally and intellectually. They study the same courses, they draw on the same literature, they join the same divisions of APA.

Experimental and correlational psychologists, however, grew far apart in their training and interests. It is now commonplace for a student to get his PhD in experimental psychology without graduate training in test theory or developmental psychology, and the student of correlational branches can avoid experimental psychology only a little less completely. The journals of one discipline have small influence on the journals of the other (Daniel & Louttit, 1953). Boring even dares to say (1950, p. 578) that there is a personality difference between the fields: the distinction being that correlational psychologists like people!

Certainly the scientific values of psychologists are sharply divided. Thorndike (Clark, 1957; Thorndike, 1954) recently asked American psychologists to rate various historic personages by indicating, on a forced-choice questionnaire, which have made the greatest contributions to psychology. A factor analysis of the ratings

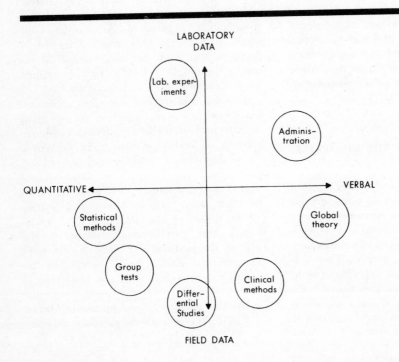

Fig. 1 *Factors accounting for esteem of leaders in psychology by American psychologists (based on correlations presented by Thorndike [1954] corrected for attenuation and refactored).*

shows two distinct factors (Figure 1). One bipolar factor (irrelevant to our present discussion) ranges from verbal to quantitative psychologists. The other factor has at one pole the laboratory experimenters like Stevens, Dodge, and Ebbinghaus, and at the opposite pole those like Binet, May, and Goodenough who collect and correlate field data. A psychologist's esteem for the experimenters is correlated −.80 (−1.00, corrected for attenuation) with his esteem for scientists who use correlational methods.

There was no such schism in 1913 when Yerkes stated the program of correlational psychology. Genetic psychology and experimental psychology were hard at work on the same problems. Terman demonstrated in his 1923 presidential address (1924) that the mental test was within the tradition of experimental, fundamental research in psychology, and had quotations to show that the contemporary experimentalists agreed with him. Wells and Goddard, in 1913, had been asked to lecture on mental tests within the Holy Temple itself, the Society of Experimental Psychologists. And, in 1910, the High Priest Titchener had said:

Individual psychology is one of the chief witnesses to the value of experiment. It furnishes the key to many, otherwise inexplicable differences of result, and it promises to allay many of the outstanding controversies. . . . There can be no doubt that it will play a part of steadily increasing importance (1910).

But when Terman spoke in 1923, the common front had already been fatally breached. Watson had announced that experimental treatment could make and unmake individual differences at will, thus stripping them of scientific importance. Thurstone had taken the first firm stride in the opposite direction:

I suggest that we dethrone the stimulus. He is only nominally the ruler of psychology. The real ruler of the domain which psychology studies is the individual and his motives, desires, wants, ambitions, cravings, aspirations. The stimulus is merely the more or less accidental fact . . . (1923, p. 364).

The personality, social, and child psychologists went one way; the perception and learning psychologists went the other; and the country between turned into desert.

During the estrangement of correlational and experimental psychology, antagonism has been notably absent. Disparagement has been pretty well confined to playful remarks like Cattell's accusation that the experimental psychologist's "regard for the body of nature becomes that of the anatomist rather than that of the lover" (1898, p. 152), or the experimentalist Bartlett's (1955, p. 210) satire on the testers emerging from World War I, "chanting in unaccustomed harmony the words of the old jingle

'God has a plan for every man
And He has one for you.' "

Most correlationists have done a little experimenting in the narrow sense, and experimenters have contributed proudly to testing work under wartime necessity. But these are temporary sojourns in a foreign land. (For clear expressions of this attitude, see Boring, 1950, pp. 570-578 and Woodworth, 1938, p. 24.)

A true federation of the disciplines is required. Kept independent, they can give only wrong answers or no answers at all regarding certain important problems. It is shortsighted to argue for one science to discover the general laws of mind or behavior and for a separate enterprise concerned with individual minds, or for a one-way dependence of personality theory upon learning theory. Consider the physical sciences as a parallel. Physics for centuries was the study of general laws applying to all solids or all gases, whereas alchemy and chemistry studied the properties and reactions of individual substances. Chemistry was once only a descriptive catalogue of substances and analytic techniques. It became a systematic science when organized quantitative studies yielded principles to explain differences between substances and to predict the outcomes of reactions. In consequence, Mendeleev the chemist paved the way for Bohr the physicist, and Fermi's physics contributes to Lawrence's chemistry; the boundary between chemistry and physics has become almost invisible.

The tide of separation in psychology has already turned. The perceiver has reappeared in perceptual psychology. Tested intelligence and anxiety appear as independent variables in many of the current learning experiments. Factor analytic studies have gained a fresh vitality from crossbreeding with classical learning experiments (e.g., Eysenck, 1956; Fleishman & Hempel, 1954). Harlow, Hebb, Hess, and others are creating a truly experimental psychology of development. And students of personality have been designing subtle combinations of experimental and correlational method (see, for example, Lazarus & Baker, 1956) which may ultimately prove to be our parallel to the emergence of physical chemistry.

CHARACTERIZATION OF THE DISCIPLINES

In the beginning, experimental psychology was a substitute for purely naturalistic observation of man-in-habitat. The experimenter placed man in an artificial, simplified environment and made quantitative observations of his performance. The initial problem was one of describing accurately what man felt, thought, or did in a defined situation. Standardization of tasks and conditions was required to get reproducible descriptions. All experimental procedures were tests, all tests were experiments. Kraepelin's continuous-work procedure served equally the general study of fatigue and the diagnosis of individuals. Reaction time was important equally to Wundt and to Cattell.

The distinctive characteristic of modern experimentation, the statistical comparison of treatments, appeared only around 1900 in such studies as that of Thorndike and Woodworth on transfer. The experimenter, following the path of Ebbinghaus, shifted from measurement of the average mind to measuring the effect of environmental change upon success in a task (Woodworth, 1918). Inference replaced estimation: the mean and its probable error gave way to the critical ratio. The standardized conditions and the standardized instruments remained, but the focus shifted to the single manipulated variable, and later, following Fisher, to multivariate manipulation. The experiment thus came to be concerned with between-treatments variance. I use the word "treatment" in a general sense; educational and therapeutic treatments are but one type. Treatment differences are equally involved in comparing rats given different schedules of reinforcement, chicks who have worn different distorting lenses, or social groups arranged with different communication networks.

The second great development in American experimental psychology has been its concern with formal theory. At the turn of the century, theory ranged far ahead of experiment and made no demand that propositions be testable. Experiment, for its part, was willing to observe any phenomenon, whether or not the data bore on theoretical issues. Today, the majority of experimenters derive their hypotheses explicitly from theoretical premises and try to nail their results into a theoretical structure. This deductive style has its undeniable defects, but one can not question the net gains from the accompanying theoretical sophistication. Discussions of the logic of operationism, intervening variables, and mathematical models have sharpened both the formulation of hypotheses and the interpretation of results.

Individual differences have been an annoyance rather than a challenge to the experimenter. His goal is to control behavior, and variation within treatments is proof that he has not succeeded. Individual variation is cast into that outer darkness known as "error variance." For reasons both statistical and philosophical, error variance is to be reduced by any possible device. You turn to animals of a cheap and short-lived species, so that you can use subjects with controlled heredity and controlled experience. You select human subjects from a narrow subculture. You decorticate your subject by cutting neurons or by giving him an environment so meaningless that his unique responses disappear (cf. Harlow, 1953). You increase the number of cases to obtain stable averages, or you reduce N to 1, as Skinner does but whatever your device, your goal in the experimental tradition is to get those embarrassing differential variables out of sight.

The correlational psychologist is in love with just those variables the experimenter left home to forget. He regards individual and group variations as important effects of biological and social causes. All organisms adapt to their environments, but not equally well. His question is: what present characteristics of the organism determine its mode and degree of adaptation?

Just as individual variation is a source of embarrassment to the experimenter, so treatment variation attenuates the results of the correlator. His goal is to predict variation within a treatment. His experimental designs demand uniform treatment for every case contributing to a correlation, and treatment variance means only error variance to him.

Differential psychology, like experimental, began with a purely descriptive phase. Cattell at Hopkins, Galton at South Kensington, were simply asking how much people varied. They were, we might say, estimating the standard deviation while the general psychologists were estimating the central tendency.

The correlation coefficient, invented for the study of hereditary resemblance, transformed descriptive differential research into the study of mental organization. What began as a mere summary statistic quickly became the center of a whole theory of data analysis. Murphy's words, written in 1928, recall the excitement that attended this development:

The relation between two variables has actually been found to be statable in other terms than those of experiment . . . [Moreover,] Yule's method of "partial correlation" has made possible the mathematical "isolation" of variables which cannot be isolated experimentally. . . . [Despite the limitations of correlational methods,] what they have already yielded to psychology . . . is nevertheless of such major importance as to lead the writer to the opinion that the only twentieth-century discovery comparable in importance to the conditioned-response method is the method of partial correlations (1932, p. 410).

Today's students who meet partial correlation only as a momentary digression from their main work in statistics may find this excitement hard to comprehend. But partial correlation is the starting place for all of factor analysis.

Factor analysis is rapidly being perfected into a rigorous method of clarifying multivariate relationships. Fisher made the experimentalist an expert puppeteer, able to keep untangled

the strands to half-a-dozen independent variables. The correlational psychologist is a mere observer of a play where Nature pulls a thousand strings; but his multivariate methods make him equally an expert, an expert in figuring out where to look for the hidden strings.

His sophistication in data analysis has not been matched by sophistication in theory. The correlational psychologist was led into temptation by his own success, losing himself first in practical prediction, then in a narcissistic program of studying his tests as an end in themselves. A naive operationism enthroned theory of test performance in the place of theory of mental processes. And premature enthusiasm[2] exalted a few measurements chosen almost by accident from the tester's stock as the ruling forces of the mental universe.

In former days, it was the experimentalist who wrote essay after anxious essay defining his discipline and differentiating it from competing ways of studying mind. No doubts plagued correlationists like Hall, Galton, and Cattell. They came in on the wave of evolutionary thought and were buoyed up by every successive crest of social progress or crisis. The demand for universal education, the development of a technical society, the appeals from the distraught twentieth-century parent, and finally the clinical movement assured the correlational psychologist of his great destiny. Contemporary experimentalists, however, voice with ever-increasing assurance their program and social function; and the fact that tonight you have a correlational psychologist discussing disciplinary identities implies that anxiety is now perched on *his* windowledge.

Indeed, I do speak out of concern for correlational psychology. Aptitude tests deserve their fine reputation; but, if practical, validated procedures are to be our point of pride, we must be dissatisfied with our progress since 1920. As the Executive Committee of Division 5 itself declared this year, none of our latter-day refinements or innovations has improved practical predictions by a noticeable amount. Correlational psychologists who found their self-esteem upon contributions to theory can

2 This judgment is not mine alone; it is the clear consensus of the factor analysts themselves (see Laugier, 1955, pp. 321-325).

point to monumental investigations such as the *Studies of Character* and *The Authoritarian Personality*. Such work does throw strong light upon the human scene and brings important facts clearly into view. But theories to organize these facts are rarely offered and even more rarely solidified (McCandless & Spiker, 1956; McClelland, 1956, p. 55).

POTENTIAL CONTRIBUTIONS OF THE DISCIPLINES TO ONE ANOTHER

Perhaps it is inevitable that a powerful new method will become totally absorbing and crowd other thoughts from the minds of its followers. It took a generation of concentrated effort to move from Spearman's tetrad equation and Army Alpha to our present view of the ability domain. It took the full energies of other psychologists to move from S-R bonds to modern behavior theory. No doubt the tendency of correlationists to ignore experimental developments is explained by their absorption in the wonders and complexities of the phenomena their own work was revealing. And if experimentalists were to be accused of narrow-minded concentration on one particular style and topic of research, the same comment would apply.

The spell these particular theories and methods cast upon us appears to have passed. We are free at last to look up from our own bedazzling treasure, to cast properly covetous glances upon the scientific wealth of our neighbor discipline. Trading has already been resumed, with benefit to both parties.

The introduction of construct validation into test theory (Cronbach & Meehl, 1955) is a prime example. The history of this development, you may recall, was that the APA's Committee on Psychological Tests discovered that available test theory recognized no way of determining whether a proposed psychological interpretation of a test was sound. The only existing theory dealt with criterion validation and could not evaluate claims that a test measured certain psychological traits or states. Meehl, capitalizing on the methodological and philosophical progress of the experimenters, met the testers' need by suggesting the idea of construct validity. A proposed test interpretation, he showed, is a claim that a test measures a construct, i.e., a claim that the test score can be linked to a theoretical network. This network, together with the claim, generates predictions about observations. The test interpretation is justified only if the observations come out as predicted. To decide how well a purported test of anxiety measures anxiety, construct validation is necessary; i.e., we must find out whether scores on the test behave in accordance with the theory that defines anxiety. This theory predicts differences in anxiety between certain groups, and traditional correlational methods can test those predictions. But the theory also predicts variation in anxiety, hence in the test score, as a function of experience or situations, and only an experimental approach can test those predictions.

This new theory of validity has several very broad consequences. It gives the tester a start toward the philosophical sophistication the experimenter has found so illuminating. It establishes the experimental method as a proper and necessary means of validating tests. And it re-establishes research on tests as a valuable and even indispensable way of extending psychological theory.

We may expect the test literature of the future to be far less saturated with correlations of tests with psychologically enigmatic criteria, and far richer in studies which define test variables by their responsiveness to practice at different ages, to drugs, to altered instructions, and to other experimentally manipulated variables. A pioneering venture in this direction is Fleishman's revealing work (Fleishman, 1956; Fleishman & Hempel, 1954) on changes in the factorial content of motor skills as a function of practice. These studies go far beyond a mere exploration of certain tests; as Ferguson has shown (1954; 1956), they force upon us a theory which treats abilities as a product of learning, and a theory of learning in which previously acquired abilities play a major role.

Perhaps the most valuable trading goods the correlator can offer in return is his multivariate conception of the world.

No experimenter would deny that situations and responses are multifaceted, but rarely are his procedures designed for a systematic multivariate analysis. The typical experimental design and the typical experimental law employ a single dependent variable. Even when more than one outcome is measured, the outcomes are analyzed and interpreted separately. No response measure, however, is an adequate measure of a psychological construct. Every score mixes general construct-relevant variance with variance specific to the particular measuring operation. It is all right for the agriculturist to consider size of crop as the fundamental variable being observed: that is the payoff for him. Our task, however, is to study changes in fundamental aspects of behavior, and these are evidenced only indirectly in any one measure of outcome.

The correlational psychologist discovered long ago that no observed criterion is truly valid and that simultaneous consideration of many criteria is needed for a satisfactory evaluation of performance. This same principle applies in experimentation. As Neal Miller says in a recent paper on experiments with drugs:

Where there are relatively few facts it seems easy to account for them by a few simple generalizations. . . . As we begin to study the effects of a variety of drugs on a number of different behavioral measures, exceptions and complexities emerge. We are forced to reexamine and perhaps abandon common-sense categories of generalization according to convenient words existing in the English language. As new and more comprehensive patterns of results become available, however, new and more precise generalizations may emerge. We may be able to "carve nature better to the joint" and achieve the simplicity of a much more exact and powerful science (1956, pp. 326-327).

Theoretical progress is obstructed when one restricts himself to a single measure of response (1959). Where there is only one dependent variable, it is pointless to introduce intervening variables or constructs. When there are many response variables, however, it is mandatory to subsume them under constructs, since otherwise we must have a separate set of laws for every measure of outcome. Dealing with multiple response variables is, as Miller says (1957), precisely the problem with which the factor analysts have been concerned. Factor analysis, by substituting formal for intuitive methods, has been of great help in locating

constructs with which to summarize observations about abilities. It is reasonable to expect that multivariate treatment of response measures would have comparable value in experimental psychology.

Experimenters very probably have even more to gain from treating *in*dependent variables as a continuous multivariate system. The manifold treatment categories in a Fisherian design are established a priori. In agriculture, the treatment dimensions the farmer can manipulate are obvious: fertilizer, water, species of seed, and so on. In a more basic science, we require genotypic constructs to describe situations, constructs like the physical scientist's temperature and pressure. The conditions the psychologist most easily manipulates —stimulus form, injunction to the subject, strength of electric shock—are not chosen because we intend to apply these specific conditions when we get around to "controlling behavior." They are used because these conditions, we hope, embody scientifically useful constructs.

The experimenter has no systematic way to classify and integrate results from different tasks or different reinforcers. As Ferguson remarks (1956, p. 130; see also 1954, p. 100): "No satisfactory methodology has emerged for describing particular learning tasks, or indicating how one task differs from another, other than by a process of simple inspection." We depend wholly on the creative flair of the theorist to collate the experiments and to invent constructs which might describe particular situations, reinforcements, or injunctions in terms of more fundamental variables. The multivariate techniques of psychometrics are suited for precisely this task of grouping complex events into homogeneous classes or organizing them along major dimensions. These methods are frankly heuristic, but they are systematically heuristic. They select variables with minimal redundancy, and they permit us to obtain maximum information from a minimum of experimental investment.

In suggesting that examining treatment conditions as a statistical universe is a possible way to advance experimental thinking, I am of course echoing the recommendations of Egon Brunswik (1956, esp. pp. 39-58). Brunswik criticized the Fisherian experimenter for his ad hoc selection of treatments and recommended that he apply the sampling principles of differential psychology in choosing stimuli and conditions. A sampling procedure such as Brunswik suggests will often be a forward step, but the important matter is not to establish laws which apply loosely to a random, unorganized collection of situations. The important matter is to discover the organization among the situations, so that we can describe situational differences as systematically as we do individual differences.

Research on stress presents a typical problem of organization. Multivariate psychophysiological data indicate that different taxing situations have different effects. At present, stressors can be described and classified only superficially, by inspection. A correlational or distance analysis of the data groups treatments which have similar effects and ultimately permits us to locate each treatment within a continuous multidimensional structure having constructs as reference axes. Data from a recent study by Wenger, Clemens, and Engel (1957) may be used as an illustration. Figure 2 shows the means of standardized physiological scores under four different stress conditions: mental

arithmetic, a letter association test, hyperventilation, and a cold pressor. The "profiles" for the four conditions are very significantly different. I have made a distance analysis to examine the similarity between conditions, with the results diagrammed in Figure 3. There is a general factor among all the treatments, which distinguishes them from the resting state, and a notable group factor among three of them. According to these data, a mental test seems to induce the same physiological state as plunging one's foot into ice water!

Much larger bodies of data are of course needed to map the treatment space properly. But the aptness of an attempt in this direction will be apparent to all who heard Selye's address to the APA last year. His argument (1955) that all stressful situations lead to a similar syndrome of physiological changes is strongly reminiscent of Spearman's argument regarding a general factor linking intellectual responses. The disagreement between Selye and other students of stress clearly reduces to a quantitative question of the relative size of specific and nonspecific or general factors in the effects of typical stressors.

APPLIED PSYCHOLOGY DIVIDED AGAINST ITSELF

Let us leave for the moment questions of academic psychology and consider the schism as it appears in applied psychology. In applied psychology, the two disciplines are in active conflict; and unless they bring their efforts into harmony, they can hold each other to a standstill. The conflict is especially obvious at this moment in the challenge the young engineering psychology offers to traditional personnel psychology.

The program of applied experimental psychology is to modify treatments so as to obtain the highest average performance when all persons are treated alike—a search, that is, for "the one best way." The program of applied correlational psychology is to raise average performance by treating persons differently—different job assignments, different therapies, different disciplinary methods. The correlationist is utterly antagonistic to a doctrine of "the one best way," whether it be the heartless

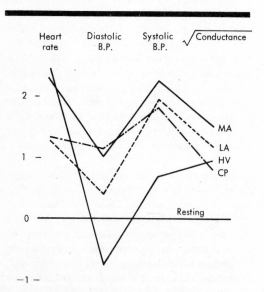

Fig. 2 *Mean response to four stressors expressed in terms of resting standard scores (data from Wenger, Clemens, & Engel, 1957).*

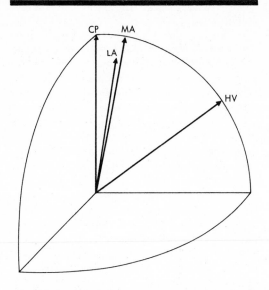

Fig. 3 *Multivariate diagram showing similarity between four stressors.*

robot-making of Frederick Taylor or a doctrinaire permissiveness which tries to give identical encouragement to every individual. The ideal of the engineering psychologist, I am told, is to simplify jobs so that every individual in the working population will be able to perform them satisfactorily, i.e., so that differentiation of treatment will be unnecessary. This goal guides activities ranging from the sober to the bizarre: from E. L. Thorndike and Skinner, hunting the one best sequence of problems for teaching arithmetic, to Rudolf Flesch and his admirers, reducing *Paradise Lost* to a comic book. If the engineering psychologist succeeds: information rates will be so reduced that the most laggard of us can keep up, visual displays will be so enlarged that the most myopic can see them, automatic feedback will prevent the most accident-prone from spoiling the work or his fingers.

Obviously, with every inch of success the engineer has, the tester must retreat a mile. A slight reduction in information rate, accomplished once, reduces forever the validity and utility of a test of ability to process data. If, once the job is modified, the myopic worker can perform as well as the man with 20/20

vision, Snellen charts and orthoraters are out of business. Nor is the threat confined to the industrial scene. If tranquilizers make everybody happy, why bother to diagnose patients to determine which treatments they should have? And if televised lessons can simplify things so that every freshman will enjoy and understand quantum mechanics, we will need neither college aptitude tests nor final examinations.

It is not my intention to warn testers about looming unemployment. If test technology is not greatly improved, long before the applied experimentalists near their goals, testing deserves to disappear. My message is my belief that the conflicting principles of the tester and the experimenter can be fused into a new and integrated applied psychology.

To understand the present conflict in purposes, we must look again at historical antecedents. Pastore (1949) argues with much justice that the testers and classifiers have been political conservatives, while those who try to find the best common treatment for all—particularly in education—have been the liberals. This essential conservatism of personnel psychology traces back to the days of Darwin and Spencer.

The theory of evolution inspired two antagonistic movements in social thought (Corwin, 1950; Spengler, 1950). Darwin and Herbert Spencer were real determinists. The survival of the fittest, as a law of Nature, guaranteed man's superiority and the ultimate triumph of the natural aristocrats among men. As Dewey put it, Spencer saw "a rapid transit system of evolution . . . carrying us automatically to the goal of perfect man in perfect society" (1910, p. 66). Men vary in their power of adaptation, and institutions, by demanding adaptation, serve as instruments of natural selection among men. The essence of freedom is seen as the freedom to compete for survival. To Spencer, to Galton, and to their successors down to the present day, the successful are those who have the greatest adjustive capacity. The psychologist's job, in this tradition, is to facilitate or anticipate natural selection. He seeks only to reduce its cruelty and wastage by predicting who will survive in schools and other institutions as they are. He takes the system for granted and tries to identify who will fit into it. His devices have a conservative influence because they identify persons who will succeed in the existing institution. By reducing failures, they remove a challenge which might otherwise force the institution to change (Tyler, 1951).

The experimental scientist inherits an interpretation of evolution associated with the names of Ward, James, and Dewey. For them, man's progress rests on his intelligence; the great struggle for survival is a struggle against environment, not against competitors. Intelligent man must reshape his environment, not merely conform to it. This spirit, the very antithesis of Spencerian laissez-faire, bred today's experimental social science which accepts no institution and no tradition as sacred. The individual is seen as inherently self-directing and creative. One can not hope to predict how he will meet his problems, and applied differential psychology is therefore pointless (Scoon, 1950, p. 37).

Thus we come to have one psychology which accepts the institution, its treatment, and its criterion and finds men to fit the institution's needs. The other psychology takes man—generalized man—as given and challenges any institution which does not conform to the measure of this standard man.

A clearer view of evolution removes the paradox:

The entire significance of the evolutionary method in biology and social history is that every distinct organ, structure, or formation, every grouping of cells or elements, has to be treated as an instrument of adjustment or adaptation to a particular environing situation. Its meaning, its character, its value, is known when, and only when, it is considered as an arrangement for meeting the conditions involved in some specific situation (Dewey, 1903, p. 15).

We are not on the right track when we conceive of adjustment or adjustive capacity in the abstract. It is always a capacity to respond to a particular treatment. The organism which adapts well under one condition would not survive under another. If for each environment there is a best organism, for every organism there is a best environment. The job of applied psychology is to improve decisions about people. The greatest social benefit will come from applied psychology if we can find for each individual the treatment to which he can most easily adapt. This calls for the joint application of experimental and correlational methods.

INTERACTION OF TREATMENT AND INDIVIDUAL IN PRACTICAL DECISIONS

Goldine Gleser and the writer have recently published a theoretical analysis (Cronbach & Gleser, 1957) which shows that neither the traditional predictive model of the correlator nor the traditional experimental comparison of mean differences is an adequate formulation of the decisions confronting the applied psychologist. Let me attempt to give a telescoped version of the central argument.

The decision maker has to determine what treatment shall be used for each individual or each group of individuals. Psychological data help a college, for example, select students to be trained as scientists. The aim of any decision maker is to maximize expected payoff. There is a payoff function relating outcome (e.g., achievement in science) to aptitude dimensions for any particular treatment. Figure 4 shows such a function for a single aptitude.

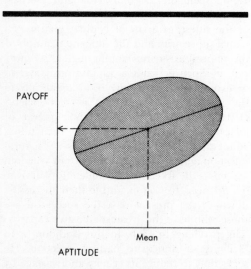

Fig. 4 *Scatter diagram and payoff function showing outcome as a function of individual differences.*

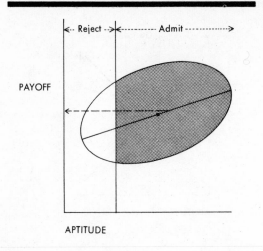

Fig. 5   *Increase in payoff as a result of selection.*

Pure selection, however, almost never occurs. The college aptitude test may seem to be intended for a selection decision; and, insofar as the individual college is concerned only with those it accepts, the conventional validity coefficient does indicate the best test. But from a societal point of view, the rejects will also go on into other social institutions, and their profit from this treatment must be weighed in the balance along with the profit or social contribution from the ones who enter college. Every decision is really a choice between treatments. Predicting outcome has no social value unless the psychologist or the subject himself can use the information to make better choices of treatment. The prediction must help to determine a treatment for every individual.

Average payoff—if everyone receives the treatment—is indicated by the arrow. The experimentalist assumes a fixed population and hunts for the treatment with the highest average and the least variability. The correlationist assumes a fixed treatment and hunts for aptitudes which maximize the slope of the payoff function. In academic selection, he advises admission of students with high scores on a relevant aptitude and thus raises payoff for the institution (Figure 5).

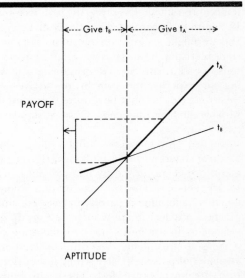

Fig. 7   *Payoff functions for two treatments.*

Even when there are just two treatments, the payoff functions have many possible relationships. In Figure 6 we have a mean difference between treatments, and a valid predictor. The predictor—though valid—is useless. We should give everyone Treatment A. In Figure 7, on the other hand, we should divide the group and give different treatments. This gives greater payoff than either treatment used uniformly will give.

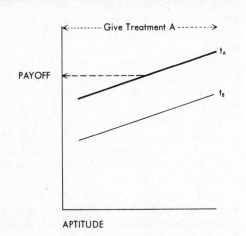

Fig. 6   *Payoff functions for two treatments.*

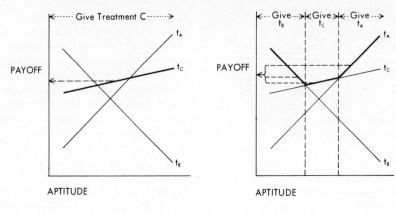

Fig. 8 *Payoff functions for three treatments.*

Assigning everyone to the treatment with the highest average, as the experimentalist tends to recommend, is rarely the best decision. In Figure 8, Treatment C has the best average, and we might assign everyone to it. The outcome is greater, however, if we assign some persons to each treatment. The psychologist making an experimental comparison arrives at the wrong conclusion if he ignores the aptitude variable and recommends C as a standard treatment.

Applied psychologists should deal with treatments and persons simultaneously. Treatments are characterized by many dimensions; so are persons. The two sets of dimensions together determine a payoff surface. For any practical problem, there is some best group of treatments to use and some best allocation of persons to treatments. We can expect some attributes of persons to have strong interactions with treatment variables. These attributes have far greater practical importance than the attributes which have little or no interaction. In dividing pupils between college preparatory and noncollege studies, for example, a general intelligence test is probably the wrong thing to use. This test, being general, predicts success in all subjects, therefore tends to have little interaction with treatment, and if so is not the best guide to differential treatment. We require a measure of aptitude which predicts who will learn better from one curriculum than from the other; but this aptitude remains to be discovered. Ultimately we should *design*

treatments, not to fit the average person, but to fit groups of students with particular aptitude patterns. Conversely, we should seek out the aptitudes which correspond to (interact with) modifiable aspects of the treatment.

My argument rests on the assumption that such aptitude-treatment interactions exist. There is, scattered in the literature, a remarkable amount of evidence of significant, predictable differences in the way people learn. We have only limited success in predicting which of two *tasks* a person can perform better, when we allow enough training to compensate for differences in past attainment. But we do find that a person learns more easily from one *method* than another, that this best method differs from person to person, and that such between-treatments differences are correlated with tests of ability and personality. The studies showing interaction between personality and conditions of learning have burgeoned in the past few years, and the literature is much too voluminous to review in passing. Just one recent finding will serve in the way of specific illustration, a study done by Wolfgang Böhm at Vienna (Rohracher, 1956, pp. 58-59). He showed his experimental groups a sound film about the adventures of a small boy and his toy elephant at the zoo. At each age level, a matched control group read a verbatim text of the sound track. The differences in average comprehension between the audiovisual and the text presentations were trivial. There was, however, a marked interaction. For some reason yet unexplained, a general mental test correlated only .30 with text learning, but it predicted film learning with an average correlation of .77.[3] The difference was consistent at all ages.

Such findings as this, when replicated and explained, will carry us into an educational psychology which measures readiness for different types of teaching and which invents teaching methods to fit different types of readiness. In general, unless one treatment is clearly best for everyone, treatments should be differentiated in such a way as to maximize their interaction with aptitude variables. Conversely, persons should be allocated on the basis of those aptitudes which have the greatest interaction with treatment variables. I believe we will find these aptitudes to be quite unlike our present aptitude measurements chosen to predict differences *within* highly correlated treatments.

THE SHAPE OF A UNITED DISCIPLINE

It is not enough for each discipline to borrow from the other. Correlational psychology studies only variance among organisms; experimental psychology studies only variance among treatments. A united discipline will study both of these, but it will also be concerned with the otherwise neglected interactions between organismic and treatment variables (Shen, 1942). Our job is to invent constructs and to form a network of laws which permits prediction. From observations we must infer a psychological description of the situation and of the present state of the organism. Our laws should permit us to predict, from this description, the behavior of organism-in-situation.

There was a time when experimental psychologists concerned themselves wholly with general, nonindividual constructs, and correlational psychologists sought laws wholly within developmental variables. More and more, nowadays, their investigations are coming to bear on the same targets. One psychologist measures ego involvement by a personality test and compares the behavior of high- and low-scoring subjects. Another psychologist heightens ego involvement ex-

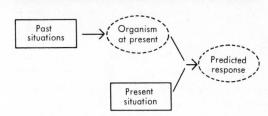

Fig. 9 *Theoretical model for prediction from a historic data.*

perimentally in one of two equated groups and studies the consequent differences in behavior. Both investigators can test the same theoretical propositions, and to the extent that their results agree they may regard both procedures as embodiments of the same construct.

Constructs originating in differential psychology are now being tied to experimental variables. As a result, the whole theoretical picture in such an area as human abilities is changing. Piaget (1950) correlates reasoning processes with age and discovers a developmental sequence of schemata whose emergence permits operational thought; Harlow (1949) begins actually to create similar schemata in monkeys by means of suitable training. It now becomes possible to pursue in the controllable monkey environment the questions raised by Piaget's unique combination of behavioral testing and interviewing, and ultimately to unite the psychology of intelligence with the psychology of learning.

Methodologies for a joint discipline have already been proposed. R. B. Cattell (1952) has offered the most thorough discussion of how a correlationist might organize data about treatment and organism simultaneously. His factor analytic procedures are only one of many choices, however, which modern statistics offers. The experimenters, some of them, have likewise seen the necessity for a united discipline. In the very issue of *Psychological Review* where the much-too-famous distinction between *S-R* and *R-R* laws was introduced, Bergmann and Spence (1944) declared that (at the present stage of psychological knowl-

3 Personal communication.

edge) the equation $R = f(S)$ must be expanded into

$$R = f(S, T, D, I)$$

The added variables are innate differences, motivation, and past experience — differential variables all. Hull (1945; 1951) sought general laws just as did Wundt, but he added that organismic factors can and must be accounted for. He proposed to do this by changing the constants of his equations with each individual. This is a bold plan, but one which has not yet been implemented in even a limited way. It is of interest that both Hull (1951, p. 116) and Tolman (1938, p. 26) have stated specifically that for their purposes factor analytic methods seem to have little promise. Tucker, though, has at least drawn blueprints of a method for deriving Hull's own individual parameters by factor analysis (1955). Clearly, we have much to learn about the most suitable way to develop a united theory, but we have no lack of exciting possibilities.

The experimenter tends to keep his eye on *ultimate* theory. Woodworth once described psychological laws in terms of the *S-O-R* formula which specifically recognizes the individual. The revised version of his *Experimental Psychology* (1954, p. 3), however, advocates an *S-A-R* formula, where *A* stands

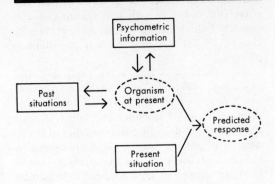

Fig. 11 *Theoretical network to be developed by a united discipline.*

for "antecedent conditions." This formulation, which is generally congenial to experimenters, reduces the present state of the organism to an intervening variable (Figure 9). A theory of this type is in principle entirely adequate to explain, predict, and control the behavior of organisms; but, oddly enough, it is a theory which can account only for the behavior of organisms of the next generation, who have not yet been conceived. The psychologist turns to a different type of law (Figure 10) whenever he deals with a subject whose life history he has not controlled or observed in every detail. A theory which involves only laws of this type, while suitable for prediction, has very limited explanatory value. The theory psychology really requires is a redundant network like Figure 11. This network permits us to predict from the past experience or present characteristics of the organism, or a combination of the two, depending on what is known. Filling in such a network is clearly a task for the joint efforts of experimental and correlational psychology.

In both applied work and general scientific work, psychology requires combined, not parallel, labors from our two historic disciplines. In this common labor, they will almost certainly become one, with a common theory, a common method, and common recommendations for social betterment. In the search for interactions we will invent new treatment dimensions and discover new dimensions of the organism. We will come to realize that organism

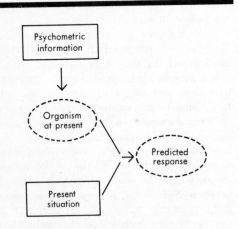

Fig. 10 *Theoretical model for prediction from historic data.*

and treatment are an inseparable pair and that no psychologist can dismiss one or the other as error variance.

Despite our specializations, every scientific psychologist must take the same scene into his field of vision. Clark Hull, three sentences before the end of his *Essentials of Behavior* (1951, p. 116), voiced just this need. Because of delay in developing methodology, he said, individual differences have played little part in behavior theory, and "a sizeable segment of behavioral science remains practically untouched." This untouched segment contains the question we really want to put to Nature, and she will never answer until our two disciplines ask it in a single voice.

REFERENCES

INTRODUCTION
*Psychological science
and human understanding*

McClelland, D. C. *The achieving society.* Princeton, N. J.: D. Van Nostrand Co., 1961

Merton, R. *Social theory and social structure.* Glencoe, Ill.: The Free Press, 1957.

Pepper, S. C. *Ethics.* New York: Appleton-Century-Crofts, 1960.

Skinner, B. F. *Walden two.* New York: Macmillan, 1948.

Skinner, B. F. *Science and human behavior.* New York: Macmillan, 1953.

Slosson, E. E. *Creative chemistry.* New York: The Century Co., 1919.

Stevenson, C. L. *Ethics and language.* New Haven: Yale University Press, 1945.

Volkart, E. H. (Ed.) *Social behavior and personality: contributions of W. I. Thomas to theory and social research.* New York: Social Science Research Council, 1951.

JOHN W. ATKINSON
*Motivational determinants
of risk-taking behavior*

Atkinson, J. W. Explorations using imaginative thought to assess the strength of human motives. In M. R. Jones (Ed.), *Nebraska symposium on motivation,* 1954. Lincoln, Nebr.: Univer. of Nebraska Press, 1954.

Atkinson, J. W., & Reitman, W. R. Performance as a function of motive strength and expectancy of goal-attainment. *J. abnorm. soc. Psychol.,* 1956, **53,** 361-366.

Brown, J. S. Problems presented by the concept of acquired drives. In *Current theory and research in motivation.* Lincoln, Nebr.: Univer. of Nebraska Press, 1953.

Clark, R. A., Teevan, R., & Ricciuti, H. N. Hope of success and fear of failure as aspects of need for achievement. *J. abnorm. soc. Psychol.,* 1956, **53,** 182-186.

Edwards, W. Probability preferences in gambling. *Amer. J. Psychol.,* 1953, **66,** 349-364.

Edwards, W. The theory of decision making. *Psychol. Bull.,* 1954, **51,** 380-417.

Eysenck, H. J. A dynamic theory of anxiety and hysteria. *J. ment. Sci.,* 1955, **101,** 28-51.

Eysenck, H. J., & Himmelweit, H. T. An experimental study of the reactions of neurotics to experiences of success and failure. *J. gen. Psychol.,* 1946, **35,** 59-75.

Himmelweit, H. T. A comparative study of the level of aspiration of normal and neurotic persons. *Brit. J. Psychol.,* 1947, **37,** 41-59.

Hyman, H. H. The value systems of different classes: a social psychological contribution to the analysis of stratification. In R. Bendix & S. M. Lipset (Eds.), *Class, status, and power.* Glencoe, Ill.: Free Press, 1953.

Lewin, K. *Field theory in social science.* D. Cartwright (Ed.). New York: Harper Bros., 1951.

Lewin, K., Dembo, T., Festinger, L., & Sears, P. S. Level of aspiration. In J. McV. Hunt (Ed.), *Personality and the behavior disorders,* Vol. 1, Chap. 10. New York: Ronald Press, 1944.

McClelland, D. C. *Personality.* New York: William Sloane Associates, 1951.

McClelland, D. C. Some social consequences of achievement motivation. In M. R. Jones (Ed.), *Nebraska symposium on motivation,* 1955. Lincoln: Univer. of Nebraska Press, 1955.

McClelland, D. C., Atkinson, J. W., Clark, R. A., & Lowell, E. L. *The achievement motive.* New York: Appleton-Century-Crofts, 1953.

Mandler, G., & Sarason, S. B. A study of anxiety and learning. *J. abnorm. soc. Psychol.,* 1952, **16,** 115-118.

Miller, D. R. Responses of psychiatric patients to threat of failure. *J. abnorm. soc. Psychol.,* 1951, **46,** 378-387.

Pottharst, B. C. The achievement motive and level of aspiration after experimentally induced success and failure. Unpublished doctor's dissertation, Univer. of Michigan, 1956.

Raphelson, A. Imaginative and direct verbal measures of anxiety related to physiological reactions in the competitive achievement situation. Unpublished doctor's dissertation, Univer. of Michigan, 1956.

Rotter, J. B. *Social learning and clinical psychology.* New York: Prentice-Hall, 1954.

Tolman, E. C. Principles of performance. *Psychol. Rev.,* 1955, **62**, 315-326.

Winterbottom, M. R. The relation of childhood training in independence to achievement motivation. Unpublished doctor's dissertation, Univer. of Michigan, 1952.

ROBERT W. WHITE
Motivation reconsidered: the concept of competence

Allport, G. W. *Personality: A psychological interpretation.* New York: Holt, 1937.

Allport, G. W. Effect: A secondary principle of learning. *Psychol. Rev.,* 1946, **53**, 335-347.

Angyal, A. *Foundations for a science of personality.* New York: Commonwealth Fund, 1941.

Ansbacher, H. L., & Ansbacher, R. R. (Eds.) *The individual psychology of Alfred Adler.* New York: Basic Books, 1956.

Beach, F. A. Analysis of factors involved in the arousal, maintenance and manifestation of sexual excitement in male animals. *Psychosom. Med.,* 1942, **4**, 173-198.

Beach, F. A. Instinctive behavior: Reproductive activities. In S. S. Stevens (Ed.), *Handbook of experimental psychology.* New York: Wiley, 1951. Pp. 387-434.

Berlyne, D. E. Novelty and curiosity as determinants of exploratory behavior. *Brit. J. Psychol.,* 1950, **41**, 68-80.

Berlyne, D. E. The arousal and satiation of perceptual curiosity in the rat. *J. comp. physiol. Psychol.,* 1955, **48**, 238-246.

Berlyne, D. E. Attention to change, conditioned inhibition (S¹R) and stimulus satiation. *Brit. J. Psychol.,* 1957, **48**, 138-140.

Berlyne, D. E. The present status of research on exploratory and related behavior. *J. indiv. Psychol.,* 1958, **14**, 121-126.

Bibring, E. The development and problems of the theories of the instincts. *Int. J. Psychoanal.,* 1941, **22**, 102-131.

Bruner, J. S., Matter, J., & Papanek, M. L. Breadth of learning as a function of drive level and mechanization. *Psychol. Rev.,* 1955, **62**, 1-10.

Bühler, C. The reality principle. *Amer. J. Psychotherap.,* 1954, **8**, 626-647.

Bühler, K. *Die geistige Entwicklung des Kindes.* (4th ed.) Jena: Gustav Fischer, 1924.

Butler, R. A. Discrimination learning by rhesus monkeys to visual-exploration motivation. *J. comp. physiol. Psychol.,* 1953, **46**, 95-98.

Butler, R. A. Exploratory and related behavior: A new trend in animal research. *J. indiv. Psychol.,* 1958, **14**, 111-120.

Butler, R. A., & Harlow, H. F. Discrimination learning and learning sets to visual exploration incentives. *J. gen. Psychol.,* 1957, **57**, 257-264.

Cofer, C. N. Motivation. *Ann. Rev. Psychol.,* 1959, **10**, 173-202.

Colby, K. M. *Energy and structure in psychoanalysis.* New York: Ronald, 1955.

Dashiell, J. F. A quantitative demonstration of animal drive. *J. comp. Psychol.,* 1925, **5**, 205-208.

Diamond, S. A neglected aspect of motivation. *Sociometry,* 1939, **2**, 77-85.

Dollard, J., & Miller, N. E. *Personality and psychotherapy.* New York: McGraw-Hill, 1950.

Erikson, E. H. *Childhood and society.* New York: Norton, 1952.

Erikson, E. H. Growth and crises of the healthy personality. In C. Kluckhohn, H. A. Murray, & D. Schneider (Eds.), *Personality in nature, society, and culture.* (2nd ed.) New York: Knopf, 1953. Pp. 185-225.

Fenichel, O. *The psychoanalytic theory of neurosis.* New York: Norton, 1945.

French, T. M. *The integration of behavior.* Vol. I. *Basic postulates.* Chicago: Univer. Chicago Press, 1952.

Freud, A. The mutual influences in the development of ego and id: Introduction to the discussion. *Psychoanal. Stud. Child,* 1952, **7**, 42-50.

Freud, S. *Wit and its relation to the unconscious.* New York: Moffat, Yard, 1916.

Freud, S. Formulations regarding the two principles in mental functioning. *Collected papers.* Vol. 4. London: Hogarth Press and Institute of Psychoanalysis, 1925. Pp. 13-21. (a)

Freud, S. On narcissism: An introduction. *Collected papers.* Vol. 4. London: Hogarth Press and Institute of Psycho-analysis, 1925. Pp. 30-59. (b)

Freud, S. Instincts and their vicissitudes. *Collected papers.* Vol. 4. London: Hogarth Press and Institute of Psycho-analysis, 1925. Pp. 60-83. (c)

Freud, S. *The ego and the id.* (Trans. by J. Riviere) London: Hogarth Press, 1927.

Freud, S. *Beyond the pleasure principle.* London: Hogarth Press, 1948.

Freud, S. *An outline of psycho-analysis.* (Trans. by J. Strachey) New York: Norton, 1949.

Goldstein, K. *The organism.* New York: American Book, 1939.

Goldstein, K. *Human nature in the light of psychopathology.* Cambridge, Mass.: Harvard Univer. Press, 1940.

Gross, K. *The play of man.* (Trans. by E. L. Baldwin) New York: D. Appleton, 1901.

Harlow, H. F. Mice, monkeys, men, and motives. *Psychol. Rev.,* 1953, **60**, 23-32.

Harlow, H. F., Harlow, M. K., & Meyer, D. R. Learning motivated by a manipulation drive. *J. exp. Psychol.,* 1950, **40**, 228-234.

Hartmann, H. Comments on the psychoanalytic theory of the ego. *Psychoanal. Stud. Child,* 1950, **5**, 74-95.

Hartmann, H. Notes on the theory of sublimation. *Psychoanal. Stud. Child,* 1955, **10**, 9-29.

Hartmann, H. Notes on the reality principle. *Psychoanal. Stud. Child,* 1956, **11**, 31-53.

Hartmann, H. *Ego psychology and the problem of adaptation.* (Trans. by D. Rapaport) New York: International Univer. Press, 1958.

Hartmann, H., Kris, E., & Loewenstein, R. Notes on the theory of aggression. *Psychoanal. Stud. Child,* 1949, **3/4**, 9-36.

Hebb, D. O. *The organization of behavior.* New York: Wiley, 1949.

Hebb, D. O. Drives and the c.n.s. (conceptual nervous system). *Psychol. Rev.,* 1955, **62**, 243-254.

Hebb, D. O. The motivating effects of exteroceptive stimulation. *Amer. Psychologist,* 1958, **13**, 109-113.

Hebb, D. O., & Thompson, W. R. The social significance of animal studies. In G. Lindzey (Ed.), *Handbook of social psychology.* Vol. I. Cambridge, Mass.: Addison-Wesley, 1954. Pp. 532-561.

Hendrick, I. Instinct and the ego during infancy. *Psychoanal. Quart.,* 1942, **11**, 33-58.

Hendrick, I. Work and the pleasure principle. *Psychoanal. Quart.,* 1943, **12**, 311-329. (a)

Hendrick, I. The discussion of the 'instinct to master.' *Psychoanal. Quart.,* 1943, **12**, 561-565. (b)

Hill, W. F. Activity as an autonomous drive. *J. comp. physiol. Psychol.,* 1956, **49**, 15-19.

Johnson, E. E. The role of motivational strength in latent learning. *J. comp. physiol. Psychol.,* 1953, **45**, 526-530.

Kagan, J. Differential reward value of incomplete and complete sexual behavior. *J. comp. physiol. Psychol.,* 1955, **48**, 59-64.

Kagan, J., & Berkun, M. The reward value of running activity. *J. comp. physiol. Psychol.,* 1954, **47**, 108.

Kardiner, A., & Spiegel, H. War stress and neurotic illness. New York: Hoeber, 1947.

Lashley, K. S. Experimental analysis of instinctive behavior. *Psychol. Rev.,* 1938, **45**, 445-471.

Lashley, K. S. The problem of cerebral organization in vision. In H. Klüver, *Visual mechanisms.* Lancaster, Pa.: Jaques Cattell, 1942. Pp. 301-322.

Leuba, C. Toward some integration of learning theories: The concept of optimal stimulation. *Psychol. Rep.,* 1955, **1**, 27-33.

Lilly, J. C. Mental effects of reduction of ordinary levels of physical stimuli on intact, healthy persons. *Psychiat. res. Rep.,* 1956, No. 5.

Maslow, A. H. *Motivation and personality.* New York: Harper, 1954.

Maslow, A. H. Deficiency motivation and growth motivation. In M. R. Jones (Ed.), *Nebraska symposium on motivation, 1955.* Lincoln, Neb.: Univer. Nebraska Press, 1955. Pp. 1-30.

McClelland, D. C., Atkinson, J. W., Clark, R. A., & Lowell, E. I. *The achievement motive.* New York: Appleton-Century, 1953.

McDougall, W. *Introduction to social psychology.* (16th ed.) Boston: John Luce, 1923.

McReynolds, P. A restricted conceptualization of human anxiety and motivation. *Psychol. Rep.,* 1956, **2**, 293-312. Monogr. Suppl. 6.

Miller, N. E. Learnable drives and rewards. In S. S. Stevens (Ed.), *Handbook of experimental psychology.* New York: Wiley, 1951. Pp. 435-472.

Miller, N. E. Central stimulation and other new approaches to motivation and reward. *Amer. Psychologist,* 1958, **13**, 100-108.

Mittelmann, B. Motility in infants, children, and adults. *Psychoanal. Stud. Child,* 1954, **9**, 142-177.

Montgomery, K. C. The role of the exploratory drive in learning. *J. comp. physiol. Psychol.,* 1954, **47**, 60-64.

Montgomery, K. C., & Monkman, J. A. The relation between fear and exploratory behavior. *J. comp. physiol. Psychol.,* 1955, **48**, 132-136.

Morgan, C. T. *Physiological psychology.* New York: McGraw-Hill, 1943.

Morgan, C. T. Physiological mechanisms of motivation. In M. R. Jones (Ed.), *Nebraska symposium on motivation 1957.* Lincoln, Neb.: Univer. Nebraska Press, 1957. Pp. 1-35.

Mowrer, O. H. *Learning theory and personality dynamics.* New York: Ronald, 1950.

Munroe, R. *Schools of psychoanalytical thought.* New York: Dryden, 1955.

Murphy, G. *Personality: A biosocial approach to origins and structure.* New York: Harper, 1947.

Murray, H. A. *Explorations in personality.* New York & London: Oxford Univer. Press, 1938.

Murray, H. A., & Kluckhohn, C. Outline of a conception of personality. In C. Kluckhohn, H. A. Murray, & D. M. Schneider (Eds.), *Personality in nature, society, and culture.* (2nd ed.) New York: Knopf, 1953.

Myers, A. K., & Miller, N. E. Failure to find a learned drive based on hunger; evidence for learning motivated by "exploration." *J. comp. physiol. Psychol.,* 1954, **47**, 428-436.

Nissen, H. W. A study of exploratory behavior in the white rat by means of the obstruction method. *J. genet. Psychol.,* 1930, **37**, 361-376.

Olds, J., & Milner, P. Positive reinforcement produced by electrical stimulation of septal area and other regions of rat brain. *J. comp. physiol. Psychol.,* 1954, **47**, 419-427.

Piaget, J. *The origins of intelligence in children.* (Trans. by M. Cook) New York: International Univer. Press, 1952.

Rapaport, D. *Organization and pathology of thought.* New York: Columbia Univer. Press, 1951.

Rapaport, D. On the psychoanalytic theory of thinking. In R. P. Knight & C. R. Friedman (Eds.), *Psychoanalytic psychiatry and psychology.* New York: International Univer. Press, 1954. Pp. 259-273.

Rapaport, D. The theory of ego autonomy: A generalization. *Bull. Menninger Clin.,* 1958, **22**, 13-35.

Rosvold, H. E. Physiological psychology. *Ann. Rev. Psychol.,* 1959, **10**, 415-454.

Schachtel, E. G. The development of focal attention and the emergence of reality. *Psychiatry,* 1954, **17**, 309-324.

Sheffield, F. D., & Roby, T. B. Reward value of a non-nutritive sweet taste. *J. comp. physiol. Psychol.,* 1950, **43**, 471-481.

Sheffield, F. D., Roby, T. B., & Campbell, B. A. Drive reduction vs. consummatory behavior as determinants of reinforcement. *J. comp. physiol. Psychol.,* 1954, **47**, 349-354.

Sheffield, F. D., Wulff, J. J., & Backer, R. Reward value of copulation without sex drive reduction. *J. comp. physiol. Psychol.,* 1951, **44**, 3-8.

Skinner, B. F. *Science and human behavior.* New York: Macmillan, 1953.

Steller, E. The physiology of motivation. *Psychol. Rev.,* 1954, **61**, 5-22.

Tolman, E. C. Cognitive maps in rats and men. *Psychol. Rev.,* 1948, **55**, 189-208.

Welker, W. L. Some determinants of play and exploration in chimpanzees. *J. comp. physiol. Psychol.,* 1956, **49**, 84-89.

Whiting, J. W. M., & Mowrer, O. H. Habit progression and regression—a laboratory study of some factors relevant to human socialization. *J. comp. Psychol.,* 1943, **36**, 229-253.

Wolfe, J. B., & Kaplon, M. D. Effect of amount of reward and consummative activity on learning in chickens. *J. comp. Psychol.,* 1941, **31**, 353-361.

Woodworth, R. S. *Dynamics of behavior.* New York: Holt, 1958.

Yerkes, R. M., & Dodson, J. D. The relation of strength of stimulus to rapidity of habit-formation. *J. comp. Neurol. Psychol.,* 1908, **18**, 459-482.

Young, P. T. Food-seeking drive, affective process, and learning. *Psychol. Rev.,* 1949, **56**, 98-121.

Young, P. T. The role of hedonic processes in motivation. In M. R. Jones (Ed.), *Nebraska symposium on motivation 1955.* Lincoln, Neb.: Univer. Nebraska Press, 1955. Pp. 193-238.

Zimbardo, P. G., & Miller, N. E. Facilitation of exploration by hunger in rats. *J. comp. physiol. Psychol.,* 1958, **51**, 43-46.

SEYMOUR FESHBACH
The drive-reducing function of fantasy behavior

Allport, G. W. *Personality.* New York: Holt, 1937.

Atkinson, J. W., & McClelland, D. C. The projective expression of needs: II. The effect of different intensities of the hunger drive on thematic apperception. *J. exp. Psychol.,* 1948, **38**, 643-658.

Dembo, Tamara. Anger as a problem of dynamics. In Translations of eight experimental studies in personality directed by Kurt Lewin. Unpublished manuscript, Yale Univer. Library, 1940.

Dollard, J., & Miller, N. *Personality and psychotherapy.* New York: McGraw-Hill, 1950.

Escalona, Sibylle. Play and substitute satisfaction. In R. G. Barker, J. S. Kounin, & H. F. Wright (Eds.), *Child behavior and development.* New York: McGraw-Hill, 1943. Pp. 363-378.

Freud, Anna. *The ego and mechanisms of defense.* New York: International Universities Press, 1946.

Freud, S. The relation of the poet to day-dreaming. In *Collected papers.* Vol. IV. London: Hogarth, 1949. Pp. 173-183.

Lewin, K. *A dynamic theory of personality.* New York: McGraw-Hill, 1935.

McClelland, D. C., Clark, R. A., Roby, T. B., & Atkinson, J. W. The projective expression of needs: IV. The effect of the need for achievement on thematic apperception. *J. exp. Psychol.,* 1949, **39**, 242-255.

Mahler, W. Studies of the substitute function of different levels of reality. In Translations of eight experimental studies in personality directed by Kurt Lewin. Unpublished manuscript, Yale Univer. Library, 1940.

Rotter, J. B., & Willerman, B. The Incomplete Sentence Test as a method of studying personality. *J. consult. Psychol.,* 1947, **11**, 43-48.

Symonds, P. M. *The dynamics of human adjustment.* New York: D. Appleton-Century, 1946.

Tomkins, S. S. *The Thematic Apperception Test.* New York: Grune & Stratton, 1947.

Wittenborn, J. R., & Eron, L. D. An application of drive theory to TAT responses. *J. consult. Psychol.,* 1951, **15**, 45-50.

JANET A. TAYLOR
A personality scale of manifest anxiety

Ahana, Ellen. A study on the reliability and internal consistency of a manifest anxiety scale. Unpublished master's thesis, Northwestern Univer., 1952.

Cameron, N. *The psychology of behavior disorders: a*

bio-social interpretation. Boston: Houghton Mifflin, 1947.

Lucas, J. D. The interactive effects of anxiety, failure, and intraserial duplication. *Amer. J. Psychol.,* 1952, **65,** 59-66.

Peck, Ruth. The influence of anxiety upon effectiveness of counseling. Unpublished doctor's dissertation, State Univer. of Iowa, 1950.

Spence, K. W., & Taylor, Janet. Anxiety and strength of the UCS as determiners of the amount of eyelid conditioning. *J. exp. Psychol.,* 1951, **42,** 183-188.

Taylor, Janet A. The relationship of anxiety to the conditioned eyelid response. *J. exp. Psychol.,* 1951, **41,** 81-92.

Taylor, Janet A., & Spence, K. W. The relationship of anxiety to performance in serial learning. *J. exp. Psychol.,* 1952, **44,** 61-64.

Thorndike, E. L., & Lorge, I. *Teacher's word book of 20,000 words.* New York: Teachers College, Columbia Univer., 1941.

Wenar, C. Reaction time as a function of manifest anxiety and stimulus intensity. Unpublished doctor's dissertation, State Univer. of Iowa, 1950.

Wesley, Elizabeth L. Perseverative behavior in a concept formation task. Unpublished doctor's dissertation, State Univer. of Iowa, 1950.

I. E. FARBER
Response fixation under anxiety and non-anxiety conditions

_____

Everall, E. E. Perseveration in the rat. *J. comp. Psychol.,* 1935, **19,** 343-369.

Festinger, L. A statistical test for means of samples from skew populations. *Psychometrika,* 1945, **8,** 205-210.

Hamilton, J. A., & Krechevsky, I. Studies in the effect of shock upon behavior plasticity in the rat. *J. comp. Psychol.,* 1933, **16,** 237-253.

Hull, C. L. Mind, mechanism, and adaptive behavior. *Psychol. Rev.,* 1937, **44,** 1-32.

Klee, J. B. The relation of frustration and motivation to the production of abnormal fixations in the rat. *Psychol. Monogr.,* 1944, **56,** 1-45.

Kleemeier, R. W. Fixation and regression in the rat. *Psychol. Monogr.,* 1942, **54,** 1-34.

Maier, N. R. F. The specific processes constituting the learning function. *Psychol. Rev.,* 1939, **46,** 241-252.

Maier, N. R. F., Glaser, N. M., & Klee, J. B. Studies of abnormal behavior in the rat: III. The development of behavior fixations through frustration. *J. exp. Psychol.,* 1940, **26,** 521-546.

Maier, N. R. F., & Klee, J. B. Studies of abnormal behavior in the rat: XII. The pattern of punishment and its relation to abnormal fixations. *J. exp. Psychol.,* 1943, **32,** 377-398.

Martin, R. F. 'Native' traits and regression in rats. *J. comp. Psychol.,* 1940, **30,** 1-16.

McClelland, D. C. Functional autonomy of motives as an extinction phenomenon. *Psychol. Rev.,* 1942, **49,** 272-283.

Miller, N. E., & Dollard, J. *Social learning and imitation.* New Haven: Yale University Press, 1941.

Mowrer, O. H. A stimulus-response analysis of anxiety and its role as a reinforcing agent. *Psychol. Rev.,* 1939, **46,** 553-565.

Mowrer, O. H. An experimental analogue of 'regression' with incidental observations on 'reaction formation.' *J. abnorm. soc. Psychol.,* 1940, **35,** 56-87. (a)

Mowrer, O. H. Anxiety-reduction and learning. *J. exp. Psychol.,* 1940, **27,** 497-516. (b)

Mowrer, O. H. The Freudian theories of anxiety: a reconciliation. 1941. Address given before Monday Night Group of the Institute of Human Relations.

Mowrer, O. H., & Jones, H. Habit strength as a function of the pattern of reinforcement. *J. exp. Psychol.,* 1945, **35,** 293-311.

O'Kelly, L. I. An experimental study of regression: I. The behavioral characteristics of the regressive response. *J. comp. Psychol.,* 1940, **30,** 41-53. (a)

O'Kelly, L. I. An experimental study of regression: II. Some motivational determinants of regression and perseveration. *J. comp. Psychol.,* 1940, **30,** 55-95. (b)

Sanders, M. J. An experimental demonstration of regression in the rat. *J. exp. Psychol.,* 1937, **21,** 493-510.

Sears, R. R. Survey of objective studies of psychoanalytic concepts. *Bull. Soc. Sci. Res. Coun.,* 1943. No. 51.

Tolman, E. C. *Drives toward war.* New York: D. Appleton-Century, 1942.

CHARLES McARTHUR
Personality differences between middle and upper classes

_____

Davis, A. Child training and social class. In R. G. Barker, J. S. Kounin, & H. F. Wright (Eds.), *Child behavior and development.* New York: McGraw-Hill, 1943. Pp. 607-621.

Davis, A. *Social class influences upon personality.* Cambridge: Harvard Univer. Press, 1948.

Davis, A. American status systems and the socialization of the child. In C. Kluckhohn & H. A. Murray (Eds.), *Personality in nature, society, and culture.* New York: Alfred A. Knopf, 1949. Pp. 459-470.

Davis, A., Gardner, B., & Gardner, M. *Deep South.* Chicago: Univer. Chicago Press, 1949.

Davis, A., & Havighurst, R. J. Social class and color differences in child-rearing. In C. Kluckhohn & H. A. Murray (Eds.), *Personality in nature, society, and culture.* New York: Alfred A. Knopf, 1949. Pp. 252-264.

Edwards, A. L. On "The use and misuse of the chi-square test"—the case of the 2 × 2 contingency table. *Psychol. Bull.,* 1950, **47**, 341-346.

Ericson, M. C. Social status and child-rearing practices. In T. M. Newcomb & E. L. Hartley (Eds.), *Readings in social psychology.* New York: Henry Holt & Co., 1947. Pp. 494-502.

Fisher, R. A. *Statistical methods for research workers.* New York: G. E. Stechert & Co., 1941.

Gorer, G. *The American people.* New York: Norton, 1948.

Henry, W. E. The Thematic Apperception technique in the study of culture-personality relations. *Genet. Psychol. Monogr.,* 1947, **35**, 3-135.

Hollingshead, A. *Elmtown's youth.* New York: John Wiley & Sons, 1949.

Kluckhohn, C., & Kluckhohn, Florence. American culture: generalized orientations and class patterns. In L. Bryson, L. Finkelstein, & R. Maciver (Eds), *Conflicts of power in modern culture.* New York: Symposium of Conference in Science, Philosophy, and Religion, 1947. Pp. 106-128.

Kluckhohn, Florence. Dominant and substitutive profiles of cultural orientations: their significance for the analysis of social stratification. *Soc. Forces,* 1950, **28**, 376-393.

Lewis, D., & Burke, C. J. The use and misuse of the chi-square test. *Psychol. Bull.,* 1949, **46**, 433-489.

Marquand, J. P. *The late George Apley.* Boston: Little, Brown & Co., 1937.

Marquand, J. P. *Point of no return.* Boston: Little, Brown & Co., 1949.

Mead, Margaret. *And keep your powder dry.* New York: William Morrow & Co., 1942.

Mead, Margaret. *Male and female.* New York: William Morrow & Co., 1949.

Milner, Esther. Effects of sex role and social status on the early adolescent's personality. *Genet. Psychol. Monogr.,* 1949, **40**, 231-325.

Mitchell, H. E. Social class and race as factors affecting the role of the family in Thematic Apperception Test stories of males. *Microfilm Abstracts,* 1951, **11** (2), 428-429.

Morley, C. *Kitty Foyle.* New York: The New American Library, 1944.

Murphy, G. *Personality.* New York: Harper, 1947.

Murray, H. A. *Explorations in personality.* New York: Oxford Univer. Press, 1938.

Rosenzweig, S. Types of reaction to frustration. *J. abnorm. soc. Psychol.,* 1934, **29**, 298-300.

Sargent, S. (Ed.) *Culture and personality.* New York: The Viking Fund, 1949.

Tomkins, S. S. *The Thematic Apperception Test.* New York: Grune & Stratton, 1947.

Warner, W., & Lunt, P. *The social life of a modern community.* New Haven: Yale Univer. Press, 1941.

J. STACY ADAMS AND A. KIMBALL ROMNEY
A functional analysis of authority

Bruner, J. S., Goodnow, J. J., & Austin, G. A. *A study of thinking.* New York: Wiley 1956.

Grice, G. R. The relation of secondary reinforcement to delayed reward in visual discrimination learning. *J. exp. Psychol.,* 1948, **38**, 1-16.

Perin, C. T. A quantitative investigation of the delay-of-reinforcement gradient. *J. exp. Psychol.,* 1943, **32**, 37-51. (a)

Perin, C. T. The effect of delay of reinforcement upon the differentiation of bar responses in white rats. *J. exp. Psychol.,* 1943, **32**, 95-109. (b)

Skinner, B. F. *Verbal behavior.* New York: Appleton-Century-Crofts, 1957.

Verplanck, W. S. A glossary of some terms used in the objective science of behavior. *Psychol. Rev.,* 1957, **64** (6), Part 2.

B. F. SKINNER
Teaching machines

Menger, K. New approach to teaching intermediate mathematics. *Science,* 1958, **127**, 1320.

Pressey, S. L. *School and society,* 1926, **23**, 586.

Pressey, S. L. *School and society,* 1932, **36**, 934.

Skinner, B. F. *Science and human behavior.* New York: Macmillan, 1953.

Skinner, B. F. The science of learning and the art of teaching. *Harvard Educational Rev.,* 1954, **24**, 2.

Skinner, B. F. The experimental analysis of behavior. *Am. Scientist,* 1957, **45**, 4. (a)

Skinner, B. F. *Verbal behavior.* New York: Appleton-Century-Crofts, 1957. (b)

SIDNEY L. PRESSEY
Teaching machine (and learning theory) crisis

Ausubel, D. P., & Fitzgerald, D. Meaningful learning and retention: Intrapersonal and cognitive variables, *Rev. educ. Res.,* 1961, **31**, 500-510.

Baskin, S. *Quest for quality: Some models and means.*

Washington, D. C.: United States Department of Health, Education, and Welfare, 1960.

Brownell, W. A. The development of children's number ideas in the primary grades. *Suppl. educ. Monogr.*, 1928, No. 35.

Gagné, R. M. Military training and principles of learning. *Amer. Psychologist*, 1962, **17**, 83-91.

Hilgard, E. R. *Theories of learning.* (2nd ed.) New York: Appleton-Century-Crofts, 1956.

Jones, R. S. Integration of instructional and self-scoring measuring devices. *Abstr. doct. Dissert., O. State U.*, 1954, **65**, 157-165.

Lumsdaine, A. A., & Glaser, R. *Teaching machines and programmed learning.* Washington: National Education Association, 1960.

Piaget, J. *The construction of reality in the child.* New York: Basic Books, 1954.

Pressey, S. L. A third and fourth contribution toward the coming "industrial revolution" in education. *Sch. Soc.*, 1932, **36**, 668-672.

Pressey, S. L. Basic unresolved teaching machine problems. *Theory Pract.*, 1962, **1**, 30-37.

Silberman, H. F. Self-instructional devices and programmed materials. *Rev. educ. Res.*, 1962, **32**, 179-193.

Horst, P. Pattern analysis and configural scoring. *J. clin. Psychol.*, 1954, **10**, 3-11.

Little, K. B., & Shneidman, E. S. Congruencies among interpretations of psychological tests and anamnestic data. *Psychol. Monogr.*, 1959, **73**(6, Whole No. 476).

McArthur, C. C., Meehl, P. E., & Tiedeman, D. V. Symposium on clinical and statistical prediction. *J. counsel. Psychol.*, 1956, **3**, 163-173.

Meehl, P. E. *Clinical versus statistical prediction.* Minneapolis: Univer. Minnesota Press, 1954.

Meehl, P. E. Wanted—a good cookbook. *Amer. Psychologist*, 1956, **11**, 263-272.

Meehl, P. E. When shall we use our heads instead of the formula? *J. counsel. Psychol.*, 1957, **4**, 268-273.

Meehl, P. E. Some ruminations on the validation of clinical procedures. *Canad. J. Psychol.*, 1959, **13**, 102-128. (a)

Meehl, P. E. A comparison of clinicians with five statistical methods of identifying psychotic MMPI profiles. *J. counsel. Psychol.*, 1959, **6**, 102-109. (b)

Meehl, P. E., & Dahlstrom, W. G. Objective configural rules for discriminating psychotic from neurotic MMPI profiles. *J. consult. Psychol.*, 1960, **24**, in press.

PAUL E. MEEHL
The cognitive activity of the clinician

Campbell, D. T., & Fiske, D. W. Convergent and discriminant validation by the multitrait-multimethod matrix. *Psychol. Bull.*, 1959, **56**, 81-105.

Cattell, R. B. *Description and measurement of personality.* Yonkers: World Book, 1946.

Cattell, R. B. *Personality.* New York: McGraw-Hill, 1950.

Cronbach, L. J., & Meehl, P. E. Construct validity in psychological tests. *Psychol. Bull.*, 1955, **52**, 281-302.

Fleeson, W., Glueck, B., Heistad, G., King, J., Lykken, D., Meehl, P., & Mena, A. The ataraxic effect of two phenothiazine drugs on an outpatient population. *Univer. Minn. med. Bull.*, 1958, **29**, 274-286.

Garfield, S. *Introductory clinical psychology.* New York: Macmillan, 1957.

Hoffman, P. J. Criteria of human judgment ability: I. The "clinical" assessment of intelligence and personality. *Amer. Psychologist*, 1958, **13**, 388. (Abstract) (a)

Hoffman, P. J. Human judgment as a decision process. *Amer. Psychologist*, 1958, **13**, 368. (Title) (b)

Hoffman, P. J. The prediction of clinical prediction. *Amer. Psychologist*, 1959, **14**, 356. (Title) .

J. McV. HUNT
Experience and the development of motivation: some reinterpretations

Beach, F. A. Current concepts of play in animals. *Amer. Naturalist*, 1945, **79**, 523-541.

Bechterev, V. M. *La psychologie objective.* (Translated by N. Kostyleff) Paris: Alcan, 1913.

Berlyne, D. E. Novelty and curiosity as determinants of exploratory behavior. *Brit. J. Psychol.*, 1950, **41**, 68-80.

Berlyne, D. E. The arousal and satiation of perceptual curiosity in the rat. *J. comp. physiol. Psychol.*, 1955, **48**, 238-246.

Bernard, C. *Leçons sur les propriétés physiologiques et les alterations pathologiques des liquides de l'organisme.* Paris: Ballière, 1859. 2 vols.

Bexton, W. H., Heron, W., & Scott, T. H. Effects of decreased variation in the sensory environment. *Canad. J. Psychol.*, 1954, **8**, 70-76.

Butler, R. A. Discrimination learning by rhesus monkeys to visual-exploration motivation. *J. comp. physiol. Psychol.*, 1953, **46**, 95-98.

Butler, R. A. Discrimination learning by rhesus monkeys to auditory incentives. *J. comp. physiol. Psychol.*, 1957, **50**, 239-241.

Canestrini, S. Über das Sinnesleben des Neugebornen. [Alzheimer, A. & Lewandowsky, M. (Eds.)]

Monogr. Gesamt. Neurol. Psychiat. (Heft 5). Berlin: Springer, 1913.

Cannon, W. B. *Bodily changes in pain, hunger, fear, and rage.* New York: Appleton-Century, 1915.

Dashiell, J. *Fundamentals of objective psychology.* Boston: Houghton Mifflin, 1928.

Davis, R. C., & Buchwald, A. M. An exploration of somatic response patterns: stimulus and sex differences. *J. comp. physiol. Psychol.,* 1957, **50,** 44-52.

Dollard, J., & Miller, N. E. *Personality and psychotherapy.* New York: McGraw-Hill, 1950.

Festinger, L. *A theory of cognitive dissonance.* Evanston, Ill.: Row, Peterson, 1957.

Freud, S. The interpretation of dreams (1900). In *The basic writings of Sigmund Freud.* (Translated by A. A. Brill) New York: Modern Library, 1938. Pp. 179-548. (a)

Freud, S. Three contributions to the theory of sex (1905). In *The basic writings of Sigmund Freud.* (Translated by A. A. Brill) New York: Modern Library, 1938. Pp. 553-629. (b)

Freud, S. Instincts and their vicissitudes (1915). In *Collected papers,* Vol. IV. London: Hogarth, 1950. Pp. 60-83.

Freud, S. *Inhibition, symptom and anxiety* (1926). (Translated by H. A. Bunker as *The problem of anxiety.*) New York: Norton, 1936.

Granit, R. *Receptors and sensory perception.* New Haven: Yale Univer. Press, 1955.

Harlow, H. F. Learning and satiation of response in intrinsically motivated complex puzzle performance by monkeys. *J. comp. physiol. Psychol.,* 1950, **43,** 289-294.

Harlow, H. F. Motivation as a factor in the acquisition of new responses. In *Current theory and research in motivation: a symposium.* Lincoln: Univer. of Nebraska Press, 1953. Pp. 24-49.

Harlow, H. F. The nature of love. *Amer. Psychologist,* 1958, **13,** 673-685.

Harlow, H. F., Harlow, M. K., & Meyer, D. R. Learning motivated by a manipulation drive. *J. exp. Psychol.,* 1950, **40,** 228-234.

Hebb. D. O. On the nature of fear. *Psychol. Rev.,* 1946, **53,** 259-276.

Hebb, D. O. *The organization of behavior.* New York: Wiley, 1949.

Hebb, D. O. Drives and the CNS (conceptual nervous system). *Psychol. Rev.,* 1955, **62,** 243-254.

Helson, H. Adaptation-level as frame of reference for prediction of psychophysical data. *Amer. J. Psychol.,* 1947, **60,** 1-29.

Helson, H. Adaptation-level as a basis for a quantitative theory of frames of reference. *Psychol. Rev.,* 1948, **55,** 297-313.

Holmes, Frances B. An experimental study of the fears of young children. In A. T. Jersild & Frances

B. Holmes, Children's fears. *Child Develpm. Monogr.,* 1935, **20,** 167-296.

Hull, C. L. *Principles of behavior.* New York: Appleton-Century, 1943.

Hunt, J. McV. The effects of infant feeding-frustration upon adult hoarding in the albino rat. *J. abnorm. soc. Psychol.,* 1941, **36,** 338-360.

Hunt, J. McV., Schlosberg, H., Solomon, R. L., & Stellar, E. Studies on the effects of infantile experience on adult behavior in rats: I. Effects of infantile feeding frustration on adult hoarding. *J. comp. physiol. Psychol.,* 1947, **40,** 291-304.

Jasper, H. H. Electrical signs of cortical activity. *Psychol. Bull.,* 1937, **34,** 411-481.

Jones, H. E., & Jones, Mary C. A study of fear. *Child Educ.,* 1928, **5,** 136-143.

Kelly, G. A. *The psychology of personal constructs.* New York: Norton, 1955.

Lacey, J. I., & Lacey, Beatrice C. The relationship of resting autonomic activity to motor impulsivity. In *The brain and human behavior.* Baltimore: Williams & Wilkins, 1958. Pp. 144-209.

Levine, S. Infantile experience and consummatory behavior in adulthood. *J. comp. physiol. Psychol.,* 1957, **50,** 609-612. (a)

Levine, S. Infantile experience and resistance to physical stress. *Science.* 1957, **126,** 405. (b)

Levine, S. Noxious stimulation in infant and adult rats and consummatory behavior. *J. comp. physiol. Psychol.,* 1958, **51,** 230-233.

Levine, S., Chevalier, J. A., & Korchin, S. J. The effects of shock and handling in infancy on later avoidance learning. *J. Pers.,* 1956, **24,** 475-493.

Lilly, J. C. Mental effects of reduction of ordinary levels of physical stimuli on intact, healthy persons. *Psychiat. Res. Rep.,* 1956, No. 5, 1-9.

Lindsley, D. B. Psychophysiology and motivation. In M. R. Jones (Ed.), *Nebraska symposium on motivation.* Lincoln: Univer. of Nebraska Press, 1957. Pp. 44-105.

McClelland, D. C., Atkinson, J. W., Clark, R. A., & Lowell, E. L. *The achievement motive.* New York: Appleton-Century-Crofts, 1953.

McDougall, W. *An introduction to social psychology.* Boston: Luce, 1915.

Miller, N. E. An experimental investigation of acquired drives. *Psychol. Bull.,* 1941, **38,** 534-535.

Miller, N. E. Studies of fear as an acquirable drive: I. Fear as motivation and fear-reduction as reinforcement in the learning of new responses. *J. exp. Psychol.,* 1948, **38,** 89-101.

Miller, N. E., & Dollard, J. *Social learning and imitation.* New Haven: Yale Univer. Press, 1941.

Montgomery, K. C. The relation between exploratory behavior and spontaneous alternation in the white rat. *J. comp. physiol. Psychol.,* 1951, **44,** 582-589.

Montgomery, K. C. The effect of the hunger and

thirst drives upon exploratory behavior. *J. comp. physiol. Psychol.*, 1953, **46**, 315-319.

Montgomery, K. C., & Monkman, J. A. The relation between fear and exploratory behavior. *J. comp. physiol. Psychol.*, 1955, **48**, 132-136.

Mussen, P. H., & Conger, J. J. *Child development and personality.* New York: Harper, 1956.

Olds, J. Physiological mechanisms of reward. In M. R. Jones (Ed.), *Nebraska symposium on motivation.* Lincoln: Univer. of Nebraska Press, 1955. Pp. 73-139.

Olds, J., & Milner, P. Positive reinforcement produced by electrical stimulation of septal area and other regions of the rat brain. *J. comp. physiol. Psychol.*, 1954, **47**, 419-427.

Pavlov, I. P. *Conditioned reflexes.* (Translated by G. V. Anrep) Oxford: Oxford Univer. Press, 1927.

Piaget, J. *The origins of intelligence in children.* New York: International Universities Press, 1952.

Piaget, J. *The construction of reality in the child.* (Translated by Margaret Cook) New York: Basic Books, 1954.

Pratt, K. C. The neonate. In L. Carmichael (Ed.), *Manual of child psychology.* (2nd Ed.) New York: Wiley, 1954. Pp. 215-291.

Prosser, C. L. Action potentials in the nervous system of the crayfish: I. Spontaneous impulses. *J. cell. comp. Physiol.*, 1934, **4**, 185-209.

Richter, C. P. Animal behavior and internal drives. *Quart. Rev. Biol.*, 1927, **2**, 307-343.

Rogers, C. R. *Client-centered therapy.* Boston: Houghton Mifflin, 1951.

Sheffield, F. D., Roby, T. B., & Campbell, B. A. Drive reduction versus consummatory behavior as determinants of reinforcement. *J. comp. physiol. Psychol.*, 1954, **47**, 349-355.

Sheffield, F. D., Wulff, J. J., & Backer, R. Reward value of copulation without sex drive reduction. *J. comp. physiol. Psychol.*, 1951, **44**, 3-8.

Solomon, R. L., & Brush, Elinor S. Experimentally derived conceptions of anxiety and aversion. In M. R. Jones (Ed.), *Nebraska symposium on motivation.* Lincoln: Univer. of Nebraska Press, 1956. Pp. 212-305.

Solomon, R. L., & Wynne, L. C. Traumatic avoidance learning: acquisition in normal dogs. *Psychol. Monogr.*, 1953, **67**, No. 4 (Whole No. 354).

Thorndike, E. L. *Educational psychology.* (Vol. I, *The original nature of man;* Vol. II, *The psychology of learning.*) New York: Teachers Coll., 1913.

Watson, J. B. *Psychological care of the infant and child.* New York: Norton, 1928.

Watson, J. B., & Raynor, Rosalie. Conditional reactions. *J. exp. Psychol.*, 1920, **3**, 1-4.

Woodworth, R. S. *Dynamic psychology.* New York: Columbia Univer. Press, 1918.

Young, P. T. The role of hedonic processes in motivation. In M. R. Jones (Ed.), *Nebraska symposium on motivation.* Lincoln: Univer. of Nebraska Press, 1955. Pp. 193-237.

LEE J. CRONBACH
The two disciplines of scientific psychology

Bartlett, F. C. Fifty years of psychology. *Occup. Psychol.*, 1955, **29**, 203-216.

Beach, F. A. The snark was a boojum. *Amer. Psychologist*, 1950, **5**, 115-124.

Bergmann, G., & Spence, K. W. The logic of psychophysical measurement. *Psychol. Rev.*, 1944, **51**, 1-24.

Bindra, D., & Scheier, I. H. The relation between psychometric and experimental research in psychology. *Amer. Psychologist*, 1954, **9**, 69-71.

Boring, E. G. *History of experimental psychology.* (2nd ed.) New York: Appleton-Century-Crofts, 1950.

Brunswik, E. *Perception and the representative design of psychological experiments.* Berkeley: Univer. California Press, 1956.

Cattell, J. McK. The biological problems of today: Psychology. *Science*, 1898, **7**, 152-154.

Cattell, R. B. *Factor analysis.* New York: Harper, 1952.

Clark, K. E. *America's psychologists.* Washington, D. C.: APA, 1957.

Corwin, E. S. The impact of the idea of evolution on the American political and constitutional tradition. In S. Persons (Ed.), *Evolutionary thought in America.* New Haven: Yale Univer. Press, 1950. Pp. 182-201.

Cronbach, L. J., & Gleser, Goldine C. *Psychological tests and personnel decisions.* Urbana: Univer. Illinois Press, 1957.

Cronbach, L. J., & Meehl, P. E. Construct validity in psychological tests. *Psychol. Bull.*, 1955, **52**, 281-302.

Cronbach, L. J., & Neff, W. D. Selection and training. In Com. on Undersea Warfare Panel on Psychology and Physiology, *Human Factors in Undersea Warfare.* Washington, D. C.: Nat. Res. Coun., 1949. Pp. 491-516.

Daniel, R. S., & Louttit, C. M. *Professional problems in psychology.* New York: Prentice-Hall, 1953.

Dashiell, J. F. Some rapprochements in contemporary psychology. *Psychol. Bull.*, 1939, **36**, 1-24.

Dewey, J. *Studies in logical theory.* Chicago: Univer. Chicago Press, 1903.

Dewey, J. *The influence of Darwin on philosophy and other essays.* New York: Holt, 1910.

Eysenck, H. J. Reminiscence, drive and personality theory. *J. abnorm. soc. Psychol.*, 1956, **53**, 328-333.

Ferguson, G. A. On learning and human ability. *Canad. J. Psychol.*, 1954, **8**, 95-112.

Ferguson, G. A. On transfer and human ability. *Canad. J. Psychol.*, 1956, **10**, 121-131.

Fleishman, E. A. Predicting advanced levels of proficiency in psychomotor skills. In *Proc. Sympos. on Human Engng.* Washington, D. C.: Nat. Acad. Sci., 1956. Pp. 142-151.

Fleishman, E. A., &' Hempel, W. E., Jr. Changes in factor structure of a complex psychomotor test as a function of practice. *Psychometrika*, 1954, **19**, 239-252.

Ford, C. S., & Beach, F. A. *Patterns of sexual behavior.* New York: Harper, 1952.

Harlow, H. F. The formation of learning sets. *Psychol. Rev.*, 1949, **56**, 51-65.

Harlow, H. F. Mice, men, monkeys, and motives. *Psychol. Rev.*, 1953, **60**, 23-32.

Hull, C. L. The place of innate individual and species differences in a natural-science theory of behavior. *Psychol. Rev.*, 1945, **52**, 55-60.

Hull, C. L. *Essentials of behavior.* New Haven: Yale Univer. Press, 1951.

Laugier, H. (Ed.) L'analyse factorielle et ses applications. Paris: Centre National de la Recherche Scientifique, 1955.

Lazarus, R. S., & Baker, R. W. Personality and psychological stress—a theoretical and methodological framework. *Psychol. Newsletter*, 1956, **8**, 21-32.

McCandless, B. R. & Spiker, C. C. Experimental research in child psychology. *Child Develpm.*, 1956, **27**, 75-80.

McClelland, D. C. Personality. In P. R. Farnsworth (Ed.) *Annu. Rev. Psychol.*, 1956. Stanford: Annual Reviews, 1956. Pp. 39-62.

Miller, N. E. Effects of drugs on motivation: The value of using a variety of measures. *Ann. N. Y. Acad. Sci.*, 1956, **65**, 318-333.

Miller, N. E. Liberalization of basic S-R concepts: Extensions to conflict behavior and social learning. In S. Koch (Ed.), *Psychology: A study of a science.* Vol. II. *General systematic formulations, learning, and special processes.* New York: McGraw-Hill, in press. [Published in 1959—*Editor's note.*]

Miller, N. E. Objective techniques for studying motivational effects of drugs on animals. In E. Trabucchi (Ed.), *Proc. Int. Sympos. on Psychotropic Drugs.* Amsterdam, Netherlands: Elsevier Publishing Co., in press. [Published in 1957 by Van Nostrand, New York; edited by S. Garattini & V. Ghetti—*Editor's note.*]

Murphy, G. *An historical introduction to modern psychology.* (3rd ed.) New York: Harcourt, Brace, 1932.

Pastore, N. *The nature-nurture controversy.* New York: Kings Crown Press, 1949.

Piaget, J. *Psychology of intelligence.* M. Piercy and D. E. Berlyne (Trans.). London: Routledge and Kegan Paul, 1950.

Rohracher, H. Aus der wissenschaftlichen Arbeit des Psychologischen Institutes der Universität Wien. *Wiener Z. Phil., Psychol., Pädag.*, 1956, **6**, 1-66.

Scoon, R. The rise and impact of evolutionary ideas. In S. Persons (Ed.), *Evolutionary thought in America.* New Haven, Yale Univer. Press, 1950. Pp. 4-43.

Selye, H. Stress and disease. *Science*, 1955, **122**, 625-631.

Shen, E. The place of individual differences in experimentation. In Q. McNemar and M. A. Merrill (Eds.), *Studies in personality.* New York: McGraw-Hill, 1942. Pp. 259-283.

Spengler, J. J. Evolutionism in American economics. In S. Persons (Ed.), *Evolutionary thought in America.* New Haven: Yale Univer. Press, 1950. Pp. 202-266.

Terman, L. M. The mental test as a psychological method. *Psychol. Rev.*, 1924, **31**, 93-117.

Thorndike, R. L. The psychological value systems of psychologists. *Amer. Psychologist*, 1954, **9**, 787-790.

Thurstone, L. L. The stimulus-response fallacy in psychology. *Psychol. Rev.*, 1923, **30**, 354-369.

Titchener, E. B. The past decade in experimental psychology. *Amer. J. Psychol.*, 1910, **21**, 404-421.

Tolman, E. C. The determinants of behavior at a choice point. *Psychol. Rev.*, 1938, **45**, 1-41.

Tucker, L. R. Determination of parameters of a functional relation by factor analysis. *ETS Res. Bull.*, 1955, **55**, No. 10.

Tyler, R. W. Can intelligence tests be used to predict educability? In K. Eells et al., *Intelligence and cultural differences.* Chicago: Univer. Chicago Press, 1951. Pp. 39-47.

Wenger, M. A., Clemens, T. L., & Engel, B. T. Autonomic response patterns to four stimuli. Unpublished manuscript, 1957.

Woodworth, R. S. *Dynamic psychology.* New York: Holt, 1918.

Woodworth, R. S. *Experimental psychology.* New York: Holt, 1938.

Woodworth, R. S., & Schlosberg, H. *Experimental psychology.* (2nd ed.) New York: Holt, 1954.

Wundt, W. *Principles of physiological psychology.* Vol. 1. (5th ed.) E. B. Titchener (Trans.) New York: Macmillan, 1904.

Yerkes, R. M. Comparative psychology: A question of definitions. *J. Phil. Psychol., and sci. Methods*, 1913, **10**, 580-582.

Yerkes, R. M. The study of human behavior. *Science*, 1914, **29**, 625-633.

1 2 3 4 5 6 7 8 9 10 11 12 13 14 15 16 17 18 19 20 21 22 23 24 25   Ph   70 69 68 67 66 65 64